Social Reform Movements to Protect
America's Vulnerable 1830–1940

WOMEN & CHILDREN *First*

Edited by David J. Rothman and Sheila M. Rothman

A Garland Series

Documents Relative to the House of Refuge, Instituted by The Society for the Reformation of Juvenile Delinquents in the City of New York, in 1824

Garland Publishing, Inc.
New York & London
1987

For a complete list of the titles in this series
see the final pages of this volume.

This facsimile has been made from a copy in
the Library of Congress.

Library of Congress Cataloging-in-Publication Data

Documents relative to the House of Refuge, instituted by the Society for the Reformation of Juvenile Delinquents in the City of New York, in 1824.

(Women & children first)
Reprint. Originally published: New York : N.C. Hart, Superintendent, Board of Managers, 1832.
1. House of Refuge (New York, N.Y.) 2. Rehabilitation of juvenile delinquents—New York (N.Y.) I. Title. II. Series.
HV9106.N61D693 1987 365'.42 86-7608
ISBN 0-8240-7675-3 (alk. paper)

The volumes in this series are printed on
acid-free, 250-year-life paper.

Printed in the United States of America

E. S. Mesier's Lith.

DOCUMENTS

RELATIVE TO THE

HOUSE OF REFUGE

INSTITUTED BY

The Society for the Reformation of Juvenile Delinquents

IN THE CITY OF NEW-YORK,

IN 1824.

COMPRISING

1st. MEMORIAL TO THE LEGISLATURE OF THE STATE, INTERSPERSED WITH FACTS FROM THE REPORTS OF THE "SOCIETY FOR THE PREVENTION OF PAUPERISM."
2d. ACT OF INCORPORATION.
3d. THE SEVEN ANNUAL REPORTS OF THE SOCIETY.
4th. RULES AND REGULATIONS FOR THE GOVERNMENT OF THE HOUSE.
5th. AN ADDRESS DELIVERED BY THE REV. DR. STANFORD, ON THE OPENING OF THE FIRST NEW BUILDING.
6th. LAWS AND STATUTES OF THE STATE RELATIVE TO THE HOUSE OF REFUGE.

PUBLISHED BY PERMISSION
OF THE
BOARD OF MANAGERS,
BY NATHANIEL C. HART, SUPERINTENDENT.

New-York:
PRINTED BY MAHLON DAY,
376 PEARL-STREET.

1832.

CONTENTS.

PREFACE.

The subject of Penitentiary Discipline is of great and increasing importance to civilized communities. As the dictates of humanity gain an ascendency over the feelings of revenge in penal inflictions against crime, the judicious substitution of milder punishment in place of the more severe and sanguinary, is a matter which must necessarily engage the attention of wise and prudent Legislators.

The welfare of society is deeply involved in the question of the most effectual mode of restraining vice, and preventing the commission of crime; and whether we consult the pages of sacred or profane history, or compare nations with each other in every stage of advancement from the savage to the most civilized, the soundest induction appears to be, that the most effective Legislation is that which is most conformable to the precepts of Christianity.

In moral as well as corporeal diseases, it is a sound maxim, that "prevention is better than cure." A slight observation of the nature of the crimes which disturb society, and of the character of the criminals, will convince any intelligent observer, that the greater portion of those crimes originated in early moral debasement;—in the contamination of youth by vicious associations. It is on this ground that the Refuge establishments are founded—on the conviction that they will save to the communities in which they are erected, by their conservative and reformatory influence, a much greater sum than the cost of their maintenance.

The House of Refuge in the city of New-York, being the first of the kind in the United States, by which the experiment of Juvenile Reformation has been fairly attempted, it has been thought desirable that the several papers and reports which relate to its rise and progress, should be brought together, in order to prevent their being scattered and lost, and to this end the present volume makes its appearance.

MEMORIAL

TO THE LEGISLATURE OF THE STATE OF NEW-YORK, BY THE SOCIETY FOR THE REFORMATION OF JUVENILE DELINQUENTS, WITH AN ABSTRACT FROM A REPORT OF A COMMITTEE APPOINTED BY THE SOCIETY FOR THE PREVENTION OF PAUPERISM, IN THE SAID CITY, ON THE SUBJECT OF ERECTING A HOUSE OF REFUGE, FOR VAGRANT AND DEPRAVED YOUNG PEOPLE.

To the Honorable, the Legislature of the State of New-York, in Senate and Assembly convened:—The Memorial of the Society for the Reformation of Juvenile Delinquents, in the City of New-York, respectfully sheweth,

THAT having received an Act of Incorporation, at the last session of the Legislature, your Memorialists, with such means as were placed at their disposal, by the liberality and public spirit of such of their fellow-citizens as were applied to for their assistance, have proceeded to the fulfilment of the objects of their Institution. They have procured from our City Corporation a lease of a piece of land eligibly situated for the establishment of a HOUSE OF REFUGE, which had been formerly used for the purpose of a National Arsenal. And they have purchased from the Government of the United States, a cession of their improvements, consisting of various buildings, outworks, sheds, &c. These improvements, the Society have put in the best state of temporary repair possible, and they are now ready to receive under their care, a limited number of young persons, whose vagrancy, or whose crimes, may have rendered them fit objects for the care and discipline of this Society.

But in the very commencement of their operations, they are presented with the fact of a treasury nearly exhausted by the purchase of the above-mentioned improvements, and the necessary repairs of them, and the furnishing of a quantity of materials with which to employ the objects of their care, in the great purpose of their reformation and amendment. And the small amount of their funds has enabled them to prepare accommodations for the number only of about seventy persons.

Under these circumstances it is evident, that, in the course of a few months, at most, the proceedings of this Society, having for their object the reformation and restoration to society, under circumstances favorable to their future prosperity, of the hundreds of youth who are annually thrown upon our municipal government for correction and punishment, must be entirely suspended, and the humane effort that has been made under the protection and fostering care of your Honorable Body, and the no less distinguishing liberality of our private citizens, must be abandoned, unless the bounty of the State shall be added to the private contributions that have already been made in behalf of this Society.

We therefore address your Honorable Body, as the guardians of all portions of the community, and particularly of those institutions which are formed for the benign and necessary purpose of reforming the abandoned and profligate, of rescuing them from the deplorable consequences of ignorance, of bad example, and of guilt; and of mingling the salutary lessons of reformation, with the indispensable administration of punishment, especially to those young and inexperienced convicts, of whose future usefulness a reasonable hope may be entertained.

And when your Honorable Body shall take into consideration, the peculiarly exposed situation of the city of New-York, to the migrations of the wandering and restless subjects of poverty and vice, not only from foreign parts, but from our own country and state, the Managers of this Society entertain the confident expectation, that your Honorable Body will feel the necessity and propriety of extending towards them such portion of the patronage of the State, as shall enable them to erect the necessary buildings, and to introduce extensive and permanent plans for the employment and education of such juvenile offenders as shall be committed to their charge.

The Society beg leave to refer your Honorable Body to the annexed Abstract of a Report of a Committee of the Society for the Prevention of Pauperism in the city of New-York, for a full account of the origin of their Association, and a developement of the principles and objects which are to govern them in its administration.

CADWALLADER D. COLDEN, President.
Robert F. Mott, *Secretary*.

REPORT, &c.

It will be admitted by every person conversant with human nature, and with the great objects of political association, that there are few judicial considerations of greater importance, than the wise adaptation of punishment to crime. The safety of life and property; the enjoyment of personal liberty; the blessings of social intercourse; and the strength and stability of governments themselves; are essentially interwoven with those penal regulations, which coerce the refractory, and operate as dissuasives from the indulgence of passions, hostile to the general good. Of the various institutions of civil government, there are none, perhaps, which more clearly mark the progress of refinement, and the growth of enlightened feeling, than the meliorations which are visible from time to time in the criminal code of nations. In the savage and barbarous state, vengeance is the ruling principle in the infliction of punishment, and death is seldom decreed, without the accompaniment of lingering and merciless torture. As knowledge increases, men learn to discriminate more clearly between actions and their motives: and although the divisions of the statute book become more artificial, there is an obvious attention to the natural distinctions of crime; a more cautious inquiry into the *quo animo*—the nature and force of the temptation; and more humanity in the retributions of legal justice. But the most important step in the enactment and administration of penal laws, is the full admission of the principle, that it is not revenge which stimulates society to the infliction of punishment, and arms the law with its severest denunciations;—that neither in the prescriptions of the Legislature, nor in the progress of juridical investigation and decision, are the vindictive passions to be allowed to operate:—but that the great ends of punishment are, to deter others from crime, to prevent the aggressor from the repetition of his offences, and, if possible, to effect the moral reformation of all those who become amenable to the laws.

It cannot but afford the highest gratification to every humane individual, to witness the solicitude which now prevails in relation to this subject. The zeal which is observable in various countries, with respect to the improvement of prison discipline, to the reformation of abuses, to the perfection of criminal laws, and to the more discreet and consistent treatment of those whom offended justice visits with its severe but needful inflictions, is an indubitable indication of that expansive benevolence which is the genuine fruit of Christianity. It is creditable to this country, young as it was in experience, to have given to the world one of the first effective impulses in this new sphere of wise and charitable regulation—the Penitentiary System of Prison Discipline. Had that system been pursued among us with the same intelligent and disinterested zeal with which it was commenced, our prisons would at this time exhibit the best models for the world to imitate;—their influence would be far more decisive upon the public welfare; and we should not now have to lament that disrepute into which the Penitentiary System has partially fallen, in consequence of doubts of its superiority.

Among the evils and abuses which obstruct the operation of this system, and most powerfully counteract the reformatory influence of imprisonment, is the want of classification among prisoners, the indiscriminate assemblage of persons of all ages and degrees of guilt, and the inevitably corrupting tendency of such an intercourse. The very imperfect structure, and the crowded state of our prisons, absolutely forbid the application of an adequate remedy for this deplorable evil. So notorious is the demoralizing nature of some of those institutions which are called Penitentiaries,—so generally do those who are liberated from them come out more vile and corrupt, and more skilful in the various modes of depredation than when they entered;—and so seldom do they manifest any signs of reformation, that these places have acquired the appellation of *Schools* and *Colleges* of crime. The amount of injury sustained by the lamentable defects in the regulations of our city and state prisons, is so great,—to such an extent is the younger class of prisoners initiated in the mysteries of wickedness, by this exposure, it is a questionable point, in the estimation of many persons, whether the present system, with all its expensive apparatus, and all its show of lenity and moral treatment, is not more inauspicious to public tranquillity, than the simple incarceration and corporal chastisements, the whipping-posts, pillories, and croppings of former times. The experience, nevertheless, of some of the prisons of the United States, whose discipline is the most exact, and where classification is an object of careful attention; and the growing experience of England, and other countries of Europe, where the sanguinary codes which have been for ages in operation, are beginning to yield, in practice, to the more rational and humane substitution of hard labor, restricted diet, solitary confinement, and judicious classification, afford unquestionable evidence, that the energies of the law in the suppression of crime, are most potent and availing, when directed with a constant reference to the moral faculties of our nature; and when clothed with that spirit, which seeks to restore, in order that it may safely forgive.

The great object of the institution of civil government, is to advance the prosperity, and to increase the happiness of its subjects. The agents of the government, become, in this point of view, the fathers of the people; and it may surely be ranked among the duties incident to this paternal care, not only that those who are guilty of crime should receive the chastisement due to their offences, but that no pains should be spared to remove the causes of offence, and to diminish, as far as possible, the sources of temptation and corruption. This obligation applies with peculiar force to the case of juvenile offenders;—a class whose increasing numbers, and deplorable situation in this city, loudly call for the more effective interposition of its police, and the benevolent interference of our citizens in general.

To this class of guilty unfortunates, the Society for the Prevention of Pauperism, beg leave to solicit the attention of their fellow-citizens, in the earnest hope, that means may be devised to rescue from the lowest degradation, and from the danger of utter ruin, hundreds and thousands of the youth of this city, of both sexes, whose crimes and misery arise, in a very marked degree, from the neglect of those who ought to be their guardians and protectors.

Every person that frequents the out-streets of this city, must be forcibly struck with the ragged and uncleanly appearance, the vile language, and the idle and miserable habits of great numbers of children, most of whom are of an age suitable for schools, or for some useful employment. The parents of these children, are, in all probability, too poor, or too degenerate, to provide them with clothing fit for them to be seen in at school; and know not where to place them in order that they may find employment, or be better cared for. Accustomed, in many instances, to witness at home nothing in the way of example, but what is degrading; early taught to observe intemperance, and to hear obscene and profane language without disgust; obliged to beg, and even encouraged to acts of dishonesty, to satisfy the wants induced by the indolence of their parents,—what can be expected, but that such children will, in due time, become responsible to the laws for crimes, which have thus, in a manner, been forced upon them? Can it be consistent with real justice, that delinquents of this character, should be consigned to the infamy and severity of punishments, which must inevitably tend to perfect the work of degradation, to sink them still deeper in corruption, to deprive them of their remaining sensibility to the shame of exposure, and establish them in all the hardihood of daring and desperate villainy? Is it possible that a christian community, can lend its sanction to such a process, without any effort to rescue and to save? If the agents of our municipal government stand towards the community in the moral light of guardians of virtue,—if they may be justly regarded as the political fathers of the unprotected, does not every feeling of justice urge upon them the principle, of considering these juvenile culprits as falling under their special guardianship, and claiming from them the right which every child may demand of its parent, of being well instructed in the nature of its duties, before it is punished for the breach of their observance? Ought not every citizen, who has a just sense of the reciprocal obligations of parents and children, to lend his aid to the administrators of the law, in rescuing those pitiable victims of neglect and wretchedness, from the melancholy fate which almost inevitably results from an apprenticeship in our common prisons.

In order to arrive at a more correct understanding of the amount of the evils alluded to, the committee have to state, that they have been furnished by the District Attorney, H. Maxwell, Esq. with an abstract of those persons who were brought before the Police Magistrates, during the year 1822, and sentenced either to the City Bridewell from 10 to 60 days, or to the Penitentiary from 2 to 6 months. The list comprehends more than 450 persons, all under

25 years of age, and a very considerable number of both sexes between the ages of 9 and 16. None of these have been actually charged with crime, or indicted and arraigned for trial. It includes those only, who are taken up as vagrants, who can give no satisfactory account of themselves;—children, who profess to have no home, or whose parents have turned them out of doors and take no care of them,—beggars and other persons discovered in situations which imply the intention of stealing, and numbers who were found sleeping in the streets or in stables. These miserable objects are brought to the Police Office under suspicious circumstances,—and, according to the result of their examinations, they are sentenced as before mentioned. Many of these are young people on whom the charge of crime cannot be fastened, and whose only fault is, that they have no one on earth to take care of them, and that they are incapable of providing for themselves. Hundreds, it is believed, thus circumstanced, eventually have recourse to petty thefts; or, if females, they descend to practices of infamy, in order to save themselves from the pinching assaults of cold and hunger. The list furnished us, affords numerous instances, especially of females, who request to be sent to the Penitentiary, as a favor—as their only resource and refuge from greater evils.

The District Attorney, in the explanations which accompany his abstract, observes, "that many of each description might be "saved from continued transgression, no one can doubt, who will "examine the statement that I have made from the records of the "Police Office for the year 1822. This abstract contains the names "of more than 450 persons, male and female, none over the age "of 25, many much younger, and *some so young as to be presumed* "*incapable of crime.*

"All these have been convicted by the Police Magistrates as "disorderly persons, and imprisoned as such.

"Many others not mentioned, have been discharged, from an "unwillingness to imprison, in hope of reformation, or under pe-"culiar circumstances.

"Many notorious thieves, infesting the city, were at first idle, "vagrant boys, imprisoned for a short period to keep them from "mischief. A second and a third imprisonment is inflicted, the "prison becomes familiar and agreeable, and at the expiration of "their sentence, they come out accomplished in iniquity.

"I have already mentioned," observes the District Attorney, "that this statement does not include prisoners, indicted and tried "at the Court of Sessions. At each term of the Court (the terms "are once a month,) the average number of lads arraigned for pet-"ty thefts, is five or six; and I regret to state, that lately high "crimes have been perpetrated in several instances, by boys not "over 16, who, at first, were idle, street vagrants, and, by degrees, "thieves, burglars, and robbers."

From further information it appears, that about 60 persons are, upon an average, indicted and arraigned at each term of the Court of Sessions, for misdemeanors and felonies; and that out of this number, four or five are boys under sixteen years of age. A large proportion of them, amounting to fifty or sixty per annum, are found guilty and condemned, either to the City or State Penitentiary, there to associate with others more hardened in crime, and who are ever ready to impart their instructions in the arts of deception and wickedness.

It is now generally admitted, that in none of our prisons,—in the Bridewell,—the City Penitentiary—or the State Prison—as they are at present constructed, and conducted, is it possible to introduce those subdivisions, and restrictive regulations, which are absolutely essential to the prevention of mutual contamination, and independently of which, the prospect of reformation is really preposterous.

In the City Prison or Bridewell, it is not only impossible to separate the juvenile offenders from those that are old in crime, but the rooms are so small, and very often so crowded, as to produce an atmosphere both physically and morally disgusting in a high degree, and certainly adapted to the debasement of every virtuous sentiment, and almost inevitably ruinous to the natural sensibilities of youth. The condition of this prison, in our estimation, calls loudly for the attention of the police; and were its actual condition known to the citizens of the neighborhood, we think the notice of Grand Juries would be often directed to it, as a nuisance, disreputable to the character of the city. In rooms about eighteen feet square, there are often thirty or forty persons, confined together without any discrimination except that of sex and color—boys of nine years of age and upwards, sharing the same dismal fare, and mingling in conversation with aged villiany,—and girls of ten or twelve exposed to the company and example of the most abandoned of the sex. This prison has no yard excepting for the use of the keeper. The prisoners' rooms have no outlet whatever, not even by pipes or conduits, and no ventilation excepting by the door and windows. The convicts in these small, close rooms, are employed in picking oakum. The period of confinement is from a few days to a year or more, and it is not unusual for them to remain several months. The present keeper, *Mr. Thorpe*, evidently conducts the prison with as strict an attention to cleanliness and order, as the construction of the house and the nature of his charge will admit; but both in verbal and written communications to the committee, he states unequivocally his opinion of the impossibility of classifying the prisoners in the present confined and very imperfect building, and the consequent injury to the morals of juvenile offenders. "The number of boys," he observes, "committed to "this prison, as nearly as it can fairly be estimated, is from three "to four hundred in the course of a year, and at one time from six "to nine. They are committed generally for trifling offences, such "as vagrancy, misdemeanors, &c. and some for petit and very few "for grand larcenies. The proportion that are committed here for "the second and third time, is about two-thirds of the whole, chief-"ly owing to a want of residence, or a return from transportation, "or an escape from the Alms-house. This prison," he adds, "is "so constructed that there can be no suitable place for the confine-"ment of this class of prisoners, separate from old and hardened "offenders, with which it generally abounds; and what induces or "leads them to the commission of crime, is the education they re-"ceive from the before mentioned offenders. There have been a "multiplicity of instances where boys have been sent here as va-"grants, destitute of parents, &c. and have either been discharged, "transported, or sent to the Alms-House, and have returned char-"ged with crime, and when examined, they have proved to have "had or received their education in this prison. They are confi-"ned with old and hardened offenders, by day and night, because "the prison is so constructed that it will not admit of keeping them "otherwise."

It may well be submitted to the judgment of a discerning public, whether an exposure of a few weeks, or even of a few days, to such company and fare as are here represented, is not sufficient to suppress, in youthful minds, all virtuous emotions; to reconcile the feelings to a life of guilt, and even of suffering, shame, and degradation. Sleeping upon the bare floor, without covering, or at best with only a coarse and dirty blanket, they soon learn to brave the exposure, and to disregard the privation.

That an institution of this nature, in a building so entirely inadequate to its object, and exhibiting so much that is repulsive to the senses, and deplorable in moral regulation, should be suffered to occupy one of the most prominent and beautiful situations in the city, we cannot but consider as a reflection upon the humanity and public spirit of our citizens; and we indulge the hope, that the period is not distant, when the city prison will be removed to a situation of greater seclusion, and erected upon a plan which will admit of every facility for cleanliness, ventilation, classification, employment, and perfect inspection.

The Penitentiary at Bellevue, three miles from the City Hall, is destined for convicts from the city, whose period of confinement does not exceed three years. This prison, though comparatively of modern erection, does not, we regret to say, possess those requisites for convenient distribution, employment, instruction, moral government and easy inspection, which the present improved plans for prisons so readily afford. The boys, it is true, are here separated from the old offenders; but this, though it is the first important step in classification, is entirely insufficient to answer the desired end of reformation. No principle of our common nature is better established, than that "evil communications corrupt good manners." It is certainly as necessary, in order to preserve the moral sensibilities of youth, to keep them from the society of corrupt persons of their own age and class, as it is from the company of older criminals. Boys imitate each other, both in virtue and in vice, more naturally and more rapidly than they do those who are much their superiors in age. They may not, indeed, receive from each other, such profound lessons in the science of crime, nor hear from the lips of their equals, observations, which will tend so effectually to blast every germ of compunctive feeling, and establish the guilty soul in the principles of infidelity and misanthropy; but with associates of their own cast, they will more readily assimilate, and their initiation in depravity may prove the more certain. It is well known, that when vagrant children are taken up, on their first offence, and threatened with imprisonment, they frequently evince great penitence and contrition, entreat forgiveness on the promise of better conduct, and deprecate a confinement in gaol with cries of distress and horror. But a familiarity with the company they find there, soon wears off this repugnance, and renders a second conviction a thing of comparative indifference. Hence, to convert a prison into a real Penitentiary, there ought to be, in a collection even of juvenile offenders, at least half a dozen different classes, not regulated by age; for it is obvious that a prisoner of eighteen may be far less guilty, less hardened, and more open to the visitations of remorse and shame, than others of twelve or fourteen. The divisions should therefore depend upon an experimental inquiry into their moral character and dispositions, and a knowledge of their previous habits.

The most important facts relative to the Bellevue prison, as connected with the objects of this report, will be best understood from the following answers of Arthur Burtis, Esq., superintendent of that extensive establishment, to questions sent to him from this committee.

Ques. 1. What number of boys are sent to the Penitentiary in the course of a year, and of what ages; and what is the average number at one time in the prison?

Ans. The average number of boys sent to the Penitentiary for the last three years, has been seventy-five per year, from twelve to sixteen years old. The average at one time in the house is about thirty-five.

Ques. 2. For what offences generally are they imprisoned?

Ans. Most generally for petit larceny and vagrancy.

Ques. 3. What proportion of them are sent there for the second or third time?

Ans. About one-half are in for the second and third time; but it is impossible to be exact, as the same boys come in by so many different names.

Ques. 4. How far are the boys instructed?

Ans. They are taught the catechism, and to read and write.

Ques. 5. How far are they put to labor, in the Penitentiary?

Ans. We have not put them to labor, except a part in the Pin Factory.

Ques. 6. What effect has the present treatment upon them, in reference to their reformation and future usefulness?

Ans. The effect of their present condition *is deplorable.* Instead of reformation, they must become worse, as we are compelled to put a boy for his first, perhaps small crime, with the old offender, if not in years, *in crime*, in the same room.

Ques. 7. What proportion of them are destitute of parents, or other persons to take charge of them?

Ans. About two-thirds have one or more parents, but in almost every case their parents have taken very little or no care of them.

Ques. 8. As far as you have experience, what is the origin, or what leads to the commission of offences by boys of those ages?

Ans. The principal cause of Juvenile Delinquency, is, first, the bad example they have from their parents and guardians; when small, they are allowed to run at large without restraint. No child will be a vagrant, if put and kept steadily to a well-regulated school, but for a few years.—But the reason why their parents will not send them, is, the encouragement which our citizens give, (and no doubt from the best motives,) *to begging.* When a poor child calls at a gentleman's house for a little cold victuals, who can refuse, when they have it, and especially, since, if not given it must be thrown away? But if our citizens were aware of the evil, I am sure they would make a universal stop. I can not learn of one child that has been in the habit of begging, who has not turned out a prostitute, or vagrant; and their begging serves only to keep their parents in idleness and profligacy: for they find it so profitable, that, if they have one or two good begging children, (as they term it,) it is all they want; all they can get by other means, goes for drink. Another cause, is, sending small children round the docks, under the pretence of picking chips, and whatever they can find; in peddling small articles on board of sloops, and through the streets, &c. These habits introduce them into bad company, and prove an almost certain cause of their ruin. It is hoped that they may be discountenanced by all good citizens.

Ques. 9. What proportion of them can read and write, at the time of their committal?

Ans. About one in eight.

Ques. 10. How far are the boys separate from old offenders by day and by night?

Ans. They are kept entirely separate, except a few who are in the Pin Factory, and they are under the care of a keeper.

From the exposition thus given of the subjects referred to their consideration, the Committee cannot but indulge the belief, that the inference which will be drawn by every citizen of New-York, from the facts now laid before him, will be in perfect accordance with their own,—that it is highly expedient that A House of Refuge for Juvenile Delinquents, should, as soon as practicable, be established in the immediate vicinity of this city.

The subject presents itself to the minds of your Committee, as one of the deepest importance. Such a proposition appears to us to come forward at the present time, clothed with all the authority which can be derived from considerations not only of humanity, of mercy, of christian tenderness, and parental feeling; but of a due regard for the honor and reputation of this metropolis. To suffer such a building as the present Bridewell to remain in activity for a single year, after the appalling facts have been fairly disclosed of its total inadequacy to the purposes of such an institution, and the inevitable corruption of our youth, which results day by day, and hour by hour, from its continuance,—what is this but to view with complacency, and even to sanction by our apathy, a school, whose lessons of moral turpitude and of dark iniquity, must assuredly render its pupils adepts in crime, and lost to all rational expectations of happiness as social and accountable beings. What parent or guardian, who has had to contend in the execution of his charge, with the innate perversities of human nature, and to enlist in the struggle between the powers of light and darkness, but must shudder at the bare possibility, that the child of a near and valued connexion, should, through the enticements of wicked associates, chance to fall into the hands of the officers of justice in this city, and be placed as an apprentice in this school!

The present is emphatically an age of humanity,—of unusual sympathy, on the part of the wise and virtuous, not only for those who are suffering from the unavoidable calamities of the world, but for those who, untaught and unprotected, are left to struggle with its manifold temptations. It is a period in which science is displaying its vast and increasing resources, not only in the conveniences and embellishments of life, but in advancing the interests of humanity, and facilitating the means by which men may become wiser and better. Prisons and hospitals have felt and are feeling its benign influence. The diseases of the body and the maladies of the mind, have experienced its relieving hand,—and even the moral disorders of our corrupt nature, have fallen within the circumference of its beneficent energies. Abroad and at home, there is a spirit of more than ordinary benevolence, seeking for the means by which it may invade more effectually, the domains of prejudice and folly, and relieve the sufferings which they have entailed for ages upon their victims. In that quarter of the field which it has been our object to explore, much has been done in other places, and unless this city shall speedily renew its efforts, we shall soon be left greatly in the rear in this progress of humanity.

That the views of your committee, in relation to a House of Refuge, are not unsupported by the opinion of many of their fellow-citizens, who have had the most extensive opportunities of forming a correct estimate of its importance, they can confidently affirm. The District Attorney, in reference to a House of Refuge, remarks, in his communication to the committee, "That many of each de-" scription might be saved" by it, "from continued transgression, " no one can doubt who will examine the statement which I have " made from the records of the Police Office for 1822. This ab-" stract contains the names of more than four hundred and fifty " persons, male and female, none over the age of 25, many much " younger, and some so young as to be presumed incapable of crime. " Many others not mentioned have been discharged; from an un-" willingness to imprison, in hope of reformation, or under peculiar " circumstances. Such facts," he adds, "must satisfy every one of " the necessity of a House of Refuge. It would be indeed difficult " to determine who would and who would not be influenced by such " an institution, to leave the paths of vice: unworthy objects might " be received,—imposition practiced; yet surely out of three or " four hundred miserable beings, some would be found worthy of " protection, and desirous of amendment.

" Legislative interference must be had to carry into full effect the " objects of your institution.

" The law under which the Police Magistrates convict as va-" grants, &c., ought to be amended to authorise them in proper ca-" ses, when the culprit consents, to deliver the party to the direc-" tors of the House of Refuge. The court ought to be empowered, " when boys under fourteen shall have been acquitted of a theft, " on account of their tender years to dispose of them in like man-" ner; always consulting the views of the persons who may have " charge of your proposed institution." Thus far the District At-" torney.

The keeper of the City Prison (Bridewell,) says in his letter; " The proposition of the society for erecting a House of Refuge, " meets my warmest approbation. Of the boys who are committed " here, I presume there might be, with care and attention, about " one-third received in a House of Refuge, with hopes of reforma-" tion. The expense of supporting boys in a House of Refuge " would not materially vary from 15 to 20 cents per day."

The Superintendent of the Bellevue establishment, thus replies to the queries of the committee in reference to this immediate object:—

Ques. 11. What is your opinion of the expediency of establishing a House of Refuge for Juvenile Delinquents?

Ans. I believe it feasible and necessary; or we must continue to have our city thronged with young, idle vagrants. I think it charitable, humane, and economical.

Ques. 12. Of the boys who are in general committed to the Penitentiary, what proportion do you think might be received into a House of Refuge with a fair prospect of their reformation?

Ans. I think two-thirds may be made useful to themselves and the public.

Ques. 13. To what mechanical, or other employments could boys be put, in a House of Refuge, to the most advantage?

Ans. What mechanical employment will be the most advantageous, it is impossible for me to say. I should however suggest that they be put to different trades as application is offered for their labor.

Ques. 14. Would it be more economical to hire out their services by contract, to labor in the Establishment, or to procure raw materials, and work them on account of the House of Refuge?

Ans. I have no doubt that hiring them out by contract would be the most economical.

Ques. 15. What is the expense of supporting a boy per day in the Penitentiary?

Ans. About 9 cents per day.

Ques. 16. What do you think would be the expense of supporting them in a House of Refuge?

Ans. In a Temporary Refuge it will cost at least 12 cents per day, but in a Permanent, I should hope they would maintain themselves.

Ques. 17. Would it be necessary to deprive them of their liberty by restraints of walls or otherwise?

Ans. They must be kept secure until the keeper and committee are well acquainted with their wishes and character.

Ques. 18. What proportion of them do you think would consent to be bound by indentures to go to sea, or to the country.

Ans. They will all consent; that must be left to the judgment of the committee.

In answer to your general inquiry, I should suggest a Temporary and a Permanent Refuge: the Temporary to receive all Juvenile Offenders—to contain separate apartments for Classification; there to have them taught and employed at such trades as may be found convenient, and not burthensome, with proper rewards and punishments, and from these bind out all that after a proper acquaintance with their characters and wishes, give a reasonable hope of reformation, to merchants, farmers, or as seamen; with an assurance, if they should behave improperly again, they will have to go into the Permanent Refuge.

The Permanent Refuge should receive all those in whom there is no reasonable hope of reformation, and those that should return to bad practices, after being put out of the Temporary Refuge; these should be taught such trades as will be found most useful and convenient, as applications may offer.

JULY 3, 1823.

Thus supported in their views of the importance of a House of Refuge, by a mass of interesting facts, and by men, whose opportunities of practical information and judgment entitle their opinions to much respect, the committee cannot but indulge the belief, that the proposition of the society will meet with the prompt and cordial support of their fellow-citizens, with the unhesitating patronage of the Corporation, and the approval of the Legislature. It remains for them to state more particularly their views of the plan of such an institution, and to enter into a few details, relative to its arrangement, and to advert to the success which has been obtained in some other countries, in the erection and progress of similar establishments.

The design of the proposed institution is, to furnish, in the *first place*, an asylum, in which boys under a certain age, who become subject to the notice of our Police, either as vagrants, or houseless, or charged with petty crimes, may be received, judiciously classed according to their degrees of depravity or innocence, put to work at such employments as will tend to encourage industry and ingenuity, taught reading, writing, and arithmetic, and most carefully instructed in the nature of their moral and religious obligations, while at the same time, they are subjected to a course of treatment, that will afford a prompt and energetic corrective of their vicious propensities, and hold out every possible inducement to reformation and good conduct. It will undoubtedly happen, that among boys collected from such sources, there will be some, whose habits and propensities are of the most unpromising description. Such boys, when left to run at large in the city, become the pests of society, and spread corruption wherever they go. To expect the reformation of such, by the ordinary chances of Sunday schools, churches, or admonitions from Magistrates, would be vain and fruitless. There may be some, who, in the best regulated institution, would prove altogether incorrigible. But if placed in a situation in which their dress, their food, their labor, their privations, and enjoyments, are all made to depend on their conduct; and in which every important step in the progress of improvements, advances them into a better class, and greater comforts,—when they learn to know that a daily register is made of their conduct, that this register is inspected by the governors of the institution, and by respectable visiters,—that the public eye is thus fixed upon them, and their future welfare has become the subject of public concern—is it not probable that in a majority of cases, the latent sparks of emulation may be elicited, and fanned into a goodly desire that they may yet live to honor their country, and to reward the assiduity which thus labors to save them? Such an institution would, in time, exhibit scarcely any other than the character of a decent school and manufactory. It need not be invested with the insignia of a prison. It should be surrounded only with a high fence, like many factories in the neighborhood of cities, and carefully closed in front.

Second.—In addition to the class of boys just mentioned, the committee have no doubt that were such an institution once well established, and put under good regulation, the Magistrates would very often deem it expedient to place offenders in the hands of its Managers, rather than to sentence them to the City Penitentiary. The gradations of crime are almost infinite; and so minute are the shades of guilt, so remote, or so intimate the connexion between legal criminality, and previous character, it would often be judged reasonable to use all the discretion which the law would possibly admit, in deciding upon the offence and the destination of juvenile delinquents; and every principle of justice and mercy, would point, in numerous cases of conviction for crime to such a refuge and reformatory, rather than to the Bridewell or City Prison.

A third class which it might be very proper to transplant to such an establishment, and to distribute through its better divisons, are boys, (some of whom are of tender age,) whose parents, either from vice or indolence, are careless of their minds and morals, and leave them exposed in rags and filth, to miserable and scanty fare, destitute of education, and liable to become the prey of criminal associates. Many of such parents would probably be willing to indenture their children to the managers of a House of Refuge; and far better would it be for these juvenile sufferers, that they should be thus rescued from impending ruin. The laws of this state, do not, as in Massachusetts and some other places, authorize magistrates to use compulsory measures with parents who thus grossly abuse their charge, and, at the same time, absolutely refuse to resign their children to the hands of the guardians of the poor; but it is surely presumable, that were suitable provision made for the economical support and instruction of such children, a law for this purpose might readily be obtained.

There is still a fourth description of youthful delinquents for whom the contemplated establishment would afford a most seasonable and essential refuge from almost inevitable suffering and deterioration: that is those youthful convicts, who, on their discharge from prison, at the expiration of their sentence, finding themselves without character, without subsistence, and ignorant of the means by which it is to be sought, have no alternative but to beg or steal. They may, perhaps, be provided for at the Alms-House during a few days, or they may receive the admonitions and advice of the superintendents how to conduct themselves, but this can avail them but little, and with their previous habits unaltered, and their vicious propensities aggravated by corrupt intercourse, they again become depredators, and are again consigned to the same, or to some other prison, and most probably under a different name. Your committee, cannot but consider a House of Refuge for such outcasts from society as a desideratum called for by every principle of humanity and christian benevolence. Here they will be put to work, and treated acoording to their dispositions and behavior; their capacities for useful service will become known; habits of industry will be acquired; moral precepts will be implanted; and suitable places will be eventually obtained for them, in which they may have every opportunity of becoming honest and useful members of the community.

There remains to be noticed but one more class, for whom a House of Industry and Correction, under the management we contemplate, would be an appropriate place for reformation and improvement. We allude to that class of delinquent females, who are either too young to have acquired habits of fixed depravity, or those whose lives have in general been virtuous, but who, having yielded to the seductive influence of corrupt associates, have suddenly to endure the bitterness of lost reputation, and are cast forlorn and destitute upon a cold and unfeeling public, full of compunction for their errors, and anxious to be restored to the paths of innocence and usefulness. That there are many females of tender age just in those predicaments in this city, none can doubt who surveys the list of last year's culprits, furnished by the District Attorney. In this list, are the names of thirteen females, of 14 years of age, fourteen others of 15 and 16, and about forty of 17 and 18. The ages of a considerable number in this appalling catalogue have not been inserted, and it is by no means to be supposed that even a majority of those unhappy females who are in the predicament we have alluded to, have become the subjects of police investigation.

It is very far from the intention of the Committee, to propose, that the contemplated Refuge should become the receptacle of females whose ages and habitudes in the paths of guilt, render their restoration to society a question of dubious result. However desirable it may be, that an institution should be formed for the special purpose of affording the means of reformation, to those who are sincerely desirous to abandon a life of such debasement and wretchedness, we have no hesitation in expressing the belief, that it ought to be altogether detached from every other concern, and conducted by a separate association, and with the most prudent attention to delicacy and retirement. But within the ages and under the circumstances we have alluded to, it is our decided opinion,—an opinion founded not only upon the reasonableness of the proposition, but upon the result of similar institutions in Europe, that destitute females might form one department of the establishment, with the greatest benefit to themselves, and with advantage to the institution. Occupying apartments entirely distinct from those of the other sex, and separated from them by impassable barriers, the females might contribute, by their labor, to promote the interests of the establishment, and at the same time, derive from it their full and appropriate share of benefit. On this point, however, the Committee only mean to express their opinion, without urging it as an indispensable part of the concern.

The idea suggested by the Superintendent of the Alms-House of two distinct institutions, a Permanent and a Temporary Refuge, seems naturally to have sprung from the consideration of a distinction which will doubtless be found to prevail among the inmates of such a Penitentiary, viz.—a separation of those who are obviously susceptible of reformation, from those whose vicious propensities appear to be incorrigible. But we do not conceive it necessary to carry this principle to the length of having two distinct erections;—nor is it apprehended that two classes will by any means be sufficient. Even if there should be no more than forty or fifty inmates of the House of Refuge, we believe that there ought to be at least six classes, in order to form such a separation of character, and establish such a gradation of treatment, as to afford a perpetual and powerful stimulus to improvement and reformation. We would make a distinction in each of these classes in their dress, diet, lodging, hours of labor, recreation, &c., and we doubt not that these and other modes of treatment, would be found quite sufficient to break down the most stubborn dispositions, without having recourse to flagellation, or other personally degrading modes of punishment. The middling and lower classes, should in no wise differ in appearance from a decent and well ordered school and manufactory. But we should rely above all in the reformation of our subjects, upon a careful, unabated, and judicious course of moral and religious instruction. The Bible should become familiar,—the admirable events which it records, and the Divine precepts which it contains, should be the subject not merely of weekly but of daily enforcement; and, in order to render the moral and also the economical government of the institution more efficient, your committee would strongly recommend that a suitable number of ladies should be appointed to take a share in its administration. Of the special and very important advantages of associating the skill, the discretion, the tenderness, and fidelity of females, in concerns of this nature, we have not the least doubt. In those countries of Europe, in which penitentiary institutions, and establishments for the support of the poor, are under the best management, women are associated in the direction. In Holland, there is not, perhaps, an alms-house, or a house of correction, in which the females do not take an active share; and in no part of the world, it is believed, are the concerns of charity, and economical government more wisely managed. In England, Scotland, and Ireland also, since the illustrious example of Mrs. Fry and her associates in Newgate, the humane design of ladies' associations has been greatly encouraged, and accordingly we are informed by the late reports, that female visiting committees have been formed in the prisons at Bedford, Bristol, Carlisle, Chester, Colchester, Derby, Durham, Dumfries, Exeter, Glasgow, Lancaster, Liverpool, Nottingham, Plymouth, York, and Dublin.

The Committee would therefore deem themselves very deficient, did they not hold up, in a prominent point of view, the benefits to be derived from an enlistment of the services of judicious females in this moral warfare against the vices of society; and they would beg leave further to express the opinion, that if an association of ladies were once formed for this purpose, essential benefits might result from inviting them to appoint a committee for the regular visitation and inspection of our City Penitentiary and Alms-House. Their influence and assistance would, we presume, prove acceptable and grateful to the superintendents of those departments.

The introduction of labor would constitute an important feature in the concern, not only as a means of diminishing its expense and promoting its moral influence, but in order to supply its subjects with that instruction and with those habits which would enable them, on leaving the house, to procure a decent and honest livelihood. Various kinds of manufactories and trades might, doubtless, be introduced with advantage, and experience would soon enable the managers to decide upon the most profitable and eligible.

Although we are not apprised of there being any where in the United States, a House of Refuge established and conducted upon the principles now proposed; yet it is known to your Committee that philanthropic individuals, in various places, have deemed such an establishment a desideratum in each of our large cities. In Boston there is an institution approximating in its object, to that under consideration. It consists of a house, to which are sent those children, whose parents, through culpable and vicious neglect, leave them to roam through the streets untaught and unprotected. By the laws of Massachusetts, children thus neglected, may be taken from their parents, at the discretion of persons duly authorised, and placed at school, or at trades with suitable masters. In this asylum, their time is divided between the exercises of a school and manufactory, and when they have attained to a sufficient degree of skill and learning, places are obtained for them as apprentices at some useful art or trade.

But London and Dublin afford examples, quite in unison wit that which your Committee is anxious to see erected in this city. In London there are several establishments of this nature, but the one instituted in the borough, appears to come nearest in its general system to that which we would recommend. It "originated from the extent of Juvenile Depredations in the metropolis, and from a desire to ascertain the causes and arrest the progress of this great and growing evil. A large committee is appointed who meet every fortnight; and sub-committees, with confidential agents, are employed to investigate the cases of individuals, and to register the particulars. The building consists, first of a range of workshops of one floor, upwards of 500 feet in length, under which is a rope-walk, where every kind of lines, twines, and cord are manufactured; secondly, of a separate enclosure, used as a house of probation or reform, for the criminal classes of boys; thirdly, of a similar receptacle for the same description of girls; fourthly, of a chapel for religious worship; fifthly, of an eating-room, and also for an evening school-room; sixthly, of a warehouse, for the reception, delivery, and sale of the manufactured articles; seventhly, of the general kitchen, bakehouse, and dormitories; and, lastly, of the requisite accommodations for the superintendents. The quality of the food is proportioned to the gains of the youth, or the hardness of their labour. The boys are bound apprentices for a certain number of years to the master workmen employed within the institution. They have a particular dress, and a badge, which is left off after a certain period. The hours of work are from six in the morning till six in the evening in summer, and from day light till half past seven in winter. The school is open four evenings in the week for reading, writing, and arithmetic. The elder boys are allowed to go out one day in the month, and the younger, one day in three months, to return before dark. If any one escapes and is retaken, he is treated as a refractory apprentice. The task assigned, is such as can easily be performed; and of the extra labor, one-half is allowed as a reward, a small part being given in money, and the rest placed to his credit, to be paid at the end of his apprenticeship. Work of almost every trade is done by the boys. The girls are employed in making, mending, and washing the boys' clothes, and in different kinds of needle-work; and at the age of about 16, they are placed out as house servants, receiving a quarterly gratuity afterwards for good behavior during a certain period.

There are about 200 boys and girls in the place, and the result, as to conduct is extremely gratifying."

Some modifications of this plan would be requisite to adapt it to the local circumstances of this city; but in its general character it exhibits a cheering evidence of the blessings which flow from well-directed efforts to inure young people to habits of industry, regularity, sobriety, and morality. One of your Committee who went through the various wards of this institution, confirms the account which has been here given. The cheerful animation of the youthful laborers, and the neatness of their manufactured articles, were, in the highest degree, encouraging. Who can duly appreciate the importance of taking from the streets, boys who are under no parental or guardian control, who are "exposed to every temptation, "addicted to every vice, ignorant of all that is good, and trained by "their associates to the perpetration of every crime;" and training them during several years in such an institution, and then providing them with situations, in which their corrected habits will, in all probability, render them examples worthy of the imitation of others?

The annual reports of the committee detail at length, numerous striking cases of the efficacy of this Refuge, in producing an entire change in the character of individual boys and girls, and their obtaining situations of comfort and respectability.*

"They are," they observe, "more happy to allude to the suc-"cess of this establishment in reclaiming the youthful character, as "much difficulty is stated to be felt in managing juvenile offenders "in ordinary prisons. But boys in fact require a species of disci-"pline distinct from that of men; and as the gaols of the metropo-"lis, from their crowded state and imperfect construction, do not "admit, without considerable alterations, of such arrangements as "are necessary to reclaim these delinquents, it becomes of great "importance, that, at a period when crime is making such rapid "progress among the rising generation, a prison should be built "solely for the confinement of such offenders. It is not the wish "of the Committee that one of these boys should escape correction; "on the contrary, they would inflict a punishment that would be "severely felt as such, but of an opposite character and tendency "from that now experienced; imprisonment in the gaols of the "metropolis, being at present regarded by youthful criminals, with "comparative indifference."

It will doubtless be acknowledged by the society, that these important truths apply, with almost equal pertinency, to the state of the prisons and of juvenile criminality in the city of New-York; and our authorities and our citizens at large, may echo the sentiment contained in another part of the same report, that, "it is the "ordination of Divine Wisdom that man cannot suffer from the neg-"lect of man, without mutual injury; and, by a species of moral "retribution, society is punished by the omission of its duties to the "ignorant and the guilty. The renewed depredations of the offen-"der when discharged from confinement, the crimes which he pro-"pagates by his seduction and influence, spread pollution among "all with whom he associates, and the number of offenders thus "become indefinitely multiplied."

* See Appendix B.

From the views which they have thus laid before the society, your Committee cannot but cherish the lively expectation, that when the public mind comes to be impressed with the nature and importance of these various considerations, there will be but one opinion of the necessity and expediency of providing a place in this city, which shall serve as a real penitentiary to the younger class of offenders; as a refuge for the forlorn and destitute, who are on the confines of gross criminality; and as a temporary retreat for the discharged criminal, where he may find shelter, labor, and religious instruction, until some way can be pointed out to him of obtaining subsistence, without a recurrence to dishonesty and crime. If the actual situation of these several classes of criminal and destitute beings in this city, does not open a door for christian benevolence, as inviting in its promises of good, as any of the various kinds of charity, either at home or abroad which claim the attention of our citizens, your Committee think they might in vain seek to explore the miseries of their fellow-creatures, with the hope of exciting the feelings of commiseration, and the energies of active and unwearied humanity. Can it be right that we should extend our views to the wants of those that are thousands of miles from us, and close our eyes upon the condition of the worse than heathen, that wander in our streets?—Shall our hands be opened, with distinguished liberality, to the means of civilizing and reforming whole nations in the remotest quarters of the globe, and closed to the obvious necessities of the outcasts of our own society? Your Committee mean no reflection whatever on the schemes so actively prosecuted of doing good in distant parts of the earth;—but surely, if this we ought to do, the other we ought not to leave undone.

We venture upon those remarks, under the strongest impression of the importance of the subject upon which we have undertaken to dilate. Much more might be said in the way of elucidation and argument, but this is deemed unnecessary: and we cannot terminate our report more to the satisfaction of our own minds, than by quoting the conclusion of the last year's report of the London Committee for the improvement of Prison Discipline and the reformation of Juvenile Offenders. "We live in times in which extraor- "dinary efforts are in action for the moral welfare of mankind; "when the state of Europe opens channels of extensive usefulness, "and presents occasions for immediate exertion, which could "scarcely have been anticipated, and which it would be criminal "to neglect. There seems, too, at the present time, to prevail "among the benevolent of different nations, a unity of thought and "design, which cannot fail to strike a considerate beholder: and "he must be dead to sensibility, who can contemplate, without "emotion, the intercourse which now subsists between men of va- "rious countries who are laboring for the public good, and whom "national differences have too long kept asunder. Enlightened "principles and practical benevolence are taking deep root. As- "sociations, originating in public feeling and sanctioned by public "authority, are forming in countries, where co-operation in deeds "of mercy, has hitherto been but little known. The moral effects "of these institutions will be vast, and indeed incalculable not only "by the accomplishment of that which it is their professed object "to promote; but such associations call into action the latent seeds "of public virtue,—bring together the pious and the good of every "religious sentiment and political opinion, and eradicate those pre-"judices which too often alienate affection, and separate man from "man. In the exercise of their duties, prison societies bring into "benevolent contact the educated and the enlightened, with the "ignorant and the debased; the great and the powerful, with the "lowly and the oppressed; the pure and the elevated, with the ab-"ject and the guilty. They supply an important chasm in the "widely extended circle of human charities; connecting those who "most need, with those who most effectually can dispense mercy. "To behold nation after nation thus catching the spirit, and enga-"ged in the arduous struggle, of self-improvement; to trace the "progress of civilization and refinement, by the establishment of "institutions which have for their direct object the reformation of "the vicious and the succour of the oppressed; to observe the rig-"or of antiquated custom, and the relics of barbarism yielding be-"fore the advancement of knowledge, and the humanizing influence "of christian principles—this is a moral spectacle which it is indeed "a privilege to witness, and in which it is a glory to share.

"To diffuse principles, and cherish feelings, which are directly "calculated to insure respect and obedience to the laws—meliorate "the state of society, and promote the present and eternal well-"being of man—is the aim of the society for the improvement of "Prison Discipline; and surely an object of greater importance "cannot engage the attention or impress the heart. Of the various "obligations due to the community, the prevention of crime, may "be ranked among the most sacred:—whether regarded as a duty "enjoined by religion, urged by enlightened policy, or impelled by "benevolent feeling, it is one which involves the great interests of "human nature, and demands exertions from which no man is enti-"tled to consider himself exempt."

APPENDIX
A.

The following list is extracted from the four hundred and fifty cases of Juvenile Offences, furnished by the District Attorney, from the Records of the Police Office, for 1822.

Henry H. aged 15, came out of Bridewell, now charged with stealing, vagrant thief; sentence 6 months to the Penitentiary.

David B. aged 12, brought up by the watch, charged with stealing, vagrant thief; 6 months Penitentiary.

William H. goes about begging, no home or business, a vagrant; 6 months Penitentiary.

John T. aged 12, no parents, boards with a woman in Thomas-street, cannot tell her name, came from Newburgh a week ago, arrested in coming out of a house where he went to steal, vagrant thief; 6 months Penitentiary.

Henry M. aged 12, no place to live at, goes out to beg, charged with stealing fat, vagrant thief; 6 months Penitentiary.

Joseph P. aged 13, no parents, no home, goes a begging, charged with stealing, vagrant thief; 6 months Penitentiary.

Oliver R. aged 14, father lives in Flushing, stays with a woman in Mulberry-street, no home; vagrant thief; 6 months Penitentiary.

George D. aged 14, father dead, mother in Baltimore, picks up chips, begs for victuals, and steals, vagrant thief; 6 months Penitentiary.

Thomas Y. and James M'D. boys, wandering about idle, no home, and thieves; 6 months Penitentiary.

Thomas H. C. aged 12, father is dead, mother lives at service, never went to school, been twice in Bridewell, once in Penitentiary, charged with stealing; 6 months Penitentiary.

Martha Van C. aged 22, taken up by the watch, out of Penitentiary last week, often in Bridewell, three or four times in the Penitentiary, no means of living, a vagrant; 6 months Penitentiary.

Eliza M. aged 15, has no parents, came out of Penitentiary in December last, been there twice, charged with stealing; 4 months in the Penitentiary.

Hetty S. aged 13, goes to beg, found in a house with another stealing; 6 months Penitentiary.

Francis J. aged 17, has no money, no clothes, no residence; 4 months Penitentiary.

Jacob B. aged 17, came out of the Penitentiary in October last, is now indicted for burglary; 6 months Penitentiary.

Jane Ann S. aged 14, has been twice in Bridewell; 6 months Penitentiary.

Alexander G. aged 18, no occupation, no particular place of abode, vagrant thief; 6 months Penitentiary.

Peter W. and John W. ages 19, both noted vagrants, and idlers, vagrant thieves; 6 months Penitentiary.

Phebe Ann M. aged 19, no honest means of living; 60 days City Prison.

Mary Ann T. aged 18, has no honest means of support; 60 days City Prison.

John C. aged 19, no particular place of residence, charged with stealing; 60 days City Prison.

Samuel S. aged 14, has no means of support, came out of the Alms-House, vagrant; 6 months Penitentiary.

Sally B. brought up by the watch, was taken from under the stoop of the Alms-House; 60 days City Prison.

John B. brought up by the watch, has no place of residence, and is very filthy.

Hannah M. has no home, and has lodged in the watch-house for two nights past; 60 days City Prison.

George, alias Rodolph T. aged 19, has no particular place to live at, no money, no clothes, charged with stealing; 6 months in the Penitentiary.

Alfred C. aged 13, was brought up, having been found sleeping in some shavings, destitute, and no home; 6 months Penitentiary.

Samuel C. was found drunk in the street, without clothes to cover his nakedness, no means, no money; 60 days City Prison.

Jane B. aged 18, came from the Penitentiary a year ago; 6 months Penitentiary.

Thomas P. aged 15, has just come out of Bridewell, has been in the Penitentiary, has no particular place to live at; 6 months Penitentiary.

Charles M., John B. and Jacob B., ages 14, were found sleeping at night in a boat, no homes, no parents; 6 months Penitentiary.

William S. aged 11, his father turned him out of the house, was found sleeping in a boat at night; 6 months Penitentiary.

Sophia H. aged 14 years, was charged with stealing, goes about begging, has been in Bridewell 6 times, no means; 6 months Penitentiary.

Alexander C. has no money, no business, just come out of prison, no particular place to sleep at; 6 months Penitentiary.

Etienne S. aged 21, came from Canada five months ago, first offence, has no place to live at; 60 days City Prison.

Rachel S. aged 18, has no particular place to live at, is poor and ragged, was found in the street, said she was sick; 3 months Penitentiary.

Susan J. aged 18, has no home or means of taking care of herself, very filthy, and nearly naked; 3 months Penitentiary.

Mary B. aged 16, has been a vagrant about two years; 30 days City Prison.

Harriet B. aged 18, has no clothes, most of those on her back are borrowed; 60 days City Prison.

Edward Van C. aged 13, was found at night sleeping on the side-walk, has been once in Bridewell, no parents; 6 months Penitentiary.

John H. aged 13, was found at night sleeping on the side-walk, no parents; 6 months Penitentiary.

Lucinda D. aged 16, came out of Bridewell about two months ago, is a prostitute, no home; 6 months Penitentiary.

Robert T. a boy, brought up charged with stealing, has been in Bridewell and Penitentiary, no home; 6 months Penitentiary.

John C. aged 14, has no parents, was found sleeping in a yard on some shavings; 6 months Penitentiary.

Maria W. aged 18, lives with her parents at the Hook, has been a prostitute for six months; 4 months Penitentiary, &c. &c. &c.

B.

EXTRACTED FROM THE LONDON REPORTS.

TEMPORARY REFUGE.

The following Cases are given, as an outline of the description of characters which have been relieved by the Committee:—

1.—A. B. aged fourteen, was discharged from the New Prison, Clerkenwell. When received under the care of the Society, he had been in the commission of crime for eight months. During this period, he had plundered to a considerable amount, and had been engaged in purchasing and passing forged notes, picking pockets, and shop-lifting. He was in the Temporary Refuge for four months, and his conduct satisfied the Committee of the sincerity of his professions, and the earnestness of his desire to amend his life. He was consequently admitted into the Permanent Establishment, where his conduct continued to afford great satisfaction. He was discharged to his father-in-law, who is by trade a weaver, and who is teaching the lad his own trade. The accounts of his conduct are extremely favourable, and such as to justify the expectation, that he will become an honest and industrious member of society.

2.—C. D. aged seventeen, was discharged from the Borough Compter. He had been apprenticed to a paper-stainer, but having misconducted himself, left his master, and engaged himself as a gentleman's servant. He was tried in Horsemonger-lane, for stealing lead, in company with other bad characters, and sentenced to one month's imprisonment. When in his master's service, he defrauded him to a considerable amount. On the discharge of the boy from prison, he applied to one of the visiters of the Society, who placed him in the Temporary Refuge, where his general conduct and demeanor have given general satisfaction. He has been bound apprentice for seven years: and the accounts received of his conduct are very favourable.

3.—E. F. aged twelve, was discharged from the Borough Compter. The father of this youth deserted his wife, and left her with five children to maintain, entirely destitute. This boy defrauded his mother, from whom he stole the implements of trade, which his father had left at home. For this offence, his mother caused him to be committed to the Borough Compter for a week. On his discharge, he was admitted into the Temporary Refuge, and after conducting himself with propriety for six months, he was received into the Permanent Establishment. He has been bound apprentice to a captain in the merchant service, and has lately returned from a voyage of eight months, and presented himself to the committee, with an excellent character from his master.

4.—J. S. aged fourteen. This youth has been for eight months engaged in the commission of crime, during which time he had plundered and defrauded to a great amount. He had been engaged in purchasing and passing forged notes, shoplifting, picking pockets, &c. After having been four months in the Temporary Refuge, he was admitted into the Permanent Establishment, where he made considerable progress as a tailor. He has since been given up to his father-in-law, a weaver, who is teaching him his own trade, and reports to the Committee that he is going on very well, and conducts himself with great propriety.

5.—B. M. aged sixteen. This youth was about three years in the service of different gentlemen as a footboy. After having left his last place, he was taken up for picking pockets, tried at Newgate, and sentenced to six months imprisonment in the House of Correction, Cold Bath Fields. He is now in the Permanent Establishment, making considerable progress in his trade as a tailor, and conducts himself with great propriety.

6.—W. V. aged seventeen. This lad was apprenticed to a paper-stainer for some time, and afterwards engaged as a gentleman's servant. He was tried at Horsemonger-lane for stealing lead, in company with some other lads, and sentenced to one month's imprisonment, and to be flogged. Whilst in the employment of one of his masters, he defrauded him to a considerable amount, but for this offence he was not tried. He was in the Establishment for three months, and gave great satisfaction by his general conduct and demeanor. He was then bound apprentice for seven years to a merchant in Honduras, and the account both from himself and others, as to his industry and integrity, is very satisfactory.

7.—J. S. aged sixteen, is a natural child; he never knew his father, and his mother has been dead for some years. He was in three several employments; the first with a stationer, where he learnt part of the business, and in the two others as an errand boy. Unfortunately for him, two of his emyloyers became bankrupts, and upon the failure of the last, this lad was thrown upon the town completely destitute. He then fell into evil courses, and was imprisoned twice; once for passing forged notes, and the second for picking a gentleman's pocket. Upon his discharge from Newgate, he solicited admission into the Temporary Refuge, and after remaining there four months, was received into the Permanent Establishment. He is now engaged in the book-binding department, where he takes a leading part, and bids fair to be a useful and respectable member of society.

8.—J. W. aged sixteen. His father is a schoolmaster, and in consequence of the misconduct of the lad, who had become connected with some bad boys, he turned him out of doors, about a year before he solicited an asylum in the Temporary Refuge. From that period until his admission, he was engaged in the commission of crime, and was twice in Newgate, but was discharged the last time by proclamation, none appearing against him; from the Temporary Refuge he was received into the Permanent Establishment, where he behaves very well, and is making considerable progress in his trade of a shoe-maker.

9.—H. R. aged eighteen. This lad was received into the Temporary Refuge, upon the recommendation of the Sheriffs of London. He had wandered from the paths of rectitude twelve months before he was received, six months of which had been passed in prison. He behaved orderly and well whilst in the Establishment, and as there was every reason to believe that he might be trusted again in the world, he was recommended to a captain of an East Indiaman, and is now on his voyage.

10.—R. I. aged twelve years, Both the parents of this boy are dead. He was for some time in the work-house of his parish, from whence he was placed out as an errand boy. In this situation he robbed his master of a one pound note, and was sent to prison for two days by the magistrates. He was recommended to the Temporary Refuge, and pity being taken upon his destitute situation, he was immediately received. He is now in the Permanent Establishment, and has made good progress in his trade. He conducts himself perfectly well, and there is every reason to expect that he will turn out an honest and useful man.

11.—J. H. aged twenty; this young man was in the navy for two years as servant to a warrant officer. Having obtained his discharge, he was employed in different situations, and latterly as a potboy in different public houses. Having embezzled some property belonging to the master whom he last served, he was apprehended, but discharged upon trial, in consequence of a flaw in the indictment. He solicited admission into the Temporary Refuge, and after having conducted himself very well there for some time, was placed on board a ship bound to India, and is now on his voyage.

12.—M. C. aged twenty-five; a man of colour, was born in Jamaica, and had been in England fifteen years. He lived nine years in the family of the gentleman who brought him to this country, and five years in another gentleman's service. He embezzled some wearing apparel of his last master, who immediately dismissed him from his service, but did not prosecute him. After being in some other employment, he was apprehended for theft, and sent to prison. From thence he was received into the Refuge, and when an opportunity offered, was placed aboard a ship in the coal trade. With this situation he was not satisfied; but his first master having met with him, and feeling convinced that he was a reformed character, he has taken him into his service again, and he is now on his voyage to India with him.

13.—J. A. aged sixteen. This lad is entirely destitute, having no father or mother, or any friend who could assist him. He was twice imprisoned, first for a petty theft, and the second time as a vagrant. After having been six months in the Temporary Refuge, he was admitted into the Permanent Establishment, where he is now occupied in the shoemaker's shop. He conducts himself very well, and is making a good progress in his trade.

14.—W. B. aged fourteen; this lad was corrupted by some bad boys in the neighborhood where his parents resided. They persuaded him to abscond from his home; and by them he was initiated into the ways of vice. After having been a short time in prison, he was received into this Establishment. Having expressed a wish to go to sea, he was sent on a voyage in the merchant service. He conducts himself well, and to his master's satisfaction.

15.—J. G. aged twelve: this child absconded from his father's house, and associated with bad boys for two months. He was then taken up for theft, and after trial was received into the Temporary Refuge, where he remained eight months, when he was delivered to his father. He now conducts himself extremely well, and works at his father's trade. Twelve months have elapsed since his discharge.

16.—H. P. aged thirteen; the father of this boy has been separated for many years from his mother, and now lives with another woman. She declared she would not continue with him, if his child remained under the same roof. In consequence of this, the unnatural father turned him out of doors. He maintained himself for about six weeks by begging and holding horses in the street; at length, in a state of starvation, he stole a loaf of bread out of a baker's shop. He was apprehended and sent to prison for one month. From the Temporary Refuge he was after some time, sent on a voyage in a merchant vessel, and has behaved so well that the captain has desired that he might be apprenticed to him.

17.—T. F. aged twelve years. This child robbed his father, who is a poor man, of some money which he had saved to pay his rent. Having absconded from his home, he was picked up in the

5

streets by a boy who took him to his lodgings, where he remained till he had spent the greater part of the money, and been robbed of the remainder. He then returned to his father's house, who sent for an officer, when he was taken to Worship-street Police Office, and from thence to New Prison, Clerkenwell. Being recommended by the magistrates, he was received into the Temporary Refuge, where he remained nine months. He is now in the Permanent Establishment, where he behaves very well and is learning the trade of a tailor.

18.—J. B. aged sixteen; this boy who was in a stationer's warehouse, was prevailed upon by a man who had formerly been in the same employ, to rob his master. The theft being discovered, he was apprehended and was sent to Clerkenwell Prison; from thence he was received into the Temporary Refuge, and after being there for nine months, was admitted into the Permanent. In both institutions his conduct has been good, and he is now in the shoemaking department.

19.—B. B. aged fourteen: this lad had been employed in two or three different manufactories in the neighborhood where his mother resided, his father being dead. In going to and from his mother's house to the place of his employment, he became connected with some bad boys, and was apprehended for stealing a pint pot from a publican's door. He remained in the Temporary Refuge four months. From thence he was apprenticed to a baker by his mother; he has been in this situation seven months, and his master gives him an excellent character.

20.—J. U. aged sixteen. This lad, whose parents are dead, appears to have conducted himself respectably whilst he was in different situations as an errand boy, &c. Being out of employment, he became connected with some bad characters, and unfortunately was prevailed upon by them to commit a theft. For this he was apprehended and commited to Newgate, where he lay twelve weeks. After his discharge, he was received into the Temporary Refuge, from whence, after eight months, he was admitted into the Permanent. There he is engaged in the shoemaking shop: he conducts himself well, and makes great progress in his trade.

21.—C. E. aged sixteen years. This lad, whose father is an honest and industrious man, was employed for some time as an errand boy; but having become acquainted with some bad boys, he was induced by them to become a partner in their depredations. Happily for him he was soon stopped in his career; for being apprehended for a theft, he was, after a short confinement, received into this asylum. Here he remained six months, and is now in the Permanent Establishment. He is learning the trade of a shoemaker, in which he makes considerable progress, and conducts himself with great propriety.

22.—W. J. was born at sea; his father was for many years in the naval service. At the age of 14 years, he was apprenticed to a trade. He fell into the company of bad characters, and joined them in committing depredations. His case was made known to the Committee; he was received into the Temporary Refuge, and having remained a considerable time in that asylum, was apprenticed to a captain of a merchantman. His conduct on board has been most exemplary, and entirely to the satisfaction of his employers.

He lately presented himself to the Committee, and returning thanks for the kind assistance which he had received, said, with much emotion, "This House has saved me from ruin!"

23.—T. H. 16 years of age, was received into the Temporary Refuge, having been in confinement for picking pockets. He was discharged by the Magistrates, because no prosecutor appeared against him. After remaining some time, he was admitted into the Refuge for the Destitute, and has since been apprenticed, at his own request, on board of a ship in the merchant service.

24.—W. J. aged 16 years; at 12 years old he went to the service of a pawn-broker, and was with him eight months; was afterwards 20 months as a pot boy, and three months in the employ of a harness-maker; got acquainted with some young thieves, who persuaded him to join them, and he commenced picking pockets in September, 1819; has been three times in confinement; once in Tothill fields, once in Clerkenwell, and for the last offence, robbing a child's neck of coral beads, at Sadler's wells, was confined seven weeks in Newgate, tried at the Old Bailey, and sentenced to three months imprisonment in the House of Correction. Having been admitted into the Temporary Refuge, he has been since transferred to the Permanent Establishment, where he is learning the tailoring business, and is going on very well.

25.—W. A. aged 13 years: his father is dead, mother a poor woman supports herself by charing and washing. This boy has been two years in the practice of thieving, but has been imprisoned but once, for picking a gentleman's pocket, and was discharged in consequence of the prosecutor not appearing against him. He has been transferred to the Permanent Establishment, in which he has conducted himself with great propriety, and shows much gratitude for the assistance afforded him.

26.—D. W. aged 13 years: his father is dead, mother is a book-folder. This boy robbed his master of eight books, which he sold for 3s6d. Was in confinement one month at Newgate, and tried at the Old Bailey. He has been placed in the Permanent Establishment, where his conduct has been most exemplary.

27.—C. D. aged 16 years. This lad was two years a clerk in a respectable counting-house, but having stolen some property belonging to his master, he lost his situation; his employers declined to prosecute. He was received into the Temporary Refuge, where having conducted himself with great propriety, his former master has again taken him into his employ.

28.—C. B. 16 years of age: his parents are both dead. He worked several years at a cotton factory in Cheshire. Having found his way (about three years since) to London, has been employed in the brick fields, in summer, and in the winter, in several dust yards. Being in company with three boys, he was apprehended with them for robbing a till in a shop, and was committed to the New Prison, Clerkenwell, where he was confined a week. His conduct, during his residence in the Refuge was most exemplary, and he has been apprenticed for 7 years to a respectable house at Honduras.

FEMALES.

E. S. was deprived of her father at an early age, and was brought up by her mother, a poor charwoman. At the age of fourteen years, she obtained a situation as servant in a decent family, from whose house she soon absconded, through the persuasion of some wicked girls in the neighborhood, taking away with her apparel to a considerable amount. She was immediately apprehended, taken before the magistrates, and committed for a second hearing. The prosecutor having declined to appear against her, she was discharged.—She was immediately placed in the Temporary Refuge, and has since been received into the Refuge for the Destitute, where her conduct induces the hope that she will ultimately be restored to society, as a reformed character.

E. W. 19 years of age, was convicted of robbing her master's house, and was sentenced to twelve months imprisonment in the House of Correction, Cold Bath Fields. On her discharge from prison, she was placed in the Temporary Refuge by this society, and has been since restored to her relatives, and continues to conduct herself with propriety.

M. R. 26 years of age, was convicted of picking pockets, and was sentenced to seven years transportation. This sentence was, subsequently, on account of some favorable circumstances in her case, commuted for two years imprisonment in the House of Correction, Cold Bath Fields. Upon the expiration of her sentence, she was sent to the Temporary Refuge by this Society, under whose care she still remains. Her friends have since been reconciled to her, and are now endeavoring to procure for her a reputable situation.

Officers of the House of Refuge.

CADWALLADER D. COLDEN, *President.*

STEPHEN ALLEN,
PETER A. JAY,
JOHN T. IRVING,
JOHN GRISCOM,
HENRY I. WYCKOFF,
CORNELIUS DUBOIS, } *Vice Presidents.*

RALPH OLMSTED, *Treasurer.*
ROBERT F. MOTT, *Secretary.*
JOSEPH CURTIS, *Superintendent.*

Managers.

Stephen Allen,	Thomas Eddy,	Robert F. Mott,
Arthur Burtis,	John Griscom,	Hugh Maxwell,
C. D. Colden,	James W. Gerard,	Henry Mead,
Isaac Collins,	Joseph Grinnell,	Ralph Olmsted,
Samuel Cowdrey,	John E. Hyde,	John Stearns,
Gilbert Coutant,	Ansel W. Ives,	John Targee,
John Duer,	John T. Irving	J. M. Wainwright,
Cornelius Dubois,	Peter A. Jay,	Henry I. Wyckoff.
Cornelius R. Duffie,	James Lovett,	

FIRST ANNUAL REPORT, &c.

1825.

WITH a heart-felt interest in the cause which has been committed to their charge, the Managers of the Society for the Reformation of Juvenile Delinquents meet their constituents and the public, in the needful formality of a first annual Report. At no period since their appointment (on the 19th of December, 1823,) has the question of the establishment of a House of Refuge, on the plan indicated in the Report of the Society for the Prevention of Pauperism, (which led to the formation of the Society they now represent) been for one moment regarded as an object unworthy of their anxious solicitude, and their earnest and unremitted efforts. If any thing could have been necessary to stimulate them to diligence and perseverance in the accomplishment of the desired object, the generous sympathies which were promptly manifested on the distribution of that report, and the benevolence which flowed spontaneously from their fellow citizens into the channel first opened to receive it, were abundantly sufficient to excite the Board of Managers to a zealous discharge of the trust reposed in them. It was obvious that throughout our whole community, the evils which were accumulating upon destitute children and young people, were regarded as truly deplorable. The exposure to which they are subjected, in the streets and lurking places of the vicious, and more especially in the prisons to which they are sentenced as a punishment,, when once made known, called forth, from every humane bosom, a burst of feeling in favour of some more efficient protection from the pit of destruction which yawned beneath their feet. To sentence individuals of a tender age and of either sex, for crimes into which they may have been drawn, by the almost irresistible impulse of circumstances to them unavoidable, to a penalty which tends immediately to prepare them for deeper guilt, was perceived to be not only a solecism in legal justice, but a departure from every principle of enlarged humanity and sound discretion. The protection of society from the depredations of the vicious, is the main object of penal legislation. Not only to correct the criminal in his unprincipled course, but as far as possible to eradicate the habit and the desire of vicious indulgence, is the concurrent aim of all well devised schemes of penal jurisprudence. Reformation is, or ought to be an object dear to every man, who votes for a penal statute. In the case of the young it is almost every thing; for who can deny that juvenile offences proceed almost entirely from the influence of bad example. To neglect the reformation of this class of delinquents,—to punish those who are young in years and in crime, by dungeons, compulsory indolence, and wretched fare, without any attempt to break in upon the darkness of their understandings by the radiance of knowledge and religion,—and this with a view of affording protection to society,—of rendering property secure and public morals uncontaminated, is surely to neglect the plainest maxims of prudence and common sense. Such, nevertheless, has been the course pursued in our own and in other countries, in relation to one of the most important considerations embraced in the whole circle of criminal law. In what code shall we find a just discrimination between adult and juvenile crimes, and an adequate provision for withdrawing young offenders from the vortex of corrupt association, for enlightening their minds, changing their habits and inclinations, and restoring them to society, prepared to increase the amount of industry, morals, and virtue. That a far more ample provision of this nature is absolutely necessary to complete the reformatory system of prison discipline, so happily commenced in this country, few persons we think will entertain a doubt;—that such is the tenor of public opinion in this city, is most obvious from the evidence which has been afforded us, by the cheerfulness with which contributions were made, for the commencement of an institution, which we trust will be not less permanent, than beneficent in its operation and example.

The first concern of the Managers, after being duly

organized, was to ascerain to what extent they might rely upon the bounty of the city, for the means requisite to carry into effect the proposed asylum for vagrant and depraved young people. For this purpose the city was divided into districts, and with such assistance as we found it not difficult to obtain, a personal application was made to those of our citizens, who, it was believed, would be likely to respond to the views and objects of the Society. The result was an amount of subscriptions and donations, of about 15,000 dollars, and a universal expression in favour of the contemplated institution. Thus encouraged, the Board proceeded to solicit of the corporation, the appropriation of some suitable site, for the erection of a House of Refuge, and in conference with the committee of that honourable body, the ground and buildings held by the general government as an Arsenal, near the head of Broadway and the Bowery, was stated to be the most eligible of any in the city, especially as it was reported that the United States had no occasion to continue much longer in the occupation of it at least as a depot of arms and ammunition. The manner in which this application to the city authority was received, was manifest by the report of its committee, a copy of which is hereunto subjoined.

The officers of the War Department, including the present Vice President of the United States, to whom application was made in favour of a relinquishment of the said ground and buildings, for the purposes of this Society, received the proposition with cordiality, acknowledged their conviction of the utility and importance of the proposed institution, and agreed to convey the government title to the premises and buildings for as small a sum as was consistent with the nature of their public duties. An arrangement being thus amicably concluded with both the authorities concerned, the Board of Managers was put in possession, upon terms which must be regarded as extremely favourable, of ground and buildings better adapted to their wants than any other within their knowledge.

From the erratic and vicious habits of the boys who would necessarily be sentenced to a House of Refuge, it was easily foreseen that a high wall around the premises would be indispensable. The arsenal not only afforded this important advantage, but it contained a suitable dwelling for a superintendent and his family, and a building which has furnished temporary accommodations for a limited number of subjects. The outer wall includes a space of 320 feet by 300, which is quite sufficient for any extension of the institution, which will be required at any future time.*

The unavoidable delay attendant on the removal of the government stores, and the making of such alterations as were requisite to adapt the building to the purposes intended, together with those preliminary steps relative to the collection of subscriptions, the procuring of a charter, &c. which were not to be omitted, the Board was not prepared to open the institution until the commencement of the present year.

On the first day of January last, the board met and opened the Institution, in presence of a considerable concourse of citizens, (among whom were several members of the Corporation) who assembled to witness the ceremony of the introduction of a number of juvenile convicts, the first in this city, if not in this country, into a place exclusively intended for their reformation and instruction. The ceremony was interesting in the highest degree. Nine of those poor outcasts from society, 3 boys and 6 girls, clothed in rags, with squalid countenances, were brought in from the Police Office, and placed before the audience. An address appropriate to so novel an occasion was made by a member of the board, and not an individual, it may safely be affirmed, was present, whose warmest feelings did not vibrate in unison with the philanthropic views which led to the foundation of this House of Refuge. Thus commenced, our institution assumed a standing among the charities of our city and state, and the managers confidently believe, will prove inferior to none in the satisfaction which its operation will afford to a benevolent public, and

*An application to the Legislature, for an act of incorporation met with no obstacle. The act received its final sanction on the 29th day of March, 1824, and a grant of $2000 per annum, for five years, to aid in the support of the Institution, was made the last session of the Legislature.

in its moralizing influence upon the most degraded portions of our community. The number of its delinquent inmates continued to increase until it amounted to 58—beyond which the present limited accommodations for the males, at least, admit of no extension. Of this number, 44 were boys and 14 girls. Of the former, the oldest, at the time of his admission, was 18, and the youngest 9.—The whole number admitted into the house, from its commencement to the present time, is 73. They have been received from the following sources, viz:—

From the Court of Sessions, for grand larceny - -	1
————————, for petit larceny - - -	9
From the Police Magistrates, for stealing and vagrancy -	47
From the Commissioners of the Alms-House, for stealing, vagrancy, and absconding - - - -	16
Total	73

Of this number,	6 have never been in Bridewell,
————————,	49 have been in that prison from 1 to 7 times,
————————,	19 have been confined in the City Penitentiary.
Total	73

Of those who have been confined in the Penitentiary,

9	have	served	1	term of	- -	2 to 12	months
3	do.	do.	2	terms	amounting	to 12	do.
1	do.	do.	2	do.	do.	24	do.
1	do.	do.	2	do.	do.	8	do.
1	do.	do.	2	do.	do.	9	do.
1	do.	do.	3	do.	do.	18	do.
1	do.	do.	4	do.	do.	33	do.
2	do.	do.	5	do.	do.	36	do.
19							

Of the whole number received in the house, 30 are the children of foreigners, and 43 are from the city and various parts of the state.

They have been thus disposed of:—

BOYS.

Returned to their parents - - - - - - -	2
Indented - - - - - - - - - -	5
Absconded - - - - - - - - -	4
At present in the house - - - - - - - -	43
	54

GIRLS.

Sent to the Alms-House - - - - - - - -	1
Discharged, being of age - - - - - - -	1
Indented - - - - - - - - - -	4
In the house - - - - - - - - - -	13
	19
Total	73

Of the 5 boys who have been indented, 2 were placed with farmers, and the other three were bound, as seamen, to a person in whom the Managers and Superintendent place entire confidence. From one of the boys, a favourable report has been received,* the others having been recently indented, no account from them has been obtained.

From two of the girls, the Superintendent has received acceptable information.* The others have but lately left the house.

The subjects, on their admission, have proved, with a few exceptions, to be very ignorant. Some of them

* The following letters from the respectable persons to whom these children were indented, afford encouraging hopes of their continued good conduct.

P——e, June 21st, 1825.

Dear Sir,

Believing that the Managers of the House of Refuge, as well as the patrons generally of that Institution, feel a lively interest in the welfare of those intrusted to your care, and sufficient time having elapsed since I recieved J. and J. to become acquainted with their dispositions, I write to acquaint you with their deportment. Joseph for about ten days, behaved extremely well—always attentive; but after church he came to me and asked permission to take a walk; as he had been more than a mile to church, I did not consider it necessary; and being extremely cautious that he should not become acquainted with the town boys, I refused him permission to go, and he gave out some threats to one of the servants, and refused to eat his supper. The next morning I called him to me and conversed with him for a considerable time, telling him that he must look to me for protection, which he would be sure to find whilst he conducted himself with propriety; and that he would be equally sure of punishment when his conduct was bad; and as he had been angry enough to go without his supper, he must take the field without his breakfast, and at noon I would inform him whether he could have his dinner. At 12 he came in with my man, evidently humbled and weak for want of food. I asked him if he was sorry for his conduct, he said he was; and after a promise of better behaviour, for the future, I gave him his dinner. Since that I have not had cause of complaint. Jane has shown nothing of that temper which I have discovered in Joseph, and I am pleased to say, her conduct has been unexceptionable up to the present time. Wishing that all those that are bound out from that Institution may conduct themselves as well as these two have so far done,

I remain respectfully, Your Friend,

J. W.

Extract from a Letter from the same dated 18*th October*.

Since my last, under the date of 21st June, J. continues to conduct himself as well as boys generally who have been creditably educated. He is attentive to church and to school, and appears anxious to improve. As respects J. her conduct has been uniformly good, and I am informed by her teachers she is the best scholar in her class.

D——i, August 30,1825.

Dear Sir,

You may recollect that when I took Diana from the House of Refuge, I engaged to give you information respecting her behaviour in my family; and it is with no little satisfaction that I can with truth state to you that her conduct has been good. She has given less cause of complaint since being here, than we should have reason to expect, from a girl of her age taken from one of our well regulated families in this part of the country. The lessons taught her while under your care appear to have made a proper, and I think lasting impression on her mind. She evinces a disposition to learn what is good, and such kinds of work as is proper to employ her in, she performs with ingenuity and neatness. She is not by an irregular attendance at schools, had learned to read, but had acquired no relish for intellectual improvement. Their habits, as it respects skill and useful industry, were still more deplorable. With one exception, there has not been a girl received, who could sew even well enough to make an apron. Of washing, ironing, cooking, or baking, they knew but very little, and indeed, were unable to do any thing without instruction. But such has been the progress of the females in these important attainments, the Superintendent has been enabled to have every garment, which his subjects have required, made without charge to the Institution. The employment of the girls, in addition to the needful domestic occupations, has been chiefly the plaiting of grass; and although they have not yet advanced sufficiently to render their skill of much pecuniary advantage, many of them have made attainments, in this branch, which justify the belief, that it may become a source of profit to the Institution, and the means of honest support to them when discharged.

The most considerable occupation of the boys, has been the clearing up of the premises, by the removal and disposal of the lumber, sheds, &c., clearing and cultivating a small garden, and more especially in waiting upon, and assisting the masons and carpenters that have been engaged in various repairs, elevating the wall, and erecting a new building within the enclosure. In this exercise, they have been very efficient; a number of them have evinced a becoming spirit of ambition and desire of improvement, and cannot fail to have laid the foundation of future industry.

able, (and perhaps never will be) to perform any heavy work, yet I consider it a fortunate acquisition that I obtained her from you, and if the want of order and regularity in my family should not tend to weaken or do away the habits she acquired while under your care, we should have reason to be thankful. From the cursory view I had of your establishment, a very favourable impression was made on my mind respecting the beneficial effects it might produce in society. Since that time, I have reflected much on the subject; from which, and the facts I have learned from little D. I have been led to consider the Institution as one of the most wise, humane, and (as respects your city in particular) the most beneficial of any I am acquainted with, and cannot but hope and believe that it may receive from both the corporation and the legislature, that fostering care and aid which in my opinion it so justly merits —and

I am, Sir, with sentiments of respect and esteem,

Your Friend, &c. &c.

E. F.

The principal in-door employment has been shoe-making and tailoring. In these, the boys have made no inconsiderable advancement;—one hundred and twenty-nine pair of shoes having been made, in addition to forty-one pair used in the family. With respect to manual employment, it therefore appears that although nothing has yet been done, as a source of income to the Institution, the work accomplished by both sexes has produced a positive saving, and afforded a promise, under a more favourable circumstances, of a useful and profitable extension of manufacturing skill and activity.

About two hours in the day, one in the morning and one in the evening, are devoted to mental improvement. During the first hour, they are occupied in learning to spell, read, write, and cypher, and in this exercise the system of mutual instruction is followed, and they are divided into classes agreeably to the method pursued in the Lancasterian schools.

On that system the
1st Class learn the Alphabet.
2d " words and syllables of two letters.
3d " words and syllables of three and four letters.
4th " words and sentences from Scripture of five and six letters.
5th " words and sentences from Scripture of two syllables.
6th " words and sentences from Scripture of three syllables.
7th " words and sentences from Scripture of four syllables.
8th " includes the best readers, who spell and write words, with their meanings attached, and read the Old and New Testaments. Arithmetic, as far as Compound Division, is divided into nine classes, each class advancing a single rule. This explanation will enable us to understand the following statement of the Superintendent, relative to the improvement of a number of his subjects.

BOYS.

	Date of Entry.		Class of Entry.	Class advanced to.		Date of Entry.		Class of Entry.	Class advanced to.
W. C.	Jan.	1	1	4	J. B.	Feb.	16	1	5
J. B.	"	1	3	8	L. S.	March	5	5	8
J. R.	"	1	1	4	D. S.	"	5	1	5
S. C. B.	"	7	5	8	T. S.	"	14	1	5
J. H. T.	"	13	5	8	W. S.	"	19	6	8
A. T.	"	12	1	4	J. L.	"	23	4	6
E. M.	"	15	1	8	J. G.	April	7	1	5
A. M.	"	21	1	5	J. B.	"	5	3	5
J. P.	"	27	1	6	T. S.	"	7	5	6
E. E.	"	27	1	6	C. J.	"	20	1	4

GIRLS.

	Date of Entry.	Class of Entry.	Class advanced to.
M. A. Y.	Jan. 1	5	8
C. A. A.	" 1	1	5
M. S.	" 1	5	8
A. M'C.	" 1	1	4
M. A. C.	" 12	5	8
M. A. P.	" 29	5	8
J. A. B.	" 22	5	8

The advancement in learning, exhibited as above, affords a very satisfactory promise of the intellectual benefit that will be likely to ensue from the present arrangements; and the Managers are further encouraged in their views of these advantages, by knowing that the Superintendent is in the daily practice of lecturing to the boys on the subject adapted to their intelligence, such as various objects of natural history, and the useful arts, availing himself of the opportunity thus afforded of enforcing moral and religious truths, and inculcating desires, which tend to elevate their minds above the low and degraded habits to which they had been accustomed, and to implant the ambition of entering upon an honourable and useful course of life. By the liberality of several citizens, a number of books have been presented to the Institution, suitable for the instruction of those who can read; thus laying the foundation of a library for the benefit of the House of Refuge which, it is hoped, will be enlarged by further appropriate donations, from benevolent individuals. To excite in those delinquent youth a fondness for spending their leisure hours, in profitable reading, will be to gain no small ascendency over their idle and corrupt propensities. The last of the two hours of the day devoted to instruction, is chiefly employed, by the Superintendent, in reading, lecturing, explaining, and questioning.

Agreeably to a suggestion held out in the original report, the board of managers have availed themselves of the auxiliary superintendence of a committee of ladies, whose watchful care and enlightened counsel have entitled them to the sincere thanks of the board. Their benovolent attentions are producing conspicuous effects in relation to the domestic economy and to the deportment and improvement of the female delinquents. In their weekly visits, a portion of their time is employed in hearing the girls recite portions of Scripture, and other pieces, which they have committed to memory; an exercise in which several of them have distinguished themselves by laudable and remarkable exertions. The advantages to be gained by the continued superintendence of the Ladies' Committee, as the institution becomes enlarged, and the employment and exercises of the girls are multiplied, cannot be anticipated without feelings of particular satisfaction. In addition to their oversight of the domestic regulations, and of the employment of the girls, their conversations with these unfortunate children, their admonitions, their encouragement, their patient efforts to gain upon their sensibilities, to enlighten their judgments, and to implant, however slowly and discourageingly, the pure principles of integrity and religious obligation, all strengthened by their clear and pertinent explanations of Scripture truths,—cannot fail to come powerfully in aid of the instructions of the matron in effecting the moral improvement of her charge.

Upon the whole, as it respects the important and *main* question of moral reformation, the managers have abundant reason to congratulate the society on the evidences, which their short experience has afforded, of the substantial benefit which may be expected to flow from the operation of this institution. The superintendent, (whose vigilant and judicious attentions to the untried duties of his station have given much satisfaction,) speaks in the most decisive terms of encouragement, with respect to the moral improvement of the children of both sexes. Some of the boys who appeared for a considerable time to be the most obstinately depraved, began at length to yield to the application of the moral remedies which were patiently and steadily applied, and now rank among the very best in the institution,—docile, industrious, and so useful by their example and correct deportment, as to have gained upon the esteem and affections of their care-takers.

The same observations apply to several of the girls.

It was ascertained by an investigation of the circumstances of those who first entered, that their depraved condition was, in several instances, to be attributed to the example and persuasives of a young female, who, though well known in the haunts of vice, had never rendered herself absolutely amenable to the criminal laws. To abstract such an example as this from the company to which the unguarded youth of the city were daily exposed, was considered by the superintendent as important to the objects which the society have in view, and the officers of the police were requested to have her secured and placed in the House of Refuge as soon as they could find a lawful occasion for such a commitment. It was not very long before she was brought in; and proved by her deportment in the house, that she had abandoned the principles of feminine propriety. Her case was difficult and discouraging; but, restrained in conversation and behavior, by the salutary rules of the institution, her habits became changed, and she appeared to feel sensible of the superior excellence of virtue. In the course of a few months, her conduct was so altered, and evinced so many proofs of thorough amendment, that she was considered eligible to the station of a domestic in a respectable family in Connecticut with whom she has been indented.

This, with other cases of an analogous nature, have sufficiently demonstrated that among the neglected and profligate children of our metropolis, there is at least a large proportion who need only the reclaiming hand of such an institution to secure their abstraction from the delusions and horrors of vice, and establish in their minds a decided preference for a life of honest industry. The managers are thus encouraged to believe even from the short period of their operations, that the influence of the society, and its institution, will produce a decided effect upon the moral habits of the children of poverty and neglected education, in this rapidly increasing city;—that it will contribute to render its streets more decent, and its magistrates, judges, and jurors, less occupied with painful and perplexing cases of juvenile criminality. Its effects in this important relation, are believed to be already conspicuous. On inquiring of the District Attorney, whose station enables him to judge correctly of these effects, he expresses himself thus:—"I am happy to state, that the House of Refuge has had a most benign influence in diminishing the number of juvenile delinquents. The most depraved boys have been withdrawn from the haunts of vice, and the examples which they gave, in a great degree destroyed.

"I find no difficulty now in checking the young offenders. Before the establishment of the House of Refuge, a lad of fourteen or fifteen years of age might have been arrested and tried four or five times for petty thefts, and it was hardly ever that a jury would convict. They would rather that the culprit acknowledged to be guilty should be discharged altogether, than be confined in the prisons of the state or county.

"This disposition so frequently exercised by magistrates and jurors, rendered the lad more bold in guilt; and I have known instances of lads now in the House of Refuge, being indicted half a dozen times, and as often discharged to renew their crimes, and with the conviction that they might steal with impunity.

"The consideration, however, that there is a charity which provides for objects of this character, has removed all objections to convictions in cases of guilt.

"Formerly, too many citizens were reluctant in bringing to the police-office, young persons who were detected in the commission of crimes. This operated as an encouragement to depraved parents to send very young children to depredate on the community, —if detected they knew no punishment would follow. This is one cause of the small number of juvenile offenders during the last year. I might enlarge on the benefits of this noble charity, were it necessary. Of this I am certain, that no institution has ever been formed in this country by benevolent men, more useful and beneficent.

"I am very truly your obedient servant and friend,

"HUGH MAXWELL."

Oct. 21, 1825.

Of the nature and tendency of such an institution, nothing further it is presumed, need at present be urged. While them anagers console themselves with the persuasion, that it has thus far equalled, in effect, all that could reasonably have been anticipated, they need not dissemble the fact, that a few of the subjects appear to evince but little fruits of the efforts made to reform and meliorate their character. Of the whole number in the house, the superintendent reports that eleven are still restless and refractory. Considering their previous habits this is no cause of surprise. As the Refuge was considered by them all as a place of durance, it was not to be expected that they would enjoy the greater liberty of this new prison without the most ingenious efforts to escape its bounds. The alteration of the walls, the erection of the new building, and the liberty of the yard, necessarily granted them during the day, greatly facilitated the means of escape. A number of them from time to time continued to elude the vigilance of their guards. With the exception however of the four cases already mentioned, those who absconded were brought back, and in some instances within a few hours. Of those four, one is in the state-prison for stealing, one is in the Philadelphia county-prison, one in the city-penitentiary, and from the other no account has been received.

This restlessness and desire to escape, has been the greatest source of anxiety and difficulty which the superintendent has had to encounter. It has rendered a constant guard necessary; but since the first of May, there has been a sufficient number of trust-worthy boys in the house, who were able and willing to act as guards over the others; and at present, there is much less desire among them to run away, than at any previous time. In two instances, boys who absconded, returned voluntarily to the house, from a conviction that it was better for them there to remain, than to expose themselves again to their old associates.

With respect to the means by which this Institution is to be supported, and to take a permanent stand among the concerns of beneficence which every christian nation finds it necessary to cherish, the Managers wish that they could give to the Society definite and conclusive information. The benevolence of the city has indeed given to it an excellent "local habitation;" and in the confidence of acknowledged utility, and as essential to the success of the experiment, the board felt itself bound to lay such a foundation for the reception of juvenile delinquents as could alone satisfy their own views and those of their most intelligent fellow-citizens, of the importance of such an establishment. The building which they found on the premises, although it has answered a good temporary purpose, is totally inadequate to the wants of such a school of industry and reformation as the society has contemplated, and the occasion demands. Accordingly, after repairing and elevating the wall around the premises, the managers contracted for the erection of a new building, designed exclusively for boys. This building is in a state of forwardness, and will probably be completed by the first of December. It is a stone edifice, 150 feet long, by 38 feet wide, and two stories high. The lower story is to be arranged for workshops and kitchen, and the upper for school-rooms, hospital, and dormitories, and calculated for the separate lodgment of 132 male subjects. This building will cost, when completed, independently of school-room and other fixtures, $10,000. The expense of raising the wall, and making needful repairs and alterations, has been upwards of $3,000. Two thousand have been paid to the United States, and $4,000 more remain to be paid, being the valuation of the buildings and materials relinquished by the War Department. As soon as the new building is in readiness for the male subjects, it is intended to appropriate the one now occupied, to the use of the females. But it will be easily foreseen by the society, that after assigning suitable accommodations to the matron, this building which at best is not well constructed for the present object, is quite too small to admit of that extension of the female department of the institution which is so desirable. A building, corresponding with that now in progress for the males, is therefore a great desideratum in the completion of the plan, and the board cannot but indulge the earnest hope, that the enlightened bounty of the city and state will speedily authorize its erection. It will be perceived by a statement of accounts, that the funds of which the Board has been put in possession, are all pledged in the erection of the building on hand, and will scarcely be adequate to its completion. The House of Refuge has been brought into existence by the animating sympathies of our city for the destitute objects whom it embraces. But how it is to be supported,—by what unquestionable means its continuance and its prosperity are to be secured, are considerations which call for the deliberate attention of the Society, and which cannot but excite a feeling in the breast of every enlightened member of our community, who has turned his attention to the nature and tendency of this institution. That the free-will offers of benevolent citizens will, when called for, still flow to its support, cannot be doubted from the manifestations already obtained of heart-felt interest in our cause. The same liberal hands that have given us a place and a name, are able to insure our continuance, and even to enlarge the sphere of our useful activity. But the question will naturally arise,—Ought such an institution as this to rest for its support on the voluntary contributions of a city, whatever may be the extent of the benevolence which it is calculated to excite? Is it of that local and incidental character which places it in the class of those objects which are fitted merely to awaken the impulse of spontaneous charity? We would venture to call upon the members of our Corporation and of our state Legislature, to view the facts in relation to this question. Can there be a more legitimate and worthy object of legislative provision than the education of the destitute? And of all classes of the destitute, have not they the most emphatic claim to the charity of public instruction, who have the misfortune to be drawn into the vortex of crime, by the force of inevitable suffering, by the urgency of guilty parents, by the excitement of wicked associates? Our state is beginning to stand in the very front of those countries which view the question of education under the most truly enlightened aspect;—which conceive it to be a solemn duty to provide liberally for the instruction of all its children,—and to spare the hand of correction, and the brand of infamy, from those whose juvenile delinquencies spring from the combined influence of ignorance and wretchedness. On the importance of a legal provision for the education of the poor, there is hardly at present a divided opinion. But how are the peculiar objects of your bounty to be educated, unless they are entirely withdrawn from the purlieus of wickedness, and their habits radically changed, by the impossibility of criminal indulgence? We would appeal to the good sense of every citizen who hears or reads our statement. And above all we would appeal to those who have visited our House of Refuge, imperfect as it still is, and have witnessed the altered countenances, the modest demeanour, the cheerful industry, and the promising indications which its inmates exhibit. Ought such a school to be left to the casual charities of the kindhearted—annually to be sought after,—with difficulty gathered—and of doubtful efficiency? Can it be questioned that the redemption of all such children from such schools of crime as our Bridewell and County Prison, and sending them forth, in due time to the world, honest, intelligent, and industrious, will be to strike at the root of those alarming evils which fill our State Prisons, and greatly augment the numbers of our city and county paupers? Will not then, such a provision as ours for juvenile delinquents prove a real saving to the state? We have the satisfaction to know that this question is affirmatively answered by most, if not all of those who have viewed the subject in all its bearings. Considered either as a school, a prison, or a work-house, it is deemed to have as just a claim upon the protection of municipal and state authority as any establishment of a similar denomination. With respect to the educational part of our system, we trust there will not be the least hesitation in any quarter. The state has already embarked in the glorious purpose of educating its children, and especially its poor. The only point which can suggest the least difficulty, is the question of a public maintenance of these children,—of supplying them with food, clothing, lodging, and all the apparatus of a perfect domicil. But when we reflect that these pitiable beings must be somehow maintained, and that by their depredations, and the expense necessary to restrain them, they are the occasion of greater actual cost to society, than they will be when made to contribute by their own labour, under the guidance of experience and system, to their own support, the saving policy of such a provision cannot, we think, admit of a doubt. It will be proper to observe, that from the best estimates that can be drawn from the facts at present before the Board, it appears that the daily average cost of each subject, for clothing, food, fuel, light, hospital and school expenses, is 13 and 1-10 cents. This estimate is formed from the average number of 41 children, from the first of January to the first of October, embracing the first nine months of the first experiment of such an establishment. With a greater number and longer experience, the amount would in all probability be diminished. It includes also no other allowance for the work of the children than the saving of expense in the making of shoes and other garments. But when the Institution is well organized, it is the belief of the Managers, that the profits of their labor will cover a considerable portion of the expense of their maintenance. A little time and experience will enable the Managers to decide upon the most eligible occupation, for each and all of the inmates, and, it is presumed, to adapt their exercises to the difference of genius and capacity which may be found amongst them. We are encouraged therefore, —nay emboldened and animated in the belief, that upon the face of our unvarnished statement, there will not be found an individual member either of our city or state Legislature, who will say that an institution erected for such objects, and commenced under such auspices, ought to be left to struggle with the embarrassment of an uncertain support, but rather that it ought to enjoy that ample countenance, which the wealth and prosperity of our state enable it so freely to extend to institutions exclusively beneficent.

The Society for the Reformation of Juvenile Delinquents, in Account Current with Ralph Olmsted, Treasurer.

Dr.

Date	Particulars	$	cts.
1825	To Cash, paid drafts of the Acting Committee, viz—		
Jan. 1 to Nov. 1.	For first payment to the United States, on account of the purchase of the present site	$2000	00
	For Repairs and additions to the buildings upon the premises	3177	06
	For Clothing, for the Children	456	52
	For Food and Provisions, for the Children	720	54
	For Furniture, Beds and Bedding, Cooking Apparatus, &c.	528	15
	For Medicine and Hospital Expenses	150	39
	For Shoe Manufacturing Expenses, Leather, Tools, &c	177	01
	For Grass Manufacturing Expenses, Stock, &c.	149	54
	For School Expenses, Books, Stationary, &c	50	19
	For Tools, Agricultural, Manufacturing, and Mechanical	48	98
	For Horse, Cow, Wagon, and Cart for the use of the Institution	254	54
	For Society Expenses, Printing, Fuel, Stationary, &c....	126	43
	For Contingent Expenses, Insurance, Fuel, &c	72	35
	For Salaries to Superintendent, Assistant, and Matron	1104	16
	For New Building, paid on account thereof	5881	44
	For New Building, balance due on contract when finished 1st December, 1825	4073	16
		$18970	46
	To Balance, brought down, due the Treasurer	768	30

Cr.

Date	Particulars	$	cts.
1824 Jan. 1 to 1825 Oct. 1.	By Nett amount received from collection of Donations and Subscriptions from the Citizens of New-York	$16202	16
1825 May 1.	By Cash, grant from the Legislature of the State of New-York	2000	00
	By Balance due the Treasurer 1st Dec. 1825	768	30
		$18970	46

Note.—The Balance due to the General Government, on the Real Estate purchased is $4000.

An Estimate of the Funds that will be required to support the House of Refuge to 1st May, 1826.

For Food, Clothing, Shoes, School, and Hospital Expenses, for 60 Children - - - - - -	$1666 32
For additional Furniture, Beds and Bedding - -	248 65
For Fuel and Light, Alterations necessary to enlarge the Girl's Apartment, &c. - - - - - -	460 49
For Salaries of Superintendent, Assistant, and Matron	1124 99
	3501 45

If the Society should receive into the House of Refuge, as many children as the two buildings can accommodate, (and which they intend to do, provided sufficient funds for their support can be obtained,)

viz:—Boys 130
Girls 40

Making 170

It would cost for their maintenance in addition to the above sum, viz:

For 110 additional Children, Food, Clothing, &c. - - - - - - -	$1729 20	
For Beds, Blankets, Crockery, &c. - -	521 92	
		2251 12
	Total	$5752 57

IN COMMON COUNCIL,

March 1st, 1824.

The special Committee to whom was referred the Memorial of the Board of Managers of the Society for the Reformation of Juvenile Delinquents, presented the following Report which was adopted.

The Committee to whom was referred the Memorial of the Board of Managers of the Society recently formed in this city, for the Reformation of Juvenile Delinquents, report,

That they have taken the subject into consideration, and conferred with gentlemen appointed on behalf of said Board, and they feel a pleasure in expressing their approbation of the laudable objects, which they have in view. Perhaps no institution is more desirable in our city, than one which affords a place of refuge for neglected and depraved children, just entering upon the paths of vice, where they may be reclaimed from their bad habits, their minds instructed in the rudiments of learning, and their time devoted to some useful employment. Also a refuge for those juvenile convicts, continually discharged from the Bridewell and Penitentiary, many of whom have neither friends, parents, nor employment to return to.

The Committee believe that such an institution, properly regulated and conducted, would not only tend to improve the condition of society, by lessening the commission of crime, and the number of convicts sent to our prisons, but would have a tendency to diminish the expenses of the city, incurred on that account. Under the direction of the intelligent and judicious individuals who now superintend its concerns, the Committee feel satisfied that the institution and necessary erection of buildings, will not only be commenced upon an economical footing, but conducted in a manner calculated to produce permanent advantages.

The immediate aid which the Memorialists solicit from the Corporation, is a grant of land or a piece of ground for the purpose of locating their establishment, and commencing their operations. To this subject the Committee have turned their attention, and are of opinion that the wishes of the Memorialists can be accommodated without much inconvenience to the city.

The piece of ground lying at the junction of the Bloomingdale and old post roads, on which the United States Arsenal is situated, was on the seventeenth of November, eighteen hundred and seven, granted by the Corporation to the General Government, upon the express condition and understanding, that the same should be used for the purpose of an arsenal and deposite of military stores; and whenever it should cease to be used for such purpose, it was to revert to the Corporation.

This piece of ground, which, together with the triangular plot in front containing about three acres, the Memorialists are of opinion, will be an eligible place for their establishment, and they have stated to the Committee, that if the Corporation will grant, to the Memorialists, the right and title to said piece of ground, they are induced to believe that they can make an arrangement with the General Government, by which they can obtain their interest in the same, and the improvements thereon erected. This request your Committee consider reasonable, and are of opinion that it ought to be granted, and therefore offer the following resolution:—

"*Resolved*, That whenever the Board of Managers of the Society for the Reformation of Juvenile Delinquents, shall obtain from the General Government, a conveyance of their interest in the piece of ground, lying at the junction of the Bloomingdale and Old post roads, the Corporation will convey to the said Board of Managers, the said piece of ground, and the triangular plot in front, by a proper deed for that purpose, to be used by said Managers for the purpose of a House of Refuge for Juvenile Delinquents; On condition, that if it shall cease to be used for that purpose, it shall then revert to the Corporation.

(Signed) JAMESON COX.
ALPHEUS SHERMAN.
GEO. ZABRISKIE.
THOMAS BOLTON.
SHIVERS PARKER."

SELECTION OF CASES.

BOYS.

S. C. B.—Committed from the Police-Office, aged fourteen, was born in Newtown, Conn. His father moved to New-York, and died before his memory, his mother died about a year ago, and left him friendless. He early commenced a career of stealing and depredation, to which he was led by the company of older boys, and his brief life exhibits one of the most extraordinary instances of juvenile depravity that has come under the notice of the board. His thefts, as admitted by himself are almost beyond number. He has twice served out his sentence in the Penitentiary. He was much encouraged in his thefts by the facilities afforded him in selling the articles he stole to persons who must have been aware of the manner in which he got them. His depredations upon entries were numerous. The Circus and Theatre also presented a wide field for his dexterity in picking pockets.

The reformation of such a character, was a bold undertaking by the institution, but as he was young, and his offences had been the result of bad company, his case was not considered hopeless. He found means to escape the first week, but was brought back: his temper was obstinate and he was determined upon opposition. Severe remedies and punishments were then applied to bend his spirit, and the managers have reason to believe with success. Since April he is much improved in temper and has evinced a disposition to behave well; he is now one of the most agreeable and pleasant boys in the house, and is apparently quite happy: should application be made for him for a proper place where he would be strictly attended, the Board think they could bind him out with safety.

A. T.—Aged 16 years, was committed to this establishment by the Police under the vagrant act. Although he was once taken up for being in company with a boy who had committed theft, yet it does not appear that he himself had ever stolen. He lost his parents when very young, and was thus thrown upon the world. He has lived at several places, and worked for short periods at several employments. Latterly he lived in Bancker-street, where his sole employment was to pick chips, and play in the streets. The first week of his commitment to this establishment, he found means to escape by the aid of carpenter's tools, the next day he returned unexpectedly, and to the great satisfaction of the superintendent—said that he had no desire of leaving the house, but was persuaded by another; that he wished to see his sister, whom he had heard was sick; he is sensible that this is the place for him, and the only means of ridding himself of his former associates and his evil propensities. He has for several months been in the confidence of the superintendent, and principally employed as a guard over the other boys: he has also frequently been sent to the city on errands, which he has discharged faithfully. The managers think that they could bind him out to a proper place with confidence.

J. H.—Now about 12 years of age, was born in the city, his parents died in his infancy, and he was successively taken by several of his relations. He was one year in the Alms-House, and has been left to follow pretty much his own inclinations, without a friendly hand to guide him. So far as we know he has never been arraigned for crime or put in prison. He was sent to this establishment by the Police under the vagrant act. He was in May last indented to a farmer in Poughkeepsie.

From the time he was received into this asylum up to his leaving it, his conduct was almost unexceptionably good: to his fellows he was pleasant and agreeable, to his superiors obedient and humble. Two letters have been received from the gentleman to whom he is indented, which give satisfactory accounts of his behavior.*

E. M.—Aged 15 years. His parents are now living in this city, and with whom he has always lived. He used to pick chips in the street, and the first thing he ever stole was chips from other boys. About two years since, he, in company with an older boy who had been in the Penitentiary, stole from a man in the street who was intoxicated, a bundle containing many articles; he was taken up, tried for highway robbery, and sent to the Penitentiary for six months, when his time was out, he commenced thieving again. He was again taken up and put in Bridewell, (where he has been three or four times,) convicted and sentenced to the House of Refuge. He escaped in a short time, and was found in Bridewell, where he had been committed under a feigned name, under suspicion of shop-lifting. Severe remedies and punishments were applied for nearly two months. He was put to the shoe maker's bench. Since April, his conduct has been such as to give much satisfaction. He is unremitted in attention to his work, and evinces much ambition. In short, his uniformly good conduct since the above time "impress us with the belief," says the superintendent, "that the steps taken for his preservation will prove successful; in him we anticipate the realization of our wishes."

J. P.—Aged between fourteen and fifteen, was born in Boston; his father being dead, his mother removed to this city, and married again; she takes in washing, and his step-father is a laborer, and works along shore. He has been to sea four months, on his return he lived with his mother, has not lived at any other place; he used to sell oysters and clams, and play about the streets. About two years ago, he stole a goose from on board a sloop, and was sent by the Police six months to the Penitentiary. He stayed out his time, and stole nothing (he says) afterwards: he was taken up in January last on a Sunday, for getting with other boys into the cabin of a steam-boat: he was put in Bridewell and then committed to this establishment. He was never at school. His conduct at first was very refractory; evincing a settled determination to escape, in which he once succeeded, but was retaken. Appearing bent on his purpose, and making several ineffectual efforts, it was found necessary to apply severe and continued punishments and confinement to break the obstinacy of his temper.

Since April, his conduct has been very good, he has been one of the guard for some months, and has frequently been sent to town with the cart.

M. W.—Between 15 and 16 years of age, from the Police—he has no mother but his father is living in this city: without his father's consent he went to sea; on his return, he lived at various places and employments for short periods, in wandering in the

* See Page 42.

streets and picking chips, by which he was exposed to constant temptation. He was at length taken up for stealing a turkey, and sent to the Penitentiary for six months. When he came out he strolled through the streets, and commenced pilfering as an occupation, and was three times committed to Bridewell.

His conduct from the day he was received into this establishment, was uniformly good: he was one of the guard for about three months, the duties of which he performed vigilantly. After having given many evidences that he would not return to his former malpractices, he was at his own request indented to a farmer in Broome County, on the 14th of October.

G. D.—Between 14 and 15 years of age—was born in this city, his parents are living, and he has always staid with them; he was brought up in idleness, which led to habits of pilfering. He was charged with stealing clothes, tried, and sentenced for six months to the Penitentiary, at the expiration of his sentence, as his parents had neglected him, he was sent to the Refuge by the commissioners of the Alms-house.

He has conducted himself better than we had a right to expect, considering the manner in which he has been brought up. He has a cheerful and obliging disposition, and does much to obtain the good-will of the other boys. He is engaged to a person in the country.

T. B.—Aged 17, committed by the Police under the vagrant act. He was born in this city; his father is a laborer. He was some years in the Alms-House, whence he was bound to Paterson, but having permission to spend a fourth of July in town, he did not return: the winter following, he was again sent to the Alms-House, and indented to a gentleman in one of the western counties, who removing to New-York, brought the boy with him, who left his master and went to live with his father, where he staid until his mother died, when he began to lead an irregular life. The first theft he ever committed was in stealing some silver from his young brother. About four years since in company with another boy, he stole a bundle of clothes, for which he was sent to the Penitentiary for six months. He has been in the habit of drinking, in which his parents encouraged him. He says he drank one day twenty-two glasses and was not intoxicated.

Since he has been in the house, the superintendent has not had much cause to complain of him. He has frequently been heard to express his gratitude that he was snatched from the vortex of dissipation into which he was fast hastening, and to exclaim "what would have become of me by this time, if I had not been brought here."

R. F.—About 16 years old. Was born in this city. His parents, with whom he has lived most of the time, allowed him to be a street idler. He early commenced stealing, which seems to have been with him a passion. He has been tried for it four several times, and served out in the Penitentiary four different terms of punishment, and was finally sent to this Refuge.

As he has had no opportunities of gratifying his vicious propensity since he has been here, it is not possible to say how far good principles and virtuous examples have had an effect on him. The superintendent reports that his conduct has been such as to give him much satisfaction; he is in possession of his confidence, and has occasionly been on guard.

J. T. E.—aged 17 years, is a young man of good parentage, and who has lived in several respectable places in this city. His first temptation to error was the sudden attainment of money by drawing a prize in a lottery, which led him into dissipation and evil company. He became acquainted with women of loose character, who led him into extravagance, which induced him to commit theft to support his manner of living when his lottery money was expended. The Court considering his youth, the respectability of his family, and it being the first offence, thought fit to sentence him to the House of Refuge. He says he never knew a moment's happiness from the time he committed the first offence, to his being taken up.

Since his admission into the establishment, his conduct has been such as we have reason to be satisfied with. The abhorrence he appears to feel at, and the contrition he evinces for, his former conduct, give strong encouragement to believe that he will yet become a useful and respectable member of society.

GIRLS.

C. A.—Aged between 15 and 16, has a mother in this city, with whom she has always lived. This girl was brought up to no other employment than picking chips for her mother, which led her to live in the streets, and be exposed to every species of crime. She was taken up with other girls for stealing a watch. She made two several attempts to escape, and her conduct was such as to require confinement and punishment. The misconduct of this girl, we think, may with justice be attributed to the example of a depraved mother and elder sister, who are now in the Penitentiary, as well as to an impaired mind, occasioned by an epileptic affection with which she has been afflicted since a child. Our physicians have prescribed for her, and have been successful in suspending her fits: since July she has not had a return of them. From which time she has behaved much better. The improvement of her mind is also sufficient to give flattering hopes of her yet becoming a respectable woman.

A. M. C.—Between 13 and 14 years of age. Her mother lived in Bancker-street, but is now in the Alms House; the girl has lived for short periods in several places. She afterwards became associated with girls of bad character, was in the habit of picking chips, running about the docks, stealing small articles and selling them to market women. She, in company with other girls, committed several robberies upon strangers in the public streets, of an aggravated nature, which indicated a degree of daring and vice beyond her years. It may not be proper to give a detailed account of the life of this girl and several others hereafter mentioned; suffice it is to say, that to reform such characters requires no ordinary patience and talent.

Upon reading her history, it will naturally be supposed that from one so early depraved, much was not to be expected. Since her reception into this establishment, she has frequently been visited by her mother, from whom we have learned sufficient to justify our saying that her conduct may rather be ascribed to her bad example, than to any intrinsic or natural propensity to evil. Yet notwithstanding her early disadvantages, we feel pleasure in saying, that within the last three months, a great change in her feelings, as well as her conduct, has been effected, and she bids fair to become entirely reformed.

J. M. C.—Twelve years old, born in this city, is sister of the preceding. With such an example, and such company, and without any controul from her mother, a different fate from her sister's could not be expected. She became vicious and criminal, and was taken up as an accomplice in her sister's robberies. Being younger in crime and years than her sister, there were much greater hopes of her reformation; nor have they been disappointed. She was indented to a gentleman in Poughkeepsie some months ago, from whom very flattering accounts of her conduct have been received. He states that "her conduct has been unexceptionable, and he is informed by her teachers, that she is the best scholar in her class."

D. W.—Aged fifteen; was with the last two girls on the commission of their robberies, and was sent to this place by the police on her being detected.

After remaining a sufficient time to convince the superintendent that she felt a desire to reform, agreeably to her own wishes she was bound to a gentleman in the western part of the state. In a letter under date of the 30th August last, he states "that her conduct has been good. She has given less cause of complaint than he should have reason to expect from a girl of her age taken from one of our well regulated families in this part of the country. The lessons taught her while under your care appear to have made a proper, and, I think, a lasting impression on her mind. She evinces a disposition to learn what is good; and such work as is proper for her, she performs with ingenuity and neatness."

M. A. C.—Aged sixteen years. Both her parents are dead. She has been to service in several places in this city. Being out of place, she formed acquaintance with girls who led her into vicious courses. She was sent one day with others of errands; after being absent some hours she returned, and said she had been to see her relations. She stated that from the moment she had left the house until her return she was unhappy, and that she wished to remain here until it was thought best for her to leave. Her improvement is such as to give much satisfaction. She appears determined upon becoming a respectable woman. She has acquired the art of manufacturing grass into hats, and has a happy faculty of teaching others.

S. A. R.—Aged between thirteen and fourteen years, was born in this city. Her parents having died, she was put to several places, at none of which she remained any time, or received any improvement. She was taken up by the watch and sent to this establishment. Her conduct since June has been more than ordinarily good: she is very ambitious, and frequently exerts herself beyond her strength. She, in a few days, is to be bound out.

J. G.—Aged between 16 and 17. She has lived in several places but in none to any advantage to her principles or habits. Her last place, in Bancker-street, led her to form evil associates. She was taken up by the watch, being in bad company, and committed to this house. With her conduct since in the house, the superintendent has had better reason to be satisfied than with that of any other of our female subjects, notwithstanding the vicious life she led the last year before she came into this establishment. She has many good principles. After being in the house a few weeks, she became willing to yield to restraints and attend to advice given her. She has a good disposition, and pleasant manners. She was indented the beginning of last month.

Subscribers and Donors

TO THE

HOUSE OF REFUGE.

LIFE SUBSCRIBERS.

Israel Corse	$100
Harriet Douglass	100
Thomas Gibbons	100
William Jauncey	100
James Lovett	100
John Watts	100
Moses Allen	50
John Adams	50
George Arcularius	50
Stephen Allen	50
William B. Astor	50
David Austin	50
Saul Alley	50
Thomas Allen	50
Cornelius M. Allen	50
Heman Averill	50
Divie Bethune	50
Daniel Berrien	50
Henry Brevoort, jun	50
Thomas S. Byrnes	50
Robert Brown	50
William Bayard	50
Henry Barclay	50
Joseph Blackwell	50
Isaac Bronson	50
James Boggs	50
Floyd S. Bailey	50
Henry Booraem	50
James Byers	50
Hyppolite Barrere	50
F. Barretto	50
Abraham Bell	50
M. W. Brett	50
Gurdon Buck	50
Robert Bogardus	50
Dr. William Barrow	50
James Boorman	50
G. W. & H. Bruen	50
Thomas Buckley	50
Isaac Collins	50
C. D. Colden	50
Robert C. Cornell	50
Matthew Clarkson	50
Mrs. Costar	50
Borden Chase	50
John G. Costar	50
Isaac Carow	50
Lynde Catlin	50
Barney Corse	50
Henry Carey	50
Duncan P. Campbell	50
Henry A. Costar	50
Levi Coit	50
Gilbert Coutant	50
Joseph F. Carroll	50
T. S. Clarkson	50
J. J. Coddington	50
John B. Coles	50
Robert Cheesebrough	50
Cornelius Du Bois	50
M. Douglass	50
John F. Delaplaine	50
E. C. Delavan	50
Daniel B. Dash	50
Henry Eckford	50
Moses Field	50
Benjamin De Forest	50
John Flack	50
Samuel Falconer	50
Andrew Foster	50
John Fleming	50
Augustus Fleming	50
William W. Fox	50
Hickson W. Field	50

Name	Amount
Joseph Grinnell	50
N. L. Griswold	50
John J. Glover	50
J. Graff	50
J. A. Graff	50
John C. Halsey	50
Elijah Humphreys	50
William Howard	50
Wager Hull	50
H. Hendricks	50
Peter Harmony	50
L. T. & C. Hammersley	50
G. G. & S. Howland	50
Philip Hone	50
John Hone	50
D. G. Hubbard	50
Timothy Hedges	50
Samuel Hicks	50
Isaac S. Hone	50
John Haggerty	50
John H. Howland	50
John A. Hamilton	50
William C. Holly	50
Jacob Harvey	50
David Hadden	50
John Hone, jun.	50
Fisher How	50
John Hunter	50
Dr. D. Hosack	50
John Johnson	50
Edward R. Johnson	50
Peter A. Jay	50
Jacob Isaacs	50
S. Jones	50
James J. Jones	50
Alice Johnson	50
John T. Irving	50
Andrew Jackson	50
Edward Kellogg	50
Henry Kneeland	50
Joseph Kernochan	50
George Klotts	50
David Lovett	50
Gideon Lee	50
William H. Leggett	50
G. Ludlow	50
John B. Lawrence	50
John Leonard	50
Samuel Leggett	50
A. H. Lawrence	50
Rufus L. Lord	50
George Lorillard	50
Aaron Leggett	50
Isaac Lawrence	50
Herman Le Roy	50
Inlay Lecke	50
Nicholas Low	50
Cornelius Low	50
Nicholas Low, jun.	50
Henrietta Low	50
John L. Lawrence	50
William Lawton	50
David Lydig	50
Thomas Lord	50
Abner Lord	50
Jabez Lovett	50
Lindley Murray	50
Benjamin Marshall	50
John Mason	50
William F. Mott	50
H. M'Farland	50
James M'Bride	50
Catharine Murray	50
Ann M. Adams	50
O. Mauran	50
E. Morewood	50
E. Malibran	50
E. H. Nicoll	50
R. H. Nevins	50
F. H. Nicoll	50
George Newbold	50
Ralph Olmsted	50
Francis Olmsted	50
John Oothout	50
Jonathan Ogden	50
William Osborn	50
John R. Peters	50
John Pintard	50
Anson G. Phelps	50
J. G. Pierson & Brothers	50
N. Prime	50
Amos Palmer	50
Henry H. Paxton	50
William Paulding	50
Henry H. Panton	50
Thaddeus Phelps & Co.	50
Charles Porter	50
Matthew Reed	50
P. Remsen	50
Moses Rodgers	50
David Rodgers	50
William Rhinelander	50
M. Robinson	50
William M. Russell	50
R. M. Russell	50
William Roberts	50
H. C. De Rham	50
Thomas H. Smith	50

John O. Sullivan	50
Edmund Smith	50
J. Suydam	50
Thomas Suffern	50
David Stebbins	50
Samuel St. John	50
Nathaniel Smith	50
Sands, Spooner, & Co.	50
J. S. Schermerhorn	50
Richard Sadlier	50
Nicholas Schureman	50
Anthony Steinback	50
Frederick Sheldon	50
Peter Sharpe	50
Arthur Tappan	50
James Thompson	50
Jeremiah Thompson	50
Gideon Tucker	50
Najah Taylor	50
Francis Thompson	50
Robert Tillotson	50
M. Ulshoeffer	50
Richard Varick	50
G. C. Verplanck	50
John Watts	50
Charles Wright	50
John R. Willis	50
Augustus Wynkoop	50
John G. Warren	50
Samuel Ward	50
William Weyman	50
Thomas Woodruff	50
James D. L. Walton	50
E. Wainwright	50
Henry Walton	50
Henry I. Wyckoff	50
John Waite	50
Charles Wilkes	50
William W. Woolsey	50
Samuel Whittemore	50
M. Willit	50
William Wallace through the Savings Bank	53

ANNUAL SUBSCRIBERS.

Charles Anthon	10
D. Anderson	3
John Anderson	3
C. C. Andrews	3
Daniel Bache	10
William G. Bucknor	10
J. W. Bleecker	10
Robert P. Bell	10
Frederick R. Bunker	10
J. & L. Brewster	10
James A. Burtis	10
William Baldwin	10
Thomas Brooks	10
E. Byrne	10
Benjamin Bailey	10
Lewis Bancel	10
Arthur Burtis	10
William Bleakley	3
R. C. Barfree	3
John Burk	3
Joseph Bayley	3
E. W. A. Bailey	3
Gaston Barnard	3
William Bryce	3
G. Bancker	3
Enos Baldwin	3
Smith Bloomfield	3
Mrs. Banks	3
Thomas Browning	3
James Bertine	3
J. W. Brown	3
L. Binnse	3
Isaac Bell	5
Silas Brown	3
N. Benjamin	3
J. M. Bruce	3
B. C. Burdett	3
Ira Barnum	3
James Bogart, jun.	3
James Benedict	10
John S. Crary	10
Jacob B. Clark	10
D. Crassous	10
William Calder	10
N. Comstock	10
William M. Carter	10
Francis Cochran	10
Joseph Curtis	10
Dr. Thomas Cock	10
Samuel Cheesman	10
J. Couzins	10
Peter Cooper	10
J. W. Corlies	10
John Clapp	3
G. Chichester	3
J. Cummings	3
John Curtis	3
John Cassilear	3

Name		Name	
S. D. Craig	3	Robert Gracie	3
Joseph Corlies	3	Samuel Hannay	10
Ebenezer Cauldwell	3	John E. Hyde	10
W. & H. Chardyne,	3	Jacob Houseman	10
W. R. Cook	3	John Hancock	10
Oliver L. Clark	3	Alexander Henderson	10
A. Canter	3	Eldad Holmes	10
Benjamin Davids	10	John Halsey	10
Mahlon Day	10	Charles H. Hall	10
John Dean	10	W. Hall	10
Evert Duyckinck	10	M. Hoyt	10
James W. Dominick	10	James Hopson	3
D. E. Dunscomb	10	G. F. Hopkins	3
John Demon	10	Hugh Holmes	3
Miss H. Disabaye	3	Oliver Holden, jun.	3
G. S. Duryea	3	Henry Hinsdale	3
Elizabeth Duryee	3	D. J. Hubbs	3
J. E. Dekay	3	John R. Hurd	3
John F. Doland	3	J. H. Hetherington	3
J. L. Dunning	3	J. J. Ingersoll	10
E. G. Dunnell	3	William Israel	5
J. Duffee	3	D. S. Jones	10
Enoch Dean	3	James Jarvis	10
John C. Davenport	3	D. Jacot	3
Ogden Edwards	10	Joseph Johnson	3
Robert Emmett	10	Napthali Judah	3
George Englehart	3	Richard Jennings	3
Thomas Eddy, jun.	3	Silvester Judson	3
S. Flewwelling	10	John Kemp	10
Thomas Freeborn	10	Francis Kane	3
Lockwood Feeks	10	William Kemble	3
N. Fellows	10	Isaac Keeler	3
Martha Farrier	3	John D. Keese	3
Ferris Finch	3	H. T. Kiersted	3
Job Furman	3	Henry Lowery	3
Theodosius Fowler	3	H. B. Lambert	3
William Forrest	3	William B. Lowery	3
William Frazer	3	T. F. Livingston	3
James Fellows	3	Rufus Lockwood	3
John A. Franklin	3	Richard Loins	3
D. A. Frost	3	Walter Langdon	3
John Griscom	10	J. Lockwood	3
James W. Gerard	10	Allen C. Lee	10
J. & C. Gascoigne	10	John W. Leavitt	10
Jonathan Goodhue	10	Henry Laverty	10
Charles Guyer	10	Hugh Laing	10
Henry E. Grinnell	3	Charles Lawton	10
F. Gebhard	10	Lebbeus Loomis	10
Samuel L. Governeur	10	C. L. Livingston	10
Isaac Greenwood	3	Matthias Luff	10
James Grey	3	J. Lucas	10
Samuel Gesmon	3	J. W. Lent	10
James Guion	3	George Lovett	3
William Geib	3	T. Lovett	3

Name	Amount
Mrs. P. Lawrence	3
Peter Lorillard	10
R. M. Livingston	10
John De Lancey	10
George Mackie	10
Robert I. Murray	10
Dr. V. Mott	10
D. M'Carthy	10
James M'Gee & Co	10
George Manold	10
Reuben Munson	10
Richard Mott	10
Robert F. Mott	10
Hugh Maxwell	3
D. M'Laughlin	3
William M'Neil	3
J. Mount	3
Asher Martin	3
B. P. Meleck	3
Alexander M'Donald	3
Oliver Morse	3
Daniel Mersereau	3
David Marsh	5
Samuel Marsh	3
Casper Meier	3
M. Mulden	3
N. Mead	3
T. W. Moore	3
William W. Miner	3
S. Nathan	10
J. & C. Nichols & Co	10
Andrew S. Norwood	10
William Neilson	3
M. Nicholl	3
John Ogden	10
Jacob Ostrom	10
Samuel Osborn	3
F. Olmstead	3
James F. Palmer	10
John Poillon	10
P. Perit	10
E. T. Pinckney	10
Walter Peck	3
Stephen Peck	3
William Prior	3
Richard E. Purdy	3
N. Smith Prentiss	3
George Pardon	3
Joel Post	3
Thompson Price	3
Lemuel Pitman	3
R. Pardesses	3
Joseph Parker	3
Rodger Prout	3
F. Place	3
Josiah B. Quinby	3
G. S. Robbins	10
J. F. Randolph	10
James Roosevelt	10
David Reynolds	10
William C. Rhinelander	10
Henry Rodgers	10
Beverly Robinson	10
George Robson	3
Henry Robinson	3
S. F. Randolph	3
C. N. S. Rowland	3
John Robins	3
John S. Roper	3
N. Rodgers	3
F. W. Rhinelander	3
P. Rhinelander	5
John Redfield	3
George Seaman	10
Stephen Smith	10
J. P. Simpson	10
David Seaman	10
Henry Sheldon	10
Benjamin Strong	10
Peter Stagg	10
G. H. Stanton	10
J. Shepherd	3
Dr. G. Smith	3
William Stephens	3
Morris Shipley	3
S. Seaton	3
James S. Slover	3
W. W. Shirley	3
Mrs. G. Smith	5
Dr. James Stewart	3
P. N. Strong	3
Philip Smith	3
James Stewart	3
William Scott	3
Thomas Stevens	3
William F. Stevens	3
William Schureman	3
Henry D. Sedgwick	5
Bishop Sherwood	5
Jacob Tier	10
Frederick Tracy	10
James Tessier	10
Orin Thompson	10
Henry Thomas	10
John G. Tibbits	5
Samuel H. Turner	5
William Thompson	3
J. C. Totten	3

Peter S. Titus	3	Dr. H. W. Webb	10
Walter Underhill	10	William Wright	10
George Upfold	3	Elijah Whipple	10
Eli Vail	10	James Wallace	10
M. M. Valentine	10	L. Wyckoff	3
A. M. Valentine	10	Salem Wines	3
Cornelius Van Allen	10	Henry Wyckoff	3
N. Van Antwerp	10	Eliphalet Wheeler	3
H. Van Wagenen	3	Lewis Wiseburn	3
L. Van Antwerp	3	Elizabeth Walsh	3
Thomas Van Antwerp	3	Jonathan M. Wainwright	3
Abraham Van Buskirk	3	H. Worrall	3
William Waring	3	George Wragg	3
E. J. White	3	Henry Wendall	3
Francis P. Videl	3	R. N. Wenman	3
M. Valangcas	3	Thomas Waring	3
W. Van De Water	3	Joseph Walker	5
J. Webb & Co.	10	J. S. & R. Comstock	10
Charles Wardell	10		

DONORS.

William Agnew	10	Col. Barclay	3
B. Armitage	5	Thomas Barrow	10
N. T. Arnold	2	Andrew Bowden	1 50
Hugh Auchincloss	5	David Briggs	2
D. J. Anderson	2	T. G. Bull	2
Ezra Ayres	2	George Brooks	3
M. Allison	3	James Bleecker	5
B. Andariese	3	R. H. Bowne	5
J. Auchincloss	5	D. Brooks	10
S. & J. Angevine	2	Mrs. D. Brinckerhoff	10
William Acheson	2	Peter Burtsell	5
N. Allen	3	Lyman Betts	15
Benjamin Andreoin	2	John Buckley & Son	2
Henry Arcularius	10	R. V. Beekman	3
Dr. S. Akerley	5	T. H. Bogart	5
Benjamin Aymar	10	C. Bostwick	3
Daniel Alley	3	Samuel A. Bascom	5
Jacob Aimes	3	William Berrian	3
Obadiah Ayres	1 50	William Brown	3
Joanna Bethune	5	Thomas Brown	5
E. Bliss & E. White	20	J. Blackfan	3
Anna Braithwaite	20	Richard Berrian	5
Nathan Bailey	25	Joseph Baggot	2
James Bailey	10	Samuel Brown	2
James Boyd	10	J. V. B. Barricklo	2
Andrew Brunn	5	J. Bolton	10
Mrs. A. Brown	5	Burrell	1
William Burtsell	10	George W. Brown	5
Noah Brown	20	B. & L.	3
Jas.& Th. Beatty & others	21 25	Peter Bartine	3
D. I. Boyd	10	Abraham Bogart	5

Name		
Richard Bird	5	
Miles Bacon	5	
Jacob Benderhajer	1	
Edward Breman	3	
J. K. Boyd	8	
Joseph Barnes	8	
Henry Bunce	3	
David Brooks	10	
William Butler	3	
Isaac Brewster	3	
Isaac Brown	3	
C. C. Blatchley	3	
Peter Burdet	3	
William J. Bunker	20	
John Corlies	10	
Benjamin Corlies	10	
Cash	10	
Sarah Collins	20	
David Clarkson	5	
John Conger	10	
Cash	5	
William Cooper	20	
Levinus Clarkson	10	
William Civill	2	
Robert Center	5	
Francis Cochran	10	
Cash	5	50
Benjamin Clapp	1	
Mrs. Currie	2	
R. H. Cummings	3	
Cash	25	
D. D. Crane	3	
C. Cadell	2	
William Corech	10	
Cash	16	
Cash	36	
Abraham Coursen	10	
John Colgate	3	
T. S. Clark	3	
Cash	17	
James Casey	5	
William A. Cook	3	
John Concklin	1	
John Cowan	3	
P. Clendining	20	
Cash	13	50
J. H. Cowperthwaite	3	
Charles O'Connor	5	
Mr. Cahoone	1	
Captain Coffee	3	
Benjamin Crane	5	
Alexander Cascaddon	1	
W. & T. C. Chardavoyne	2	
Cash	3	

Name		
William S. Capper	10	
David Crowther	5	
Thomas Collins	20	
William Craig	10	
J. G. Collins	10	
Amsy Chapman	3	
Henry Calam	3	
John Camm	3	
John B. Cheesman	3	
Henry Coit	10	
Cash	1	
Dennis H. Doyle	20	
John Day	10	
Lyman Dennisson	5	
T. C. Doremus	3	
J. P. Dervent	10	
Joseph Depew	5	
Davis & Smith	6	
William Du Bois	3	
Robert Dickson	5	
B. Deming	2	
John C. Dillon	2	
Mrs. Mary Dale	3	
John Drake	3	
R. Dyson	5	
John Darg	5	
Thomas Doyle	2	
John M. Dow	3	
Charles Dusenbury	2	
E. Dudley	5	
Archibald Davie	2	
Philo Doane	2	
Andrew Dooley	5	
John Duncase	3	
Mrs. Doyer	3	
Benjamin Disbrow	5	
John Dean	2	
Miss H. Dessabaye	4	
Edward Doughty	3	
Dagget & Kinsett	1	50
Richard Dunn, jun.	3	
Paul Dominge	3	
Cornelia Edgar	10	
John L. Embree	5	
Thomas A. Emmet	5	
George Ehrenger	4	
Daniel Ensley	10	
John Ely, jun.	2	
Joseph D. Evernghim	10	
John Emmons	3	
Robert Edwards	2	
Joseph D. Fay	3	
A Female Friend	50	
James Fox	3	

Mr. Foot	2	
George S. Fox	20	
A. Falconer	2	
William J. Forbes	3	
Gilbert Fowler	5	
Arnest Fisk	5	
A Friend	1	
Joseph Flower	1	
Orlando Fish	3	
Mrs. Forrest	3	
Fink	0	50
A Friend	10	
Gabriel Furman	10	
A Friend	30	
Female Friend	20	
John Fream	10	
Alexander S. Glass	10	
George Gallagher	20	
Sarah Gerard	2	
John Graham	2	
Robert Gill	10	
John Greenfield	5	
J. Boonen Graves	10	
T. A. Gill & Co.	3	
James Gilbert	1	
Griffin	3	
Mr. Gammell	3	
John F. Gardiner	0	50
A. Greele	20	
Eli Goodwin	3	
William B. Gilley	10	
C. W. Gallagher	3	
Peter G. Hart	20	
Harriet Howell	10	
Silas Hicks	20	
Benjamin Haight	10	
James Heard	10	
Cornelius Heyer	10	
Abner Higgins	10	
E. Holbrook	15	
A. P. Hamlin	10	
Mrs. Halthouse	1	
H. Hone	10	
Murray Hoffman	2	
E. Hamilton	3	
O. Hull	3	
John Herriman	3	
Philo Hillyer	25	
Herriman & Nash	5	
James R. Harned	2	
O. Holmes	10	
J. Hay, jun.	5	
H. & P.	7	
V. G. Hall	1	
E. Higgins	5	
G. M. & W. Hinchman	2	
Eli Hart	20	
Peter Hattrick	25	
A. P. Halsey	3	
Elvin Hunt	3	
James C. Haviland	3	
J. Hauptman	2	
William Hilton	5	
Edmund Haviland	3	
Isaac Hatch	3	50
Mrs. Charles Hall	10	
Charles Harlett	3	
N. C. Hart	9	
Willet Hicks	20	
William Hogeland	5	
Thomas Hewitt	3	
Gideon Hewitt	3	
Walter Howell	10	
Dr. Horne	10	
Isaac Halsey	10	
A. W. Ives	10	
D. Johnson	10	
George Ireland	5	
William Jones	3	
T. W. Jenkins	20	
Henry James	3	
Thomas Jeremiah	3	
Dr. Ireland	3	
James Jenkins	5	
Chester Jennings	20	
Joseph Kissam	10	
Leonard Kip	25	
Isaac L. Kip	10	
Joseph Kirby	3	
Keeler & Luff	5	
R. V. Kissam	3	
Leonard W. Kip	3	
Mrs. B. Kenan	3	
James G. King	5	
H. H. Lawrence	20	
Thomas H. Leggett	25	
James Lowery	3	
Isaac H. Lawrence	5	
John Ledyard	1	
P. W. Livingston	2	
Catharine Lawrence	20	
Daniel Lord	3	
Mrs. S. Lee	5	
George Long	2	
Mrs. Elizabeth Ludlow	3	
Z. Lewis	5	
Thomas Lawrence	20	
Mrs. E. Lewis	5	

Mrs. F. Ludlow	5
William Langdon	5
Philo Lewis	3
C. W. Lawrence	10
Richard Lawrence	5
Mrs. Isaac Lawrence	10
Samuel W. Laverty	3
Thomas Lyon	1
Mrs. Elizabeth Lewis	10
Mrs. Jane Livesay	20
James W. Lent	5
Francis B. Lynch	3
Lynch & Clark	10
William W. Mott	20
Samuel Millbank	10
Hannah Murray	5
Mary Murray	10
Hannah L. Murray	10
Charles M'Evers	10
Daniel M'Cormick	20
Dr. H. Mott	20
John M'Donald	5
A. M'Clure	5
Mrs. A. Morris	3
R. Morris	2
Mr. Munn	1
Charles Miller	10
A. Mather	3
L. I. Maroin	3
Ralph Mead	5
H. I. Megary	2
J. M. Moore	3
Mrs. Manning	5
John B. Martin	5
Milford Martin	3
Nath'l. G. Minturn	10
John Moore	5
Thomas W. Marshall	2
Ezra W. Miller	5
John Morehead	5
James Montgomery	2
Mordecai Myers	1
James Megham	1
Abraham M. Martling	2
Thomas Mooney	1
Charles Mills	3
A. M'Cullum	3
Leander Mead	2
Mr. Marsh	1
Jonas Mapes	10
Samuel Manning	10
James Morgan	1
Hugh Miller	1
John Moran	0 50

Abraham Merrill	1
Benjamin Merrit	10
Samuel Martin	3
Samuel Marsh	3
Stephen B. Munn	5
David Marsh	10
William Marshall	10
John M'Vicker	10
James M'Cready, jun.	3
Thomas Masters	5
Peter I. Nevius	10
J. Nicholl	0 50
H. W. Nicholl	5
Magdeline Oothout	10
Daniel Oakey	10
Peter Ogilvie	12
Charles Oakley	10
Alexander Ogilvie	3
Silas Olmsted	1
Charles Osborn	10
William P. Page	20
Peter Pinckney	3
Jonathan Pinckney	3
James Palmer	20
Robert Pearsall	20
H. Parrish	20
Allen Peck	5
J. Pittsbury	3
J. S. Platt	5
Philopon	5
Samuel Penny & Son	5
Dr. Perkins	3
John Penot	4
F. S. Peet	3
Laurence Proudfoot	10
John Peterson	3
M. Parker	5
Henry Post	10
John Poiner	3
Mrs. Pool	0 50
Isaac Peckford	2
Peter Powell	1
Joseph Petit	3
Peter A. Peshine	3
Henry Peters	3
Robert M. Pennoyer	3
William Paluck	3
Tunis Quinby	5
Susan A. Remsen	10
Collin Reed	20
A. Richards	10
Laman Read	20
Thomas Richards	5
Dr. J. S. Rodgers	10

Robert Ray	3	William Scudder	3
Thomas A. Ric	2	W. H. Sacket	5
D. L. Rapelye	2	Harris Scovel	2
B. S. Rowland	2	Joseph P. Smith	2
Frederick Richard	3	C. Swan	10
W. H. Robinson	10	Daniel Spader	3
J. Robertson	2	John Simonson	3
Thomas A. Ronalds	10	P. Simmons	3
Mr. Robinson	2	E. Secor	1
T. O. Richards	5	James Suydam	5
H. Remsen	10	Daniel D. Smith	5
Moses Ritter	3	Thomas Stokes	5
James B. Reguire	3	Mark Spencer	5
Robert Le Roy	10	George Tredwell	20
George Suckley	25	Seabury Treadwell	20
James Swords	10	Stephen Thorn, jun.	20
Isaac T. Storm	25	Adam Tredwell	20
Francis Saltus	20	Richard T. Tucker	25
L. Saltus	10	John B. Thorpe	10
Thomas Skelding	10	Mrs. Turner	1
H. H. Schieffelin	5	Charles W. Taylor	2
William Schott	5	John G. Tardy	3
Samuel Stillwell	10	Robert Thompson	5
Henry Shelters	10	Mrs. Templeton	2
S. Seaman	1	Grant Thorburn & Son	1
Isaac Sayre	5	Peter C. Tappan	5
Charles G. Shipman	5	John Telfair	10
Mr. Shapter	1	Mrs. Catharine Jones	25
Peter H. Schenck	10	George T. Trimble	10
Miss Shaw	3	John G. Tibbitts	10
J. C. Sigourney	10	Samuel Turney	5
J. D. Steele	3	Walter Titus	10
Jacob Smith, jun.	3	Luke Torboss	25
William Stewart	10	Jonah Tilley	5
Ira Smith	2	Hester Tauzer	2
J. A. Snyder	2	George B. Thorp	5
Thomas T. Storm	3	Bela Tiffany	3
Samuel Sawyer	3	John S. Timmins	10
Dennis Stryker	3	Samuel Thompson	5
Abraham Stagg	3	John B. Thorpe	10
John Stuart	5	Isaac Tucker	5
Joseph Sandford	10	Thomas Thomas	10
John Snedecor	2	P. B. Van Beuren	3
George Schmelzel	1	William L. Vandervoort	10
Richard A. Stryker	1	John Van Beuren	20
Selfe & Conklin	1	Mrs. C. Valentine	2
L. L. Sturges	2	Abraham Voorhees	2
R. Sevanton	5	T. Van Tine	2
Abraham Shoemaker	15	Vreeland & Embree	3
B. Skaats	10	James J. Van Allen	5
James A. Sackett	3	William P. Van Ness	5
Mr. Sinclcare	1	S. Van Dozer	3
George L. Storer	10	Eli White	20
Mrs. Stewart	3	Timothy Whittemore	10

Name	Amount
P. H. Wendover	10
Ezra Weeks	10
C. & I. D. Wolfe	25
Andrew C. Wheeler	10
J. M. Willard	5
John E. Wise	2
Mrs. Wall	1
N. Weed	10
John Wilson	3
W. & M. Wilber	5
J. P. Whittelsey	5
Wisner & Gale	10
William & Harriman	2
M. Q. Wood	5
Alexander Wiley	5
John G. Wendall	3
J. & O. Williams	10
H. Wheeler	3
Stephen Ray	0 50
Lewis Wilcox	3
D. West	2
Ann White	3
Wyckoff, Brown, & Co.	3
T. V. Winckle & Co.	3
J. R. Wheaton	3
James Walker	2
Robert T. Walker	5
J. & H. Waterbury	2
White	0 50
E. Watholf	1
Mrs. Wadsworth	10
William Winins	1
R. White	0 50
M. Wirckmister	3
William Wilber	0 50
H. Waterbury	1
Reuben Withers	10
Tunis B. Waldron	3
William C. Wales	3
John Williams	3
Henry Wicker	5
C. P. White	20
William C. Yarwood	2
George Youle	1
George Zabriske	1

The preceding List exhibits a gratifying testimonial of the benevolence of our fellow citizens towards the House of Refuge for Juvenile Delinquents. There may possibly be some errors or omissions in it, and the Managers would be obliged to Subscribers to point out such as may appear to them, that it may be rendered more complete in the next annual report.

The Managers tender to the liberal patrons of this Institution generally, their acknowledgments for the prompt manner in which the subscriptions have been paid in, so as to enable them to pursue the objects of the association. Mr. *Peter Barker* is appointed to collect the sums yet unpaid, and to procure additional subscriptions, in the confidence of the continued extension of public benevolence to this important charity.

The payment of 50 dollars or of 10 dollars per annum for six years, constitutes a person a member of the Society for life; and an annual subscription of 3 dollars, a member so long as it is continued to be paid

Officers of the Society for the Reformation of Juvenile Delinquents.

CADWALLADER D. COLDEN, *President.*
STEPHEN ALLEN,
JOHN T. IRVING,
JOHN GRISCOM,
HENRY I. WYCKOFF,
CORNELIUS DUBOIS,
JAMES LOVETT, } *Vice Presidents.*
RALPH OLMSTED, *Treasurer.*
ROBERT F. MOTT, *Secretary.*

Managers.

STEPHEN ALLEN,
ARTHUR BURTIS,
C. D. COLDEN,
ISAAC COLLINS,
SAMUEL COWDREY,
ROBERT C. CORNELL,
WILLIAM A. DAVIS,
CORNELIUS DUBOIS,
THOMAS EDDY,
JOHN GRISCOM,
THOMAS GIBBONS,
JAMES W. GERARD,
JOSEPH GRINNELL,
JOHN E. HYDE,
ANSEL W. IVES,
JOHN T. IRVING,
JAMES LOVETT,
WILLIAM F. MOTT,
ROBERT F. MOTT,
HUGH MAXWELL,
RALPH OLMSTED,
RICHARD RIKER,
JOHN STEARNS,
FRED'K SHELDON,
PETER SHARPE,
ARTHUR TAPPAN,
J. M. WAINWRIGHT,
HENRY I. WYCKOFF,
GABRIEL WISNER,
SAMUEL WOOD.

Acting Committee.

CORNELIUS DUBOIS,
ROBERT C. CORNELL,
JOHN E. HYDE,
ISAAC COLLINS,
PETER SHARPE,
JAMES LOVETT,
WILLIAM F. MOTT,
ARTHUR BURTIS.

Ladies' Committee.

MRS. ANN SHIPLEY,
" ISABELLA STEELE,
" MARTHA WILLIS,
" CHARLOTTE FOX,
" MARY BOSTWICK,
" REBECCA M'COMB,
" ANN WARNER,
MRS. ABIGAIL BARKER,
" MARIA HYDE,
" ALMY CORNELL,
" ALICE TOWNSEND,
" MARGARET PRIOR,
MISS SARAH COLLINS.

House of Refuge.

JOSEPH CURTIS, *Superintendent.*
HENRY MILLER, *Assistant.*
PHEBE CURTIS, *Matron.*

*** Donations to the House of Refuge will be thankfully received by the Officers and Managers of the Society.

SECOND ANNUAL REPORT, &c.

1827.

It is with great satisfaction that the Managers of the Society for the Reformation of Juvenile Delinquents, in the city of New-York, report the state of this Institution, at this second anniversary of its establishment. This satisfaction arises, as well from the liberality with which a fund, during the last year, has been provided by the Legislature for its support, as from a thorough conviction, that the good, which it was hoped would result from its establishment will be amply realised.

It is but a proper tribute of grateful recollection to mention that the public is indebted for this Institution to the philanthropic labours of the Society for the Prevention of Pauperism. The attention of that Society which was composed of a number of our most valuable citizens, had been awakened by the condition of the many vagrant children, who appeared to be cast upon the public, destitute of protectors, a home, or the means of support. Our court for the investigation of criminal offences was monthly engaged in the trial of children, and the consciences and feelings of jurors were shocked, on being continually called upon to decide on the guilt or innocence of those who were arraigned before them almost unconscious of their situation, and some of them incapable of truly appreciating the criminality of the offences with which they stood charged. In truth, to them an acquittal or a conviction, was attended with the like disastrous consequences. If acquitted, they were returned destitute, to the same haunts of vice from which they had been taken, more emboldened to the commission of crime, by their escape from present punishment. If convicted, they were cast into a common prison with older culprits to mingle in conversation and intercourse with them, acquire their habits, and by their instruction to be made acquainted with the most artful methods of perpetrating crime, and with the surest means of avoiding its detection.

By the report of a committee of that Society, made in June, 1823, it appears that during the year, 1822, more than 450 persons, under 25 years of age, had been sentenced in the Court of Sessions, either to the City Bridewell or to the Penitentiary, and that of those a considerable number were between the ages of 9 and 16 years. That the average number of lads, arraigned at the sessions for petty thefts, was five or six monthly. And that 75 a year, for the three preceding years, had been sentenced to the Penitentiary, and one half of that number for the second and third offences. It was therefore evident from these melancholy facts, that motives of public good, as well as of private benevolence, called loudly for the devising of some means by which this great and growing evil might be remedied.

Children among us were becoming accustomed to the admission of crime, before they were fully aware of its iniquity. The moral sense became hardened or corrupted almost before it had began its monitory admonitions. Those sensibilities which ever cling to the first season of life, and which are as well the nurse as the guards of virtue, were cowered, broken down, and destroyed by suffering, degradation and punishment; when dismissed from prison, those wretched culprits had neither a character, a shelter, or any to care for them. As perfect derelicts, they appeared to be placed beyond the pale of confidence, and almost of commiseration: debased and destitute, they became prepared, from the very hopelessness of their condition, and also from its necessities, to make fresh depredations upon society.

May it not be asked, was not the public, from this very course of treatment, in some measure accessary to their accumulated guilt?

The arraignment and trial of children, is often a mere compliance with the forms of law, in order to produce a legal conviction. The accused themselves, are usually inattentive spectators of the formalities observed in their respective cases, without capacity properly to comprehend the investigation which is taking place; or, if unjustly accused, to assert and demonstrate their innocence. Even when guilty, jurors have strained their consciences to find some ground for their acquittal. Their youth, their helpless situation, and a heartfelt repugnance to consign them over to the common herd of malefactors, has often plead powerfully and successfully in their behalf, when truth and justice exacted their conviction. Yet this acquittal proved no salvation to them; again left to join their dissolute companions, and to unite and indulge with them in the same vicious employments, they only by a course of deeper depravity, became prepared and ripened for a second arraignment, without the hope of escaping condemnation.

If we follow them into the prisons to which they are consigned, how demoralizing the scene which that prison discloses. The work of depravity, began when they were at large, here progresses with a more than double rapidity; they listen, with that eager curiosity which belongs to their years, to the escapes and adventures of old and fearless offenders, admire what appears to be daring and chivalric in their exploits, receive and treasure up their advice, and when enlarged, are prepared to enter with them upon the same course of bold and desperate villainy.

Reformation, in our enlightened day, is considered one of the main objects of punishment; and surely, towards the young, it can be the only legitimate object: their years and their inexperience forbid the idea of making them the subjects of retributive justice. The vengeance of the law, when inflicted upon them as a terror to others, is altogether misplaced, and has neither vindication for its justice, nor apology for its severity. But réformation in a place like that we have described, and in the midst of such associates, so far from being accomplished, will never have a beginning. The prison, instead of becoming the school of reform, becomes the nursery of crime. The place where bad morals are taught, bad counsel given, and bad examples set. Nothing can be expected from such a system of retribution but the increase of crime, and the accumulation of expense for its detection and punishment.

Indeed, this subject cannot be placed in a clearer point of light, or the advantages which will result to the state from a separate imprisonment of adult and juvenile offenders, be more forcibly illustrated, than has been already done in the report of a committee, of the Senate of this state to that body at its last session. To this committee had been referred the petition to the Legislature from the managers of this Institution, praying assistance from the state, towards the building of a house for females, and which was then erecting, and also an annuity of eight thousand dollars towards the support of this Institution. The committee, after remarking upon its utility and success, as far as the experiment had been made with its limited means, observe: " Your Committee are fully persuaded, that a better disposition of the funds of the state to these amounts, could not be made. If the House of Refuge were to be considered merely as a place where so many children may be rescued from poverty, reclaimed from the haunts of vice and wickedness, protected, instructed, and reformed, it would be a charity having the highest claims to the liberality and bounty of government. But when viewed as a means by which the perpetration of crimes will be prevented, and the increased number of criminals, which without it, the state would be obliged to support in our state prisons, it is believed, that a regard to economy alone would require the support of this Institution. There is hardly a child who will be condemned to it, who, if left to the course which would bring him to the House of Refuge, would not finally be supported by the state as a convict. The evidence of this is, that a very large proportion, as your committee have been informed, and as they believe, who are now confined in our state prisons, commenced their career in crimes when they were children, in the city of New-York, or some other of our large cities. One person in particular, who is now confined in the prison at Auburn, was first convicted when he was only ten years old, and has since been, at different times, twenty-eight years a convict, supported by the state, at an expense of not less than two thousand dollars. This case, which is by no means singular, except as to time, shows at once what may be the advantages, even in point of economy, of an Institution which will arrest young persons in their progress and crime, and at the same time is an evidence that confinement in the state prisons, was ill calculated to produce reformation in young offenders."

But apart from these considerations of public policy, which must ever condemn as inefficient any system of punishment which tends rather to increase than to diminish the evil; we are called upon by a better principle to forsake a system, which has been heretofore pursued towards juvenile offenders, by a regard for the unfortunate beings, who are thus early made the subjects of penal retribution. Their youth, their ignorance, and their necessities, appeal to our best feelings, and beseech us to spare and to consider, while we compel them to account and to atone for their offences. Let them be arrested in the career of crime, and removed from the haunts of wickedness: let them be corrected, restrained, and their passions subdued: let them be made tractable and obedient. Towards them let a vigorous course of moral and corporal discipline be observed and enforced; but never let them be made the victims of the law. We can have but little commiseration for the old and hardened offender, who transgresses both against knowledge and experience, but how much can be said in palliation of him, who lacks both maturity of mind and of years; who has no judgment within, and no friend without to warn or to controul him: who through his own inexperience, the force of temptation, and by the enticements of others, may have been completely " outwitted and betrayed into evil."

And shall there be no redemption for a mind thus led astray, no separate place for reflection and atonement? Shall its conscience, freshly awakened and alarmed, be turned over to the derision of the heartless and the vile? Shall no attempt be made at a time like this to make a lodgement both upon its feelings and its fears, and to turn its shame and contrition to a good account?

The Chistian Observer contains an instance of the corruption of an innocent boy, who had been unjustly imprisoned, and whose principles were perverted by the pernicious influence of his prison associates. The case is extracted from a work entitled, "An Inquiry by Thomas P. Buxton, M. P. whether crime and misery were produced or prevented by the present system of prison discipline in England." "When I first went to Newgate," says Mr. Buxton, "my attention was directed by my companion to a boy, whose apparent innocence and artlessness had attracted my notice. The schoolmaster said he was an example to all the rest; so quiet, so reserved, and so unwilling to have any intercourse with his dissolute companions. At his trial, he was acquitted, upon evidence which did not leave a shadow of suspicion upon him; but lately I recognized him again in Newgate, but with a very different character. He confessed to me, that, on his release, he had associated with the acquaintances he had formed in prison. Of his ruin I can feel but little doubt, and as little of the cause of it. He came to Newgate innocent; he left it corrupted."

The same work also contains an address made by a man condemned to death for murder, at Douay, in France, as affectingly illustrating the evil of mingling persons of all ages together, in a common place of imprisonment. "This individual requested to speak in private with Mr. Apert, when he thus addressed him: 'I await,' said he, 'the hour of execution, and since you are the first person who has visited me, I will address you with confidence, and conceal from you nothing. I am guilty of the dreadful crime for which I am to suffer; but from my infancy my parents neglected me: I had neither a moral example nor a religious education: I was abandoned to the violence of my passions: I fell, when young, into bad company, by whom I was corrupted: but it was a prison that completed my ruin. Among the persons now in this apartment are several boys, who, with pain I observe, are preparing themselves for the further commission of offences, when the term of their confinement shall expire. I entreat you to obtain their removal into a separate ward, and snatch them from the contagion of such associates. Believe me, sir—and I speak from bitter experience—you can confer on those boys no greater favor!"*

These affecting cases prove not only the inefficiency of this mode of punishment, but the deplorable consequences which must result from mingling together adult and juvenile offenders. They urge upon us with a feeling and a truth which cannot be resisted, the absolute necessity of providing a separate place of punishment for the offences of the young. The young offender should, if possible, be subdued by kindness. His heart should first be addressed, and the language of confidence, though undeserved, be used towards him. He should be taught that his keepers were his best friends, and that the object of his confinement was his reform and ultimate good. If he is made to believe that he is still of some use and value, he will soon endeavor to act up to the character which is set upon him. Obedience thus procured, not by stripes, but by a reformation of his mind, will be willing, cheerful and lasting. His heart, which had been closed, and become almost callous, by a consciousness of its own unworthiness, softened by this course of treatment, will again expand, and made to hope better of itself; will look up with affection and reliance upon those, who, with so much consideration and mercy, have tempered its punishment.

The minds of children, naturally pliant, can, by early instruction, be formed and moulded to our wishes. An inclination can there be given to them, as readily to virtuous as to vicious pursuits. The seeds of vice, which bad advisers may have planted, if skill is exercised, can yet be extracted. Evil habits, before they have become inveterate by long indulgence, can be entirely changed; and on the mind which appeared barren and unfruitful, may yet be engrafted those principles of virtue which shall do much to retrieve the errors of the past, and afford a promise of goodness and usefulness for the future.

If we look into the bosoms of our own families, how

*This is extracted into the Christian Observer, from the 6th Report of the Society established in England for the improvement of Prison Discipline, and for the reformation of Juvenile Offenders.

much, in respect to the management of children, will be found to depend upon ourselves. How necessary to guard the purity of our own conduct, in order to preserve the purity of theirs. How closely do they watch what is passing around them, with the eye of ardent and freshly awakened curiosity. How eagerly do they imitate, not only what is meritorious and praiseworthy in those on whom they are dependent, but even their foibles and their peculiarities of character. Theirs is not the period of correct discrimination, that is the work of judgment, and belongs to their after years. If models of correct and virtuous conduct are at all times necessary and useful, they are especially so to the young. The tender mind can be easily made not only to comprehend, but to love all that is excellent in virtue itself, and to perceive the advantages which will be obtained from observing and obeying its dictates. It can be led on step by step, from one degree of goodness unto another; improved and improving, until it is prepared to launch into the world, with sufficient ability to encounter and withstand the many allurements and temptations which shall there beset it.

These little vagrants, whose depredations provoke and call down upon them our indignation, are yet but children, who have gone astray for want of that very care and vigilance we exercise towards our own. They deserve our censure, and a regard for our property, and the good of society. requires that they should be stopped, reproved, and punished. But they are not to be destroyed. The public must in some measure take the place of those who ought to have been their natural guardians and protectors. If we are parents, and look to our own children, and we know not what vicissitudes may await them; how powerful is the appeal both to our pity, and to our protection!

If it is possible then, let those children be saved. Let their unformed minds, now dark and ignorant, be made glad with the light of knowledge. Let their hearts, as yet young and tender, be softened by a mercy unexpected, and be subdued by a kindness which before they had never known. Let their voices, reclaimed from obscenity and profaneness, be raised in grateful thanks to those by whose benevolence they have been rescued from destruction: and beyond them, to that Being who has provided a refuge for them in their greatest need.

It is with these benevolent designs that this House of Refuge has been established for Juvenile Delinquents. It is here, that separated from vicious companions and pursuits, by a judicious course of restraint, instruction, and employment, their dispositions are ameliorated, their depraved morals corrected, and their idle habits changed. This has not only been the case with the children generally, confined in this Institution, but has been signally displayed in some who were termed its worst subjects.

Several cases of this nature are attached to this Report, and which have been selected from a Register which is kept by the Superintendent, and in which the age, offence, disposition, and conduct of each child in the establishment is regularly noted. We here select one instance, as illustrative of the reformation which may be produced by a course of steady discipline, even in those who appear to be the most obstinate and depraved.

"John P——s, aged about 17 years, was born in Boston: his father being dead, his mother removed to this city, and remained here. He had no opportunity in his early years, of acquiring an education, but was permitted to rove the streets, and to form such associations as he thought proper. After pursuing a vagrant course of life, he shipped as a sailor to the West Indies; and upon his return, in company with some depraved boys, committed an act of petit larceny, for which he was convicted, and sent to the Penitentiary for six months. A short time after the expiration of his sentence, he was again taken up, for being with some companions in the cabin of a sloop, for the purpose of stealing. He was sent from the Bridewell here.

"At first his conduct was such as to render him almost unmanageable. He evinced a settled determination to escape; in which he once succeeded, but was retaken. Appearing bent on his purpose, and making several desperate yet ineffectual efforts, it was found necessary to apply severe and continued punishments, in order to break the obstinacy of his spirit. With him, the discipline enforced, had a most happy effect. He became submissive and obedient. For several months, he conducted himself with the most unexceptionable propriety; he was frequently sent on errands to the city, and which he discharged faithfully. He was also placed as a guard over others, and was invariably found vigilant and impartial. In July last, he became desirous of going to sea. Considering the object of the Institution realized in him, his request was complied with, and he was indented to a respectable ship owner of this city. He has returned, after a voyage of three or four months, with an excellent character for good conduct. Such was his determination not to be influenced by bad examples, that upon one occasion during the voyage, the master of the vessel was obliged to punish the whole crew for some flagrant misdemeanor: John alone was excepted: he having refused to participate in their vicious conduct."

It will be remarked, that in the case of this boy, corporal punishment was used to subdue his vicious and turbulent disposition; this, by the rules of the Institution, is not permitted, unless absolutely necessary. Every effort is first made to influence the feelings by mild treatment, and it is only when this fails of its effect, that recourse is had to harsh and severe measures. The most judicious means the Managers could devise, are used to awaken the faculties of the children, and to excite a proper spirit of emulation. It is found that few of them are so abandoned, as not to be operated upon by shame, or that cannot be aroused to exertion by motives of ambition. Wardsmen and monitors, selected from among the most orderly and best qualified, are appointed to observe the conduct and behavior of the respective classes to which they are attached, and to see that they keep their persons clean, and their apartments and clothes in good order.

The children, according to their moral conduct, are formed into four grades or classes, each grade having its distinct badge, and which is at all times to be worn. As those in the lower grades improve in morals and behavior, they are advanced to the higher, and so also those in the higher, who relapse into bad conduct, are transferred and degraded to the lower classes.

The number of children at present in the House, is one hundred and twenty-two boys, and twenty-seven girls. The boys, when in health, are kept strictly employed during the hours appointed for labor, at chair-making, shoe-making, tailoring, brass nail manufacturing, and silver plating. The object being not only to keep them employed, but to teach them some trade, by which they may obtain a livelihood when set at large. Two school sessions, of two hours each, are held every day; at which times the children are taught reading, writing, arithmetic, geography, and book-keeping. Eight hours in each day are allotted to labor, and the residue of their time to their meals, reading, recreation, and sleep.

At night, each child has his own private sleeping apartment, which is properly ventilated, and in which he is locked during the night, and is required after he has retired, to remain silent. The only guard at night, is eight of the reformed boys, who each stand their regular watch of one hour, and this guard has been found sufficient for the purpose of its employment. When a boy by his disposition, conduct, and industry, has recommended himself to the notice and approbation of the Superintendent, he becomes eligible to the office of guard, and is also, with the approbation of the visiting Committee, occasionally permitted to visit his friends and relatives, in company with the Superintendent, or one of the Assistant Keepers. These indulgences and distinctions are found to have a powerful influence on the morals, industry, and conduct of the children. When any of them become trustworthy, and suitable situations are found for them at a distance from this, or any of our large cities, they are bound out to trades, or other suitable employments. During the last year, twenty-three boys and eleven girls have been thus apprenticed. The information received from the persons to whom they have been entrusted, has generally been very satisfactory; complaints have been made but in two or three instances, and in those, the misconduct could be traced and attributed to improper associations, which they were permitted to form in the places where they resided.

The girls are engaged in baking, tailoring, sewing, and washing for the Institution, and which engrosses almost the whole of their time; as all the clothing worn by the children is prepared in the house. They are visited by a Committee of ladies, whose kind offices are employed in instilling into their minds the principles of virtue and piety, in inculcating habits of industry, cleanliness, and strict obedience to the directions of the matron: in exciting a generous spirit of emulation amongst them, and in rewarding those who have distinguished themselves by their industry, neatness, and modest behavior.

The Managers cannot sufficiently express their indebtedness to those ladies, who have thus with so much patience, perseverance, and success, devoted themselves to the benevolent objects of this Institution. The female delinquents, addressed in that soothing and persuasive language, which so peculiarly belongs to their own sex, have appeared to be sensibly impressed with such kindness and condescension, and have evinced sooner than was expected, a change for the better in their dispositions and deportment.

In general, the children are obedient, and conform themselves to the rules and discipline of the house. No death has yet occurred among the children, which, as many of them were sent to the house diseased, is perhaps the best evidence, that the diet and regulations established there are conducive to health. Most of the boys, when committed, were in the habit of using profane language. It is very seldom that an expression of this nature is now heard, even in their hours of recreation. Their minds, before they were placed here, had been generally suffered to run to waste for want of proper culture and education. Many of them had been wanderers about our streets, destitute of parents, or, what is worse, had been under the influence of parents worthless and depraved.

With those of them who are quite young, the Superintendent has not much difficulty. They stand chiefly in need of guidance and advice. They are soon taught habits of industry and obedience, and, with but a few exceptions, become pleased and diligent in their employments. The most untractable are generally among the oldest of them, and who had become more hardened by a longer course of indulgence in vicious pursuits.

On Sundays, the whole of them attend morning and afternoon service in the chapel of the Institution; where a discourse is delivered to them, adapted to their years and situation, and suitable advice is given. On these occasions many visiters attend, and the conduct of the children has been observed to be remarkably quiet and correct. Having been taught psalmody, they principally conduct that part of the devotion, and the whole scene is solemn, impressive, and affecting.

Since the last anniversary, the Managers have to deplore the loss, by death, of Robert F. Mott, their late valuable Secretary. To those who knew him well, little need be said in favor of his worth. He was the friend of the friendless, and the advocate of the poor. Our public schools found him diligent and zealous in their support. Unobtrusive in his manners, yet steady to his purpose, nothing could swerve him from the path of duty, or divert him from the main object of his life, and which was the good and welfare of his fellow-creatures. He has early finished his course of rectitude, and has left for the approval and imitation of others, a bright example of active and disinterested worth.

It will be recollected, that this Institution was started by the bounty of individuals. The appeal which was made to our citizens in behalf of this charity, was met with a warmth, which proved how deeply they felt the necessity and propriety of the application. Seldom has there been witnessed among us, a more generous flow of feeling, than was manifested upon that occasion. Every hand appeared to be open to assist, and every heart responded its best wishes in favor of so good and benevolent a work.

In the course of a few weeks, upwards of $15,000 was subscribed and collected. This stream of benevolence has still continued to flow, and the fund from this source alone, at present amounts to upwards of $19,000.

With this fund, the Managers commenced their operations. The ground at present occupied by the Institution, was liberally granted to them, for that purpose, by the Corporation of this city. The Society at the same time, procured from the General Government the relinquishment of its interest in the improvements which had been made upon these premises. This was obtained for the consideration of six thousand dollars, two thousand of which the Managers have been able to discharge.

The fund which private benevolence had thus bestowed, though munificent, was insufficient to provide suitable buildings and conveniences, for the unfortunate inmates of the Institution, or to permit the reception of many others, who were proper subjects for its discipline. An application was therefore made to the Legislature, at its session in the year 1825, for assistance. It was conceived that few objects could be presented to them of more public interest than this, or more deserving of their attention and patronage. The application was zealously approved and supported by the Executive of the State, and met with the most cordial encouragement from both branches of the Legislature.

In 1825, an act was passed, appropriating $2000 a year, for five years, to the purposes of this Institution; and in 1826, it was provided, that young delinquents from all parts of the state should be received into it, and a source of revenue was provided for its support, being the surplus monies which annually accrued at the Marine Hospital, after defraying all its necessary expenses. The aid from this source will of course be fluctuating, as it must depend upon the amount of perquisites annually received from passengers in vessels, and from seamen, and also on the expenditures and wants of the Hospital, which are first to be amply provided for and satisfied.

The Managers believe that the revenue to be derived from those sources will not defray the necessary expenses of the Institution, if all the children are received which the present buildings can accommodate. The building for the boys can receive one hundred and forty, and that for the girls seventy children; and these have been so substantially erected, that they will need but little expense in their repair for many years. But to support the whole number which the house is capable of receiving, will, according to present calculation, require an annual income of at least thirteen thousand dollars, of which about three thousand dollars may be obtained from the labor of the children.

The Managers believe that but little more assistance can be reasonably expected at present from the State, or from individual benevolence: but they trust that the Corporation of our City, from a conviction of the great use and importance of this charity, will powerfully aid their endeavors in extending its benefits to the many juvenile delinquents, who yet stand in need of its succour.

The managers cannot close their remarks upon this occasion, without expressing, from their hearts, the pride which they feel in the interest which our State has taken in the improvement and the welfare of the young. The great appropriation made for diffusing education, while it secures the happiness and prosperity of millions, will prove the most efficient means for the preservation of order and prevention of crime.

While the school fund, therefore, ample and increasing, stands a proud monument of the character of our State, the present Institution, the first which has yet been established of this nature, shall continue a lasting memorial of its benevolence.

While a virtuous education is extended, without distinction, to the children of all, it is a solace to the philanthropist, that even those who have been considered as the outcasts of our species, not forgotten and forsaken, but reclaimed and regenerated, shall be gathered to the fold, and the whole, as far as the infirmities of our nature will permit, under the blessing of Providence, be formed into an intelligent, moral, and religious community.

STATEMENT.

The whole number admitted into the House from the commencement to the present time, is 220. They were committed from the following authorities, viz.

From the Court of Sessions, for different degrees of larceny,	36
From the Sessions at Albany and Schoharie, - - -	2
From the Circuit Court of the United States to await his trial, - - - - - - - - - - -	1
From the Police Magistrates for stealing and vagrancy, -	88
From Commissioners of the Alms-House, for stealing, vagrancy, and absconding from that institution, - -	93
Total,	220

Of this whole number received into the House, 83 are the children of foreigners, 137 are from the city and various parts of the state.

The following disposition has been made, viz.

BOYS.

Indented, - - - - - - - - -	28
Sent to the Alms-House, - - - - - -	2
Returned to parents, - - - - - -	11
Absconded, - - - - - - - -	8
In the House, - - - - - - - -	125
	169

GIRLS.

Indented, - - - - - - - -	15
Discharged, being of age, - - - - - -	3
Sent to the Alms-House, - - - - - -	4
At present in the Refuge - - - - - -	29
	51
Total,	220

Of this number,	48	never have been confined in Bridewell,
———————,	141	have been confined there from 1 to 7 times,
———————,	31	have been in the Penitentiary.
Total,	220	

Of those who have been confined in the Penitentiary,

20	have served	1	term of 2 to 12 months.			
3	"	2	"	amounting to	12	months each.
1	"	2	"	"	24	"
1	"	2	"	"	8	"
1	"	2	"	"	8	"
1	"	3	"	"	18	"
1	"	3	"	"	21	"
1	"	4	"	"	33	"
1	"	5	"	"	36	"

Of the 28 boys who have been indented, 5 were named in the last Annual Report.

Of the 15 girls, 4 were named in the last Annual Report.

The Superintendent has heard from all, except 3 or 4 who have left the House lately; and the following extracts from such letters as have been received from their masters, will enable us to judge as to the success of our labors, and the encouragement there is to persevere. From all we have favorable accounts, except 3 boys, 2 of whom, after remaining with their masters for a short time, returned to the House. One of these was discharged nearly 300 miles from the city, on account of getting intoxicated: with a few shillings in his pocket, he, in three weeks honestly worked his passage back to the House, where he now is learning a trade. The other absconded, being unwilling to eat with the blacks, while the laborers sat at the table with his master. The third boy was indented about eighteen months since as a mariner, under circumstances of expediency; after serving about six months, he absconded, and has returned to his former habits of stealing; has since been in the Penitentiary, for a six-month term.

APPENDIX.

Extract from Letters addressed to the Superintendent, during the year 1826.

"Your letter is now before me. In answer to your inquiries respecting the conduct of little D——a, I can assure you that it has been such as to merit my entire approbation. Excepting for ordinary juvenile errors, she has not given any cause for admonition. My other girl will probably leave me in the spring, and if I could procure another, either black or white, that possessed the same good qualities that D——a has, I should deem it a great acquisition, but I have no reason to expect such a thing, unless I should be so fortunate as to get another who had been instructed and disciplined in your school." E. F.

The following letter gives an account of a colored boy, the tenth subject received by us. He was committed as a vagrant, aged about thirteen years. He said his name was Jo: did not know how old he was, nor where he was born; did not know that he had a father; he believed that his mother was in the Alms-House, had never been at school, and did not know one letter from another; used to steal his victuals, when he could not get enough by begging. In short, his was a deplorable case of ignorance and vice.

"In answer to your letter on the subject of Joseph Refuge, we find him possessed of better abilities than I at first anticipated, but poorly cultivated, except the good lesson received at your valuable institution. Your first and most important rule, 'Tell no lies,' he is not apt to violate, but pays less attention to your other rule "Do as well as you know how.' He often speaks with much pleasure and confidence, of whatever you said to him as being right. Upon the whole, we think much of Joseph, and hope he will make a good boy." D. F.

The following extract gives an account of M. A. C. a girl aged sixteen, who was mentioned in the last Report. After complaint of her indolence and carelessness, the writer proceeds:—

"Her conduct otherwise has generally been good; she seems to possess a good disposition, although her temper sometimes discovers itself: she is kind to the children, and not inclined to gad about. We hope, that before her term of service expires, her conduct will authorise a different report." A. D.

"S. A. K." who was named in the last Report, "is as good a domestic as I can ever expect to have in my family. She is affectionate, respectful, generally obedient, perfectly honest, and makes satisfactory improvement in whatever branch of business she has been instructed in. The disposition to run away, which she manifested at first, has entirely subsided. She does not always exhibit a regard for truth, and is dull at learning her book. Her obliging conduct has gained her much esteem in the neighborhood, and there is a fair prospect of her becoming a useful and respectable woman."

L. W. L.

J. G. was noticed in the last Report, and is the same spoken of in the body of the Report, as the seducer of young females. Since she left us, she has uniformly supported the character given in the following letter.

"It is with great satisfaction I can say that Jane's conduct is even better than we expected to find it. Her reformation is greater than that of any person I ever knew. She has not formed any acquaintance, and is very attentive to her business: her time soon expires. She is about engaging with a missionary who moves to Ohio in the spring. M. C.

The following letter gives an account of a girl about thirteen years old, taken from a house in Bancker-street.

"I am pleased in being able to state, that we have uniformly found her of a willing and obliging disposition, and that she has proved a useful inmate of my family. I may add, that I feel encouraged with the prospect of her becoming in her riper years, an intelligent and virtuous woman. She frequently speaks of the kind treatment she received from the Superintendent of the Refuge."

J. C.

Cooperstown, Dec. 4th, 1826.

"Dear Sir,—Mr. Scott brought the little girl safe to us, we are very much pleased with her thus far, she answers your representation in every respect. She is amiable in her disposition, and very industrious—appears very contented and happy, and it will be our endeavor always to make her so. I do not feel disposed to lay myself under any legal obligation, to do for her, more than is specified in the indenture; but should she continue to manifest the same good disposition, the same industrious habits, and serve us faithfully, not prove vicious, nor leave us, until the expiration of the time for which she has to stay, I shall feel myself bound in conscience, to do well by her. This obligation will bind me as strong as any other whatever. Mary wishes to be remembered to you and Miss Andrews—she often speaks of you with gratitude—she also wishes that her mother might be informed of her safe arrival, and that she is well and happy. F. T. T.

SELECTION OF CASES.

BOYS.

W. H. O.—This boy's history exhibits one of the most striking instances of juvenile depravity that we have on the records of this institution. He, at the early age of nine years, commenced his career of stealing, and with the assistance of some, more hardened and older in crime than himself, he continued it for three years, with the most undeviating success.

Of his short life, two and a half years, in three separate terms, have been served in the Penitentiary, besides having been several times in Bridewell. The associations he formed in those schools of vice, instead of reclaiming him, served only to strengthen his vicious propensities, and at his discharge from them, he recommenced his depradatory acts with renewed skill; in short, with him, stealing seemed to be an instinctive principle.

Thus he continued until the establishment of this institution. He fortunately became one of its first inmates. Upon his introduction, he evinced a settled determination to escape, (in which he succeeded three several times.) The most rigid treatment was for a long time unsuccessfully applied. At length he began gradually to yield to the restraints, and submit to the regulations required of him. From January to December, 1826, he so far improved that we considered him one of the most amiable boys in the House. The person who contracted for his services, said, that his attention to his work was such as to afford him much pleasure; that he was entirely obedient, agreeable, and active in the discharge of his duties.

Conceiving that the object of the Institution in the effect of his reformation was completed, and that a better state of mind could not be effected in William, he was indentured to a highly respectable mechanic living in Connecticut. Some time previous to his indenture, he was asked whether he would ever redarken his character by the commission of crime, if selected to be bound out; his reply was, that he was then influenced by the *wicked one*, but that he now felt his mind to be in a different channel; and if a modest and humble deportment for several months, together with a knowledge of his frequently practising devotional exercise, are proper criterions by which to judge, we feel perfectly safe in saying that William was truly an altered boy.

Since his indenture, a very favorable report has been received from him.

S. T.—Aged sixteen years, born in Paterson, N. J.; he lost his father and mother when quite young, after which he was left to the care of guardians, who neglected him. He in a short time acquired a degree of celebrity among his companions by his skill in stealing old rope, iron, copper, &c. from around the docks. His career, however, was made short by the superintending care of the city authority, by whom he was committed to the Alms-House as a vagrant. He twice escaped from that institution, and when retaken the second time, he was sent here.

Soon after his commitment, it became evident that the discipline of the House was all that was requisite to make him obedient.

After conducting himself to the entire satisfactic of the Superintendent, he was indented to a farmer in the country. Since his indenture, we have been informed by the gentleman with whom he lives, that "he is industrious, attentive, and kind; and such is the state of his mind as relates to religion and morality, that he will reprove his men for using profane language, in a prompt, though modest and becoming manner, often referring to the precepts he received from his recent friends."

D. B. L.—Aged fifteen years, born in New-York, committed from the Police, on suspicion of having stolen a shawl. He was brought up in the vicinity of Bancker-street, and for some months played the tambourine, in those receptacles of vice and misery, the dancing-houses of Corlears Hook. He acknowledges having stolen some few articles, but denies stealing the article for which he was sent here. From the time he was committed until his discharge, he conducted in an entire satisfactory manner. In October, he was indented to a respectable gentleman residing about sixty miles north of this city.

L. S.—Aged about sixteen years, born in Ireland; his parents emigrated to this country about eight years ago. His father has since died. His education was entirely neglected by his parents, and the choice of his companions left exclusively to himself. He has worked at several mechanical branches of business, to none of which his restless disposition could attach itself. He was committed to the Refuge in March, 1825, from the Police Office, for stealing a copper kettle, for which he had been confined in Bridewell eight days, (and where he had been four times before.) The character of a notorious thief cannot with justice be attached to this boy, though he had been a habitual pilferer for several years. Upon his entry into the House, he gave no evidence of a disposition palpably wicked, yet he was a source of much trouble to the superintendent. In mischief, he was almost invariably first; to the rules and regulations of the House he was perfectly indifferent, and in one instance he absconded. After a few days he was returned, severely punished, and put in irons for forty-three days, when his irons were taken off. In December, his improvement was so great, that he was promoted to the situation of night watch and day guard, the duties of which he faithfully performed until July, 1826, when he requested to be sent to sea: his request was complied with, and he was indentured to a highly respectable ship owner of this city.

After an absence of three months, he returned to the Refuge on a visit, stated that he was perfectly contented with his situation, and that he had often reflected while at sea, that instead of enjoying the blessings of liberty, he might have now been in State Prison, had it not have been for the establishment of a House of Refuge.

D. S.—Aged fifteen years, born in New-York. His father died while he was yet an infant, his mother since married an oysterman, now living in the vicinity of Bancker-street. David has lived with three different persons, who kept oyster-cellars. After leaving them he returned to his mother. He commenced his thefts by stealing wood from about the docks; has also been in the habit of stealing old junk, copper, &c. He has been three several times committed to Bridewell; the last time for stealing a copper kettle in company with the foregoing boy: it was for this offence that he was committed to the Refuge.

He was at first very refractory, constantly plotting how to escape, and endeavoring to persuade others to accompany him. He was for some months treated with much strictness: from June, 1825, to February, 1826, his conduct was entirely satisfactory. At this time, an opportunity offering to give him an advantageous situation, it was deemed incompatible with the object of the Institution to detain him longer. He was consequently indented to a gentleman residing in the western part of this state, who, in a letter directed to his mother, two months after the date of his indenture, says he has much reason to be pleased with David's conduct.

J. D. S.—Aged eleven and a half years, born in New-York. This child, notwithstanding his extreme youth, has committed many errors. He was first led to the perpetration of crime, by the persuasion of one older than himself, in whose company he stole many articles; he was once in Bridewell for stealing, and was frequently punished by his parents, but to no effect. He was committed here at the solicitation of his father, in April, 1825. He conducted himself with uniform propriety until October, 1826, when he was returned to his parents, for the purpose of indenturing to a gentleman who was instrumental in his reformation, and who was well acquainted with his disposition.

Here is another instance in which the preservation of a child from ruin may be attributed to the establishment of a House of Refuge. Had this boy's thieving practices been permitted to degenerate into a habit, they doubtless would have procured for him a residence in our State Prison or Penitentiary, where the object is punishment, and not reformation, he must have been thrown in the company of old and hardened offenders, the contaminating influence of whose conversation, would eventually have banished every virtuous and generous sentiment from his tender bosom. What reflecting mind but must admit the utility of such an institution, and what generous soul but would contibute to its support?

G. D.—Between sixteen and seventeen years of age, born in New-York. He had been sentenced to the Penitentiary for petit larceny for six months, in October, 1824. At the expiration of his sentence, in April, 1825, being sick, and no one appearing to take charge of him, he was sent to the Refuge by the Commissioners of the Alms-House.

His conduct, from the time of his commitment until December ensuing, was uniformly good. He was at this time indentured to a gentleman residing at Poughkeepsie; and four months subsequent to his departure, we received a letter from his master, giving a very satisfactory account of his behavior.

GIRLS.

M. S.—Aged sixteen years, was committed by the Police on the day the Institution commenced its operations; for the first sixteen months of her confinement, she manifested a restless and uneasy disposition, and twice was successful in escaping, but was retaken.

After this, she appeared to reflect upon her former conduct, with regret, and gave evidence of a determination to reform. Having conducted herself well for three or four months, she was indented to a clergyman in the country, from whom the superintendent has since received a letter, in which he states, that he is very much pleased with the girl.

M. L. B.—Aged about seventeen and a half years. Some few days previous to her indenture, some one of the committee happened to express a doubt as to the reality of her reformation; this was communicated to her by a girl who heard it. She said nothing at the time, but quietly commenced her apprenticeship. In a letter subsequently directed to the Superintendent, she manifests a degree of exultation in doing well, and in disappointing those who suspected her fidelity. She also expresses much regard and friendship for those she left behind, and appears very grateful "for the good advice given her."

M. A. C.—Aged seventeen years, born in New-York. Is an orphan: was committed to the Refuge in January, 1825, at the solicitation of her aunt, in whose charge she was left by her parents.

After having been but three months here, her conduct was such as to gain the entire confidence of the Superintendent, who in one instance permitted her to go off the premises in search of greens: after having been absent about six hours, she returned, and said she had been to see her friends in town; expressed a regret that she had done so without permission, and said that she did not wish to leave the House until the Managers thought best. From this period, her conduct was very good until April 21st, 1826, when she was indented to a gentleman residing in the central part of the state. Since her indenture, we have received letters from her, expressive of her entire contentment.

J. A. B.—Aged between sixteen and seventeen years, born in Philadelphia, father and mother both dead. She was committed in February, 1825, for stealing a few articles of wearing apparel from a person with whom she lived as a domestic. She has lived at many different places, and has been in considerable bad company for about one year. After her commitment, she was almost unmanageable. She in one instance escaped, but was shortly after retaken. The frequent application of corporal punishment and solitary confinement, were finally successful. After giving evidence of a change of feeling, by conducting herself with uniform propriety for many months, she was indented to a lady living a short distance from the city, who informs us that she wants no better girl.

C. W.—Aged fourteen years, born in New-York, of Irish parents, who now keep a fruit shop in this city. This child became a victim to the seductive arts of a villain at the early age of *eleven* years. For two and a half years subsequently continued to associate with lewd and abandoned women, and has twice been in Bridewell for being found in such company. She has also been guilty of stealing many articles.

She was brought here in July, 1826, at the request of her father, for leaving his roof, and frequenting houses of ill fame. At first her conduct was such as to give little hope of reformation: she would use profane and vulgar language, was disobedient and disrespectful. She was soon given to understand, that this was not a place in which she could indulge in improprieties with impunity, and was treated as her conduct deserved.

After about two months, the treatment she received produced the desired effect, and she became directly the reverse of what she before was. The Matron now thinks her the best girl in the House, and says that if she offends in the most trivial thing, she is not content until she has asked and obtained forgiveness.

Many more cases of both sexes could be selected, but it is presumed that those mentioned will be adequate to convince every judicious person, that the House of Refuge has not been established in vain; and our subscribers, that they have not contributed their money to a useless purpose.

The Society for the Reformation of Juvenile Delinquents, in Account Current with Ralph Olmsted, Treasurer.

Dr.		$	cts.		Cr.	$	cts.
1825 Jan. 1	To Cash, first payment to the United States, on account of the purchase of the present site	$2000	00	1824 Jan. 1 to 1827	By Nett amount received from collection of Donations and Subscriptions from the Citizens of New-York....	$19177	41
1825 to 1827	For Repairs and additions to the buildings upon the premises	4420	11	Jan. 1 1825			
	For Clothing, for the Children........................	1548	13				
	For Food and Provisions, for the Children............	3544	19	May 1. to 1827	By Cash, grant from the Legislature of the State of New-York, $2000 per annum for 3 years..................	6000	00
	For Furniture, Beds and Bedding, Cooking Apparatus, &c.	2940	15				
	For Medicine and Hospital Expenses..................	350	39	May 1. 1825			
	For Manufacturing Expenses, Shoe and Grass Manufactory, and Weaving, ...	830	39	Jan. 1 to 1827	Cash from Sales of Manufactured Goods,............	394	70
	For School Expenses, Books, Stationary, Desks, Benches, Stoves, Library, &c........................	1075	98		Cash from Labor of the Children, ...	1270	40
	For Tools, Agricultural, Manufacturing, and Mechanical	48	98	Jan. 1			
	For Horse, Cows, Wagon, and Cart for the use of the Institution, &c................................	592	71	1827	Cash from Marine Hospital Fund, for the erection of a Female Refuge................................	19000	00
	For Society Expenses, Printing, Fuel, Stationary, &c....	218	43				
	For Contingent Expenses, Insurance, Fuel, &c........	772	35		Cash from Marine Hospital Fund, towards the annual support of the House of Refuge, ...	8000	00
	For Salaries to Superintendent, Assistant, and Matron..	4618	34				
	For New Building for Boys, ...	9954	60	1827. Jan. 1	By Balance due the Treasurer 1st Jan. 1827	789	19
	For New Building for Girls, Assistant Keeper's House. Store-House, Work-Shops, Walls and Fences, Vaults, Wells and Privies, Bake-House, Paving, Flagging, &c. &c.	21716	95				
		$54631	70			$54631	70
	To Balance, brought down, due the Treasurer..........	789	19				

DESCRIPTION OF THE HOUSE OF REFUGE.

The Houses of Refuge for Juvenile Delinquents, are situated about two miles north of the City Hall, at the junction of the Harlæm and Bloomingdale roads, on the ground recently occupied by the United States Arsenal. A more convenient or eligible situation could not probably have been selected. The lot of ground, 320 feet by 300, is enclosed by a stone wall 17 feet in height, and more than two feet thick. Within this enclosure, the Society has erected two stone buildings, each 150 feet in length by 38 in breadth, and two stories high. One of the houses is appropriated for Boys, the other for Girls, and the two being separated by a high wooden fence, there is no communication between them.

The first story of the Boys' Refuge is divided into five rooms, 30 by 34 feet, for Dining Room, Common Hall, Superintendent's Office, and Tailor's and Shoemaker's Shops. Three flights of stairs lead into the second story, which contains a Hospital, 30 by 34 feet, and two rows of Dormitories, each 3½ feet by 7, and 6 feet high, for the accommodation of 132 boys with separate rooms, each of which is well ventilated by openings in the rooms and stone wall. Two aisles, 10 feet by 110, are used as School Rooms, and are furnished with desks and benches, suitable for the *monitorial* plan of instruction. The Garret is one large room, 150 feet by 34, and may be occupied when required as a work-room. The whole building is well lighted and ventilated.

The Girls' Refuge is finished in a superior manner to that for the Boys. The first story is divided into four rooms, 30 feet by 34, for a Kitchen, Dining Room, and Work Rooms. The other part of this story is occupied by a neat Parlor and Chamber for the Matron, a Committee Room, and a Laundry. In the south end of the second story is a handsome Chapel, with a gallery, sufficiently large to accommodate 140 boys, 70 girls, and 300 visiters. At the north end is the Hospital, 25 feet by 34, and the intermediate space is occupied by two rows of Dormitories, furnishing 68 rooms for as many girls, which are also ventilated similar to the Boys' rooms. The Garret is 150 feet by 34, and is intended for the stowing of goods and drying of clothes, and may be used as a work-room.

A two-story brick building, 40 feet by 30, situated on the south-west corner, is occupied by the Superintendent and his family. Near to this is another brick building, 22 feet by 60, occupied by the Superintendent, and by the Assistant Keeper and his family. Adjoining this is a two-story brick Work-House, 40 feet by 80, divided into four rooms, each 40 feet square, in which 40 boys are employed in the chair-making business.

On the south-east part of the yard, is a one-story wooden building, 60 feet by 14, in which 30 boys are employed in the manufacturing of brass nails and sadlery, and in filing, &c.—to this is attached another wooden building, used as a foundry, &c. Near to the north wall is a wooden building, 80 feet by 18, used as a Bakery and Store-House, under which are large vaults for provisions, stores, and fuel; a stable and carriage-house under one roof, and some small out-buildings, complete the establishment.

A part of the ground is laid out into kitchen and flower gardens, grass plots, and gravel walks. There are four wells on the premises, of excellent soft water. Adjoining the south wall, the Society occupies an angular piece of ground, containing about one acre, as a pasture.

The whole aspect of the establishment is cheerful and comfortable, and it has little or none of the appearance of a prison.

EXTRACT FROM A REPORT OF THE COMMITTEE ON EDUCATION.

THE Sub-Committee to which was assigned the duty of providing the books, furniture, &c., required for the schools in the House of Refuge, Report—

That they selected the east and west aisles of the second story, as most convenient for the purpose intended; and the necessary arrangements for this important part of our system having been completed, the boys' school was opened, and conducted on the monitorial plan of education. The committee have frequently visited the school, and Dr. Griscom has repeatedly delivered familiar lectures on Natural History and Natural Philosophy, which have instructed and interested the children, and have been listened to with eager attention. We have no design to convey to their young minds any profound instruction, or to prepare them for the pursuit of science; but the intellectual darkness in which they have been involved, and the difficulty of inducing them to devote the requisite degree of attention to their simpler studies, make it advisable to combine in their view, the ideas of study and amusement. We are persuaded, that if such lectures were more frequent, and accompanied with simple experiments, very beneficial results would be discovered.

The Committee purchased a library of 476 volumes, comprising History, Voyages and Travels, Biography, Fables, Poetry for Children, Narratives and Anecdotes, and a few elementary Treatises of Science. Those boys who can read, avail themselves of the privilege of obtaining books from the library, and it is not unusual to observe them reading at table when their meals are finished, as well as during their leisure hours, and particularly on the Sabbath.

Soon after the girls were removed into the new building, the east aisle of the second story was appropriated as a school room, under the care of the male teacher, when he is not engaged with the boys. When the funds of the Institution will warrant the expense, and the Female Refuge shall contain its full number of 70 girls, it will be proper to employ an assistant Matron, qualified to superintend their studies.

Agreeably to the direction of the Board of Managers, four hours daily are devoted to instruction in each house, and the Committee have the satisfaction of stating, that the Teacher is assiduous in the discharge of his important duties. He informs us, that the conduct of the children is such as would reflect credit on any well regulated school, and that, in general, they are gentle, studious, and obedient, and with few exceptions, are anxious for the arrival of school hours.

Donations of books, maps, slates, globes, &c. have been received from individuals, who are anxious that a good school should be established in the Refuge.

The following are among the books used in the schools—Tytler's General History, Histories of England and of the United States, Park's Chemistry, Conversations on Natural Philosophy, American Speaker. Brief Remarker, Introduction to English Reader, Murray's Reader, Popular Lessons, Scripture Lessons, Spelling Books, Willet's Arithmetic, Hart's Geography, Daboll's Book-keeping, &c.

One hundred and twenty six boys attend the school, who can all read, with a single exception—38 of these could not read, and many did not even know the Alphabet, when they were committed to the House of Refuge—70 now write on paper, and 56 on slates; a few study Geography and Book-keeping.

Of the 29 girls, 19 read in Scripture Lessons, and 10 read and spell in the Lancastrian Lessons on boards; 7 study Geography and Arithmetic, 14 write on paper, and 15 on slates.

Each School is supplied with Maps on large and small scales, and with a pair of 13 inch Globes.

The expenditure has been $776 76, viz.

For the Library, exclusive of donations, - -	$200 00
For Stationary, Furniture, &c. - - - - -	576 76

We recommend that the weekly visiting Committee should be requested to visit the Refuge, during the school session, at least once in each week.

December 16, 1826.

THE PRESIDENT'S ADDRESS TO THE SUPERINTENDENT.

Sunday, July 2, 1826.

By request of the Acting Committee, the Managers of the Society for the Reformation of Juvenile Delinquents, assembled at the House of Refuge this day, for the purpose of attending public worship, and of transferring the superintendence of the Institution to Nathaniel C. Hart, he having been appointed to this office in place of Joseph Curtis, who had resigned.

Many visiters were present upon this interesting occasion. After prayer, and a sermon by the Rev. John Stanford; the President of the Board, the Hon. Mr. Colden, delivered the following address to Mr. Hart:—

SIR,

I am happy to address you on your assuming the Superintendence of this Institution. We know that you have left an establishment where your services have been pre-eminently useful,* and we are persuaded, that you have been induced to change your situation with a view not of personal advantage only, but by considerations of public benefit. You are no doubt aware, that the House of Refuge had its foundation in the benevolence, and zealous exertions of a number of your fellow-citizens; under whose guardianship, and the liberal patronage of the State, it has assumed its present importance.

Hitherto it has answered the most sanguine expectation of its friends, and its success must be in some measure imputed to the exertions, industry, and good conduct of your predecessor. He has

* Mr. N. C. Hart has been one of the teachers in the Male High-School.

no less share than any other member of the Institution, in its organization. While we receive you with every feeling of cordiality, and with perfect confidence, that, under your administration, the Establishment will continue to realize our anticipations, we cannot take leave of him, without those feelings which are naturally connected with a separation from a worthy brother and fellow-laborer, who so well deserves the commendation of "Well done thou good and faithful servant."

The children you will have under your care, are the victims of vice; not always resulting from their own depravity, so much as from the negligence, the bad examples, and very often the precepts of their parents, or of those from whom their immature minds would receive character and impulse. It was believed by the founders of this Institution, that many of these might be reclaimed, and instead of being left to grow in crime as they increased in years, that their young minds might be imbued with the principles of virtue and religion, and the juvenile delinquent transformed into a virtuous, religious, and industrious citizen. So far as we have had experience, we are warranted to believe that such reformations may be effected. If not in all cases, at least in such a proportion as will be an ample reward for our exertions. But our success can depend on nothing so much as upon the course pursued by those who may fill the station you are about to assume. It requires great kindness, great patience, and great firmness. The objects of your care will understand, from your attention to administer to their wants and comforts, both in sickness and in health—from your efforts to give them religious as well as moral instruction—from your making them industrious, and giving them the means of gaining an honest livelihood, that you have no motive but their welfare. When this impression is on their minds, respect and obedience follow. If unhappily it should not, then punishment must be inflicted. But this, with you, I am persuaded, will seldom be necessary, and will be a last resort. It requires much less capacity, much less knowledge of human nature, to govern a child by his corporal, than by his mental feelings. And therefore it is, that the former are appealed to so often, and frequently so injudiciously. A child may be made quiet and industrious by beating, but it seldom happens, I believe, that kindheartedness, morality, and intelligence are induced by whipping. There can be no worthy sentiment in the apprehension of corporal chastisement. But an appeal to the understanding and affections will generally awaken feelings that soften the mind and elevate the character: no human being ever gave himself credit for doing right from fear, but every one feels a self respect, when he is conscious that he does right from reason.

There may be however instances, and they are most likely to occur in an institution of this nature, where the painful necessity of resorting to punishment is inevitable. In such cases I am convinced I need not say to one of your experience, that their efficacy, either for example or reformation, must depend on their being inflicted with firmness but with temperance, and with no more than a just severity.

I know from your character that the children now to be placed under your protection, will meet with every indulgence that they can claim. If any caution on this head were necessary, it would be that they should be so treated as that they may not forget that they are placed here for their misdeeds. My own view of this establishment is, that it should be kept in the remembrance of those who are committed to our care, that they are offenders against the laws of their country, that they are in a place of punishment, and that that punishment is confinement and labor, from which they can only be redeemed by a continuation of good conduct that will give such assurance of reformation, as that they may be trusted to mix with society. I cannot think, therefore, that these children are to be treated exactly as they would be if they were the innocent inmates of a college. Were they to be treated as those deserve who are pure and innocent, they might be led to think, that vice was not odious to mankind, and that the stain of crime was too easily obliterated.

The charge that you have assumed is an arduous one, and its employments must be less agreeable than others in which you have been engaged; but, I am persuaded, you will find encouragement and reward in the considerations that there are few situations in which you could be placed where you would have it in your power to do more good. The consciousness that by your assistance a number of your fellow-creatures are rescued from perdition; that the child who was hurrying from stage to stage in the progress of vice, is turned to the paths of virtue, and instead of the hardened adult, becomes the virtuous citizen, must be a gratification not often enjoyed. But it is not only the individuals who may be here that will feel the advantages of this Institution. Society at large has experienced, and will continue to feel its benign influence. Already has it greatly diminished the number of juvenile offenders, who are brought to the bar of our criminal courts. Formerly there was no other mode of disposing of these than by sending them to the Penitentiary, or to the State Prison. There they mixed with old and hardened offenders, and after having their vices confirmed, and received new instructions in wickedness, they were turned from the doors of the prison, without character, without food, and without a roof under which they could claim a shelter. What resource had these abandoned objects, but to commit new crimes? And this they did with the less reluctance, because often they had not been taught the difference between virtue and vice. We have found in several instances, that children were encouraged to believe that there was no crime in stealing, if it were not detected. So little sense of guilt in theft do we find in some children, that it has happened, when asked how they came to the House of Refuge, they have answered, "by begging and stealing," seemingly without any consciousness that they were making a shameful confession.

Were other considerations wanting to excite our compassion towards the subjects of this Institution, and to stimulate our exertions to maintain it, we should find them in the knowledge we have, that so many of these objects owe their situation to the want of that parental care and instruction, so necessary to plant in the youthful mind, and to cherish the seeds of virtue. Many of these that are now before us, have been orphans, or abandoned by their parents from their earliest infancy. Often a child wanders to this wilderness of vice, from some remote quarter of the country. Frequently an infant of tender years is left in our streets without protection, by the death of a father or a mother. Some who might have been brought up virtuously and lived happily, had their natural guardians been spared to them, have no other recollection of their parents than is impressed on their minds by the agony with which a father or a mother bid them an eternal farewell, and left them unprotected, and in poverty to struggle for existence, and to encounter the temptations of the world.

How many may there be among these poor orphans whose mother,

"Bent o'er her babe, her eyes dissolv'd in dew,
"The big drops mingling with the milk it drew,
"Sad presage of its woes in future years!
"The child of misery baptis'd in tears."

I will not detain you further, sir, than to give you assurances, that the managers of this institution will be anxious to render your situation agreeable, and that you may at all times rely on their exertions and co-operation with you to promote the objects of the establishment.

N. C. Hart's Reply.

Sir,—

Deeply impressed with the great responsibility devolving on the superintendent of this important Institution, I cannot reflect on the confidence you have placed in me in calling me to succeed the gentleman who has so ably conducted its affairs from its commencement, without trembling.

Children without parents, some of them worse than destitute, have, by your fostering hands, been snatched from infamy. The world indeed is gazing upon your noble charity, while the community is rejoicing in hope of your success.

The weight and responsibility tower like mountains before me; but when I reflect that I shall have your wisdom in council, and, I trust, the directions of Him who prompts you to these praiseworthy acts, I console myself that I shall be enabled in a degree to be a father to the fatherless.

Yes, my dear children, I have sons, and I have daughters, and am enabled to feel for you; and often in my dealings with the children of others, solve this question for my own government,—'How should I like my child to be dealt with under similar circumstances?' This rule, I think, shall govern me here.

As to government, sir, I have no doubt but that many of these children only require to know my wishes, in order to obey them; but others will require to be more closely watched. *Virtue shall be rewarded;* while vice and immorality shall be promptly attended to. That you may understand my views on this subject, I would remark, sir, that in my opinion, the most benevolent and humane method for the management of children, is, to require prompt and implicit obedience.

RULES AND REGULATIONS FOR THE GOVERNMENT OF THE HOUSE OF REFUGE,

ADOPTED JAN. 2d, 1827.

Requisites which the House of Refuge possesses for the Reformation of Juvenile Delinquents.

1. THE MEANS OF SECURITY.
2. INSPECTION.
3. CLASSIFICATION.
4. CONSTANT EMPLOYMENT.
5. RELIGIOUS AND MORAL INSTRUCTION.
6. ALLOWANCE OF FOOD AND CLOTHING.
7. SPACE FOR EXERCISE CONDUCIVE TO HEALTH.
8. SEPARATION OF THE SEXES.
9. ATTENDANCE UPON THE SICK.

THE introduction of labor into the House of Refuge, will be regarded principally with reference to the moral benefits, and not merely to the profits, to be derived from it. If the employment should be unproductive of much pecuniary profit, still the gain to the city and state will eventually prove considerable, from the *reformation*, and consequently the reduced number of offenders.

Preference will be given to those trades, the knowledge of which may enable the prisoners to earn their subsistence, on their discharge from the House.

ACTING COMMITTEE.

The Board of Managers shall choose from their own number, an Acting Committee, consisting of seven members: one of whom may go out of office monthly, and a new member be chosen to supply his place.

The Acting Committee shall meet at least once in each month at the House of Refuge, for the transaction of business.

The Acting Committee shall appoint a Sub-Committee of two, to visit the House of Refuge weekly, one of whom shall retire each month, and a new one be appointed. The sub-committee shall record in a book, to be submitted to the Acting Committee, such observations on the cleanliness of the House, and the conduct of the officers and children, as may seem to them proper. From these records summary minutes shall be made by the Acting Committee, and laid before the stated meetings of the Managers.

The Acting Committee shall, at every meeting, appoint a chairman for the time being, whose duty it shall be to appoint all Committees, and to preserve order and decorum in the transaction of business.

The Acting Committee shall, out of their number, appoint a Secretary, whose duty shall be to keep regular minutes of all their proceedings, and to notify in writing the appointment of all subcommittees.

The Acting Committee shall be empowered to appoint an Assistant, or Assistants, for the purpose of instructing the children in the House of Refuge, in any work, manufacture, or useful employment, which they may deem expedient to introduce into the House.

The Acting Committee shall be authorised to apprentice the children out to suitable persons, under regular articles of indenture, and to enter into such contracts as they may think proper, with any person, for the employment of the children in any work, manufacture, or trade.

The Acting Committee shall have power, by a majority present, to summon special meetings of the Board of Managers; specifying the occasion upon which they are summoned.

LADIES' COMMITTEE.

The Managers will annually appoint a Committee of 13 Ladies, to visit the Female Delinquents, and to advise and confer with the Matron, relative to the affairs and management of this Department.

This Committee of Ladies will visit the House of Refuge monthly, and they will appoint in rotation a sub-committee, of two of their number, to visit it once in each week, to inspect the Female Department, to excite in the girls a sense of virtue and piety, to inculcate habits of industry, cleanliness, and strict attention to the directions of the Matron and the Rules of the House, and to reward those who shall distinguish themselves for industry and good conduct.

Minutes will be kept by the general and sub-committee, in a book provided for that purpose, in which they will note the order, cleanliness, and improvement of the girls, and make such suggestions and remarks as they may deem proper and useful. Abstracts from these minutes will be read at the meetings of the Acting Committee, and a summary of them also at the stated meetings of the Managers.

Should vacancies occur in this Committee by death or resignation, the Committee may appoint such Ladies as they shall have previously ascertained will, if elected, attend to the important duties devolving on them.

SUPERINTENDENT.

The Superintendent shall have the general superintendence of both male and female departments of the House of Refuge, and shall carry into effect all the rules and regulations adopted by the Acting Committee for their management and government.

He shall keep a register of every child committed to his custody; the name, age, and description of person; when received, by whom committed, on what charge, when discharged, and such other remarks as may be proper and useful, including a brief historical sketch.

He shall keep a regular account of the expense incurred for the keeping of the children placed under his charge, with every item properly designated; also, an inventory of the whole personal property within the House belonging to the Society, and the manner in which the same may have been disposed of, to be submitted to the Acting Committee every year, or oftener if required.

He shall keep a record of the events worthy of note that may occur, daily, during the recess of the Committee, and submit the same for inspection at every meeting.

He shall daily inspect every part of the Establishment in person, and shall not absent himself from the Establishment for a night, without permission from the Acting or Visiting Committee.

He shall exercise the authority delegated to him with firmness, moderation, and discretion; but in order that the certainty of punishment may deter from a repetition of offence, he shall permit no offence against the rules to pass without some punishment, except by consent of the Acting Committee.

He shall procure such supplies for the Establishment as may be directed by the Acting Committee.

He shall not, at any one time, allow more than four of the children to be absent from the premises, and then only in company with himself, the Matron, or one of the Assistant Keepers, who are not to lose sight of them while absent from the Refuge.

He shall have the direction of the Assistant Keeper or Keepers, in all matters relative to carrying into effect the rules, regulations, and discipline of the House; and he shall be responsible for their acts and conduct while on the premises, and in the employ of the Society.

ASSISTANT KEEPERS.

The Assistant Keepers, Teachers, and other officers and servants, shall conduct themselves in strict conformity with the rules of the Establishment: they are to receive their orders from the Superintendent, and to obey his directions. They shall not absent themselves from the House, without his permission.

LABOR.

The Children shall be employed every day in the year, except Sundays, at such labor, business, or employment, as may from time to time be designated by the Acting Committee.

A LIST OF EMPLOYMENTS THAT MAY BE CARRIED ON IN THE THE HOUSE OF REFUGE.

BOYS.	GIRLS.
Tailoring.	*Cutting out and Making Wearing Apparel for Girls and Boys.*
Shoe Making.	*Washing, Ironing, and Mending for Girls and Boys, Plain Cooking, and House Work generally.*
Comb Making.	*Plaiting Straw.*
Pin Making.	*Making Women's Shoes and Gloves.*
Broom Making.	*Knitting, and Needle Work of all kinds.*
Basket Making.	*Spinning, Weaving, &c.*
Making Rope Mats.	*Folding Sheets for Book-Binders.*
Cutting Corks and Pegs.	*Sticking Card Teeth.*
Oakum Picking.	
Straw Braiding.	
Twine Making.	
Cutting Skewers for Butchers.	
Folding Sheets for Book-Binders.	
Sticking Card Teeth.	
Turner's Work.	
Sash Cord.	
Scratches and Wigs for Hair Dressers.	
Coopering.	

FOOD.

The Children shall be fed with a sufficient quantity of coarse, but wholesome Food, in conformity with a Dietary to be established by the Acting Committee.

CLOTHING.

The children shall be clothed in coarse but comfortable apparel, of the cheapest and most durable kind. The cloth to be of a uniform color, and the clothes of the same cut or fashion. All the clothes, garments, shoes, &c. must, if practicable, be made on the premises, and by the children.

FEMALES AND MATRON.

The Females shall eat their meals and lodge in a separate building from the males, with whom they shall have no intercourse or communication, except at family or public worship.

The Females shall be placed under the immediate care and superintendance of a Matron, or Female Keeper, who shall reside in the House, and shall at no time absent herself from the premises, without the permission of the Acting Committee, or the Superintendent.

None but the Matron shall search or examine the Female Delinquents. She shall superintend their work, and take charge of the clothes and bedding of the Establishment. She shall accompany the Superintendent or Physician, whenever it may be necessary for either of them to visit the apartments of the Females. She shall endeavor to unfold to those under her charge, the advantages of a moral and religious life, and to impress them with a conviction of the evils and miseries that attend the wicked and profligate. She shall, at the season set apart for the purpose, teach them the rudiments of education, and instruct them in the business of Housewifery, &c. She shall be authorised to punish them for offences against the rules of the House, or for indecorum in their behavior towards herself or one another; and she shall keep a daily record of the occurrences, and regularly report to the Superintendent, such matters relative to their deportment and conduct, and the punishment she has inflicted, with the nature of the offence committed, as will be proper for him to lay before the Acting Committee.

PUNISHMENTS.

If any child shall refuse, or wilfully neglect, to perform the work required of him or her, or to obey the orders of the Superintendent or Matron, or Assistant Keepers, or shall use profane or indecent language, or shall assault or quarrel with a fellow-delinquent, or shall make a noise, or talk after having retired to the sleeping room, he or she shall be punished at a suitable time; and if, after this, such child persist in disobedience, he or she shall be confined in solitude, for such time as the Superintendent or Matron may direct.

If any subject shall strike or resist the Keeper, or attempt to escape from the House, or shall wilfully injure any article belonging to the Society, he or she shall be punished, except the same be remitted on application to the Acting Committee.

The Superintendent shall possess a discretionary power in awarding the punishment to offenders. He may try offenders by a jury of their peers, and inflict such punishment as they shall award, subject, however, to his revision. He shall, in all cases, enter on the daily journal, and report to the Acting Committee, a brief detail of the offence, and the punishment inflicted for the same.

If it should ever be necessary to inflict corporal punishment upon *females*, it shall only be done by or in the presence of the Matron.

KINDS OF PUNISHMENT THAT MAY BE USED IN THE HOUSE OF REFUGE.

1. Privation of play and exercise.
2. Sent to bed supperless at sunset.
3. Bread and water, for breakfast, dinner, and supper.
4. Gruel *without salt*, for do. do. do.
5. Camomile, boneset, or bitter herb tea, for breakfast, dinner, and supper.
6. Confinement in solitary cells.
7. Corporal punishment, if absolutely necessary, or if awarded by a jury of the boys, and approved.
3. Fetters and handcuffs, only in *extreme cases.*

WARDSMEN OR MONITORS.

The Superintendent may, whenever in his opinion it shall be useful, appoint for each ten or more children, one of the Delinquents as Wardsman or Monitor, who shall be selected from the most orderly, well behaved, and best qualified for the purpose.

The general duty of the Wardsmen shall be, to observe the behavior and conduct of their respective classes; to see that they daily wash their persons; that their sleeping and work rooms are regularly swept every morning, and washed or scrubbed once in each week; that the rooms and bedding be ventilated and aired, and the night utensils removed and cleansed; and that decency and good order prevail throughout the class.

The Wardsman shall be authorised to select from his class, in rotation, one of the number, to perform the duty of sweeping, scrubbing, &c., and it shall be an offence against the rules, for any of the class to disobey the reasonable commands of the Wardsman. He shall report to the Superintendent, any improper act committed by a member of his class, immediately after its occurrence, in order that it may be corrected forthwith.

ARRANGEMENT OF TIME.

A Bell shall be rung every morning, one quarter of an hour before the unlocking of the lodging rooms, and also at the hour of unlocking, when every child shall be prepared to leave his room, in order to wash, &c. previous to going to work.

The time of beginning and leaving off work, of eating breakfast, dinner, and supper, of attending school, and of retiring to sleep, shall be in conformity with a table prepared by the Acting Committee, and each time shall be designated by the ringing of the bell, as the Superintendent may direct.

A TABLE OF THE DIVISION OF TIME.

	Time to Rise.	*To go to School.*	*To Breakfast.*	*To Work.*	*To Dinner.*	*To Work.*	*To Supper.*	*To School.*	*To Bed.*	*No. of Working Hours.*	*No. of hours at School.*
January,	7	0	7½	8	12	1	4	4½	8	7	3½
February,	7	0	7½	8	12	1	4	4½	8	7	3½
March,	6	0	7	7½	12	1	4	4½	8	7½	3½
April,	5½	6	7	7½	12	1	4½	5	8	8	4
May,	5	5½	7	7½	12	1	5	5½	8	8½	4
June,	5	5½	7	7½	12	1	5	5½	8	8½	4
July,	5	5½	7	7½	12	1	5½	6	8	9	3½
August,	5	5½	7	7½	12	1	5½	6	8	9	3½
September,	5½	6	7	7½	12	1	5	5½	8	8½	3½
October,	6	0	7	7½	12	1	4½	5	8	8	3
November,	6½	0	7	7½	12	1	4	4½	8	7½	3½
December,	7	0	7½	8	12	1	4	4½	8	7½	3½

The half hour between unlocking and work, in the morning, shall be employed in washing and combing, in calling the roll, and in hearing a chapter read in the bible, and in such other moral and religious exercise as the Superintendent may direct.

On Sunday, the children after washing, combing, and shifting their clothes, shall proceed to the school or lecture-room, and shall be employed as in Sunday Schools, until the hour of breakfast; after which they shall be employed in the same manner, until the hour of religious exercises, and so throughout the day, with such relaxations, as the Superintendent may order and direct.

CLASSIFICATION.

The Boys and Girls shall be classed according to their moral conduct, and as soon as practicable there shall be four Grades or Classes formed, viz. No. 1, 2, 3, 4.

Class, No. 1. Shall include the best behaved and most orderly Boys and Girls: those who do not swear, lie, or use profane, obscene, or indecent language or conversation, who attend to their work and studies, are not quarrelsome, and have not attempted to escape.

Class, No. 2. Those who are next best, but who are not quite free from all of the foregoing vices and practices.

Class, No. 3. Those who are more immoral in conduct than Class No. 2.

Class, No. 4. Those who are vicious, bad and wicked.

Badges, bearing the number of each class, shall be worn on the arm at all times in the day.

In case of improper and bad conduct, the children in Classes No. 1, 2, or 3, shall be transferred or degraded by the Superintendent to the lower or lowest Class. And for improvement, or good conduct, in Classes 4, 3, or 2, they may be transferred or promoted to a higher class.

The children in Class No. 1, who behave well, and are orderly and correct in their conduct, shall be rewarded Monthly by the Superintendent, in the presence of all the children, and of the Acting Committee.

Those children who have behaved well for three months in succession, shall be allowed to wear a badge of distinction and approbation.

Extracts from such parts of these regulations, as relate to the several classes of delinquents, shall be printed and hung up in several parts of the House of Refuge.

GENERAL REGULATIONS.

No spirituous liquors shall, upon any pretence whatever, (excepting by order of the Physicians,) be brought into any part of the premises of the House of Refuge.

No species of gambling, nor of plays or games having a tendency thereto, shall be permitted at the House of Refuge.

The walls and ceilings of the wards, dormitories or sleeping-rooms, and passages, used by the delinquents throughout the House of Refuge, shall be white-washed and thoroughly cleaned at least twice in each year; which work shall be done by the delinquents, except on particular emergencies.

Every morning the school-rooms, hospital, work-rooms, passages, and dormitories shall be swept; the pans emptied, the dirt and ashes, and all filth and rubbish collected in the yard, removed to the place appropriated for the same. The school-rooms, work-rooms, and sleeping-rooms, shall be washed once a week, or oftener if requisite. The doors of all the sleeping-cells, and also the windows, when the weather will permit, shall be kept open during the day.

The bedding of the House shall be hung up to air, whenever the Superintendent shall require it. The straw in the Mattresses shall be changed, and the corn husk Mattresses scalded and washed as often as the Physicians may think proper. The blankets and bedding shall be washed frequently, and in all cases clean bedding shall be provided for every new delinquent.

No delinquent of any description, shall, on any account whatever, be confined in any apartment under ground, or where there is not sufficient light and ventilation.

Every delinquent, seized with any disorder, shall be forthwith removed to the Infirmary; and, in case of any putrid or infectious disorder, to the Hospital. The dormitories, from which he or she was taken, shall, immediately after such removal, be cleansed, fumigated, and white-washed.

Bibles and Testaments, and such elementary books on Natural History, Juvenile Biography, Voyages and Travels, as may be thought necessary, shall be provided for the use of the children, to be distributed among them, at the discretion of the Acting Committee.

The Superintendent shall present all written applications for apprentices and servants to the Acting Committee, by whom they shall be approved before they are granted; and no child shall be put to service out of the House, unless under regular indentures from the Society.

A Bible and printed paper of advice relative to his or her future conduct, shall be given to each delinquent when so apprenticed.

The term of the apprenticeship of the Girls shall not extend beyond the age of 18 years; they shall not be apprenticed to unmarried men, nor placed in boarding-houses, or academies for boys.

At every Anniversary Meeting of the Society, the several Boys and Girls who have been apprenticed by the Managers, and who shall appear at such Meeting, in a clean dress, and produce a written testimonial from their master or mistress of their good behavior during the preceding year of their apprenticeship, shall receive a reward or prize, as a token of approbation from the Society.

Officers of the Society.

CADWALLADER D. COLDEN, *President*

STEPHEN ALLEN,
CORNELIUS DUBOIS,
JOHN GRISCOM,
JOHN T. IRVING,
HENRY I. WYCKOFF,
JAMES LOVETT, } *Vice Presidents.*

RALPH OLMSTED, *Treasurer.*

ISAAC S. HONE, *Secretary.*

House of Refuge.

NATHANIEL C. HART, *Superintendent.*

CHARLOTTE E. ANDREWS, *Matron.*

MONMOUTH B. HART, *Teacher.*

HENRY MILLER,
JOHN MILLER, } *Assistant Keepers.*

P. SHERLOCK, *Gate Keeper.*

Managers.

Stephen Allen,	William W. Fox,	Hugh Maxwell,
Heman Averill,	John Griscom,	Ralph Olmsted,
Arthur Burtis,	James W. Gerard,	Fred'k Sheldon,
C. D. Colden,	John E. Hyde,	Peter Sharpe,
Isaac Collins,	Isaac S. Hone,	John Stearns,
Robert C. Cornell,	John T. Irving,	Benjamin L. Swan,
Samuel Cowdrey,	Ansel W. Ives,	David Stebbins,
Joseph Curtis,	James Kent,	M. Van Schaick,
Cornelius Dubois,	James Lovett,	Henry I. Wyckoff,
Thomas Eddy,	William F. Mott,	Samuel Wood.

Acting Committee.

Cornelius Dubois,	Arthur Burtis,
Robert C. Cornell,	Henry I. Wyckoff,
Isaac Collins,	David Stebbins,
William F. Mott,	Wm. W. Fox.

Ladies' Committee.

Mrs. Ann Shipley,	Mrs. Ann Warner,
" Martha Willis,	" D. Embury,
" Charlotte Fox,	" Maria Hyde,
" Sarah Hawxhurst,	" Isabella Buloid,
" Almy Cornell,	" Margaret Prior,
" Alice Townsend,	" Maria Colden.
" Rebecca M'Comb,	

*** Donations to the House of Refuge will be thankfully received by the Officers and Managers of the Society.

The payment of 50 dollars, or of 10 dollars per annum for six years, constitutes a person a member of the Society for life; and an annual subscription of 3 dollars, a member so long as it is continued to be paid.

A complete list of the Donors and Subscribers to this important Institution, will be published in the next Annual Report.

THIRD ANNUAL REPORT, &c.
1828.

The Managers of the Society for the Reformation of Juvenile Delinquents, in commencing their Third Annual Statement, cannot but congratulate the Society, on the prosperous condition of its Institution, and the beneficial results which evidently flow from its operations.

The actual condition and results of the House of Refuge have become so far the objects of public inquiry and minute examination, as to have furnished the means of a more exact appreciation of its value as an establishment of charity, and a moral instrument in the community, than can be said of, almost any other of the benevolent institutions of our state. The principles on which it is founded, and the nature of the evils which it is intended to remedy, have been commented upon by some of the ablest jurists of our country; and it appears to be conformable to the most correct views of human nature, and to the soundest principles of legal justice, that in the infliction of punishment for offences against society, there ought to be a marked distinction between juvenile and adult offenders;—that the treatment of each class, in order to be the most effectual, ought to be distinguished by those discriminations which are so clearly indicated by the natural and acquired propensities of the guilty in these different periods of human life;—and that, with respect to the greater number of youthful offenders,—those whose offences are so intimately connected with the abandoned situation to which they have been exposed, it would be a wide and grievous departure from moral justice to condemn them to a life of suffering, for crimes that might have been prevented with less expenditure to the community than that which must unavoidably be incurred in the infliction of the penalty.

The practical recognition of these principles, in

the establishment of a juvenile penitentiary, together with a knowledge of the immense degradation of character which has ensued from the mixture of young and old convicts, in the prisons of this and other states, was the leading motive in the formation of this Society; and the Managers do not fear to assert, that the call upon their fellow-citizens and the legislature for support in this undertaking, has been justified to the fullest extent in the progress and present state of the House of Refuge.

The advantages, abstractly considered, of an institution of this nature, have been so fully developed in the former Reports of the Society, that it is deemed unnecessary to insist further upon them. It is not among the least of the gratifications of the Society, that its efforts have gained the attention of the Legislature, and so far received the sanction of the highest authorities of the state, as to justify the belief, that a juvenile penitentiary will hereafter be regarded as an integral part of those institutions, which, from a due consideration of public safety and benefit, have a permanent claim to its protection and support.

The source from which its support has hitherto been chiefly derived, under the authority of law, has proved to be fully adequate to the several objects to which that fund is destined. This fund, it is well known, accumulates, mainly, from the payment of a small sum by each of the emigrants who arrive in this state from other quarters of the globe. Provision is first made for the ample maintenance of the Marine Hospital on Staten Island:—and few persons there are, it may be presumed, who will assert, that a more reasonable and fit appropriation of the surplus could be made, than to the reformation of juvenile delinquents, a large proportion of whom are the offspring of these very emigrants. The children of seamen are also as likely to partake of the benefits of the Refuge, as those of any other class; and the pursuits of seamanship under judicious captains, are considered by the Managers to be a fit destination for those of the inmates who incline thereto; and it will be seen by the reports that a considerable number have been thus apprenticed.

There have been, within the last year, ninety boys apprenticed by the Managers, and thirty-five girls. About thirty of the boys have been sent to sea, principally on whaling voyages from Nantucket and New Bedford, as apprentices to captains or owners, in whose care and guardianship the Managers have reason to confide. The others have all (with one peculiar exception) been placed in situations more or less remote from this city, under circumstances favorable to the formation of virtuous habits, and to an entire change of old associations. The masters to whom they are bound, covenant with the Society for giving them a suitable share of school learning, and for their due instruction in the art or trade in which they are engaged.

In a few cases, the children who have been thus apprenticed, have, after a trial of their new homes, returned to the Refuge, disappointed in the opportunities of improvement which were afforded them, or dissatisfied with the treatment they received. The cases appear to have been very few in which the master has been glad to relinquish his bargain from the continuance of depraved habits in the apprentice; but on the other hand, the Managers have been much gratified in the information received from various quarters, of the good conduct of those who have been thus disposed of, and of the mutual satisfaction of master and apprentice. As this is a point of vital importance, and the intelligence thus obtained affords an unquestionable evidence of the tendencies of the House of Refuge, it will not be deemed improper to introduce in this place, extracts from several letters from persons who have taken apprentices from our establishment.

LETTERS.

A.

*S*****, November* 7, 1827.

DEAR SIR,—I received your letter, dated September, inclosing an address to G——. I am much pleased to find that the Managers of the Society feel such a deep interest for the happiness, and are so solicitous for the improvement of the morals and habits of the children from under their care. G.—— was much pleased with the address sent him by his friends, containing instructions and advice* so encouraging. He keeps it as a treasure, and often reads it, as though he intended to adhere to the instructions of his much respected friends.

I shall comply with your request in as brief and plain a manner as possible. I am happy to say that G——'s conduct has been praiseworthy since he left the House of Refuge. If he continues as faithful as he has been, I think he will do honor to the Institution: he is a very industrious, obedient, and trusty boy; I have never found him to be guilty of telling an untruth, or make use of any bad language, but he reads his bible, attends public worship, and always speaks well of the House of Refuge. His improvement in learning has not been as great as I should wish, but I am in hopes he will improve faster with longer experience. He seems to be seriously inclined, and we endeavor to impress his mind with the necessity of religion.

I remain yours, &c.

B. B——.

B.

*G******, *February* 28, 1827.

Dear Sir,—Yours of the 3d of January I have just received, in which you want to know how my boy (J. H. S——) behaves;—he has spent the winter at school—his conduct as yet has met my entire approbation. You will communicate this information to Mr. Hart, if he has not received a previous letter which I have sent to him and you.

I remain yours, &c.

W. B. S.

C.

*N******, *October* 19, 1827.

Dear Sir,—I received your letter on the 17th of this month, stating that you would esteem it a favor to have a detail of R——'s conduct. With pleasure I write a few lines to inform you that R. has conducted very well; he has been very attentive to his business, and learns as fast as I can expect. He has made but very few acquaintances since he has been with me in this place, and appears to be very well contented, and has no disposition to run about the town in the evening as many boys do. He assists me in keeping my books, and I leave him the charge of my business when I am absent. On the whole, I have found him honest and industrious.

Yours, with respect,

E. C. B.

D.

*W******, *Turnbull County*, *Ohio*, *September* 17, 1827.

Dear Sir,—It affords me much pleasure to report to you the general good conduct and behavior, since his residence with me, of A. V., the young lad I took from the House of Refuge in your city, about twelve months since.

I have discovered in him no vicious habits; he is faithful, honest, and industrious; though not very active or intelligent, always willing and obedient, even-tempered, and contented: had he more sprightliness and activity, he would be a most valuable boy. I

* A printed Letter of Advice from the Managers is given to each child on leaving the Refuge.

should be, however, loath to part with him for the chance of obtaining a better.

Many of my friends in the vicinity are desirous of procuring lads from your institution, who cannot conveniently personally apply for them; could arrangements be made without their personal attendance, several persons of very respectable standing in this place would like to obtain them.

Your institution I consider of the first order amongst the numerous benevolent and humane associations of the present day to benefit mankind, and as such entitled to public and individual patronage. Enclosed I send you five dollars, accompanied with my hearty wishes that success and prosperity may attend the laudable exertions of yourself and associates to reclaim the youth of our country from the paths of vice.

Very respectfully, I am, Sir, your Obedient Servant,

L. K.

E.

*Y****town, Ohio, November* 18, 1827.

Dear Sir,—Your letter of September, I did not receive until yesterday. By some means it has been mailed at Cleveland, Ohio, which I presume occasioned the delay.

In answer to your letter, I am happy to state to you, that M—— V——, whom I took from the House of Refuge in the month of October, 1826, has behaved himself as well as any boy I ever saw. I have had him at school ever since I brought him home. He is the most attentive boy to his learning I ever saw, and his instructer informs me that he is the most attentive scholar he has in his school. I am also pleased to state to you that the impressions he has received from your excellent institution, I have no doubt, have been the means of reclaiming the youth M—— V——.

My intention is, if he remains as attentive to his learning as he has done, to make a scholar of him.

Accept of my best wishes for the success of your excellent institution. I remain yours, respectfully,

W. R.

P. S.—M—— will write to you before your next Report. I shall be pleased to hear of the success of your institution occasionally.

AA.

*F*******, February* 27, 1827.

Respected Friend,—After a full trial of the indented little girl, (C—— D——,) which I procured through your means from the House of Refuge, we have great reason to be highly pleased with her. As she was in the House of Refuge, so she is beloved by the whole family. She is useful and attentive in all the kinds of business in which we have employed her. I have no doubt, that with ordinary care, and the blessing of God, she will grow up in favor of God and man.

The great interest which you take in this interesting institution, is fully deserved by its undoubted utility. That Providence may long continue you in your successful career of practical benevolence, is the sincere prayer of your friend,

C. D. W.

BB.

*H*******, (Conn.) October* 27, 1827.

Mr. Hart,

Sir,—In compliance with the request contained in your circular, that I should give you an account of the character and conduct of E—— M. M——, a girl whom we received from the House of Refuge in March last, I address to you the following lines. In answer to your queries, I am happy to inform you, that she is a girl of good disposition, and that her conduct and deportment have been such as to meet our approbation. She is a very good domestic, faithful and industrious, and she performs expeditiously and correctly, the various duties which are entrusted to her. She goes to church every Sabbath, frequently reads aloud in the Bible, and receives moral advice and instruction from myself and from Mrs. P., which we hope has been beneficial to her. I should have written to you sooner, but my health is very poor, and I am not able, nor have I had an opportunity of writing before.

Yours, respectfully, For W. P.,
W. E. W.

CC.

*P***********, October* 18, 1827.

Sir,—In compliance with your request, and my promise made last spring, I proceed to give you an account of the deportment of E—— B——. I should have written before, but thought best to delay until a sufficient time had elapsed to test her character; and it affords me much pleasure to say, that after six months' trial, I can bear testimony to the correctness of her conduct. The fundamental rules of the institution over which you preside, appear to be indelibly impressed on her mind. I have never discovered any deviation from the truth in her, and as to the work allotted to her, she performs it as well as a child of her years can be expected to do, and expresses her gratitude to the Managers and Officers of the House of Refuge, for their interference in her behalf, and being instrumental in rescuing her from a vicious course, and restoring her to a virtuous and correct line of behavior. She does now, and I trust, by the blessing of God, will continue to do credit to that best of charities, the House of Refuge.

It must be a source of much gratification to the Managers and Officers of the Refuge, to find that in many cases their benevolent efforts have been crowned with success, in rescuing delinquents from the abyss of vice, and restoring them to the paths of virtue. Wishing every prosperity to the Institution, and temporal and eternal happiness to all connected with this invaluable establishment,

I remain, Sir, your Obedient Servant,
J. V. B. V.

As an exemplification of the characters of the youth who are the subjects of the Refuge, including those respecting whom the foregoing Letters were written, the following selection is made from the books of the superintendent.

SELECTION OF CASES.

BOYS.

G. W. B.—This boy was sentenced here from the Sessions, for being connected with that gang of youthful depredators, who created so much public excitement by store-breaking in the latter part of last fall. He was put to work in the Chair department, where his industrious and quiet disposition soon gave the Superintendent reason to believe that he had rather been a victim to bad example than to any intrinsic vicious propensity. After continuing in the House eight months, and exemplifying his determination to do as well as he knew how, he was indented to a respectable mechanic in West Chester County, whose account of him is given in the preceding letters. (A.)

M. M.—Aged about fourteen years, was born in Ireland, emigrated to this country at the age of eight years; soon after which his father died, leaving his mother in very indigent circumstances. The boy shortly after became a subject of the Alms-House, from which institution he was indented to a painter in the country, who discharged him on account of his not being sufficiently strong, and gave him a letter to Mr. Burtis, stating the reason why he had sent him back. M. instead of returning, destroyed the letter and ran away. Having no home, he in a short time commenced stealing, and pursued it for more than three years uninterruptedly. His thefts were principally confined to old rope, copper, and lead; but after a while he joined the gang of store-breakers referred to in the foregoing case, and was connected with them in entering twenty-six stores. They were all arrested excepting M. He was apprehended in the course of three months for stealing two dollars, and sent here at the recommendation of the Grand Jury.

From the information the Superintendent had previously received of his character, he anticipated much trouble from him, and in taking his examination he explained to him the object of the institution, and told him that if his conduct merited it, all his former crimes should be forgotten, and he should be treated kindly; but on the contrary should his conduct be vicious and immoral, he might depend that it should meet with prompt punishment. This lesson was evidently listened to with attention. He went to work industriously and cheerfully, and continued to merit the approbatory smiles of the Superintendent as long as he continued in the House. In August last, he was indented to a gentleman in Connecticut, who subsequently informs us that M. is a sterling good boy; that he is the quickest boy in the neighborhood at doing an errand, and that he is perfectly satisfied with his situation.

J. H. S.—Aged about sixteen years, was sent to the Refuge in March, 1826, from the Penitentiary, to which place he had been committed some few months previous for vagrancy. His conduct was entirely void of every thing of a flagitious or immoral nature; he was industrious while at work, and in his private deportment quiet, peaceable, and inoffensive. In nine months after his admission he was indented to an opulent farmer in Orange County, who after the lapse of a sufficient length of time fully to test his conduct, writes to the Superintendent that "John has spent the winter at school, and that his conduct had met his entire approbation." (See letter B.)

R. T. C.—Aged seventeen years, born in New-York, of very respectable parents. At the age of thirteen years his father put him with a merchant in the country, where he unfortunately contracted a habit of pilfering from his employer; after continuing for one year, he returned to this city, and was engaged as a clerk in a respectable dry-goods store, in Pearl-street. While there he stole about sixty dollars at different times, in sums of five dollars each, in a few months; he was suspected and discharged. His father then sent him on a voyage to Germany; he was absent five months, returned and resuming his old practices of stealing, he was put into Bridewell by his brother-in-law, for stealing a merino shawl and sundry jewels from his wife. He was tried at the Sessions, plead guilty, and was sentenced to the Refuge.

After being in the House some few months, he was promoted to the class of honor, which station he soon forfeited by a misdemeanor. A short time after this, he attempted to escape, but was arrested and punished. From this period his conduct became exemplary, and he seemed determined to obliterate the remembrance of his past misconduct, by his future good behavior, and in which he was entirely successful.

In July, 1827, he was bound an apprentice to a mechanic, in New-Jersey, whose account of him, after a few months trial, is given in letter C.

A. V.—Aged about 14, born in New-York, was a friendless orphan, entirely destitute of a home, and gave himself up as a vagrant, and at length desired to be sent to the House of Refuge. Upon questioning him as to the manner in which he had spent his past life, it was ascertained that his parents when living were poor and incapable of providing for their children; that he had worked alternately with tobacconists and boatmen; he had never stolen any article of consequence, but had commenced pilfering about the markets, whence we may infer that he would too soon have become an adept.

While in the House he appeared at all times entirely cheerful and happy. In October, 1826, he was bound to a gentleman, in the State of Ohio, who, after a year's trial of his character, speaks of him in encouraging terms. (See Let. D.)

B. W. R.—Committed from the Police in November 1826. His father was a Counsellor at Law, and unfortunate in his circumstances. B. was sent to school at an early age, and continued two or three years, after which, he accompanied his uncle on a voyage round Cape Horn, and was absent about eighteen months. When he returned, he became connected with some vicious boys, and commenced the practice of stealing. From his grandmother he stole money, in small sums, a number of books, handkerchiefs, &c. From the yards of several people, residing contiguous to his grandmother's house, he stole frequently chickens and clothes. He was finally detected, in stealing cakes from a store in the Bowery, and sentenced to the Refuge. After conducting himself, with uniform propriety, for half a year, he was indentured to a gentleman, in the State of Connecticut.

The reformatory influence of this establishment upon his mind, the following anecdote may serve to illustrate. B. on his passage in the steam-boat, up the East River, found a watch, in one of the private rooms of the boat, belonging to a passenger; he immediately sought the captain, and delivered it to him, and was solicitous that the owner might be found. The gentleman, to whom the watch belonged, struck with the honesty of the act, was led to inquire his name and residence. This gave rise to a very interesting dialogue, in which B. evinced a degree of exultation, in having been an inmate of the Refuge, and in realizing the benevolent motives which led to its establishment.

GIRLS.

C. D.—Aged about nine years, committed in April, 1825. This little girl was a very singular case of youthful female depravity. She had been in Bridewell, before she became an inmate of the Refuge, for stealing, and had been in the practice of pilfering, from her earliest childhood. After having been confined for one month in the Refuge, she was returned to her parents, by order of the Acting Committee, in order to remove some private unhappiness, between her father and mother.

Three months afterwards, she was found by the Superintendent in Bridewell, where she had been put for stealing, and returned to the Refuge.—She acknowledged that soon after her discharge, she ran away from her father's house and offered her services to a woman at Powles Hook; she continued with her three weeks, stole five dollars, absconded, and returned to the city.

She enumerated a variety of articles that she had stolen, with as much simplicity and apparent innocence, as if she was unconscious that she had done wrong.

After her return, it was frequently necessary to punish her for falsehoods, and such was her general misconduct, it was almost feared that she was incorrigibly vicious. She continued in this course for many months, without manifesting any evidence of a reformation; but some time in September, 1826, she appeared to be a subject of religious excitement, and from this period became a new girl; instead of an untractable and almost unmanageable disposition, she evinced an agreeable, cheerful, obedient state of mind, which endeared her to all who saw her.

In January, 1827, she was indentured to a reverend gentleman, residing in the central part of this state, who after the lapse of a few months, in a letter addressed to one of the managers, speaks of her in flattering terms. (See letter A. A.)

S. I. F.—Aged about seventeen, committed in November, 1826. This girl was the daughter of pious and respectable parents, residing in the central part of this state. She was persuaded to come to this city to learn the mantuamaking business, by a female, who, after she had arrived here, introduced her to a house of ill fame, where her inexperienced youth was soon persuaded to relinquish her greatest treasure, for the glittering vanities offered her. She was kept by a young man, who indulged her in every thing she wished for, but he soon died and left S—— friendless. Soon after this, she was taken by Mr. Hays, and sent to the Refuge.

She acknowledged that she never experienced a moment's happiness, while living in the haunts of vice, and, that the parting advice of her kind mother was constantly in her mind.

Her conduct in the house was at all times good; in conversation she frequently spoke of her lost reputation, with the most poignant anguish and apparent heart-felt contrition.

When her time of confinement had nearly expired, she earnestly solicited that a place of service might be procured for her, in the country, where she would be out of the reach of the persuasions of her former associates, and where by her future good conduct, she might create the forgiveness of the past. Her request was complied with, and she voluntarily consented to bind herself, for a period of one year over the general time, in order to secure the situation.

Some few months after her indenture, we received from her master, a very flattering account of her conduct; he states that she is a good and industrious girl, and that he is much pleased with her.

E. M. M.—Aged fifteen years, committed by the Commissioners of the Alms House, for vagrancy. Her mother kept one of the brothels of Corlaers Hook, and E—— resided with her. With such examples and associates, it was not to be expected that she would be free from error—she was daily in the practice of running the streets, and associating with women of the most abandoned character. Her mother's house was indicted, and she and her daughter were put in Bridewell, from which place, E—— was sent to the Refuge.

Her conduct, when she first came into the House, was such as was anticipated; she was wild and indolent, and gave the matron much trouble; she was frequently reprimanded, and in one or two instances punished. After a while, however, the discipline of the House was productive of the desired effect, and E—— became a very good girl. For the last six months of her residence here, she never gave the matron occasion to find fault with her, but was always quiet and industrious.

In March last she was bound to a gentleman of Connecticut, who, in the ensuing September, furnished the statement contained in letter BB.

E. B.—Aged about thirteen years, born in Liverpool, (Eng.) The predominant propensity of this girl was a restless disposition; she repeatedly absconded from her father's house, but was as often found and taken home.

In one instance she ran away, and was taken up and put in the Alms House, from which place she was bound out on Staten Island, where her father found her and took her home; in a few weeks afterwards, she stole some articles from her father, and again ran away, she was then taken, and a second time became a subject of the Alms House, from which place she was sent here.

After being in the House nearly two years, she was indentured to a gentleman residing in Dutchess County. (See Letter CC.)

S. A. M'C.—Aged about sixteen years.—At the age of twelve years, she was put, by her father, to live with a woman, who kept a sailor boarding-house; her association in this place naturally tended to the corruption of her morals, and after continuing three years, she quit, and became a prostitute. She had been living, in this abandoned course, six months, when she was arrested by the watchman, for being very noisy in the streets, taken to the Police, and from thence sent here.

Upon her entry into the Refuge, she appeared entirely callous to every principle of shame or morality; but the rigid enforcement of the discipline of the House were productive of a happy influence, in correcting her vicious propensities, and it is hoped in effecting her entire reformation.

In May, 1826, she was indentured to a gentleman in West Chester County, who after sixteen month's trial informs us that S—— is a very good girl, and a faithful and industrious domestic.

Numerous other cases of an analagous nature might be related, but it is believed that those already quoted will be sufficient to satisfy the public.

STATEMENT

Of numbers admitted, destination, &c.

The whole number of subjects received into the House, from the commencement of its operations to the present time is 377, viz:—

Boys	270	
Girls	107	
		377

They have been committed by the following authorities, viz:—

From the Court of Sessions	42	
—— U. S. Court	1	
—— Ballstown Saratoga Sessions	1	
—— Albany Sessions	8	
—— Schoharie Sessions	1	
—— Troy Sessions	3	
—— Washington Co. Oyer and Terminer	1	
—— Newburgh Sessions	2	
—— Police of this City	122	
—— Commissioners of N. Y. Alms House } —— Bridewell }	196	
		377

Of the above number, one hundred and forty-nine are the children of foreigners, and the remaining two hundred and twenty-eight were born in the city and in various parts of the adjacent states.—

They have been disposed of as follows:—

BOYS.

Indentured	118	
Sent to the Alms-House,	4	
Returned to friends	14	
Deceased	1	
Of Age	5	
Permanent Escapes	5	
Now in the House	123	
		270

GIRLS.

Indentured	50	
Of Age	8	
Sent to the Alms-House	8	
Returned to friends	2	
Permanent Escape	1	
In the House	38	
		107
		377

Of the 118	boys Indentured,	28	were included in	last	Report.
4	sent to Alms H.	2	do.	do.	do.
14	ret'd to friends,	11	do.	do.	do.
5	perm't escapes,	3	do.	do.	do.

Of the 50	girls indentured,	15	were named	last	year.
8	of age,	3	do.	do.	do.
8	sent to Alms H.	4	do.	do.	do.

Of the whole number, 109 never have been in Bridewell,
225 have been there from 1 to 7 times,
43 have been in Penitentiary from 1 to 3 times.

The boys have been apprenticed, as follows, viz:—

Farmers,

8 in Putnam County, N. York.		7 in West Chester Co. N. York.	
1 Queens do. do.		1 Sullivan do. do.	
4 Saratoga do. do.		2 Orange do. do.	
3 Delaware do. do.		2 Greene do. do.	
3 Ulster do. do.		1 Clinton do. do.	
14 Dutchess do. do.		2 Somerset do. do.	
1 Livingston do. do.		2 State of Connecticut,	
1 Genessee do. do.		2 State of New-Jersey,	
2 Steuben do. do.		2 State of Ohio.	
1 Oneida do. do.			

2 Assistants, in an Oil and Candle Store, in Nantucket, Mass.
2 Chair Makers, in Syracuse, Onondago Co. New-York.
2 Paper Makers, in New Prospect, New-Jersey.
1 Potter, in Norwalk, Connecticut.
1 Weaver, in Poughkeepsie, Dutchess Co. New-York.
1 Cabinet Maker, in West Chester Co. New-York.
2 Printers, 1 in West Chester Co. and 1 in Suffolk Co. (L. I.)
2 Shoe Makers, 1 in Stamford, and 1 in Fairfield, Con.
2 Tanners and Curriers, 1 in Orange Co. and 1 in Somerset Co. New-York.
1 Tin Smith, in Newark, New-Jersey.
1 Hatter, in West Chester Co. New-York.
1 Provision Dealer, in the city of New-York.
4 Blacksmiths, 1 in West Chester Co. 2 in Nantucket, and 1 in Dutchess Co.
35 Seamen, 5 for European voyages, 30 for the Nantucket Whale Fishery, in the Pacific Ocean, and on long voyages.

The girls have all been indented, as domestic servants, in the following places:—

2	in Delaware	Co.	N. York.	1	in Ontario	Co.	N. York.
10	Dutchess	do.	do.	6	Ulster	do.	do.
2	Wayne	do.	do.	1	Jefferson	do.	do.
4	Steuben	do.	do.	4	Sussex	do.	do.
1	Courtlandt	do.	do.	3	State of Connecticut.		
4	Rensselaer	do.	do.	1	State of New-Jersey.		
9	West Chester	do.	do.	1	State of Ohio.		
1	Sullivan	do.	do.				

NOTE.—It is an invariable rule, that no child is indented, except by his own consent.

From the foregoing statement, it will be perceived, that while the labors of the Society in the support and management of the House of Refuge, are affording a local convenience to the city of New-York, it is at the same time acquiring the character of more general usefulness in becoming the receptacle of youthful convicts from other parts of the state. In proportion as its benefits are thus perceived by the courts and magistrates of interior counties, the necessity will arise of more extended accommodations than the present limits can supply. The house for boys has been for some time past, nearly full; and some restriction is of necessity placed on the number and character of those who are now admissible from our city authorities. Whatever may be thought by those who indulge in cold and abstract speculation on the relative amount of good which this or any other benevolent institution may produce upon the great mass of our population, there cannot, as the Managers fully believe, be a doubt remaining in the mind of a sound political economist, of the meliorating, protecting, and reformatory influence of such an establishment as the House of Refuge. Its positive effects on those who partake of its coercions, its persuasions, and instructions, and the terror which is inspired by a knowledge of its incarcerations and its penalties, all tend to increase in the minds of our youth, a sense of the magnitude of crime, and to diffuse throughout the neglected and misguided portion of our juvenile community a better feeling in relation to their social and moral duties. This effect is already obvious to the magistrates, attornies, and officers whose duty it is to arraign such young criminals at the bar of justice. Nor ought we to omit, in the enumeration of its benefits, the important fact that it strengthens the too feeble hands of parents, (many of whom are widows,) over their ungracious and disobedient children, furnishing them with a final resource altogether new, and almost altogether exempt from the insuperable objection which lies against the commitment of young people to the common prisons.

The Managers are induced, from these considerations, to turn the attention of the Society and the public to the means of enlarging the sphere of their operations. One hundred and forty boys are all that the present buildings can accommodate. Two hundred and seventy is the whole number upon which the institution has been in operation. If within these narrow limitations, advantages so decisive have resulted to this populous city, and to the adjacent counties, as the letters and other cases contained in this Report clearly prove, what might not be expected from an adequate extension of such a salutary system of juvenile reform? That it would eventually diminish the increasing number of those adult convicts who crowd the cells of the state prisons, and whose established career of vice is generally found to have been connected with, and preceded by, a youth of neglect and abandonment, is nearly as certain as that effects proceed from established causes in the moral as well as in the physical world.

Buildings adapted to at least double the number of male Delinquents, may on these accounts become desirable. Nor are we so enthusiastic as to suppose, that, with a population so rapidly augmenting, congregated from so many parts of the world, and comprising so great a variety of character, and amidst so many sources of temptation to criminality, the utmost exertions of the benevolent by this and all other modes, will be able to exterminate vice, or remove the necessity of penal inflictions.

It seems obvious to the Managers, that while the New-York Refuge is thus interposing its shield against the devastations of crime within the limits of this metropolis, it ought to be the timely concern of magistrates and other enlightened citizens in the interior districts of the state, to devise the means of erecting a similar institution, in some one of the most populous or central places within their confines. We shall do no more than make this suggestion, indulging the hope that it will in due time meet the views of those who are competent to estimate its importance, and to give it all the efficiency which it may deserve.

The following is an account of the manual operations in the shops of the Refuge during the past year.

STATEMENT OF MANUFACTURES,

Done on the Premises, from January 1st, 1827, to Jan. 1st, 1828.

IN THE SHOE DEPARTMENT.

1214 pair of Pumps have been completed.
4341 " Pump Uppers closed.
39 " Boots completed.
4262 " Boot Legs crimped and closed.
1556 " Brogans and Shoes closed.

IN THE CHAIR SHOP.

9834 Cane Seats for Plain Frames.
864 " " for Maple Frames.
330 " " and Backs for large Arm Chairs.
132 " Settee Bottoms, caned.

IN THE BRASS NAIL SHOP.

14976 M. Brass Nails.
228 doz. Bits,
2196 pair Stirrups,
396 " Holster Tips,
104436 feet of Moulding,
660 gross Ornaments,
156 " Buckles,
732 pair Wheelbands,
780 " Spanish Gig Steps,
108 " Hames,
408 " Gig Handles,
396 " Cavessons,
1200 " Ferrets.

IN THE DOMESTIC SHOE-SHOP.

394 pair of new Shoes for the subjects, besides mending.

IN THE TAILOR'S SHOP.

350 pair Canvass Pantaloons, for summer.
175 Round Jackets of Satinett, for winter.
175 pair Pantaloons, " "
Besides all the requisite mending for 135 or 140 subjects.

In addition to the above, it may be observed, that much has been done by the boys in improving the walks, garden, and grounds within the walls. The work assigned them is in general performed with great alacrity, and some of them have acquired no inconsiderable dexterity in the trades in which they are employed.

But valuable as is the labor performed in the work shops, both in a moral and physical point of view, it will be perceived by the Society, that this labor cannot be relied upon as a source of profit, to so great an extent as might at first be anticipated from the evidence of industry which the shops exhibit. Nearly as soon as the boys acquire a dexterity at their trades which renders their labor increasingly valuable, they are sent into the country, and inexperienced hands succeed to their places. On this account, it has been found impracticable to obtain for them steady employment, at higher wages than an average of twelve and a half cents per day, of eight hours each; the remainder of the twelve hours being devoted to their school exercises. A few of them are also too small to be considered as entitled to any reward. From the work of the females, no other profit is obtained than that which is saved by the performance of domestic duties.

Their number, since the increase of the boys to their present amount, has been only sufficient to accomplish the varied routine of cooking, cleaning, making of garments, and other work, incident to so large a family.

But although it is desirable to direct the employment of the youth so as to render it an important item in the pecuniary concerns of the institution, it is not, and cannot be the main object of the Refuge, to cause those juvenile offenders to support themselves. To inflict upon them a suitable punishment for their offences, and to effect that moral reformation which will restore them to the world, enlightened and regenerated, are the great objects of this Society. Accomplish this, and we hold it to be a demonstrable truth, that, whatever the cost of such an institution within the bounds of practicable economy, it cannot but prove in its ultimate effects, an essential advantage to the finances of the state.

The School, we believe to be in a prosperous condition; and that it forms an invaluable department of the institution, not only as the means of literary improvement, but of intellectual and moral culture. The following is the teachers' report.

SCHOOL REPORT.

There are now in the Male School, 123 pupils. Of this number, when they entered the House, the greater part could not read, and many did not know their letters.

At present 13 spell words of one and two syllables on Boards,
23 read on boards select sentences from Scripture,
14 " in Spelling-books and Moral Monitor,
7 " Jack Halyard and Popular Lessons,
30 " Murray's Introduction and Reader,
13 " History of the U. States. (Goodrich's.)
11 " History of England, and American Speaker,
12 " Natural Philosophy and Parkes' Chemistry.

123

Of the 101 Boys indented and otherwise disposed of within the last year, 9 had made considerable proficiency in Geography; 77 could read, write, and cypher; and 15 had not been in the House sufficiently long to make much improvement.

Of the number at present in the House, very few were acquainted with the first principles of Arithmetic.

22 now Cypher in Addition,
9 " " Subtraction,
8 " " Multiplication,
10 " " Short Division,
7 " " Long Division,
21 " " Compound Rules,
7 " " Rule of Three,
1 " " Tare and Trett,
1 " " Vulgar Fractions,
37 Studying the Tables preparatory to Cyphering.

123

46 write very legibly on paper, and 75 on slates.

The Female School may be said to be in a like good condition; there being 38 Girls, the most of whom read and write, and a few are somewhat advanced in Arithmetic.

Four hours in each day, are devoted in both Houses, to instruction.

The Schools are in good order, and the children tractable, obedient, submissive, and with few exceptions, fond of learning.

Each Sabbath morning, previous to church hours, the teacher is assisted by two or three pious gentlemen from the city; the children are then organized, and taught in the manner of a Sabbath School. In addition to this, one hour between meetings, is appropriated to reading the Scriptures, and the general and silent attention the children appear to give to this exercise, to a spectator is solemn and impressive.

The teacher feels a pleasure in saying, that though the children under his tuition, are generally from the lowest classes of society, they evince in their conduct, a degree of decorum, equal to that which is discovered in well regulated schools: and though they are at first wild, and sometimes almost incorrigible, nothing is requisite but steady discipline, to inure them to habits of perfect order.

The health of the Refuge since the last Report, has been remarkably preserved, notwithstanding the prevalence of fevers in several parts of the vicinity. But one death has occurred since the opening of the institution, and that was the result of vicious imprudence on the part of the sufferer. In the momentary absence of the Assistant Apothecary, this boy swallowed a portion of the tincture of cantharides, designing, as is supposed, to take some laudanum. To the skill and benevolent attention of the physicians, Drs. Stearns and Ives, the Institution is greatly indebted for its relative exemption from disease, and for which these gentlemen are entitled to the thanks of all those who are interested in the health of its inmates.

With respect to that kind of improvement which constitutes by far the most important experimental part of the Discipline of the Refuge,—its moral influence upon the minds and dispositions of its subjects, the Managers are persuaded they may congratulate the Society on the evidence of no inconsiderable amount of actual good. The Superintendent, whose vigilant attention to this part of his charge, affords the strongest assurance of that general fidelity with which the Managers have hitherto been highly gratified, appears to be much encouraged by the temper and feeling which are now prevalent in the House.—The Sabbath exercises are performed with solemnity. The meetings are attended by ministers of various denominations; the gospel is often preached with power by those who take a deep and lively interest in the children's welfare, and their appeals to the understandings and consciences of their hearers, are often productive of an awakened sensibility, on the part of both sexes. There has been, within the last three months, an indication of the power of religious impressions, in the case of some, whose minds, it was feared, would prove impregnable to every effort that could be made to arouse them to a sense of their moral danger. Both the Superintendent and Matron indulge the hope, that in some of these hardened and desperate cases, a conversion has been experienced, which will eventuate in an entire change of temper and inclination. "J. C., who had been one of the most notorious villains of his day—notorious in all the criminal courts, professed last spring, at the time of a religious excitement, to find mercy, and to make his peace with God. He has ever since evinced all he professed. Nor have we, (says the Superintendent under date of November 20th,) had occasion to reprove him since. He was a few days ago bound to a respectable mechanic. Also, J. McD., who was perhaps one of the most accomplished thieves that ever entered the House, and who boasted last winter, that we should never have it to say, that the House of Refuge had done him any good,—was also a subject of hopeful conversion last spring,—lived several months in the House accordingly—was some time since bound to a mechanic in Westchester county, and the information respecting him is very flattering.

"D. B., who was left an orphan, became connected with bad boys in this city, and commenced stealing about the docks, was taken up and sent here. At first he promised but little, but in a few months it was found that he possessed talents of a sterling quality, which, like the ornamental veins in the marble, needed only the proper culture to bring them conspicuously to view. In proportion as he was trained in regularity and order, he gained confidence, and he, as well as the two above named, became members of the class of honor, who alone are suffered to be our night-guard, and he never betrayed his trust, but was industrious and vigilant. I saw his master, to whom he was bound, this morning, who informs me that he never had such a boy in his shop; industrious, ingenious, obedient, and kind, and that he wants no better."

Cases of a similar nature have occurred among the females, and upon the whole, the Superintendent remarks, "the moral influence which pervaded the minds of the wickedly disposed, (at the time of a religious awakening in the spring,) even to this day is not easily described."

The Managers are aware that in resting their conclusions of a decided reformation, in the subjects of the House, on an incidental or special appearance of religious excitement, considering that impressions thus made, upon minds habitually corrupt, are too often transitory and illusive, would be very unsafe; yet from the general demonstrations of order and cheerful obedience which are observable to every visiter, the decorous attention of the children during religious service, the frequent instances which occur of private devotion after they have retired to their cells, and are unseen by their fellows, and the testimonials furnished by the letters, of which extracts have been given, we think it may be safely inferred, that under judicious management, a House of Refuge for Juvenile Delinquents may become a *true penitentiary*,—and that at least during the period of childhood and adolescence, no mind of ordinary native powers, however debased by vice, should be considered as beyond the reach of moral discipline and the admonitions of religious truth.

The assembling together of so large a number of the vagrant, corrupt, and wicked youth of the city as are collected in the House of Refuge, the entire confidence which the Superintendent is able to gain in his conversations with them, and the full confessions, which, in due time, they make of their past lives and actions, furnish data from which it is easy to deduce conclusions relative to the principal causes of that degradation and abandonment to vice which lead the culprit to prison or to infamy. There is no truth of sacred writ more fully confirmed by the testimony of ages, than that "evil communications corrupt good manners." A propensity to steal and to evade the truth, is often manifest at an early age, and appears to exist in different degrees of native force. But the temptation to these vices, might, it is believed, in all common cases, be easily checked, were it not for the power of associations, and the encouragement afforded by companionship in vice. The motives to thieving are therefore those principally which lead to vicious gratifications of a social character. The thief is often prodigal of his money. He squanders it to purchase a transient enjoyment with boon companions. Whatever holds out to him this lure, excites his unprincipled passion, and plunges him into the vortex of habitual indulgence. Among these causes of vicious excitement in our city, none appear to be so powerful in their operation as theatrical amusements. The mention of the number of boys and young men who have become determined thieves in order to procure the means of introduction to the theatres and circuses, would appal the feelings of every virtuous mind, could the whole truth be laid open before them. A small sum is at first pilfered, to obtain a single sight of amusements respecting which they hear so much, and whose entertainments the street advertisements exhibit in such conspicuous and alluring characters. The first gratification prompts powerfully to the means of renewal,—new acquaintance is formed—the secrets of others still deeper in crime become known—other passions are elicited—dishonesty and falsehood, once rendered habitual, and the vicious propensities of the mind gaining a complete ascendency—the barriers of the law, and a regard for character, present no further impediments, than a desire to evade the one and to conceal the abandonment of the other.

In the case of the feebler sex, the result is still worse. A relish for the amusements of the theatre, without the means of honest indulgence, becomes too often a motive for listening to the first suggestions of the seducer, and thus prepares the unfortunate captive of sensuality for the haunts of infamy, and a total destitution of all that is valuable in the mind and character of woman.

The two following cases, selected from the examination of the boys of the Refuge, by the Superintendent, will tend to corroborate the opinion entertained by the Managers, that no greater evil could have befallen our city, in relation to the morals of its youth, than the extraordinary increase which has recently taken place in the number and variety of its theatres and other analogous places of public amusement. From the rivalship which prevails between these places, and the necessity of resorting to some means in order to sustain a reputation for numbers, the terms of admission are reduced to a modicum; and, if our information be correct, tickets of admission, even in some of the largest of these establishments, are freely granted to that class of females which it is expected will be able to bring companions with them, and thus add to the emoluments and appearance of the house.

June 24th, 1827.

H—— S——, from the Commissioners, by the intercession of his mother and friends, aged eleven years the third of March last, born in Yonkers, Westchester Co. N. Y. His father has been dead six or seven years, his mother keeps a boarding house, on the corner of B. and R. street, is to pay one thousand dollars rent annually, and has twenty-seven boarders.

H. lived two years with his uncle R. M., at H**** N****, Connecticut; returned to his mother in September last.

His first theft was sixpence from his mother; the second was two shillings from her, with which he went to the Chatham Theatre, and told his mother that he had been playing with boys in the street; then six shillings from his mother, which he spent in going to the Bowery Theatre twice; next five dollars from his aunt H. M., of which he spent three dollars, in going to the Park Theatre three times, and concealed the rest under his mother's back stoop; then four shillings from Miss J. M., which he spent in going to the Chatham Theatre, including ice cream, oranges, &c. &c.; then five dollars from Miss S., one of his mother's boarders—spent three dollars in going to the Bowery Theatre, and concealed the rest as before; next two dollars from Mrs. D., which he hid under the back stoop as before; then ten dollars from his mother, spent the greatest part in going twice to the Chatham Theatre, put the balance as before under the back stoop. The object of his hiding these little amounts, was, that he might have a sufficiency on the ensuing fourth of July.

January, 1827.

J—— M'I——, from the Commissioners, at the request of his step-father, E. W. H. J. was born in Philadelphia; his father, who died about fourteen years since, was president of the N. A. I. C. He has four sisters and one brother living. About nine months since, his mother married E. W. H., a shipping merchant, who has since failed in business, and is now employed by R., and has a salary of sixteen hundred dollars per annum. J. appears to have had opportunities for a fair English and German education; was three years and a half at the Nazareth School, is naturally bashful and timid, submissive and quiet: has lived thirteen months in his brother-in-law's printing office, and some time in the office of his step-father. He removed from Philadelphia to this city, about three months since.

The first thing he recollects to have stolen, was six large silver spoons from his mother, about four years since, for which he obtained nine dollars; the half of it he gave to his cousin, and spent the remainder in gambling on the fourth of July. The next was five dollars from his father, after which he ran away, and was absent about one week; he then took a large six dollar atlas, which his step-father gave him, and sold it for three dollars, and spent it by going to the Theatre; then, a box of mathematical instruments from his father, which he sold for three dollars; at different times, a large number of books from his father's library, one of which he sold for five dollars, it being full of valuable plates; next, his mother's gold watch, which he pawned for ten dollars, but his mother obtained it again by paying the sum for which it was pawned. He stole his sister's necklaces, offered them for sale, and the man detaining them, his sister obtained them again. His father then found him in the Theatre, and sent him to his brother-in-law's, with a view to save him; he continued there thirteen months, as above, and then returned to Philadelphia. On his departure from his brother-in-law's, Mr. G. T., he stole two watches, which, upon his arrival in Philadelphia, he sold for twelve dollars and a half, and as his father was in New-York on business, he spent it in going to the theatre, &c. It appears that as he came to New-York, on his return from his brother-in-law's, by the way of Philadelphia, he commenced his old trade with renewed vigor; the first commencement was in sacrificing his father's library, by selling Rollin's Ancient History, breaking a set of the Encyclopedia, by selling eight volumes out of forty, French and German books, dictionaries, &c. ; next, a suit of his mother's bed curtains, for which he obtained seven dollars. He, about this time, formed an acquaintance with a thief, by the name of C. A. Crossing from Brooklyn one night, on their way he made an agreement with A. to meet him at his father's house, very early next morning, and he would furnish him with some of his mother's bed clothes ; A. came, and J. gave him a load, which he sold and returned him half the proceeds.

It would be well here to remark, that it was now in the summer season, and J's mother had put away her curtains, sheets, blankets, &c. in trunks in their garret. A. and J. continued for a week or more to lug off these articles, until they had stripped the house pretty thoroughly: the last articles that A. was furnished with, were Mrs. H's cloth coat, silk frock, white dress, &c, which he kept and returned no more. The greatest amount that J. ever received from Allen, at any one time, was ten dollars for his mother's goods stolen. J. also stole his father's saddle and bridle, for which he obtained seven dollars ; then he went to a neighboring clerk, and by stratagem, persuaded him to sign a merchant's name to five checks, one for forty-five dollars, two for thirty-five dollars each, one for twenty-five dollars, and another for fifteen dollars. He went to different shops where his father dealt, and changed the greater part of them, and raised about one hundred dollars, and stole fifty dollars more from his father. This occurred on a Saturday evening, and on Sunday morning he started for Philadelphia. His father, accidentally received early information of his departure, and overtook him at Elizabeth Town, in the afternoon; had him locked up one day, and on the following day told him that he could trust him no longer, and that he should be obliged to send him to sea. J. did not wish to go, therefore he went to a house where Mr. C. President of the L. S. boarded, and told the landlady, that Mr. C. had sent him for his coat, which he obtained and sold in the Bowery for eleven dollars; then a pair of boots from his father, for which he obtained three dollars and a half; then a coat from his cousin G. H. for which he obtained seven dollars, and ran away from his father and took private board, to avoid being sent to sea. His father found him in the Chatham Theatre, about seventeen days since, put him in Bridewell, and from thence to the House of Refuge.

His friends and himself all say that his great thirst for visiting theatres and places of amusement, was the leading passion which induced him to steal so much.

It is not believed that these are very rare or very peculiar cases. The number of boys that occupy the lower seats of the theatres and of those too whose ragged appearance indicates the poverty in which they live, is said to be very great; and the examinations of the Refuge would lead to the conclusion, that these places are the resort almost universally of those, who, by the dishonesty of their lives become candidates for the Refuge and City Prison. But it is much easier to point out these evils than to prescribe the remedy. It would not perhaps be extravagant to assert that were the theatres and circuses made to contribute an amount equal to the maintenance of the city prison, they would do no more than compensate for the extent of the moral evil which they entail upon the inferior classes of our population.

In the management of the female part of the institution and in the domestic arrangements of the whole establishment, the Managers can cordially acknowledge the assistance which has been derived from the Ladies' Committee. Their attentions have been steadily directed, in weekly visits to the Refuge, to the moral and religious improvement of the females, and to the strengthening of the hands of the Matron in her delicate and important duties. Although it may not be probable that the number of female subjects will much exceed its present proportion, yet every instance of restoration to virtue, or protection from the horrors of vice in this class of its subjects, cannot fail to yield the blessing of an ample reward for all the labor and care it may have cost. "The benevolent interests of the Matron, (observes the Sixth Report of the London Society for the improvement of Prisons, &c.) will not be confined to the walls of her gaol. There is not perhaps in the whole range of human destitution, a more genuine object of compassion, than the friendless girl, who quits a prison, with the desire, yet without the means of reformation. Satisfactory may have been her conduct during confinement, and gratifying the proofs of her moral improvement;

yet what can reasonably be expected, if at the expiration of her sentence, she is thrown upon the wide world? She is surrounded by temptation, and even the distinction of her sex, and the helplessness of her condition—which constitute the strongest claims upon protection—are too often the most fatal sources of her moral ruin and hopeless degradation. How many thus circumstanced, feel at this moment the wretchedness of guilt in the loss of character, the abandonment of friends, the pressure of want, the pangs of disease, and the bitterness of despair; and how many have quitted confinement in a state of entire destitution, whom the hand of kindness might have saved from ruin, and rescued from an untimely and dishonorable grave! To devise means for the relief of the repentant and distressed criminal, on her discharge, may form no part of the official instructions of a prison matron; but her own feeling will prompt her to the execution of duties which are enjoined by the most sacred obligations of religion, and the strongest dictates of humanity; and it will be her care to anticipate the wants of the discharged female; and to remove, as far as may be practicable the temptations to which she is about to be exposed."

It is also well observed in the same valuable Report, that, "The peculiar relation in which a prison matron stands towards the objects of her care, ought to inspire her with no ordinary share of interest and compassion. In the exercise of her duties she is at once the representative and guardian of her sex, and she ought to be a bright example of its purity, disinterestedness, and love. To win affection, yet enforce authority,—to inspire confidence, yet command respect,—to war against the vices, yet make just allowance for the frailties of humanity,—are qualities of mind in an eminent degree essential to her who would reclaim the thoughtless, subdue the stubborn, and heal the broken heart. She must be prepared to encounter disappointment from ingratitude, indifference and deceit; yet if she do not always attain success, it will be her care uniformly to deserve it: nor will such discouragements easily repress exertions that flow from the convictions of duty, and derive strength from the influence of Christian principles. A pious and judicious effort to reclaim the vicious is seldom wholly lost; and a prison matron may be assured, that to the faithful discharge of her interesting duties, the blessing of Heaven will never be denied."

The government of the Refuge, as far as is deemed compatible with the penitentiary objects of the institution, is strictly paternal. On their first admission, the subjects are made acquainted with the rules of the House and the duties that will be required of them. These are so clearly explained that none can plead ignorance as an excuse for violation. They are informed that cheerful and punctual obedience to these duties, will ensure them kind treatment and all the benefits which the institution and the interests of the Managers can procure for them. But that punishment, prompt and severe if necessary, will inevitably be the consequence of disobedience. These engagements are strictly observed on the part of the Superintendent. Those who distinguish themselves by undeviating good conduct for a certain length of time, are enrolled in the class of honor, and wear the badge of this class on the left arm. Certain privileges are granted to this class. From them the night-guards are chosen, who are officers of considerable trust. The Superintendent finds no difficulty in procuring boys of fourteen or fifteen years of age who are worthy of this confidence. If they betray it, (which has seldom been done except for the purpose of escaping from the premises,) they know that the punishment will be proportionably heavy. This punishment consists in flagellation, with a whip of strings, in solitary confinement to their cells, either with or without the accompaniment of a low diet, in forbidding any one to hold communication with the offender without permission, and in extraordinary cases of flagitious conduct, in wearing an iron on one side,* fastened to the waist at one end and to the ankle at the other. By a judicious alternation, or use of these punitive measures, no difficulty, of a formidable character, has occurred, in supporting a system of perfect order, among boys, who, from their age and crime are well entitled to the

* Under their pantaloons.

appellation of ruffians, without the use or display of dangerous or destructive weapons of any kind. To dispense with any one of these correctives would not as we believe contribute in any way to diminish the amount of punishment and suffering, or subserve the cause of humanity. Punishment by whipping, when apportioned with tempered firmness by him who is known by the culprit to be his friend, is received with feelings altogether different from that which proceeds from useless violence or untempered severity. When rightly administered, the sting is felt upon the conscience as well as upon the nerves; and we hold it to be possible in every case of flagellation, when there is a consciousness of disobedience, for the culprit to part from the keeper without any increase of dislike or aversion.

The subject of penitentiary discipline is a topic which has recently claimed an unusual share of public attention, and the discussion of it by distinguished philanthropists on both sides of the Atlantic, has elicited a very animated controversy with respect to the mode of treating convicts so as to accomplish most effectually the various objects for which they are sentenced to the confines of a prison. These objects are admitted to be, first, *labor,* so that the prisoner may contribute to the expenses of his maintenance; second, *moral reformation*, so that on his discharge, he may renew his intercourse with the world with a determination to avoid the errors of his past life, and become an honest man; third, *punishment*, to an extent sufficient to deter others from the commission of crime, and thus promote the safety and well-being of society. The experience of the most enlightened nations appears to have established the conclusion, that sanguinary laws and cruel or vindictive punishments answer no valuable purpose as instruments of terror, and that crimes are least numerous when the whole system of penal legislation is conducted upon principles of humanity and with a reference to the nobler motives which can be made to operate upon the human mind. The penitentiary system in this country has, it must be admitted, experienced a retrogression from the bright promise and happy influences under which it was first exhibited to the world. But it has unquestionably again experienced a revival; and it may we think with justice be doubted whether that system was ever more efficaciously administered, and with less expence to the feelings of humanity, than it is now exercised in the Auburn prison, under Mr. Powers, and in the new prison at Mount Pleasant, under the direction of Captain Lyndes. The government of those prisons is conducted essentially upon the principles practised at the House of Refuge. The variations are such as the more hardened criminality and the greater physical strength of the culprits so obviously require. Solitary night cells, and labor and meals performed in perfect silence are found to be effectual securities against mutual contamination and concerted schemes of mischief. There is enough of society to prevent the dreariness and corrosive gloom of entire solitude, and not enough to admit of its demoralizing perversions and abuses. Insubordination is promptly punished by corporal chastisement of which the prisoner has been amply forewarned, and which being meted to him in proportion to the manifestations of his disobedience, it is received as the inevitable consequence of a departure from duty, and hence it falls as nearly as possible in the rank of those physical miseries which result from a man's own imprudence or intemperance. Its moral impressions are thus brought home to the feelings of the sufferer in his hours of sober reflection, and associating the penalty with the crime, he soon learns to avoid the latter from the sense of its immediate and inseparable connexion with the former. Hence in his mind there prevails an incipient reformation, which results in an habitual and submissive acquiescence in the circumstances in which he is placed. The pains and privations he endures come to be regarded as the consequences of his follies and crimes,—his keeper as the minister of the law, whose duty it is to fulfil its provisions—and the law itself as a decree of necessity which it is in vain to resist.

It is perhaps possible that these moral deductions may be made by a person sentenced to exclusive solitude without the intervention of the whip, and of course without any conflict between his passions and his relative duties to his keeper and to his fellow-prisoners. But of the comparative efficacy of the two modes in producing reformation, no doubt remains upon our minds. Nor have we less hesitation on the question of humanity,—or in other words on the relative amount of suffering which the prisoner would have to endure when confined absolutely to solitude, cut off entirely from all intercourse with his fellow men, or when obliged to submit to a seasonable castigation for disobedience. The experience of the Refuge, notwithstanding the difference which may exist between young and old offenders, does in our opinion throw light on this important question. The most weighty argument against investing the keeper of a prison with the power to chastise, is the danger of abuse. This danger it would be unreasonable, in the abstract, to deny. It is however found reasonable and salutary in society at large to acknowledge this power, as one of the rights of a parent over his children, a teacher over his scholar, a master over his apprentice, the captain of a ship over his hired men. It may in all these cases be grievously abused,—but there is a remedy in other principles of our social compact, which, in a healthy state of society, cannot fail to be speedily applied. When therefore a keeper of a penitentiary is selected with a special eye to the nature of his duties,—with reference to his intelligence, his moral and religious character, his reputation for benevolence as well as firmness, and when moreover he is surrounded with a well chosen body of inspectors, and acts constantly in the presence of under keepers, we think that the hazards of an abuse of power, are not to be put in competition with the actual advantages of a system of energetic parental government. The abuses which were alleged to have taken place at Auburn a few years since, vanished into almost nothing, when a strict investigation was made by a committee of the Legislature, conducted with all the solemnity of a judicial tribunal, and affording ample opportunity for those who had made the charges, to substantiate them by adequate testimony. The publication of this inquiry, appears in the view of the Managers to have removed entirely the objections to this system of government arising from the charge of abuses at the Auburn prison. We advert to this subject on the present occasion, from a belief that it constitutes an important question in the practical management of the state prisons of this country, and in relation to which, every fact drawn from actual experience affords additional light and facilitates the means of a correct solution of the problem.

We conclude with an extract from an "INTRODUCTORY REPORT TO THE CODE OF PRISON DISCIPLINE, &c., PREPARED FOR THE STATE OF LOUISIANA," by the HON. EDWARD LIVINGSTON. The opinion of so enlightened and experienced a judge of penal law, cannot fail to add weight to the evidence contained in the preceding statements.

"One other institution remains to be described; one of perhaps quite as much importance as any other in the system. It is the SCHOOL OF REFORM; designed for the confinement, discipline, and instruction of juvenile offenders and young vagrants. Of all the establishments suggested by the charity, and executed by the active and enlightened benevolence of modern times, none interests more deeply the best feelings of the heart. Whether we consider the evil avoided, or the positive good bestowed, it is equally worthy of our admiration."

After pointing out the injustice and inhumanity of including in the same system of penalties, the crimes of childhood and those of adult age, the author proceeds:

"To argue the utility, or to descant on the humanity, of this establishment, after demonstrating its justice, would be a useless task.

"Every mind that has investigated the causes and progress of crime, must acknowledge the one; every benevolent heart must feel the other. And even economy, cold, calculating economy, after stating the account in dollars and cents, must confess that this is a money saving institution.

"If it is wise to prevent a hundred atrocious crimes by removing the opprobrium of a venial fault, and substituting instrucuon for punishment; if it is the highest species of humanity to relieve from the miseries of vice and the degradation of crime; to extend the operation of charity to the mind; and snatch with its angel arm innocence from seduction; if it be a saving to society to support an infant for a few years at school, and thereby avoid the charge of the depredations of a felon for the rest of his life, and the expense of his future convictions and confinement, then is the School of Reform a wise, a humane, and an economical institution.

"I need not enlarge this report by the details for the government of this School; they are minutely contained in this code. One principle pervades the whole, which has been sufficiently enlarged upon; that the offences of children may be sufficiently corrected, both for the ends of punishment and example, by education and employment. If this be wrong, the whole plan must be remodelled; but in establishing it, I have been guided by something better than the best reasoning. In the city of New-York, there is an establishment of this kind, which can never be visited but with unmixed emotions of intellectual pleasure. In now contains one hundred and twenty-five boys and twenty-nine girls, for the most part healthy, cheerful, intelligent, industrious, orderly, and obedient; animated with certain prospect of becoming useful members of society, who, but for this establishment, would still have been suffering under the accumulated evils attendant on poverty, ignorance, and the lowest depravity, with no other futurity before them than the penitentiary or the gallows. I ought not to omit mentioning here, that the female department is superintended by a visiting committee of ladies, who, at regular and frequent periods, examine the school, converse with the scholars, encourage the diffident, reprove the disorderly, reward the industrious, and inspire all with their own virtues. The code I submit invites a similar superintendence, from which the highest advantages, such as nothing but the benign influence of female character can give, are expected.

"The plan of indenting the scholars to useful trades has been recommended, from the practical effect that has been observed at New-York. It might at first be supposed, that an aversion would be found to taking apprentices from such a place; but experience has proved that the confidence inspired by the mode of education pursued, is so great, that applications are more numerous, for children of both sexes, than the rules of the institution will permit them to supply. And, although twenty-eight boys and fifteen girls have been indented, the most favorable accounts have been received of their behavior; two having received what they thought ill usage from their masters, left them and returned to the school: and only one has resumed his former bad habits. What renders the reformation of these children the more extraordinary, is, that thirty of them had before been sentenced to the penitentiary from one to five different times. A register is kept of the behavior of the different boys, and as much of their previous history as can be discovered. Extracts from this are annually published, and they contain a number of facts of the most interesting kind, all proving the practical utility of the plan."

The Society for the Reformation of Juvenile Delinquents, in Account Current with Ralph Olmsted, Treasurer.

Dr.

Date		$	cts
1827 Jan. 1	To Balance due the Treasurer, January 1, 1827	$789	19
to 1828 Jan. 1	To Cash, Repairs and additions to the buildings upon the premises,	3180	88
	" Clothing, for the Children	1356	60
	" Food and Provisions, for the Children	3543	01
	" Furniture, Beds, Bedding, &c.	455	93
	" School and Hospital Expenses, Books, Paper, Stationary, Medicine, &c.	796	16
	" Wood, Coal, Oil, &c.	854	22
	" Horse, Cows, &c. for the use of the Institution,	369	57
	" Salaries to the Superintendent, Assistants, Schoolmaster and Matron	3441	42
	To sundry notes received for the labor of the children, not yet due	640	03
	To Balance in the Treasury	644	57
		$16071	58

Cr.

Date		$	cts
1827 Jan. 1	By Nett amount received from collection of Donations and Subscriptions from the Citizens of New-York	$1512	34
to 1828 Jan. 1	By Cash, grant from the Legislature of the State of New-York,	2000	00
	Cash from Sales of Manufactured Goods,	300	56
	Cash received from the Labor of the Children in the different Work Shops	3258	68
	Cash from Marine Hospital Fund, towards the annual support of the House of Refuge,	9000	00
		$16071	58
	By Balance, brought down, in the Treasury	$644	57

Officers of the Society.

CADWALLADER D. COLDEN, *President.*

STEPHEN ALLEN, CORNELIUS DUBOIS, JOHN GRISCOM, JOHN T. IRVING, HENRY I. WYCKOFF, JAMES LOVETT,	*Vice Presidents.*

RALPH OLMSTED, *Treasurer.*
ISAAC S. HONE, *Secretary.*

JOHN STEARNS, M. D. ANSEL W. IVES, M. D.	*Physicians and Surgeons*

House of Refuge.

NATHANIEL C. HART, *Superintendent.*
HENRY MILLER, *Assistant Superintendent.*
CATHARINE GOWEY, *Matron.*
MARY WEAVER, *Assistant Matron.*
J. M'CONNELL, *Teacher.*
P. SHERLOCK, *Gate Keeper.*
J. BIRMINGHAM, *Cartman.*

Indenturing Committee.

WILLIAM F. MOTT,
HEMAN AVERILL,
BENJAMIN L. SWAN.

Managers.

STEPHEN ALLEN,
HEMAN AVERILL,
ARTHUR BURTIS,
C. D. COLDEN,
ISAAC COLLINS,
ROBERT C. CORNELL,
SAMUEL COWDREY,
JOSEPH CURTIS,
CORNELIUS DUBOIS,
THOMAS EDDY,
WILLIAM W. FOX,
JOHN GRISCOM,
JAMES W. GERARD,
JOHN E. HYDE,
ISAAC S. HONE,
JOHN HUNTER,
JOHN T. IRVING,
ANSEL W. IVES,
JAMES LOVETT,
WILLIAM F. MOTT,
HUGH MAXWELL,
RALPH OLMSTED,
FRED'K SHELDON,
PETER SHARPE,
JOHN STEARNS,
BENJAMIN L. SWAN,
DAVID STEBBINS,
M. VAN SCHAICK,
HENRY I. WYCKOFF,
SAMUEL WOOD.

Ladies' Committee.

MRS. ISABELLA BULOID, *First Directress.*
" SARAH HAWXHURST, *Second Directress.*
" CHARLOTTE FOX, *Treasurer.*
" MARIA HYDE, *Secretary.*

MRS. MARTHA WILLIS,
" ALMY CORNELL,
" ALICE TOWNSEND,
" REBECCA M'COMB,
" ANN WARNER,
MRS. D. EMBURY,
" MARGARET PRIOR,
" MARIA COLDEN,
" ANNA MOTT.

⁂ Donations to the House of Refuge will be thankfully received by the Officers and Managers of the Society.

The payment of 50 dollars, or of 10 dollars per annum for six years, constitutes a person a member of the Society for life; and an annual subscription of 3 dollars, a member so long as it is continued to be p

FOURTH ANNUAL REPORT, &c.

1829.

With another anniversary, the duty of the Managers of the Society for the Reformation of Juvenile Delinquents to present a Report, for the information of the members of the Institution and of the public, recurs. This is a task which it must always be a gratification to perform, as long as the Managers are able to state, as they can now do, that the establishment continues to realise the most sanguine expectations of its friends and advocates.

After the Institution has been in operation several years, and its objects, its principles, and its system have been so often developed in former annual reports, it might be unnecessary to discuss, at this time, at any length, its policy, its humanity, and its justice. It would be necessary, on this occasion, to do no more than to make known the proceedings of the Society for the last year, and the results of the efforts of the Managers to accomplish the designs of the establishment; but as the unexpected state of the funds, and the resources of the Society, will oblige them again to apply to the legislature for more certain means of support, it is thought that it will be proper in this report, to present some general views of the merits of the Institution.

It must be satisfactory to those with whom this charity originated, and to those by whose exertions it has been, and is supported, to find that it is not only approved at home, but that it has attracted the attention of those in other countries, whose minds are bent on the amelioration of the condition of mankind. If it were possible that any feelings but those of pure benevolence could mix with the consideration of this subject, we might feel a pride in the reflection, that our young country which has so lately assumed the rank of an independent nation, was the first to adopt with any efficacy, the penitentiary system of prison discipline, and the first to attempt to prevent the commission of crimes, by seeking out the youthful and unprotected, who were in the way of temptation, and by religious and moral instruction, by imparting to them useful knowledge, and by giving them industrious and orderly habits, rescuing them from vice, and rendering them valuable members of society. Several of our neighboring states are profiting by our example, and we cannot but hope that our success in this new system of wise and charitable regulation, will induce a more extensive adoption of it in our own state.

Though by a recent law, the establishment is opened for the reception of Juvenile Delinquents from every county in the state, yet owing to this provision not being sufficiently known, or possibly, owing to objections which there are to transporting young offenders for petty crimes, to a distance from their homes, there have been but few subjects in the House of Refuge sent from elsewhere than the city and county of New-York. If the happy effects of this establishment, on the community where its influence is immediately felt, were better and more generally known and considered, it could not fail to insure the adoption of similar institutions in other districts of our state.

Previously to the establishment of the House of Refuge, there were more than five hundred young persons annually committed, in the city of New-York, either as criminals or vagrants; now the officers of justice do not find half that number, of these descriptions; so that the effects of the institution are not only felt by those who are committed to its care, but the community at large feels its benign influence in the diminution of crime. Its operation, in this respect, is not only in the present time, but future generations will be rendered more pure and virtuous, by the reformation of the depraved youths of the present race, who, if they were left to their ordinary course, would have been matured in vice. The laws which provide for the punishment of aged criminals, are not more important than those which regard Juvenile Delinquents. If the young can be rendered virtuous, there will be comparatively but few crimes, for how seldom does it happen that a person in advanced life is criminal, who was not vicious when he was young?

If there could, at this time, be a question as to the humanity and justice of the institution, the condition of the objects of its care, previously to and after they are received into the House of Refuge, might be exhibited, in a manner that would appeal to the most obdurate feelings. Very generally, the children who are committed to this asylum are orphans, or if not, they are so neglected, or misled by their parents, as to be in a worse condition than if they had none—deserted and in poverty, often in absolute want, and without a roof under which they can claim shelter; not only without religious or moral instruction, but in many instances taught to be vicious by precept as well as by example, these unfortunate children are found offending against the laws. Frequently the younger persons who are received in the House of Refuge are so totally devoid of moral instruction, that they evince an entire want of a knowledge of right and wrong. It has happened that when one has been questioned as to his former course of life, and asked how he obtained means of subsistence, he has answered, by begging and stealing, with apparently, as little consciousness that he was making a disgraceful confession, as if he had said that he had found a support from some honest employment. Under such circumstances, what could be more unjust than to visit the young delinquent with the same kind or degree of punishment, which would be due to a deliberate offender of mature years?

To confine these youthful criminals in our loathsome and crowded prisons, where no, or scarcely any, distinction can be made between the young and old, or between the more and less vicious, where little can be learned but the ways of the wicked, and from whence they must be sent to encounter new wants, new temptations, and to commit new crimes, is to pursue a course, as little reconcileable with justice as humanity; yet, till the House of Refuge was established there was no alternative. The unfortunate child, though hardly beyond the years of infancy who had committed the least offence was doomed to a confinement, not only without hope of his reformation, but with almost a certainty that, when he was discharged, he would again be obnoxious to punishment; and that thus, a course would be pursued, every step in which, would lead to new and greater crimes.

The value of the institution of which we are the guardians, will not be duly appreciated, unless this retrospect be taken, and this dismal, but true picture be compared with that, which it is our happiness to be able to present.—The forlorn, helpless, abandoned or misled child, finds a comfortable home under our roof. He is supplied with food and raiment, and is surrounded by friends who devote themselves to his instruction. He acquires habits of industry and regularity; and soon sees in his fellow-creatures, who are around him, not as he formerly did, in the whole human race, beings whom he considered as regardless of him and his misery, as he was of them, but beneficent guardians, administering to his necessities, endeavouring to render him virtuous, to give him the means of future independence and happiness in this world, and to show him the right path to the next.

In almost every case, we do not say in all cases, the discipline of the institution works a reformation. The moral faculties are awakened, the thoughts of the young offender are turned, often with regret, upon his past life, and he is led to resolve on a better course. In many instances, the child not only thinks of his future condition in this world, but his mind is filled with a concern for his eternal, as well as his temporal welfare; a conviction is produced that our happiness in this life, as well as in that which is to come, depends on a due application of our moral and physical faculties. The transition of a being from a life of want, ignorance, idleness, corruption and hopelessness, to the enjoyments in the Refuge of comfort, to the relief which is afforded to the mind, by constant and useful employment, to the knowledge of good and evil, to the hope of obtaining an honest living, and to the consolations of religion, must be to him as a new birth.

That these are not visionary or exaggerated views of the effects of the institution, will, in some measure, appear from the statements, furnished by the Superintendent, of the cases of some of the children who have been received into the House of Refuge, and by the letters from some who have been apprenticed, and from persons to whom they have been bound. These statements and letters will appear in the Appendix. It is true they relate to but a few cases. Did the occasion permit, many more of the same nature might be presented; and it may be said with great truth, that, very generally, the children who have been taken from the House of Refuge, as apprentices, have evinced the benefit they derived from the institution, and have merited the commendations of those to whose care they have been entrusted. It is worthy of remark, that several of those who appeared the most depraved, when they came into the Refuge, and for some time afterward appeared incorrigible, have subsequently given the best hopes of their entire reformation.

Since the establishment was opened, on the first of January, 1825, to the commencement of the present year, five hundred and twenty-seven subjects have been received, of these two hundred and seventy-five have been bound out, and of the latter, only twenty-two have been returned on account of their having given dissatisfaction to those to whom they were apprenticed.

The feeling manifested by the letters from the children, towards those who have the immediate care of them, is very general, while they are in the house, and is not always lost when they leave it. Many who have been discharged or apprenticed, have seemed anxious to avail themselves of an opportunity of visiting the place, and the parents of their reformation. In several instances reformed youths, after an absence, which they were conscious they had advantageously employed, have presented themselves to greet those to whose care they were indebted, with filial affection, and with full hearts to express their gratitude.

The course of these remarks leads to a fit occasion

for the Managers to state, that they are always watc ful of their officers, who have the immediate care and charge of the children. They have been led, by recent circumstances, to a severe scrutiny of the conduct of their Superintendent, and they think it due to him to avail themselves of this opportunity to say, that they have been confirmed in their opinion of his strict integrity, his capacity, his zeal for the prosperity of the institution, and his entire devotion to the important station he fills. By a mild, but firm conduct, he maintains order and discipline. He does not hesitate to resort to severity, where it is necessary. His punishments are inflicted with discretion and moderation, and always with an appeal, as well to the moral, as to the corporal feelings of the delinquent; so that he kindles no animosity; but on the contrary, the offenders and their companions, while they acknowledge the justice of the chastisement, do not regard him by whom it is inflicted, otherwise than as their friend and benefactor. The Managers would not be understood as applying these remarks, as to the effect of punishments, to every case where it has been necessary to resort to the severest measures: but they are warranted as being applicable in most instances, and as presenting generally, the true character and efficacy of the system of discipline the Managers have adopted.

The rules of the House have lately been revised, and are now arranged under the following heads:—Employment, Arrangement of Time, Food, Female and Matron, Punishments, Wardsmen and Monitors, Classification, Superintendent and Keeper, Teachers and Assistant Keepers, Acting Committee, Indenturing Committee, and Divine Service. The titles to these regulations indicate the subjects to which the attention of the Managers has been particularly directed. Experience has led to improvements in relation to most of them.—The occasion does not admit of details, but the rules have been printed and published, and those who feel an interest in the establishment are invited to examine them. It will be seen, that though the Managers chiefly rely on a system of moral discipline, yet, moderate corporal chastisement is not prohibited.—It rarely happens, but there are some natures who can be made to feel only through their corporal senses; and the Managers have not been willing to suffer these to be sacrificed to notions of ultra-philanthropy, which would abolish all punishments.

The introduction of the supervision of a Committee of Ladies, for the female department, is an improvement, the benefits of which are constantly felt.

To those ladies who have been unremitting in the discharge of the duties they have assumed, the Managers feel themselves bound to make their acknowledgements. Their last annual report will appear in the Appendix, and will best explain what services they render, and the manner in which they are performed.

There have been in the House of Refuge, during the last year, including those who were left there the preceding year, three hundred and thirty-seven boys and girls, of whom one hundred and forty-eight have been bound out, and one hundred and sixty-one remained at the close of the year. For information in relation to the respective children who have been apprenticed, and in relation to the employment of the subjects, while they are in the House, as well as for other information, the Managers must refer to the subjoined tables, for particulars which would swell this report to too great an extent.

It is to be regretted that this report can not be closed, without adverting to a subject, which is very far from affording any grounds of satisfaction—it is the state of the funds and the revenue of the institution. In 1826, a law was passed, by which the surplus of the receipts of the Commissioners of Health, after paying all the expenses of the Marine Hospital and leaving an ample provision for repairs and contingencies, was appropriated to the maintenance of this charity. As it was ascertained that the expenses of the Marine Hospital did not, at that time, exceed seventeen thousand dollars a year, that the receipts were upwards of thirty-six thousand dollars and were annually augmenting, it was thought ample and certain means were provided for the House of Refuge. The

Managers, however, have not been able to realise their expectations from this source, and find themselves now short of the necessary funds. They can not doubt but that the legislature will put their revenue on a certain and permanent footing. This establishment must be considered as an integral part of the penitentiary system which has been adopted by the state; it may be said to be the foundation on which the whole superstructure rests; and there can be no more reason to believe that the legislature will withhold from it an adequate support, than there is to believe that they will abandon the principles of a penal code, which marks the advancement of mankind in knowledge, civilization, and humanity.

The Managers, while on this subject, beg leave to present some extracts from a report of a Committee of the Senate, which introduced the law of 1826.

The Committee say "If the House of Refuge were to be considered merely as a place where so many children may be rescued from poverty, reclaimed from the haunts of vice and wretchedness, protected, instructed, and reformed, it would be a charity having the highest claims to the bounty and liberality of the government; but when viewed as a means by which the perpetration of crimes will be prevented, and if the increased number of criminals be considered, which, without it, the state would be obliged to maintain in our prisons, it is believed that a regard to economy alone would require the support of the institution. There is hardly a child who will be condemned to the House of Refuge, who if left to the course, which will bring him there, would not finally become a charge to the state as a convict. The evidence of this is that a very large proportion, as your Committee are informed and believe, of the persons who are now confined in our state prisons, commenced their career in crime, when they were children, in the city of New-York, or in some other large cities. One person, in particular, who is now confined in the prison at Auburn, was first convicted when he was only ten years old, and has since, at different times, been twenty-eight years a convict, supported by the state at an expense of not less than two thousand dollars. This case which is by no means singular, except as to time, shews, at once, what may be the advantages, even in point of economy, of an institution which will arrest young offenders in their criminal course, and at the same time is an evidence that confinement in our state prisons is ill calculated to produce reformation in young persons.

"Since the House of Refuge was opened," continues the same report, "the number of children who have been brought to the bar of the criminal courts in New-York, has lessened in the proportion of four to one."

The institution, it will be recollected, was set on foot, and was for some time maintained by voluntary contributions, to the amount of upwards of twenty-thousand dollars, from inhabitants of the city of New-York; adverting to this circumstance, the report from which the above quotations are made, adds, "it is not to be expected that this institution will longer be supported by private charitable contributions. It would be unjust to require that an establishment of such public benefit should be sustained at the expense of individuals. Unless the state affords it efficient aid, it must fall. If this were to happen, while other states, under a conviction of its great utility, are adopting similar institutions, entirely at the public charge, we must be deprived of the great advantages ours must afford."

The Managers will add, in the language of a memorial they presented to the legislature, last year, that in such an event, "the children who have found refuge in this asylum, must be turned upon society to pursue a course which must again bring them to the bars of our criminal courts, from thence to be sent to our penitentiaries and state prisons, there to be maintained, as irreclaimable criminals, at a greater expense to the state than would be required to continue the support of an institution, in which they may receive moral and religious instruction, acquire habits of industry, be reformed, and fitted to be useful members of society."

As there has been much misunderstanding, in relation to the application to the House of Refuge, of a portion of the money collected by the Commissioners of Health, a copy of a memorial presented to the legislature last year, containing a full elucidation of that matter, is subjoined in the Appendix. It will be seen that no part of the contribution of mariners, to the Hospital fund, was ever touched; but that on the contrary, the Managers of the House of Refuge could only receive a part of what was paid by passengers, the most of whom are foreigners. How just and appropriate a disposition, of this contribution from emigrants, was made by the law of 1826, will appear by the fact, that of the five hundred and thirty-three subjects, who have been received into the House of Refuge, two hundred and ninety-six, that is very considerably more than half, were born abroad, or were the children of foreigners. And of one hundred and fifty-nine received last year, ninety-three or nearly two-thirds were of European parents.

That it may be seen in what manner the Managers exercise the power given to them, to bind out the children committed to their care, they subjoin, in the Appendix, circular letters, copies of which go with every apprentice taken from the institution.

In conclusion, the Managers have only to say, that they desire nothing more than the moderate means necessary to support the institution; and relying on the disposition which has been heretofore manifested by the legislature, to support an establishment which, the Managers believe, was justly characterised by the late governor, as "the best penitentiary institution ever devised by the wit, and established by the beneficence of man;" and relying on a continuance of their own zeal and exertions, which have hitherto overcome every difficulty, they cannot but hope that the establishment will be maintained, and transmitted to posterity, as an evidence of the wisdom and humanity of their ancestors

APPENDIX.

SELECTION OF CASES AND LETTERS

From Apprentices, and from Persons to whom Apprentices have been bound.

BOYS.

September 17, 1826.

J. B.—from a court of General Sessions, aged 16 years the 25th of July last. Born in New-York—his father is dead, his mother keeps a confectionary store in New-York. About two years since J. went to live with Mr. M., a tailor in Philadelphia, where he continued but a short time, and quit; being an only child, was greatly indulged; soon after he went on board of a packet, that sailed from New-York to Baltimore, &c.

His first thefts were small amounts of money from his mother, then old rope, copper, &c. with his companions, who were of the worst class of thieves, passers of counterfeit money, &c. A man by the name of King, informed him where he could steal a watch, which he succeeded in obtaining: King sold the watch for ten dollars, and divided the money with J. He also took from the money drawer of a grocer in Grand-street, twenty-five dollars. Once in company with J. C. and H. H., they went to Philadelphia on a cruise; they there stole several pieces of linen and muslin; by going into gentlemen's kitchens after dinner, they stole two or three dozen silver spoons; he then entered a house in the day time, finding the front door not fastened, went up stairs, shook the trunks to find where he could get the most valuable articles, cut the leather hinges of a trunk, took from it twelve dollars in silver, a valuable silver repeating watch, which he sold for eighteen dollars, two coats, linen shirts, and pantaloons.

In New-York, he went with A. D. a butcher, they entered houses and stole clothing. Once in Philadelphia, he was taken up and put into the work-house, for having a gentleman's coat which he knew and swore to; but when the court came to look for the marks that the owner had described, they were not to be found, J. having taken them out; he in consequence was discharged. In company with H. T. and R. D., they stole, near Fulton market, 18 gold watch keys—on the following Monday morning about three o'clock, they broke open the same store, and took all the valuable property they could find, amounting in value, he thinks, to about three hundred dollars: he has been in Bridewell three times.

For several months after J. became an inmate of this Institution, he evinced an unhappy, discontented turn of mind, and was fixed on making his escape, if an opportunity should afford. It was found necessary to deal strictly with him, and to keep a watchful eye constantly over him; by degrees we discovered his feelings to change, until he became one of the most pleasant and agreeable boys in his class. We find the following remark posted to his history.

1828, January 2,—J. was this day indentured to Mr. M. P., of T. town, S. Co. New-York, farmer.

Previous to his coming here, he was a wild youth, but has conducted himself uniformly well for nearly a year; he became pleasant and agrécable in his manners, and industrious in his habits.

T———, S——— Co. February 25, 1828.

Mr. Nathaniel C. Hart,

Dear Sir,—This will inform you that I find in J. B. a very good boy; he appears to possess a modest and excellent disposition, and in my estimation bids fair to make a useful citizen. He appears to be very contented, and thinks he should not be so happy in any other situation.

He wishes to see Mr. Hart, (of whom he speaks very highly,) and also his former mates in the Refuge. He appears to be far from those vices which generally characterize boys of his class and age, and improves well in our line of business. I think he possesses all the qualities of a good moral young man, and I shall endeavor to instruct him in the way he should go.

I should be pleased to hear from either yourself or the committee at any time, and more so should you ever think proper to call on us personally.

Receive the sincere respects of Yours, &c.

(Signed) M. P.

The following is from the boy alluded to in the above letter.

My Dear Friend, Mr. Hart,

I let you know that I am well, and hope this may find you are the same, not forgetting Mr. Miller, Miss Goewey and Miss Weaver, and all my former fellow inmates.

I like the gentleman I live with better than I thought I should, and he is as clever to me as I wish him to be. Mr. Hart will please read this letter to the boys I left behind me, and I hope they may all abide by the two rules of the House; they are simple, but true to them that follow them. I shall follow them as long as I can "speak the truth at all times," and then we will find friends always. I hope I may soon return and see you all as well as I left you.

I shall never forget the House of Refuge; it is the home I was looking for, long before I came there: but I found it at last, and if I had not found it, where should I have been now, not where I now am learning a good trade.

I remain yours affectionately,

J. B.

May 10, 1826.

N. S., from the commissioners, aged 14 years the 27th June, born in New-York of Irish parents. His father died about eight years since; his mother is a widow, and has been confined to the house above a year, with the consumption.

About three years since he was sent to the Alms-House, from whence he was put to live with Lieut. B. at fort D., where he stayed about one year, when he returned to his mother; soon after he was put on board the ship I., and made a voyage to C.; after he returned, he shipped on board the C., and made another voyage to

C.; he returned about six months since, and has played about the streets ever since. He once stole a copper kettle and some old iron from his mother, which he sold—says he never stole any thing from any one else. His mother wanted him to learn a trade, but he liked to play too well to work at any trade. He says he had rather learn a trade than go to sea. Enters 6th class.

Previous to N. being brought to the House of Refuge, we knew him to be a very bad boy, associating with the worst of boys, idling about the streets, and was pointed at, as a boy swiftly running to destruction. But since he has been introduced to regular habits of industry and obedience, he has become one of the smartest boys in the shop that he works in, improved smartly in his education, was promoted to the class of honor, and left the House in a good state of mind.

March 5, 1827, He is indentured to Mr. S. H., of P. P., D. Co., Blacksmith.

*P*** P****** D******* Co., April* 14, 1828.

DEAR SIR,—Agreeably to your request, and in compliance with my promise, I address you on the subject of N. S., whom I took from the House of Refuge in November last. I shall not be under the necessity of multiplying many words on the subject, but can with propriety make the following remarks. N., while living with me, has behaved well in every respect; has been industrious and attentive to his business; has not frequented bad company, nor shown a disposition so to do; and should he pursue his present course of conduct and attention to business, I have no hesitation in saying, he will make a respectable man, and a first rate workman.

Yours Respectfully,

(Signed) S. H.

December 2, 1826.

W. C. from the Police, aged twelve years the 22d May; born in New-York; his father and mother have been dead about two years. His father, at his decease, left a lot of ground, with a front and rear house thereon for the children, six in number: his sisters occupy the rear house, and take care of the property, and the small children. He went once to live with Mr. P., a farmer in the country, disliked and quit after staying three months, then with Mr. F. in R., continued two years and quit. After his return from the country, he went to live with Mr. C. a cooper, and quit after three months. He was recently indentured to Mr. W. B., a coppersmith, continued four months, and ran away because his master punished him for a fault about two weeks since.

The first thing he stole was cakes from his mother, the next apples from a grocery; while an apprentice to Mr. B., he stole copper twice, (about six pounds) and to avoid punishment for it after being detected, he ran away from him. He used to associate with bad boys, who used to steal old rope, iron, &c.

He and seven or eight other boys, were found in an indicted grocery, playing cards, for which he was sent here.

December 2, 1826.

J. A. M. from the Commissioners, aged 14 years the 12th of July last. Born in New-York; his father has been dead nine months. His mother resides in this city; nurses for a living. The only bad trait I can find in J., is that his mother cannot control him, nor keep him at any place to which she puts him: he says he never stole any thing.

November 24, 1827.

W. C. was this day indentured to Mr. J. B. L., paper manufacturer, of N. P. (N. J.)

November 24, 1827.

J. A. M. was this day indentured to Mr. J. B. L., of N. P. (N. J.)

*N*** P*******, April* 25, 1828.

Dear Sir,—An apology is due you, for having delayed so long answering your letter, asking information in regard to the behavior of J. A. M. and W. C., from the House of Refuge, under my charge.

Had any thing censurable occurred in their conduct deserving particular notice, I should have immediately informed you on the subject: but so exemplary and praiseworthy has been their deportment, that not a single act indicative of their former abandonment has fallen under my observation or come to my knowledge.

So effectual indeed has been the treatment pursued at the Refuge, in reclaiming them from vice and vicious habits, that the most willing obedience has been rendered to all directions given them, without the necessity of punishment in any one instance.

No stronger proofs of the utility and benefits derivable from an institution, intended for the reformation of Juvenile Delinquents, need be pursued to my mind, than those cases under my immediate observation, to impress me with the hope of its prosperity and success, equal to the wishes of its most sanguine supporters.

Yours sincerely,
(Signed) J. B. L.

April 27, 1828.

J. B. C. from the commissioners, aged 15 years, the 24th of August; born in New-York, of Irish parents. His father is quite intemperate; his mother he has not seen in three months, nor does he know where she lives; he says he never stole any thing; he has been in the practice of drinking pretty freely, beer, wine, rum, and cider; he was often seen staggering about the streets, fighting and quarrelling to the great annoyance of his neighbors; he says he was sent here because he would not stay at the Alms-House, until Alderman Burtis could get him a place.

Remarks.

Proved to be one of the most troublesome boys ever sent to the House; bold and daring, influencing others to venture in his exploits; made his escape four times, and made two unsuccessful attempts to escape. In one of his attempts to escape, he made use of three sheets and a small cord that was attached to his hammock; these he fastened together, broke through the upper part of his cell, into the garret, broke out one of the circular blinds, and while in the act of letting himself down, the cord broke, and he fell twenty-eight or thirty feet, which broke six of his bones; yet he recovered and was still bent on being wicked, until the softening grace of God touched his heart, and made a deep impression: although we do not believe he is a thoroughly changed boy, yet the deep impression was visible and lasting, and notwithstanding we believe he received the worst and severest punishments of any boy in the House, yet he left us with the most cordial feelings, determined to become a man of respectability.

December 16, 1827.

J. is indentured to Mr. S. M. of N., to go a whaling voyage.

The Superintendent has since received a letter from his captain, who states, that he shall try to teach J. navigation, and "knows no reason why he should not become a captain of a ship."

Brazil Banks, on board the ship Z., in lat. 42m, 51deg. S. Feb. 29, 1828.

Dear Sir,—I embrace this opportunity, to inform you that we are all well, and if it was not for the thoughts of those friends we left behind, would be happy. Shortly after I sent you my last, we dropped down below the flats, and on the 22d of December, we weighed anchor, and set sail for the Pacific Ocean; we had pleasant weather until we were out three days, when we experienced much bad weather, until about the 30th, when we crossed the gulf stream, and got in warm weather; from then till the 14th of January, when the man from the mast head, cried out *whales!* we lowered our boats, and pulled after them; after rowing two or three hours we fastened on one, and had the pleasure of seeing him turn up; we got him alongside about one o'clock, A. M.; we got the rigging all ready, and next morning cut him in. This whale was but a small one in comparison to some, but I thought it was a *monster*.

It may not be improper to make a few remarks on this whale; he was of an immense bulk, his body is covered over with a black skin, about the eighth of an inch thick, so hard that it is difficult to cut unless the knife is very sharp, his head is long and square, and his jaws are about fifteen feet long.

This morning we fell in with the ship Ontario, of Nantucket, which ship is nearly full, and is expected to go home in a short time, so I thought I would take this opportunity to let you hear from me. Give my best respects to Mr. Collins, and all enquiring friends.

Please excuse this miserable writing, as I am so hurried on account of sending the oil we have on board of the Ontario.

We are yours, with the most perfect respect and esteem,

(Signed) J. B. C.
J. M. and W. E.

Here the Committee would remark that from another captain, who wrote to his owners in Nantucket, having five or six Refuge boys on board; he says "they are the best sailors I have in my ship;" and another who has about as many, says "they are fine fellows."

May 4, 1826.

D. M'N., from the Sessions, aged twenty years the 4th of April; born in Scotland, his parents are living. About three years since, he came to Charleston, (S. C.) to seek employment as an accountant, he was received by his uncle, a wheel-wright in that place. About one month after his arrival, he hired to J. R., a grocer, where he lived about sixteen months, then returned to his uncle, the wheel-wright, and remained with him about one year, and kept his books; in November he took passage for New-York, and took board with R. T., a ship carpenter in C. street, a man that he had known in Charleston. Until February, he did no work, but spent his time in walking the streets, and in public houses, he then took board in O. street, at Mr. B's porter-house, where there was card playing. He used to play, but not for money.

The first theft he ever committed, was in stealing nine dollars from the pocket of a fellow boarder, which money he spent, while he boarded in O. street; he became acquainted with J. H. about eighteen years of age, who was in the habit of stealing; he went with him and stole from a dwelling house, a coat, which they sold in Catharine-street, for four dollars; about one week after, in company with the same boy, stole a time-piece, for which he was taken up, tried, and sent here. Last December he stole from a fellow boarder, twenty-five dollars; he was taken up, tried, and sent to the penitentiary for four months, which time expired on the 14th of April last. Enters 9th class.

April 4, 1827.

He is sent to sea, on a whaling voyage from Nantucket.

*On board the ship P***** B**.*

Sir—I hope this will find you in good health, as this leaves me at present. The four boys aboard here, are all in good health; they send their best respects to you: please give my best respects to Mr. M. B. Hart, and to all the boys. I have seen M. W. and W. S. about three weeks ago; they were both in good health at that time. M. W. saw J. C. in a port of South America, who told him that W. P. was lost off Cape Horn. I have not seen the ship that he sailed in myself: I will write you the news more particularly when we get into port, which will be in the course of one month, from this date. We have got at this date, seven hundred barrels of sperm oil: our ship holds about twenty-seven hundred barrels. Since we came round Cape Horn, Captain C. has taken me as steward and clerk; he is a very fine man, he has told me several times, he will instruct me in the art of navigation, as much as is in his power. Excuse bad writing, as the ship by which I send this, is laying by for our letters. No more at present, but remain your affectionate servant,

(Signed) D. M'N.

P. S. I hope the boys are all getting on well with their learning; they will all find that it is most to their advantage, to pay attention to it while they have an opportunity. I wont forget the shells.

D. M'N.

18th February, 1828, lat 5 deg.
4 min. south. lon. 107 deg. west.

J. W.—from the Commissioners, aged fourteen years in September 1826. Born in New-York, of English parents.

J. lost his mother about three years since: he had attended Free School No. 1 about three years, without playing truant one day: but after the death of his mother, he was solicited by J. M. and F. M. to play truant from school, which he feared at first to do; but they at last succeeded in persuading him. He was absent one month, before he was found out, during which time, he had become pretty well initiated in the practice of stealing lead from buildings, ships, &c., old iron, copper, and the like; and has constantly been in the practice of running away from his father's house since.

After practising awhile with the M's in stealing lead, pewter, zinc, old rope, &c., the company was increased by G. S., G. B., W. S., H. and J. H., J. H., and others. In consequence of their frequently climbing to the tops of houses after lead, they discovered a way to enter stores and houses through the scuttles, at which they became very expert, insomuch that they would sometimes enter a half dozen stores in a single night. This boy, and J. H. at one time entered a store in Broad-street, and obtained $40, which they divided; it proved, (he says,) to be counterfeit. At another time, in company with M. M., they broke open an office on the corner of Spruce and Nassau-streets, broke open a desk, and stole $18 in gold, &c. Enters 7th Class.

Remark.

J. is a smart boy, and has improved very much, and if his lot should in time be cast with a prudent man, would, we trust, make a good citizen: he possesses a good bright intellect.

J. is indentured to Mr. A. B. of B. C.

B——t, July 13th, 1828.

Mr. N. C. Hart,

Sir,—Agreeably to your request, I transmit to you an account of J. W. the boy taken from the House of Refuge in March last. It is now a little over three months that he has been with me, and he has, I think, improved very much, both in work and in his studies: he has been so far faithful and obedient, and appears willing to do as well as he knows how in all things; he attends church and Sunday School regularly every Sabbath, and his evenings are employed in study, spelling, reading, writing and ciphering, as is most convenient, or as we think most proper. We do not allow him to associate with other boys of the neighborhood, therefore his time and attention must be devoted to his work or studies. He has the same treatment and privileges as one of our family, and I doubt not but he finds it a good home: he appears very well pleased with his business and situation, and if he continues to do as well as he has done, as I have every reason to suppose, he will, with proper attention, become a respectable and worthy citizen.

J. frequently speaks of Mr. Hart, and desires at this time to be remembered to you, also to the boys generally, and hopes or wishes, that they will all do better and become good. I have given J. some little trees, and some cuttings of the vine, which he appears to be much pleased with, and wishes to know how long before they will bear grapes, as he will send some to Mr. Hart. I hope he will soon be able to write sufficiently well to write to you himself. And wishing you good success, in so good a cause as that to which you are devoted, I remain your very obedient servant.

A. B.

E. M'L.—from the Commissioners, aged sixteen years the 1st of May 1827, born in N. Y. of Irish parents. His father died about one year since; his mother resides in this city, owns the house in which she lives, and receives about $3 per week rent. His first place of residence was with Mr. Z. a baker in S. street: he was employed in carrying out and selling rusk: he continued three weeks. The next and last place was with Mr. P. in N. J. to learn the shoe-making business: continued two weeks and quit. Then to selling fish, clams, &c. about the streets: would drink frequently, and occasionally become intoxicated.

The first thing he stole was sixpence from his mother, then an apple from a Mrs. S. then a fishing line from an associate, then two shillings while selling fish, next a ball from P. B. and again sixpence, &c. &c. Was a frequent visiter of theatres, circuses, &c. was disobedient to his mother, was finally taken up at a late hour drunk, while returning from Mount Pitt circus, carried to the watch-house, and sent from there here. Enters Sixth Class.

After having been in the house some months, and manifested to our satisfaction a disposition to do as well as he knew how, was advanced to the station of guard, which station he filled with faithfulness and integrity, until June 1828, when he was indentured to Mr. W. M. a hatter, at C. R., W. county, N. Y.

C. R. August 1st.

Mr. N. C. Hart,

Sir,—As it has been your wish that I should write, I now take the opportunity of informing you, that my boy, E. M'L. has been very steady and attentive to his business ever since I have had him: for so far, I must say, I never had a better boy: he gains in learning the hatting business as fast as can be expected.

Yours, respectfully,
(Signed) W. M.

December, 1828.

E. M'L. called to see us, with a very pleasing letter from his master, who in consequence of his good conduct, had permitted him to visit his mother. E. expressed his intentions to do as well as he knew how, of his pleasure in his master, and his determination to stay and learn his trade.

C. T. S., from the Commissioners, aged fifteen years the 5th of July, 1826, born in N. Y.—His father and mother removed to P., N. J. two years ago. C. returned to this city three months since, and went to live with Mr. B. a shoe-maker, in C. street; continued six or seven weeks, and absconded. He first stole fruit from the market places, next a pair of spurs from a livery stable in Bancker-street, cakes from shops, and many other things which he cannot recollect. Enters Fourth Class.

May, 1828.—C. was indentured to Mr. W. H. P. of P. O. county, N. Y.

P. August 19th, 1828.

Mr. N. C. H----,

Respected Friend and Benefactor,—Since I left your place of confinement, I have been constantly employed in the factory, with which business I am much pleased; and by strict attention to my business, I expect to become acquainted with a trade that will afford me a full employment, and of course a good living.

I have been regularly to meeting every other Sabbath, which is four miles from this place, and to Sabbath School every week, which is half a mile. At this place there is an abundance of fruit of all kinds, which I can have in any quantity by asking for it, and that without pay. I have been well and hearty since I left you.

(Signed,) C. S.

August 19th, 1828.

Mr. N. C. Hart,

Dear Sir,—The writer of the foregoing letter, C. S. appears to be well satisfied with the business he is employed at, and also with his exchange of a city for a country residence, and has never expressed any desire to return to N. Y. I think he will make an honest man, if he has proper attention paid to him, which I shall spare no pains to bestow upon him.

I am, respectfully,
(Signed,) W. H. P.

May, 1827.

T. C. from the Commisioners, aged sixteen years in April last, born in Ireland. His father, T. lives in this city, and bottles porter, cider, &c. for a living.

I believe the complete history of this boy is comprised in the following narrative: he was put to eleven different places to learn a trade, and ran away from them all, viz. three shoe-makers, two bricklayers, two looking-glass frame-makers, two carpenters, two bakers, and I believe was too lazy to work. When he came here he was filthy in the extreme. Enters Seventh Class.

August 1st, 1828. T. has become quite a good boy; has gained our confidence, and is promoted to the class of honor as night guard, which station he fills to our satisfaction.

October. He is indentured to Mr. G. R. of W. G. county, N. Y.

W——, *November 1st*, 1828.

Dear Sir,—I have the pleasure of informing you that T. C. arrived here on the 24th of October in good spirits, and appears to be a well disposed boy, is very willing to do what he can; is not at all acquainted with our business, but appears to learn very easy: he has been very ill one night, but is now healthy, and appears contented; says he likes living in the country very much; he is anxious to learn to handle the hoe and axe, and if his health is spared, will, I think, make a good farmer. I have delayed sending the indenture, in order to be able to write concerning the boy. I shall encourage him to write to you as soon as he can write a legible hand.

Yours, &c.
(Signed,) G. R——.

T. W. from the Police, aged (he says,) twelve years the 15th of May last, which we doubt; his age can be found on the books of Public School No. 2—born in England. His father, J. came to this country several years since, and died in this city soon after. His mother some years ago married again. His mother, it was supposed, was on her death-bed when he came here.

This boy was a member of Public School No. 2, four or five years since, then a notorious truant, and has continued so ever since. He informs me that he then practised pilfering about the docks; nor had he much improved in any thing except stealing. Rope, copper, lead, and the like, were the articles that he made his calculations to raise cash from by stealing, almost every day for five years past, and for which he was sent here: twice he stole money from his mother. Enters Eighth Class.

It appeared in the case of T. that he only wanted some friendly hand to place and direct him in the right way. He soon became industrious, quiet, and attentive to all his duties.

October, 1828. T. is indentured to Capt. F. B. farmer, of P. D. county, N. Y.

P——, *November* 9, 1828.

DEAR SIR,—The little boy, T. W. does very well, and appears perfectly contented and cheerful; he is up every morning of his own accord by day-light, and I can hear him whistling and singing as he makes the fire and feeds the stock, before I am out of bed.

I am, Sir, with due respect,
Your most obedient servant,
F. B.

FEMALES.

June 9th 1827.

C. N. from the Police, aged about 11 years, born in N. C. Her father, S. N. removed to this city when she was young, and died about seven years since: her mother married D. L. a cartman within a year past, and now resides near the corner of D. and E. streets. She lived with Mrs. M. in G. street a short time last summer.

She has for some time past been connected with her elder sister and others, in selling soap, needles, cotton balls, &c. about the streets. She has been in the practice of attending theatres, circuses, &c. would use profane and indecent language; was disobedient to her parents, and would steal.

The first thing she stole was one hundred needles from a shopkeeper, while pretending to praise or purchase some: this practice she often repeated. Next a silk handkerchief, which she sold for three shillings; then two or three dollars from a shop drawer, in company with four or five others, which she divided, this being their practice. She appears to be quite an accomplished thief: often stole worked vandykes, handkerchiefs, &c. and sold them about the streets. The last attempt she made to steal, was in company with several of her companions in a dry-goods store in D. street: she, being the heroine, was sent in to steal money from the drawer, inside of the counter, from which she took four or five dollars, when the shop-keeper discovered her, gave chase and caught her; for which crime she was sent here.

She has stolen much; has a bold and daring manner; she says she never would have stolen, had it not been for A. M'D. who she says steals a great deal, and lives near the Alms House. Enters Third Class.

February 4th, 1828.

Indentured to Mr. J. D. B, of W. O. county, N. Y. In this child there has been a most pleasing change. Once a champion for daring expeditions in stealing, wild and impudent, has now become one of the best girls in the house; pleasant, obedient, active, and, we trust, seriously and religiously inclined.

W———, April 22nd, 1828.

Mr. N. C. Hart,

Sir,—The bearer of this is Mr. J. D. B. from this place, who wishes a girl from the House of Refuge: Mr. W. gave him information that one would be kept for him. It is certainly an excellent place, in which a young girl would receive the best of example and precept, and be instructed in the solemn truths of our holy religion. I can recommend this situation to you with much pleaure, inasmuch as I believe, that in this family, a child would receive such information as will make them useful in after life, and a credit to themselves and to their benefactors.

We are much gratified with our little girl C. N. she answers the recommendation given me by Mr. A. she is an industrious, obedient, kind and affectionate child, and we feel entirely satisfied with her conduct thus far, and I trust, (through the blessing of God,) she may continue as she has began. She appears willing to learn and receive instruction; she progresses rapidly in reading in her Bible; she has committed about half of the shorter catechism to memory; she has altered in appearance greatly since she came to reside with me; has grown so that you would scarcely recognize her. She feels very anxious that her sister Catharine should come with Mr. B. says if she had Catharine here she would never want to see New-York: she was much pleased that her little sister Jane came with Mr. W. and was much afflicted at the death of her mother. She speaks with much feeling and affection of yourself and Miss Goewey, and continues, I believe, the duty of prayer, at least I enjoin it upon her. The sisters appear to have much affection for each other, and I hope they may prove a blessing, and not a hindrance: and I trust that your labour may not be in vain in reclaiming the lost and wandering children of obscurity, that their hearts may be regenerated. That your institution may be blessed is my heart's desire and prayer to God, and receive my assurances for your peace and felicity.

(Signed,) J. D. B.

January 9th, 1828.

C. N., from the Police, aged fifteen years the 17th of June last, born in C. Her father has been dead about eight years, since which her mother married D. L., who is now a labourer.

C. commenced to sell cotton balls about six years ago; then shaving soap, needles, almanacs, songs, &c. &c.—this practice led her to stealing. The first theft was six skeins of silk, four or five years ago, then one hundred needles, and so on, until she was sent here for being connected with two of her old associates in stealing forty dollars from Captain ———, near White Hall, which they divided among them. She enters fourth class.

When Catharine entered the House, her sister Charity took the earliest opportunity to give her the best counsel she was capable of; who by this time had greatly profited by the discipline and opportunities the House offered: from a wild and uncultivated child, she became quiet, mild, and one of the most industrious little creatures in the House, and was found often in secret places in private devotions to her Maker. Her remarks were to this amount:—You must be very particular to obey the Matron; not do as naughty girls do, but obey the two rules of the House, "Never tell a lie."

—"Do as well as you know how," and you will be happy. But a short time had passed, before Charity's influence had caused Catharine to unite in her secret devotions; and such an attachment between sisters so natural and correct, it is uncommon to witness. Catharine soon convinced us that she only wanted to be put into the right path, and she would ornament it. But a few months had elapsed after their confinement in the House, before their mother died, and they were left without any earthly parent—Charity at this time being bound out as above. Catharine was taken down to see her lifeless mother, where was found the only remaining little sister, hanging around the corpse of her mother, and none but neighbors to comfort her. Such were the strong appeals of Catharine to the Superintendent to take her little sister under his care and protection, that he went immediately to the Commissioners with the child, and related the circumstances; they at once approved and committed her as a vagrant, not having any home.

In a short time they were all indentured to superior places in W., O. county, where they can see each other every week.

November 27th, 1828.

J. D. B. Esq. of O. county, to whom Charity was indentured, called and stated that she and her two sisters, who were in the same neighborhood, were three of the finest children he knew: that he would not part with Charity for $100; and that the oldest sister, Catharine, who lived with Mr. J. B., was, in point of *mind* and *deportment*, a *superior* girl, and that they manifested much tender and kind feeling towards each other, and had no idea of ever returning to the city to live, lest they should fall into temptation's way. Mr. B. said, the children express the warmest regard for their former care-takers while in the House of Refuge, and it was in consequence of their strong solicitations that he had called to spend a few hours with us.

January 9th, 1828.

M. L., from the Police, aged sixteen years the 20th of November last, born in the western part of this state. Her father, W. L. resides at No. 83 S.-street, is poor and intemperate. This child, and her sister, have been employed several years selling soap, cotton balls, almanacs, pencils, &c., which led her to all kinds of company. The first thing she recollects to have stolen was 250 needles, in company with A. M'D. and her younger sister; then a dozen tapes, &c. &c.; so on for two or three years, dividing all they could take. Would occasionally attend theatres and circuses. She says she has frequented bad company much.

A few days since, she, her sister, and C. N. went into a grocery store near Coenties' Slip to sell soap, when a Captain B. began to carry on with them; she consented to go with him for one dollar, and while he was planning with her, she slipped her hand into his pocket and stole his pocket book, containing $40, agreed to meet him at the next corner, and ran; went up Broadway and divided the amount between them. The Captain, rather than lose his money, exposed himself, and by some means found where C. N. lived, at whose dwelling the girls were found next day in the afternoon. They however took a good twenty shilling carriage ride, drank cordial, &c. out of their money, before they were taken up. She enters the Third Class.

When M. first came to the House, she put on many important airs, and manifested a considerable degree of impudence, and our hopes in her case were not very flattering; but by steady perseverance in correcting her errors, exhibiting to her view the enormity of her crimes, and what they must eventually result in; holding up virtue and piety, and the happy consequences that must result from a virtuous course; she, witnessing the high estimation that was placed upon those that had reformed, in a few months her manners changed to mildness, industry, and obedience; she became ambitious to have an opportunity to show how highly she appreciated her new views of virtue and propriety. The result was, she was indentured to J. N. of B., B. county, P. on the 27th of August last.

A few weeks since, we were visited by Mr. N's daughter, a young married lady, who informs us that M. is a fine girl, and that she is beloved by all the family, and bids fair to make a fine woman.

January 9*th*, 1828.

S. H. L., from the Police, aged fourteen years the 25th of December; born in New-York. Her father is infirm and does no work, drinks hard—had a handsome property left him by his father, but has spent it. He was the cause of introducing his children to sell soap and the like. One of his daughters, elder than either of these, became a prostitute through the same channel; but finally found a husband on board the S. F., and is now doing better. This little girl commenced her career, about two years since, selling soap, needles, pencils, almanacs, &c. She first commenced to steal soap from Mr. H., then needles from Mr. P. in Maiden-lane —she has taken four hundred at a time; and would receive from her companions a part of their stolen property, and in turn would give them a part of hers. I judge her not to be much past twelve years of age. She however learnt the trick of getting money from men, with the promise that she would go with them, and afterwards run away: her suitors would sometimes chase her; if she found herself too closely pursued, she would run into a grocery store, and tell them that a man was chasing her. She would pick up her sweethearts at the Battery, Steam Boat Wharves, Theatres, &c. She and her associates would occasionally attend the theatres and circuses. If they took five dollars each, per day, home to their mother, she was satisfied, and they could spend the rest. Sometimes they could clear eight dollars per day, honest sales, then again 12 *s*. per day, when they were successful in stealing needles and soap. This girl also received a portion of the forty dollars. Enters Fifth Class.

This child soon gave hope in her case, was open and frank in her communications, and became modest and industrious in her habits; only wanted to know her duty, and she performed it.

She was indentured to Mr. L., of H. C., in April last.

H. April 28, 1828.

N. C. Hart,

Dear Sir,—S. H. L. arrived on Friday, and I also received from Mr. H. her indentures by the same conveyance; and also your circular address to masters. The indentures I have signed, and they are witnessed by one of my daughters, (not wishing to go out of my family for a witness to this instrument, on S's account,) one of which will be returned herein. The address of the Managers to masters, I hope and intend to comply with strictly. S. commenced Sunday School yesterday, with my children—and to the same meeting with us, is seated under our sight. She commenced a private day school this morning, under the instruction of a pious female, in company with one of my children. Our Sunday School is attended by classes of society, from those in the first standing, down to the dregs of the lowest kind. From my family I have seven children in the school, one male and two female teachers, and four pupils. S. will have much advantageous preparation for Sunday School at home, from my two daughters, who are teachers, and I trust, Christians.

It cannot be expected I should say much of S's conduct thus early, but for the little time she has been with us, the ready cheerfulness with which she performs the little required of her, has already interested us all very favorably. I hope to be able, hereafter, to give you a further good account of her.

I am very respectfully yours,

(Signed) R. L.

Since which we have been informed that she is doing well, and is a girl of promise.

September, 1827.

M. K., from the Commissioners, aged 12 years the first of April; born in Ireland. Her father and mother are both dead. Between three and four years since, her father, E. K. put her to live with Mr. J. P., a distiller, in this city, where she continued until within a few days since, when Mr. P. informs me that one of his hired men made free with her twice, the last time it was discovered by the servant woman: and as the child was young and had no friends, Mr. P. was fearful she would go to destruction, if she was not secured more closely than lay in his power; consequently obtained legal permission to send her here.

The girl simply states, that some weeks since, S., one of Mr. P's men, threw her on the floor, &c., and that a few days since, he found her in the still house, and threw her on the hogshead, but the servant woman came so soon that he did not effect his purpose. She appears perfectly honest in her confession, says she never stole any thing; and I think if placed in a small careful family, will yet make a good girl to work. Enters seventh Class.

March 5th, 1828, M. is indentured to the Rev. W. G., of S., N. J.

S———, June 23d, 1828.

Dear Sir,—The bearer of this, Mr. N. C. is anxious of obtaining a lad from the House of Refuge, should there be one at present to put out that will suit him. Mr. and Mrs. C. are members of my church. He is a farmer in easy circumstances; his family is small, and among the most respectable in this place. So far as I can judge, I think it would be a desirable situation for one of the boys; and hope you will aid him in selecting one of a pleasant disposition, of industrious habits, and in whom confidence can be placed.

Mrs. G. and myself are much pleased with M. K., she is a good girl, respectful, industrious, pleasant, and seems anxious to commend herself to our approbation. Her health is good; and from her pleasantness and cheerfulness, I have reason to believe that she is perfectly satisfied with her situation, as an inmate of our family. She frequently speaks with much feeling of the House of Refuge, and in affectionate and grateful terms of yourself and the matron; and seems to regard it as one of the favored circumstances of her life, that her lot was cast, for a season, in the House of Refuge.

From what I have witnessed in M. connected with her conversations with Mrs. G. more particularly, I am led to form a high opinion of that interesting institution, over which you preside, and hope that you will feel encouraged still to persevere in your labors of love. Rest assured, my dear sir, that the blessings of many of these unfortunate children and youth, who were ready to perish, will come upon you, and that your instructions and councils are neither forgotten nor disregarded, by many of them, though removed from your watch and care.

Yours, very sincerely,
(Signed) W. G.

March 28th, 1828.

A. E. F., from the Commissioners, aged, she thinks, twelve years the fourth of July last; born in B., of Irish parents. Her father, she says, was first partner and then foreman, to Mr. M'Q., the founder in D. street; but a few months since went to the state of O. Her mother, she says, used to drink so hard, that her father left her, and she then went to live in A. street. This child went to live with a married sister, Mrs. N., in C. street, but was taken ill and went to Trenton. When this child went to live with Mrs. H., in Y. street, near A. street, she says her step-sister, T. B., had her sent here, for going out and staying with different boys, about fourteen and fifteen years of age, in new buildings, at different times. She says that Mrs. H's daughter M. persuaded her to do so, and she used to go also; and the boys would purchase cakes and apples for them—they used to carry on badly in the streets. Enters Eighth Class.

March 27—she was indentured to the Hon. L. E., of D., S. Co., New-York.

December 4th—Senator E., with his lady, called on us this afternoon: they speak highly of A., saying she is a good girl, and they are much pleased with her.

August 25, 1828.

M. H., from the Commissioners, aged twelve years last spring; born in B., New-York, of English parents. Her father, J. H., put an end to his existence, in A. M. has no sister living, but five brothers—the mother resides in T. street, takes in washing and goes out to labor by the day.

This little girl has been three years in bad practices, by going with boys, in other girls' company first—speaks of many of the same age and practices, then by degrees with larger boys. As small as she is, and as young as she appears, she has been in the practice of receiving men's company for more than a year. In her time she has been very active and successful in winning other little girls from the paths of virtue. Had finally taken a room with Mrs.

H., in T. street—frequently attended theatres, circuses, &c., La Fayette and Mount Pit. Enters Third Class.

Since M's residence in the House, there has been an astonishing change. For nearly four months past, she has evinced the sweetest Christian spirit, mild and meek, quiet and kind; often seen to weep under religious exercises, but never discovered to show any fruits of her former life—is one of the most industrious and trusty of her class; and when a sufficient length of time shall have elapsed, for her to be settled and grounded in the way she should go, we trust to have the pleasure of transplanting this hopeful child into some soil that will be congenial to her future prosperity and usefulness.

REPORT OF THE LADIES' COMMITTEE.

The Ladies' Committee to the Female Department of the House of Refuge, respectfully Report:

That we have great satisfaction in finding ourselves able to communicate information respecting our truly excellent institution, which must be very acceptable.

Where there are so many abandoned and profligate young persons, daily entering this establishment, it must be expected that some among them will be refractory, and occasion vexation and trouble; yet these are not numerous. Within the last year we have heard few complaints from the Matron. Two or three of the girls have not behaved so well. Their improper conduct may probably be, in some measure, attributed to the nearness of a store-room, by which the boys have access to the baking room of the girls. Here they can communicate to each other and contrive mischief, only a thin partition separates them. We are glad to learn that the directors of the institution have in contemplation to turn this store room into an eating hall for the boys, where they will only be admitted at meal time. In our opinion they should be kept out of view of each other—it is certainly the best plan, and most likely to keep them orderly and well behaved.

The Female Committee have not been unmindful of the suggestions of the Indenturing Committee, in respect to the selection and recommendation of girls to be apprenticed. Four are now, in the opinion of the Ladies' Committee, qualified, by their general good conduct, to give satisfaction, in any family in which they may be placed. At the same time, we would observe, that it is most desirable that these children should be sent to some distance from the city, where they would not be likely to meet their former bad associates.

The Ladies' Committee have held their monthly and weekly meetings, without intermission, even in stormy weather. They have constantly visited the House of Refuge, inspected the apartments, heard recitations from the Scriptures, and attended to the different lessons in which the children were engaged: most of them have improved satisfactorily, and give promise, under the advantages of religious education which the House of Refuge affords, that they may become worthy members of society, and repay the friends of the institution, the expense, trouble, and anxiety they have undergone,

In our monthly reports, every particular, in regard to these children, is given with great exactness. We now only add, that we shall continue our visits, with unabated zeal. We have daily more reason to think this institution is going on well, and that it is doing much good in the community. The beneficial effects of the establishment must and will be continually seen. Under the influence of this humane institution, vice will forsake its wonted haunts, and virtue find votaries in those who were depraved—Praise be to God! through the perseverance of a few benevolent persons so much has been effected. We have nothing further to add, but to assure the Directors of the House of Refuge, that we desire not to weary in our efforts to aid them every way in our power.

ISABELLA BULOID, *First Directress.*
MARIA COLDEN, *Second Directress.*
CHARLOTTE L. FOX, *Treasurer.*
SARAH C. HAWXHURST, *Secretary.*

Managers.

ALMY CORNELL,
MARTHA WILLIS,
MARIA HYDE,
DEBORAH L. EMBREE,
MARGARET PRIOR,
REBECCA M'COMB,
ANNA WARNER,
PHEBE MOTT,
ESTHER SEYMOUR,
MARGARET BEERS.

December, 29th, 1828.

REPORT OF WORK DONE BY THE FEMALES.

A statement of the work performed by the Female subjects in the House of Refuge, from December first 1827, to the first of December 1828, inclusive, viz:

Reeling two hundred and seventy thousand skeins of cotton yarn	270,000
Shirts made	482
Stockings run in the heels, pairs	250
Ravens Duck Pantaloons made	114
Spreads for Cells	113
Woolen Pantaloons	59
Woolen Jackets	52
Sheets for Cells made	80
Sheets for Hospital	10
White Van Dykes made	79
Calico do. do.	9
Calico Frocks	9
Gingham do.	81
Chemises made	54
Brown Aprons	67
Brown Aprons for Boys	6
Night Caps	66
Night Gowns	12
White Aprons	15
Jackets	30
Brown Towels	53
Brown Rollers	20
Pillow Cases	26

Bed Ticks	50
Mattresses	17
Carpeting, yards of	65¼
Quilts for Hospital	10
Blankets mended	52
Bed Ticks mended	30

The number of stockings mended were so numerous, that to have kept an account of them would have proved tedious.

Washing and baking, are two branches of no inconsiderable importance. The washing on an average has during the year, amounted to about eight hundred pieces per week, and the mending of the same. In addition to the above estimate of work there is to be considered all the domestic work relative to themselves, and the keeping in order the female department, viz: cooking, mending for themselves, cleaning house, &c. &c. of which there cannot be a minute account given.

WORK DONE BY THE BOYS.

BRASS NAIL MANUFACTORY.

Of assorted sizes, 15,600 M. which averages 300 thousand per week.

CHAIR BOTTOM MANUFACTORY.

Cane chair bottoms, 10,844, or 907 dozen.

It will be understood that the cane is dressed, and the frames for the seats made by the boys.

WILLOW WORKERS.

Have covered	200	3	Gallon	Demijohns
"	500	2	do.	do.
"	700	1	do.	do.
"	400	½	do.	do.
"	350	quart		do.

BRUSH MANUFACTORY.

1000 dozen Shoe Brushes.
250 dozen Hair Brushes.
250 dozen Cloth Brushes.
200 dozen Tooth Brushes.
50 dozen Hatters' Brushes.
250 dozen Scrubbing Brushes.
60 dozen Crumb Brushes.
2000 weight Bristles, assorted and combed.
500 pound Bristles picked.
1000 weight Bristles washed and bleached.

CARPENTERS' SHOP.

Soap boxes, for Shipping	12,407
Windsor do.	1,722
Large brown do.	2,529
Candle do.	1,842
	18,600

SHOE SHOP.

Cacks	1,500
Pumps	500
For domestic use	450

TAILORS' SHOP.

150 Suits, jacket and trowsers for winter.
400 pairs canvass trowsers for summer.
60 Caps.

TATEMENTS.

		subjects.
There were in the house when the last report was made,		161
Of those previously disposed of, there have been returned		17
Received during the past year - - - - - -		159
		337
Of whom there have been indentured - - -	148	
Escapes - - - - - - - - - -	6	
Returned to friends - - - - - - -	13	
Returned to the Alms-House - - - -	2	
Of age - - - - - - - - -	7	
Now in the House - - - - - - -	161	
		337

The number of subjects received into the House of Re-fuge since our last report as above - - - - - 159

Committed by the following authorities, viz:

Commissioners - -	98
Police - - - - -	45
New-York Sessions -	8
Brooklyn Sessions - -	3
Albany Sessions - -	2
Utica Sessions - -	1
Newburgh Sessions -	1
Schoharie Oyer and Terminer	1
	159

Of the above number, ninety-three are foreigners, or the children of foreigners, and the remaining sixty-six are of American parentage.

SUMMARY.

	Inden-tured	Esca-ped	Returned to friends	Retur'd to A. H.	Of age.	
1828.						
January,	5	1	2	–	2	
February,	2	–	–	–	1	
March,	11	1	–	–	–	
April,	24	2	–	–	1	
May,	24	–	3	1	–	
June,	19	–	1	–	1	
July,	8	–	2	–	–	
August,	1	–	1	–	2	
September,	16	–	1	–	–	
October,	20	–	1	–	–	
November,	12	2	1	–	–	
December,	6	–	1	1	–	
	148	6	13	2	7	tot. 176

MEMORIAL.

To the Honorable the Legislature of the State of New-York.

The Memorial of the Managers of the Society for the reformation of Juvenile Delinquents, respectfully sheweth,

That your memorialists have seen, with deep concern and regret, a remonstrance addressed to your honorable body, purporting to be from shipmasters, mariners and citizens of the city of New-York, against the appropriation made by law towards the support of the House of Refuge, of a part of the moneys collected by the commissioners of health.

Your memorialists will not doubt but that the authors of the remonstrance are actuated by the best motives, nor question the sincerity of their declaration, that they are not "hostile to any charitable institution;" neither will your memorialists presume to say, that by the remonstrance, facts are intentionally misrepresented; yet it is certain the language the shipmasters, mariners and citizens have adopted, is calculated to mislead the Legislature, and to create a prejudice in the public mind against an establishment which the late Governor, in his message to the Legislature, in eighteen hundred and twenty-six, characterised as "the best penitentiary institution ever devised by the wit, and established by the beneficence of man."

In adverting to the law creating the fund, a part of which is appropriated to the House of Refuge, the remonstrance could not avoid disclosing, that it was collected as well from passengers as from mariners; yet, in the zeal of their remonstrance, this important fact is entirely overlooked, and the injustice of a diversion of any part of the moneys collected by the commissioners of health to any other purpose than the immediate benefit of mariners, is urged on the ground of the fund being "wholly earned by them, in their arduous profession. If it be meant by the remonstrance, that the money collected from passengers, as well as that which is paid by mariners, is earned by the latter because the passengers in question arrive here by sea; then seamen might, with equal propriety, claim a particular interest in the public funds derived from duties on importations in the ships they navigate.

Soon after the law of eighteen hundred and twenty-six, relative to this subject, was passed, the managers received, under an order from the late Governor, nineteen thousand dollars out of a surplus then in the hands of the commissioners. This sum was applied to the extensive buildings erected by the society, owing in some measure to the house having been opened by a late law, to the Juvenile convicts of all the counties in the State, the number of delinquents it would be proper to receive has so far increased, that an addition to the building has become necessary.—To meet the expense of an enlargement of the establishment, the managers obtained from the late Governor an order for a further appropriation of seven thousand dollars, from any surplus the commissioners might find in their hands. Of this appropriation the managers have received no more than two thousand dollars.

Soon after the law, giving the Managers a claim on the surplus of the Hospital fund, was passed, they entered into an arrangement with the Health Commissioners, to receive from them at the rate of eight thousand dollars a year, which the Managers calculated would be sufficient for the support of the House of Refuge, as it is at present established; and the Commissioners estimated that the Managers might be allowed this sum, and ample funds be left, not only for the support of the Marine Hospital, but to meet all the expense of the very extensive additions and improvements which the Commissioners are making at the establishment on Staten Island.

The Managers have received nothing more from the Commissioners of Health than what is above mentioned: and to show how far the eight thousand dollars a year, which, under the present arrangement the Managers are to receive, will be from encroaching on the contributions of mariners, your memorialists beg leave to submit the following statement:—

There was received, during the last year, as appears from the Custom-House books,

From 1465 captains and mates,	$1297 50
From 13,750 seamen,	13750 00
From coasters,	3199 50
Making the whole amount received from mariners,	19,147 00
During the same time, there was received from passengers,	17,747 26
Making the whole receipts for the year 1827,	$36,894 26
From which deduct for the House of Refuge,	8000 00
And there will be left for the use of the Marine Hospital,	$28,894 26
Whereas the contributions of mariners have been, as above stated, only,	19,147 26
Leaving,	$9747 00

More than was contributed the last year by mariners.

There is every reason to believe, that the proportion of the hospital fund, which will be contributed by passengers, will be greater than it was last year.

The receipts for the current year from passengers have been more than they were in the corresponding months of the last season, and the information from Europe is, that the emigrations from thence will be this year greater than they have been.

The sums collected by the health commissioners are not only sufficient for the support of the marine hospital, and to afford to the House of Refuge all it requires, but will enable the commissioners, from the surplus, to establish a fund to meet contingencies, and pay the expenses of further improvements.

The ordinary expenses of the hospital are, as your memorialists have been informed and believe, less than seventeen thousand dollars a year, so that however pathetic the appeal of the remonstrance in favor of mariners may be, it is obvious, that it was not required by the occasion, nor was the expression of an opinion that an application of the earning of mariners, otherwise than for their benefit, would be unjust, (from which, it is probable, no one would dissent,) called for by any circumstances connected with the subject under consideration.

It is ascertained, that by far the greater part of the collections made from passengers, are paid by foreigners, who arrive in this state from different parts of the world. Your memorialists most readily admit, that not only a liberal support should be allowed out of the hospital fund for the Marine Hospital, but that ample provision should also be reserved for contingencies. For all this the law has provided. But when this is done, your memorialists respectfully submit that there could not be a more just or reasonable appropriation of the surplus arising from the contributions of foreign passengers, than to the support of juvenile delinquents, a large proportion of whom are children of emigrants.

When the last annual report of the Managers was made (with a copy of which the members of the legislature have been furnished, and to which your memorialists pray leave to refer) the whole number of subjects received into the House of Refuge from the commencement of its operations, was three hundred and seventy-seven, of these, one hundred and forty-nine were the children of foreigners.

The Managers forbear, on this occasion, to urge the advantages or merits of the establishment under their care. This has been done at the several times when the legislature has been induced to extend to the institution its patronage and support. The House of Refuge has more than realized the most sanguine anticipations of its founders and friends. Its benefits are not only felt in our own community, but the influeuce of its example is extending to every part of the Union, and even to foreign countries. The principles on which it is founded, its management, and the advantages resulting from its operations, have been the theme of the most enlightened jurists and philanthropists, both abroad and at home. Whenever it shall be thought more politic and humane to prevent crime than to punish criminals, asylums for the protection and reformation of juvenile delinquents, must find advocates. In several states, similar establishments are forming wholly at the public expense. The House of Refuge in New-York, grew from, and was for some time supported by, private contributions, which have amounted to more than twenty thousand dollars. But so extensive an establishment can not be maintained at the cost of individuals, and is utterly incapable of supporting itself. If the appropriations made for this object be withdrawn, and no adequate revenue be substituted, the institution must be abandoned. The hundreds of children who have found refuge in this asylum, must be again turned upon society, to pursue a course which must bring them again to the bars of our criminal courts, from thence to be sent to our penitentiaries and state prisons, there to be maintained as irreclaimable criminals at a greater expense to the state, than would be required to continue the support of an institution in which they may receive moral and religious instruction, acquire habits of industry, be reformed, and made useful members of society.

The Managers of the Society for the Reformation of Juvenile Delinquents, can have no other interest in the establishment of which they have charge, than that which ship-masters, mariners, and every citizen ought to feel. Your memorialists, therefore, can have no other prayer, than that you will duly consider the importance of the institution, its situation, the consequences of its being abandoned, and that you may do what is right.

By order of the Board of Managers,

CADWALLADER D. COLDEN, President.

New-York, April, 1828.

LETTER TO THE MASTERS.

House of Refuge, New-York, 182

The Managers of the Society for the Reformation of Juvenile Delinquents.

To

Sir,

We have consented to bind one of the children under our care in the House of Refuge, to you as an apprentice, pursuant to powers given to us by an act of the Legislature of this state.

We should not have done this, had not our inquiries, as to your character, induced us to believe, that your example, and your treatment of this young person will be such as may tend to perfect the moral reformation, we have reason to hope, he has experienced since he has been in the asylum under our charge.

Great pains are taken to impress on the children, committed to the House of Refuge, a love of truth, to give them religious instruction, habits of order and industry, and to teach them to be respectful and obedient. We have found from experience, that this may be done by a steady and firm conduct, not incompatible with great kindness. We are persuaded that most children may be more easily, and more effectually, governed by proper appeals to their mental feelings, than by corporal punishments, and that where these are inflicted frequently and with severity, it oftener marks a want of sense or humanity, on the one part, than demerit on the other.

We hope the system we pursue, will have had an effect on the child you will receive from us, which will render him useful to you, and contribute to make him a worthy member of society, when his connection with you shall cease. But this can not be expected, unless you, to whose care he will now be committed, interest yourself in his welfare.

It has not been concealed from you, and ought not to be forgotten, that this child has been a delinquent. We beg, therefore, to remind you that conduct may require more attention than might be thought necessary to one who had never been led from the paths of virtue. Should your kindness and care redeem this child, and make religious, moral, and industrious, you will participate with us in those feelings, which must result from the reflection that we may have contributed to the temporal and eternal happiness of a fellow-being.

It will be very satisfactory to us, to receive from you, from time to time, an account of the conduct of this young person. This is desirable not only as respects the individual, but should behave, as we hope will, your favorable report will be serviceable to our Institution. We wish you would encourage to write occasionly to our superintendent. We are happy to say, that the accounts we have had of, and from the children, we have bound out, have been, except in a very few instances, highly satisfactory. When the child's service has expired, it is desirable that should receive from you a certificate, which may express your opinion of conduct while was under your care.

With a hope that you may find in your apprentice a worthy and useful servant, and he in you an able instructer and kind master, and with our best wishes for and your happiness and prosperity, we commit to your care.

By order and in behalf of the Board of Managers,

Superintendent.

LETTER TO THE APPRENTICE.

House of Refuge, New-York, 182

The Managers of the Society for the Reformation of Juvenile Delinquents,

To

You are about to leave the House of Refuge. You will be bound as an apprentice to a person, who, the Managers believe, will provide for you, instruct you, and if you behave well, treat you with kindness.

We should not have consented to part with you at this time, had not your conduct given us reason to hope, that the religious and moral instruction you have received, since you have been under our care, have disposed you to lead an honest, industrious, and sober life. You are now of an age when you are capable of distinguishing between virtue and vice; you have had experience that must teach you, that if you are good you may be happy, if you are bad you must be miserable. You can not but have perceived how much your welfare depends upon yourself, and upon the observance of the precepts you have seen inculcated with so much pains by your preceptors in the House of Refuge. Among these are the following:—You are always to tell the truth. You are to be obedient to those under whose care you are placed, doing your duty as well as you know how, industriously and cheerfully. You are to be civil and respectful in your manners, and to avoid all bad language. You will find time that you may employ, not only in religious reading and exercises, but in improving your mind, and in acquiring such learning as may be useful to you. If you mean to be a good and respectable man, you will not fail to avail yourself of these opportunities.

Do not be discouraged by what has happened from striving to raise yourself to a respectable station in the world. If your life be hereafter exemplary, the errors of your infancy will be forgiven or forgotten. In our happy country, every honest man may claim the rewards he merits. Many of our most distinguished citizens have been the makers of their own fortunes, and in their childhood were as poor and unprotected as you have been. There is no reason why you, if you pursue the course they have done, may not command the same good fortune. At all events, you may be sure, that if you make yourself master of your business, are diligent in your calling, establish a character, for truth, honesty, industry, and sobriety, you can not fail to obtain a comfortable living, and to be beloved and respected. Look at those you have seen in poverty, and observe those you will hereafter meet with, who are in want: you will generally, if not always, find, that they owe their condition to bad company, to idleness, and intemperance, which not only debase the individual, but often make all who have the misfortune to be connected with him, unhappy and ashamed to acknowledge any relationship.

When you see a man, and particularly a young man, frequenting bad company, given to drink, and using profane language; when you see that he neglects his business, is wasting his time, and taking no pains to learn, you may be sure he is in the road to ruin; he has no chance to be reputable; he can hope for nothing but to live all his days from hand to mouth, and to earn by mean and hard bodily labor, enough to keep himself alive, and if he should have a family, to save them from starving. On the other hand, if you see a young man attentive to his business, passing his leisure time soberly, but cheerfully, with companions of whom he need not be ashamed; if he loses no opportunity of gaining religious and moral instruction, and is obedient and civil in his manners, you may be sure that when left to make his own way in the world, he will always be beforehand. Instead of leading a life of continual toil and hardship, and of reliance on his daily labor for his daily bread, he will become independent and happy, and may have around him a family and friends who will esteem and respect him, and be proud of their connection with one who is so deserving.

You well know the evil consequences of bad company: there is nothing as to which you ought to be more on your guard. You ought particularly to avoid those with whom you associated before you was placed in the House of Refuge. That you may not be again tempted by these, you should not be too anxious to return to this city, and put yourself in a situation where you may meet with them. When your time of service is out, and you become your own master, you may have a better chance of success in the world, if you will establish yourself where you will have no friends but those you may hereafter make by your good conduct, and where the history of your early life is unknown.

It will always be gratifying to us to hear of your welfare. We shall be pleased to learn that you preserve and often read this letter. We wish you occasionally to write to our Superintendent; you will always find in him, and in us, friends ready to advise and to serve you.

Committing you to the protection of Providence, and to the care of your master, and repeating our admonition to you, to be religious, to love the truth, to be sober and industrious, and to avoid bad company, we bid you farewell.

By order and in behalf of the Board of Managers,

Superintendent.

The Society for the Reformation of Juvenile Delinquents, in Account Current with Cornelius Du Bois, Treasurer.

Dr.

Date	Item	$	cts
1828 Jan. 1 to 1829 Jan. 1	To Cash, Repairs and additions to the buildings upon the premises,	$1611	97
	" Clothing, for the Children	1480	38
	" Food and Provisions, for the Children	3041	18
	" Furniture, Beds. Bedding, &c.	597	18
	" School and Hospital Expenses, Books, Paper, Stationary, Medicine, &c.	940	07
	" Coal, Wood, Oil, Stoves, Pipes, and fixtures,	1359	92
	" Horse, Cows, &c. for the use of the Institution,	477	99
	" Salaries of the Superintendent, Assistants, Schoolmaster, Matron, &c.	3474	42
	" Premium of Insurance against Fire on buildings,	89	73
	" Interest on Money loaned to support the Institution,	54	37
	To Balance carried down,	766	86
		$13964	07

Cr.

Date	Item	$	cts
1828 Jan. 1	By Balance in the Treasury	644	57
to 1829 Jan. 1	By Cash, grant from the Legislature of the State of New-York, for 1828,	2000	00
	Cash received for the Labor of the Children in the different Work Shops	2672	20
	By Nett amount received from collection of Donations and Subscriptions from the Citizens of New-York	247	30
	By Cash, from Marine Hospital Fund, on account of a draft for 7000 Dollars, upon the Health Commissioners, by the late Governor of the state, De Witt Clinton, for the erection of an additional building,	2000	00
	By Cash from Marine Hospital Fund, towards the annual support of the House of Refuge,	6400	00
		$13964	07
1829 Jan. 1	By Balance brought down,	$766	86

Officers of the Society.

CADWALLADER D. COLDEN, *President.*

STEPHEN ALLEN,
CORNELIUS DUBOIS,
JOHN GRISCOM,
HENRY I. WYCKOFF,
JAMES LOVETT,
PETER SHARPE, } *Vice Presidents.*

CORNELIUS DUBOIS, *Treasurer.*
FREDERICK SHELDON, *Secretary.*
JOHN STEARNS, M. D.
ANSEL W. IVES, M. D. } *Physicians and Surgeons.*

House of Refuge.

NATHANIEL C. HART, *Superintendent.*
P. SHERLOCK, *Assistant Superintendent.*
CATHARINE GOEWEY, *Matron.*
MARY WEAVER, *Assistant Matron.*
DAVID TERRY, Jun. *Teacher.*

Indenturing Committee

WILLIAM F. MOTT,
ROBERT C. CORNELL,
NATHANIEL RICHARDS.

Acting Committee.

WILLIAM W. FOX,
JAMES LOVETT,
MYNDERT VAN SCHAICK,
RUFUS L. LORD,
RALPH OLMSTED,
JOHN HUNTER.

Managers.

STEPHEN ALLEN,	JOHN E. HYDE,	NATH'L RICHARDS,
HEMAN AVERILL,	ISAAC S. HONE,	FRED'K SHELDON,
ARTHUR BURTIS,	JACOB HARVEY,	PETER SHARPE,
C. D. COLDEN,	ANSEL W. IVES,	JOHN STEARNS,
ROBERT C. CORNELL,	JAMES LOVETT,	BENJAMIN L. SWAN,
CORNELIUS DUBOIS,	RUFUS L. LORD,	NAJAH TAYLOR,
WILLIAM W. FOX,	WILLIAM F. MOTT,	M. VAN SCHAICK,
JOHN GRISCOM,	HUGH MAXWELL,	HENRY I. WYCKOFF,
JOSEPH GRINNELL,	DENNIS M'CARTHY,	JOHN W. WYMAN,
JOHN HUNTER,	RALPH OLMSTED,	SAMUEL WOOD.

FIFTH ANNUAL REPORT, &c.

1830.

THE Society for the Reformation of Juvenile Delinquents, has now been in operation five years. Previously to its organization much pains were taken to explain to the public the necessity for such an institution, the principles upon which it was to be established, and the benefits it was expected to afford.

At each anniversary, the execution of the original design, and its favorable results, have been fully disclosed. In compliance with the expectations of the public, and the duty of the Managers, another report is now to be presented.

After having exhibited the usual financial and statistical accounts for the past year, and given assurances of the general prosperity and augmented usefulness of the establishment, it will be impossible to add any thing very new to former expositions. But as these may be forgotten, or unknown to many, it will not be improper, it is presumed, to notice, generally, with as little repetition as possible, the objects of the institution, its operation, and its effects. Such remarks will be offered as are suggested by the experience we have now had, or as grow out of circumstances connected with the institution.

There is a disposition in human nature, while present advantages are enjoyed, to forget the past.

We shall not appreciate the usefulness of this establishment unless we remember what was the condition before this asylum was opened, of that class of the community which is its object.

In New-York, as in every large city, there were a number of forsaken children, many of them orphans, and many who derived no protection from parents, who received no instruction from them but in wickedness and profanity, and no example but in the practice of vice and immorality. These destitute beings began life by resorting to dishonest means to maintain it and became criminal in their infancy. The law made no distinction between the minor, after a very immature age, and the adult offender; much less did it consider the education, the wants, or the temptations of the criminal. The nature of the punishment for the old and hardened sinner, and for the helpless, ignorant, starving child, was the same.—Not only was there no difference in the nature of the punishment inflicted on the old and the young, but the treatment of all while under accusation, or detained for trial, was similar. All were secluded in the same apartments. The inexperienced child was associated with the aged, and hardened criminal, under circumstances calculated to impart the contamination of bad society.

It often happened that young persons who were brought into this situation, were not accused of any crime, but were committed for no other reason than that they were vagrants; and they were vagrants only because they were houseless orphans, or were driven from their unprovided homes, by the cruelty or vices of their parents.

When the same walls enclosed old and young offenders, the consequences were such as must have been expected. From the moment a child was obnoxious to a criminal proceeding, he was lost. There could be no hope of saving him from destruction, if he were innocent, or of reforming him if he were guilty. His life was one of incessant transitions from crime to punishment, each offence more aggravated in its character, till he became a hardened villain, and ended in being a capital felon.

Benevolent men who had an opportunity of witnessing this deplorable condition of things, devised the House of Refuge as a means of alleviating, if not remedying, evils so disgraceful to humanity, and with which the savage might have reproached the boasted refinements of civilization. Many of these have left this world, and if departed spirits may look back upon the past, our Eddys, Fews, Jones, Eastburns, and Haynes, must regard with such feelings as we may believe belong to another and a better nature, the entire success, and prosperity of an institution which they had so large a share in establishing. We should not suffer the active zeal of such men in the organization of this charity to be forgotten, not only because the world owes them a large debt of gratitude, but because a remembrance of their zealous co-operation in its establishment, should subdue the hostility of some, who have endeavored to make it be believed that its principal means of support are diverted from a more legitimate appropriation of them. But the institution never has touched a cent to which there is any more lawful, more appropriate, or more conscientious claim. No one could be unfriendly to such a charity, or could desire to take from it the favor of the public or of the legislature, if he were acquainted with the great benefits it is daily affording to the community. Let the person who would question its utility, or benevolence, so far subdue his prejudices as to be induced to visit the House of Refuge. Let him see for himself within its walls, two hundred children enjoying health, comfort, and education. Let him turn to our records and learn what was the condition of these young persons before they were consigned to our care. Let him also learn how many have been redeemed and regenerated. Let him turn his thoughts back to the time when there was no refuge for the parentless, or the deserted, or seduced child of poverty. Let him imagine these brought to the bars of our criminal courts, and tried, and condemned. Let him reflect on what was their subsequent treatment. Let his imagination follow them to their prison, and keep them in view till they were again turned into the streets to starve, or to steal.—But let him further imagine that the doors of the House of Refuge are opened, and the children he sees before him left to wander without protection or home: and if he has any thing of humanity in his composition, it could not but recoil from the consequences which he must see would ensue.

While we are adverting to the founders of this merciful charity, it is just to claim for them the credit of having been the first to establish an institution on the principles we have adopted. This, because we have called our building the House of Refuge, a name which has long been applied in Europe, is often denied. But the Society for the reformation of Juvenile Delinquents, is very different in its powers, and indeed in its objects, from any institution that existed previously to its incorporation, in this or any other country.

It is true that before our society was thought of, Houses of Refuge existed in England, and probably elsewhere. But these were either pure charities to receive and comfort destitute children, so long as they should be in want of mere penitentiaries for the punishment of such as were convicted of crime. There was no authority to detain a child who was not criminal, and all the power and control over one who was so, was prescribed by his sentence, and ceased when that expired, and he quitted the walls of the prison. No provision could be made for his protection during his non-age.

The legislature has very much enlarged the objects of our institution, and entrusted to its managers powers that have not heretofore been delegated. These are essential to its beneficent action, and mark the great difference between it and other institutions that previously existed, however similar they may be in name. If a child be found destitute—if abandoned by its parents—or suffered to lead a vicious or vagrant life; or if convicted of any crime, it may be sent to the House of Refuge. There is in no case any other sentence than that it shall "there be dealt with according to law." That is, it may if not released by some legal process, be there detained, if the managers should think it unfit to be sooner discharged, until it arrives at age. Parents or guardians, from the time it is legally sentenced to the Refuge, lose all control of its person. When it is believed that a child is reformed, the managers have power, with its consent, to bind it as an apprentice, till the age of eighteen years, if a female, and if a boy till the age of twenty-one. It is these important features that mark the difference between our institution and all others that previously existed; and it is in this sense that we may say with truth, that the New-York House of Refuge was the first of its kind ever established.

The system of instruction, employment, and discipline, as developed in our former reports, is not materially changed. The attention of the children to religious and moral instruction; the assiduity with which they study; the industry with which they labor; their cleanliness and healthful appearance, cheerfulness and orderly conduct, evince the zeal, intelligence, and discretion of the superintendent, and of those to whom the immediate management of the institution is entrusted.

The education of a large portion of the children who are taken into the House of Refuge, is found to have been as much neglected as their morals. Very many of them can neither write nor read. But though by the rules of the house, only four hours a day are devoted to their schooling, they make a progress in learning equal to what is generally experienced in institutions devoted to literary instruction. In most instances, the child whose delinquencies render him a subject for this establishment, has been led to an early exercise of his mental faculties. The frauds or tricks he has practised to provide for his sustenance, or for the gratification of his vicious propensities, have obliged him to exercise thought, reflection, and ingenuity. The mind of such a one seems precocious, more so than that of a child whose wants are all supplied, who has found no necessity for the exercise of his own energies, and who has been accustomed to rely on the judgment and guidance of others. An early self-dependence prepares these children to receive instruction, and when their minds are rightly directed, that ability which would have made ingenious rogues, renders them apt scholars. There are few who leave the House of Refuge, who have not the rudiments of a common education, and very generally are so far capable of reading, writing, and ciphering, as to be able to engage in ordinary business. Many of them, as will be seen by the subjoined reports, have so profited by the instruction they have received in this institution, as to have laid, as we may hope, the foundation of their advancement to stations in society of profit, usefulness, and respect.

The managers mention with much pleasure, that

they have a means of disposing of a number of the elder boys, which is particularly advantageous to them. Eighty of these have been bound (always with their own consent, and that of their parents, when they could be consulted) to the owners, or masters of whalers from the Eastward. In this employment, the lad, for many months, and sometimes for years, is abstracted from his bad associates, and has no opportunity of returning to his former habits. On the contrary, he finds himself subject to wholesome restraint and discipline, and has the example, though they be sailors, of moral, industrious, and religious companions. He finds at once too, that he may derive a profit to himself from his own exertions; for, in this trade, even the apprentices are sharers in the loss and gain. It is very satisfactory to refer to the letters subjoined to the Reports, written from another hemisphere by lads who are from the House of Refuge, and by their masters. The first will shew how the human mind expands—how capable it is of generous and virtuous sentiments, when it feels independence, and is cheered by hope. The other letters teach us that we should never believe a young person so depraved, as that judicious treatment may not produce reformation.

The influence and efficacy which the moral system of treatment pursued in the Refuge, has on the children, may be illustrated by the following facts.

Within the walls of the prison is a pretty large piece of ground, cultivated as a fruit and flower garden, as well as for raising vegetables for the use of the House. The fruits and flowers are all within reach of the children, and indeed when they are in season, are tempting them every moment. Yet there is scarcely an instance of any thing having been touched without permission. It may be thought that this forbearance is produced by great severity. This is not the case. The youthful inmates of this institution are governed by appeals to their understandings, to their generous feelings, rather than by corporal punishments. It is rectitude, or the fear of disgrace, and not of pain, that has this happy influence. In this little community, each member of it is led to estimate the value of character, and is not only anxious to avoid a bad reputation, but is emulous of being distinguished among his fellows for his goodness, his proficiency, and his ability. Badges of distinction are here objects of ambition, are borne with pride, and regarded with deference, as they are by human nature under other circumstances. With this difference, that here they are known to be always the reward of merit, and are never the adventitious appendages of birth or good fortune.

It is not improbable that these may be considered by some, as prejudiced and exaggerated representations of the patrons of the institution. The fear that this may be the case, should not prevent our exhibiting what we conscientiously believe to be the truth. We owe to humanity a faithful and fearless testimony of the success of the experiment we are making. It is a step in the improvement of the condition of mankind, which it is so obvious Providence is permitting. When generations to come, look back to trace the amelioration of their species, they will find among the first grades our Infant and Public Schools, the reformation of Juvenile Delinquents, and our merciful penitentiary code.

Let it not be supposed that it is pretended that we are invariably successful in producing reformation; on the contrary, it is acknowledged that we sometimes meet with incorrigible wickedness; but this is so rarely the case, that we do not hesitate to say, that after some years of experience, we are warranted to present the above as faithful representations of the condition of the institution and its general effects.

The managers feel it a duty to notice particularly the female department. Though they have to regret that the ill health of their former excellent Matron, Miss Goewey, has deprived them of her services, her place is supplied by a lady in whom they have every reason to believe they may repose entire confidence. The acknowledgments of the managers are especially due to the ladies whose report is herewith submitted. A committee of the Senate of this state at the last session, offers to the benevolence of the ladies who have devoted themselves to this charity, a tribute in which the managers most cordially join. The ladies whose

Report is now presented, have been no less active, zealous, and useful, than their predecessors. Their superintending care is attended with the happiest effects, and is essential to the good management of this branch of the institution. Their Report offers suggestions well deserving consideration. It is as they have observed, extraordinary, that while we see at every corner of our streets so many youthful females abandoned to vicious courses—while so many of them are prosecuted as vagrants, and criminals, so few should be found in an asylum, where, under the guardianship of the most amiable of their own sex, they would receive religious, moral, and useful instruction, and when they left the walls that confined them, would be put into a right path.

The reports of cases of females heretofore and now submitted, shew in how many instances the hapless child was vicious, only because her virtuous dispositions were uncultivated, and how often the most hopeless depravity has yielded to the influences of the institution. There are many females who have been bound out by the managers, who are now leading exemplary lives, and who, as will be seen by the letters annexed to the reports, are gaining the confidence and good will of all around them. It happens in many instances that females, when the time for which they are sentenced expires, are so nearly of age, that they must be discharged without such provision as may be made for younger persons. A female, though she may have been reformed in the Refuge, and may have determined to lead a life of virtue and industry, if she be nearly eighteen years old, cannot be indentured—she must be discharged. Without a home, without friends, without means, and even without a character, except such as she can obtain from those who have known her only as a delinquent,—she could hardly have any choice but to starve, or to obtain a miserable subsistence by a return to her former habits,—and although benevolent persons do often interpose to rescue objects from this dire necessity, yet the managers agree with the ladies' committee, that nothing can be more desirable than that there should be some permanent resource for unhappy beings so circumstanced.

Among the benevolent projects which constantly filled the mind of our late excellent and venerable associate, Thomas Eddy, was one for establishing an asylum for those who might deserve it, and who are turned from our prisons in a desolate state. He proposed to give them a shelter and employment, by which they might earn something, until they could be offered the means of gaining an honest livelihood. It was part of his plan to obtain a law which would authorise persons who needed the benefit of such an establishment, to bind themselves to submit to its regulations, so that they might not be uncontrolled when in it, or leave it at their pleasure. There would seem to be much less difficulty in realizing such a prospect for females, than for the other sex. Possibly it wants only the patronage of the ladies, who in their report advert with so much feeling and humanity to the deplorable condition of young women discharged from the House of Refuge, to bring into existence a charity the successful operation of which would be so grateful to their feelings.

Though there be vacant room in the female apartment, the boys' house is generally so crowded that it often happens, that there are from fifteen to twenty obliged to sleep in the halls and passages,—an arrangement which is a violation of the salutary regulation that each child shall have a separate dormitory, and be secluded when he cannot be watched. It is in the silence of night, in solitude, and within the naked walls of a cell, that the mind is obliged to turn upon itself, and that reflection is awakened which gives growth to the seeds of virtue and religion, planted in the school and in the chapel.

The managers soon perceived that though the influence of the institution in society, in lessening the number of crimes, should be equal to their most sanguine expectations, the present buildings would be too small for the increase of population, and to meet the extended operation which is given to the House of Refuge, by the act of the legislature opening it for young delinquents from every part of the state.

The managers, therefore, in 1828, proposed to build an additional house, and with that view obtained from the late Governor Clinton, who was so much the friend and patron of the institution, an order on the health commissioners for seven thousand dollars, to be applied to the erection of a new building. Only two thousand dollars had been received under this order, when the law of 1829 placed the revenue of the establishment on a new footing. But this two thousand dollars has been held for the purpose for which it was designed, and forms part of the available funds on hand, as will be seen by the subjoined account. The managers are happy to find, that this year there will be some surplus, and they now hope that these funds will soon warrant them to erect the building so much required, and enable them to meet the increased expenses of an enlarged establishment.

It may be thought, that when we represent the children in the House of Refuge as enjoying all the comforts of life, and as submitting to their confinement with cheerfulness, it must lose so much of the character of a penitentiary, that to be confined in it will not be considered as a punishment, and that the fear of being sent, or returned to it, will not deter young persons from the commission of crimes. But it must be remembered, that it is by amending the heart, inspiring a love of virtue, and a conscious rectitude, that this institution is expected to produce its beneficial effects. If experience warranted the conclusion that this could only be done by terror, the House of Refuge might fail in its objects. But though it has been established now more than five years, how few are the instances of a child being re-committed after a regular discharge! Let us contrast this with the representations of the District Attorney made in 1822, when with a view to the formation of this Society, he furnished from the records of the police office, a list of upwards of four hundred and fifty cases of juvenile delinquents. This did not include the young persons who were charged with indictable offences. Fifty or sixty of these, he stated, were tried in the course of a year, and some of them not over fourteen or fifteen years of age, he had known to be indicted and tried five or six times.. But the love of liberty is as natural to man as the love of life. It may be said of incarceration as it has been of slavery—disguise it as you will, still it is a bitter draught. The cage cannot be made so fine, or so comfortable, that the bird will not covet the open air.

The frequent, and as will be seen by a subjoined document, sometimes successful attempts, to escape from the Refuge, is evidence that there is little probability that we shall ever have voluntary inmates; and there seems no reason to believe that there will not b ea fear of this prison, or of being subjected to its confinement and discipline, after they have been once experienced. Indeed we know that "the boys' prison" is very familiar in the mouths of a certain class of the younger part of our population, and is mentioned with a dread that to be sent to it may be the punishment of misconduct.

It is highly gratifying for the managers to repeat, after the experience of so many years, that the House of Refuge continues to realize the anticipations of its warmest friends and advocates. Religion, policy, and benevolence, require its support, not only in reference to the present time, but in regard to other generations, to whom, with a continuance of the liberality they have heretofore met from the legislature, and with the blessing of Providence on their zeal and exertions, the managers hope to transmit the institution.

APPENDIX.

SELECTION OF CASES AND LETTERS

From Apprentices, and from Persons to whom Apprentices have been bound.

BOYS.

A. B., the son of a dissolute mother and a runaway father,—was bound out from the Alms-House, discharged by his master, and in a few months changed his place of service in this city five or six times. This course led to idle and reckless habits; visiting Theatres, and petty thefts followed, and he came into the Refuge, with a peevish and sullen disposition and only able to spell words of one syllable. This is one of the cases in which the efficacy of a mild, firm and regular system of instruction, was soon made apparent by bringing out the good qualities of the lad. He was indentured in October, 1828. August 12, 1829, his master writes as follows: —"For the most part A. is a very good boy, and certainly we would not part with him for any consideration. He is generally faithful and steady at his work, which consists in tending my garden, &c. When he gets older, I shall put him on the farm and instruct him in all the branches of the profession, provided he proves a good boy, stays with me till he is 21, is smart and industrious, and looks to my interest as to his own, he shall never be turned off with no more than is mentioned in his indentures. I have it in my power to do as much for him as any man in this part of the country; having no children of my own and two good farms, either of which I shall be glad for him to manage after he is 21, and in a way that he shall find profitable. In fine, it is my design to make a smart business man of him, and to this end he shall have a good education. He is not suffered to spend the Sabbath day as some other boys in this place and elsewhere do, in strolling from place to place, hunting, fishing, swimming, &c.: but on such days he is generally found with his spelling book or testament, reading to me or my wife, or to himself. In fine, I shall spare no pains to make a good and respectable citizen of him, and if he does not do well, his blood shall not be upon my hands."

In another letter he says—"I have always found him remarkably quick and willing to do whatever I command him, and perhaps no boy of his age has proved himself more trusty and faithful when left alone, &c. He often speaks of Mr. Hart, and I think views him almost in the relation of a father, though nothing will cause him to shed tears sooner than to talk of sending him back again to the House of Refuge, &c. I have taken the special charge of his education, &c. He loves me dearly, and his mistress, as he loves his life."

The letter is too long to be continued, but it is filled with favorable descriptions of the boy, and there can be no doubt that his prospects of success in life are of the most animating kind. We scarcely know which most to admire, the character of the boy, or that of his christian master.

George W., at the age of 16, had accomplished so great a number of petty thefts as to make him an adept. His last feat was a burglary of a daring character, for which he was committed to the Refuge, on the 20th of February, 1827. Having grown up to man's estate in profligate habits, with thoughts bent on mischief, and being wholly unaccustomed to work, he found his situation in the house extremely irksome. Upon one occasion, it became necessary to use severe measures to reduce him to obedience. But being administered in the cautious and paternal manner which the rules prescribe, happy effects soon followed, and in 16 months after his commitment, he was considered fit to be indentured.

On the 23d February, 1829, his master writes as follows:—"I have received your letter making enquiries respecting G. W., whom I got from the House of Refuge in June last, and can say he is industrious, and that I have no knowledge but that he has a strict regard for truth, that he attends public worship and sabbath school, and reads the scriptures; that I believe he does as well as he knows how, and exceeds my expectations. He considers the House of Refuge a blessing for him, and speaks of the Superintendent in the highest terms."

Anthony C. born on the passage from France. His parents died before he was two years old.

Committed by the police in March 1825, for a petty crime. A most impracticable boy. After two years discipline in the House, he was bound out with some misgivings. But the account of him is favorable. His master writes: "C. has conducted as well as I could expect a boy of his age, he has made but very few acquaintances since he has been with me in this place, and appears to be very well contented and has no disposition to run about the town in the evening, as many boys do. I should be loth to part with him for the chance of obtaining a better."

J. R. commenced thieving at 9 years of age, and soon became notorious, being frequently instigated by older boys to enter houses to steal plate, watches, &c. "After having been in the House of Refuge more than a year, he became one of the most interesting children we had." April 17, 1829, his master writes as follows, "J. R. is in good health and very well pleased with his situation, and we are much pleased with him, we would be glad to hear from you to obtain the 1st annual report of the House, if convenient to send it. It gives J. R. new energy every time he hears you approve of his good behaviour, and on that account a line now and then would be of infinite service to the boy and gratifying to," &c.

Subsequent verbal information confirms this account, and says, "that J. R. indulges no other disposition than to make a man of himself."

J. M. B. an orphan boy, was bound out from the alms house and ran away from his conductor, before he left the city. His exploits were numerous and various, reaching almost every description of petty thefts, such as of old lead, copper, rope, porter bottles, eggs, and fruit in the markets, a shawl from a store, &c. For these and other offences, he has been in Bridewell 10 or 12 times, but always escaped conviction because no one appeared against him. When brought to the Refuge, May 9, 1827, it was soon discovered that he had one redeeming quality which has been made the foundation of a good work. "He told the truth with the utmost promptitude," and in a few months excited attention by his industry and punctuality. But such had been the extent of his depredations and so apprehensive were the Indenturing Committee that at the age of 14, the bad habits he had contracted when at large upon the world with no hand to guide and no heart to cherish him, had become too confirmed to be suddenly eradicated, that he was detained in the House 16 months before they acquired sufficient confidence in his stability to put him out.

March 15, 1829, his master writes:—"It affords me much pleasure to report to you the general good conduct and behavior of J. M. B. I have discovered in him no vicious habits, he is faithful, honest, and industrious, though not as active as I could wish; always willing and obedient, even tempered, and appears perfectly contented. He has been at school this winter, besides attending Sabbath school and church with my family. Is very attentive to his book, reads his bible, and receives good instructions from my family. He speaks very highly of the House of Refuge, and often speaks of Mr. Hart with as much respect as a child for a father. With my best wishes for your Society, &c."

A. T., had been employed in selling sweet potatoes, clams, &c. about the streets, (the most fatal business a boy can pursue) and contracted an inveterate habit of drinking ardent spirits, which led to the commission of other errors. He was sent to the House as a vagrant. After 18 months of detention, his conduct became so satisfactory, that he was indentured to learn a carpenter's trade. Poor fellow! his unhappy propensity returned upon him, and the slave of rum again became an inmate of the House of Refuge. Eighteen months training in temperate, industrious and moral habits, had not been sufficient to cure that dreadful malady, and his master with sorrow gave him back to our care. After a suitable time had elapsed, he was bound out to a Nantucket Merchant, and departed on a three years whaling voyage. His letter dated "Coast of Japan, Lat. 32, Long."— is too long for insertion, but from its cleanly appearance and fair hand, we should judge that he was kept from the use of ardent spirits.

April 7, 1825.

T. S.—from the Police, aged 13 years. His mother died three years since. This boy was and we presume is still what is technically called, a hard character. The detail of his criminal exploits, would fatigue the reader. He followed stealing as a profession, and with associates of the same age, seems to have delighted in the vocation in which he had acquired expertness and hardihood.

He remained in the Refuge more than three years, and great desire was felt to place him at a good trade. He had the fairest opportunities, but every attempt failed, and he was at length bound to a merchant of Nantucket.

He writes to Mr. Hart:— *September* 12, 1828.

I take this opportunity to let you know that I am in good health. We have had a pleasant time: we are on the Brazilian Banks, &c. You must excuse my letter. I just want to mention to the boys that want to go to sea, if they were to see me on the maintop-gallant mast, or royal yards, they would like to stay at home; but if they would like to come, let them come.

Your Refuge Boy.

W. A.—received into the House, March 8, 1828, from a Court of Special Sessions held in the country, aged 14 years. His father drinks very hard; his mother is in the Poor House, with all her children except the oldest.

W. was indentured by the Poor Masters, three or four times, and ran away as often. His thefts were trifling. Being only accustomed to a vagrant life, it was difficult to change his habits to those of order and industry. But in a few months he became what the Superintendent calls a "lovely boy." He was indentured to a farmer in Illinois, a kind and respectable man, who answers our letter, October 4, 1829. "He is both trust-worthy and industrious. He has as strict a regard for truth as children of his age commonly have. I am fully convinced he does as well as he knows how," &c.

February 10, 1827.

William, committed by the Police, aged 14 years. His parents are still more depraved than those mentioned in the last history. Their residence is the abode of dissipation and misery. A lingering recollection of former respectability, induced them to send William to school. But what could the boy do to resist the effect of so much bad example. Domestic instructions he had none; a virtuous precept he probably never heard. He ran from school, was bound to a shoemaker, ran away: was put to a chair maker, stopped a little while and quit: he then became a vagrant, and his history exhibits an acquaintance with the most depraved modes of life. After he was in the House 13 months, he was indentured to a farmer. Here he stayed only 4 months: his vicious thoughts had not been eradicated nor his heart changed. He was found in his old haunts, and returned to the House: some months after, made his escape, was recovered, and after another probation, was indentured to a respectable merchant in Nantucket. This is a bad case, and yet, thank Heaven! not without hope, for while this report is preparing, the following letters from him have been received.

Ship E———, at Cape Verd Islands, August 14, 1829.

DEAR GRANDMOTHER.—I take the first opportunity of informing you by a letter that I am in a very good state of health. We have been out now one month, and I expect I shall be gone about twenty eight or thirty months. I am very much pleased with the vessel and all the officers, they appear to be very nice men indeed, and treat me more like a son than any thing else. We have a meeting held in the cabin every Sunday afternoon, and there is no swearing allowed on board." The residue is uninteresting.

His letter to the Superintendent is written in a handsome strong hand, and is well expressed. He repeats the substance of his letter to his grandmother, and then says, "I feel very grateful indeed for the kindness which you shewed me, while under your care and instruction. I now see the errors of my former conduct, and you may rest assured that I have commenced a new beginning, and shall always endeavor to behave myself with all the propriety and decorum that I am capable. I have often read the (printed) letter which you handed me on my departure from the House of Refuge, and shall endeavor to keep in mind all the good instructions contained in said letter," &c.

I am sir, with the greatest respect,
Your most obedient servant.

There are two classes of criminals whom it is difficult to convert or save from the error of their ways. These are, dissolute girls, and drunken boys. There are no practices of which corrupt human nature is guilty, that so certainly carry their victims to destruction as these: It seems as if the soul had become tainted with so deadly a leprosy, that no mortal balm could cure it. Other stains the House of Refuge has washed away, and often in cases of so deep a dye, as to excite the highest degree of astonishment and gratification; but five years experience furnishes us with but few cases of reformation from the effects of these, the most public and destructive vices of civilized life.

GIRLS.

Catharine D. was sent to the House of Refuge by the Police Magistrates, before she was 9 years old. At this tender age, she had already been convicted of stealing, and other offences and was becoming hardened in iniquity, having been twice confined in Bridewell. The catalogue of her misdeeds is too long for minute relation, and it is not intended to give any other than a general view of each case, so as to avoid wearying the patience, or shocking the delicacy of the reader.

In the Refuge, the most strict attention was paid to the morals of this little unfortunate: we say unfortunate, for be it remembered that the parents of this child belong to that dissipated and intemperate class of beings, whose dwellings are the abodes of misery and crime. The discipline of the House was so happily adapted to the temper of her mind, that Catharine soon assumed habits of obedience, industry and regularity, and after a few months residence in the House, when her guilty thoughts began to be displaced by new hopes and aspirations, the natural sweetness of her disposition and her moral and religious feelings became so apparent, that in the language of the superintendent, "she was beloved by all who became acquainted with her."

January 3, 1827, Catharine was indentured to the Rev. Mr. W., of F. In answer to our enquiries about her, made in pursuance of rules of the establishment, this highly respectable and pious gentleman, under date of July 13, 1829, writes as follows. "I am happy that I am enabled to state that Mrs. W., myself, and all my family, still are, as they always have been, highly pleased with the temper of her mind and the tenor of her conduct. Such has been and still is our pleasure in her, that she is in my family as one of my children." The letter contains answers to six questions, respecting her behavior, character and education, and the account given of her is such as a good parent would give of a good child, and it concludes in the following manner: "She speaks with tenderness and affection of the House of Refuge. She inquires in the kindest manner concerning the Superintendent, and takes deep interest in every intelligence from that institution. Catharine is far superior to almost all the hired girls in her situation. She is very interesting in her appearance and in her manners, and bids fair to grow up in a manner which shall have effaced from her mind and deportment every trace of her origin. May God reward you and the honored patrons of your institution, and make you all and it an extended and extending blessing to your day and generation."

Before the reader indulges in those feelings of pleasure and surprise which this little history must excite in every christian bosom, we wish to inform him that when Catharine came into the Refuge, "she did not know her letters," and her conduct was leading her to "inevitable destruction." Now her moral culture is quite as perfect as is given to children of the best families, and she is getting a good education.

Sarah A. G., was received into the House at the age of 14. Its discipline and instruction saved her. A letter from her master speaks of her in terms of praise. "I have never discovered in her any bad habit; she is industrious and honest, and devotes all her leisure time to her studies, the principal of which is the Bible, &c." The writer promised to send her to school in the spring. We have no doubt this was done, and that she will be allowed a reasonable opportunity for mental improvement.

Margaret J., sent into the House for some petty crime, at the age of 12, and was thus happily snatched from the ruinous contact of a deeply depraved and bad example. What in the aberrations of the worst of Nature's works, can be so shocking and baneful as the intentional and persevering misconduct of a *mother*.

This child soon fell into our habits of regular industry, became fond of reading, gained the matron's confidence, was promoted to the class of honor, and never betrayed her trust. Her attachment to her Bible became ardent, and her knowledge of its precepts unusual. This induced a foreign gentleman of distinction to make her a present of a handsome Bible. Shortly after the house was visited by some Indians from Canada. She became acquainted with their religious hopes, and joyfully presented her new Bible to one of the aborigines to be given to *his wife*. Some months after, the Indian woman was taken sick. The child's Bible was her constant companion; she would not part with it, and she died with it in her arms. In a subsequent visit to New-York, the same people made much inquiry about "that beloved little girl of the House of Refuge."

That beloved little girl is growing up in the way she should go, is at a good trade, is pious, industrious, and happy; and writes a creditable letter to the matron, in which she says, "Oh, if I had not been sent to the House of Refuge, where would I have been this day. My dear Miss Goewey, I can hardly call you any thing else but my dear mother, I thank you and Miss Weaver for all your motherly care over me. I never can pay you for all, but I do believe that my Heavenly Father will."

September 5, 1827.

M. D., from the commissioners aged 13 years. Her mother has been dead seven years. She has been to six places of service in about fourteen months. She was a girl of talents, resolute, wayward, and apparently bent on her own destruction. Not succeeding in a bold attempt, to escape, she contrived a plan to set the female house on fire, which was detected and prevented. This led to a more rigid course of discipline, which together with the instruction of the House, subdued her temper, and in eighteen months she was considered fit to be indentured. She shall speak for herself.

Pennsylvania, Feb. 22, 1829.

"MY DEAR FATHER.—You need not feel uneasy on my account, as I have got a good place. I like my situation very much, as the lady I live with is very kind to me. I want to know if my little sister M., has got a good place, and if she has I wish her to stay to it. My dear father, do not grieve after me, my time will soon be expired, when I hope I shall be a comfort to you in your old age.

Tell my sister for me, to try and be a good girl, not to be saucy to the lady she lives with; to do all she can to please her. Tell her she must pray to God to help her, and he will hear her prayers, for his ear is ever open to the prayers of the orphan. Tell her she must never dare to take that which does not belong to her."

The letter contains three pages of pious and fervent encouragement to her father, and admonition to her sister.

Her letter to the Matron, dated March 8, is written in a similar strain.

The following is from a member of the Legislature, a gentleman of distinguished reputation, July 1, 1829.

"Sarah appears to be a kind and good girl as yet, and gives good satisfaction thus far: she is kind to the children, and they are fond of her; attends Sunday Schools, and her whole deportment thus far is perfectly satisfactory. She speaks often of you, (the matron) and appears grateful for the treatment and advice she received at the House of Refuge. I trust the instruction she has been favored with in your institution, will not be lost upon her, but that she will become a useful member of society, and prepared for that kingdom where there shall be no more trial or sorrow."

The father of this child burst a blood vessel, and upon his death her mother was removed to the Alms House. The child was thrown upon the wide world at the age of ten or eleven, and fell into the common course of idleness and petty crime. The Refuge saved her from total ruin.

December 23, 1828.

E. N., committed by the Police, aged 10 years. Her father kept a bad house. The mother employed her child in the business of begging victuals and old clothes, while she remained home in a state of intoxication.

Some of the suspicious persons who frequented her father's house, would occasionally go out begging and take this little girl with them: this was a cover for thievish practices. It is not possible to conceive a story of more sickening depravity than this would make, if related in plain language.

The Superintendent says, "when this interesting girl first entered the House, she was as black and as dirty as a chimney sweep; her muslin was the color of the earth, it being all the garment of the kind she had.

After the Matron had thoroughly cleaned her, and put on her a clean plain dress, she excited our sympathy, and we thanked the Lord that he had put it into the hearts of benevolent men, to get up a House of Refuge, for such unfortunates. The child having been accustomed to live in degradation and filth, and now beginning to enjoy the sweets of regularity, good order and cleanliness, could not be induced to say that she would like to return home.

Her parents finding that they had lost a valuable member of their fraternity, had her brought before the Recorder on a writ of Habeas Corpus. The judge examined the case with much attention, interrogated the child, discovered that she preferred the Refuge to her father's house, seemed pleased with her clean and sweet appearance, and then looked with disgust at the dirty heap of clothes in which she had come to the Refuge: and suddenly addressing the lawyer: "Sir, said he, if I should return you this child, my conscience would not let me sleep this night!"

The child's improvement in the House was rapid, and she soon became fit to be indentured. The gentleman under whose roof she leads a happy and an innocent life, writes as follows:

November 16, 1829.

"It gives me much satisfaction to state that E's conduct and disposition have been such, that I think a person not knowing from whence she came, would be induced to believe her almost incapable of committing crime, the most trivial in its nature, should it be placed within her reach. Her disposition is very mild and pleasing, her willingness to do as directed, seems to indicate there could have been no pains spared, while under your control to instil upon her mind the manner of conduct that should govern her through life," &c.

The decision of the Recorder, has probably saved this child from a life of infamy and wretchedness.

It must not be supposed that all the children sent from the House of Refuge, turn out as well as those alluded to in the preceding histories. On the contrary, our previous remarks admit that we do not always succeed in producing reform: but though we have to regret occasional failures, they are not of a character to arrest our efforts, or impair our confidence in the general results of the system. The interesting and conclusive cases of penitence and reform, which we have related, afford us ample encouragement to perseverance in this good work. To these, many other cases exhibiting instances of reformation might be added. Besides, these failures, though comparatively few in number, and of no great importance as it regards their bad example to the inmates of the House, may in some instances be traced to the unfitness of the master who has been intrusted with the care and education of a child. Though great caution is observed in the selection of situations for our children, it is not possible always to discover the true character of applicants, notwithstanding that the Indenturing Committee, consisting of three gentlemen, devote a large portion of their time, with unwearied diligence, to this responsible and laborious business.

It will be observed in one of the histories we have given, that a salutary dread of returning to the Refuge was felt by a child. This is a safe and advantageous state of mind, provided it is accompanied, as in this instance it appears to have been, by kind and respectful recollections of the officers of the House. For it must not be forgotten, that the House of Refuge is in fact a prison for children, and that whilst the greatest tenderness is due to their youth, and the greatest compassion should be displayed towards their involuntary errors, no such relaxation of discipline can be permitted, as may tend to call off their minds from the severer duties of life, or encourage the illusory expectation of exemption from wholesome restraint, and from inevitable punishment whenever it is deserved.

Other histories shew that the children love the House of Refuge, for the good it has done them. Any more happy illustration of its merits, cannot be desired than those cases display. The wish of every benevolent mind, should therefore be, that it may long continue to be a blessing, and a refuge to the houseless orphan, and the child of neglect, of bad example, and of crime.

REPORT OF THE LADIES' COMMITTEE.

To the Managers of the House of Refuge, the Ladies' Committee respectfully Report—

That, since their last Annual Report, the Monthly Meetings of the Committee have been regularly held, besides such special Meetings as circumstances appeared to require. A Sub-Committee of their number have visited the House of Refuge, at least, once in each week during the year. Minutes have been regularly kept by the Committee and Sub-Committees, a summary of which will be laid before the Managers, and to this summary, they refer for a more detailed account of their proceedings.

On this occasion it may be sufficient to remark, that, so far as opportunity has been afforded, the present Matron appears qualified to discharge the arduous duties of her station, with credit to herself, and benefit to the Institution. The girls continue to be fully employed, and their time profitably divided between the usual School exercises. Family devotions, and the numerous domestic duties of the House, such as baking, washing, making and mending their own and the boys' clothes, bedding, &c. And in each of these departments, the Committee are happy to say, there is evidence of improvements.

The Sub-Committees have, during their weekly visits to the Refuge, advised with, and assisted the Matron in the arrangement of its domestic concerns, and have not been unmindful of the highly important duty of endeavoring to instil into the minds of the girls, principles of piety and virtue, and excite them to a sense of the necessity of cultivating habits of industry, cleanliness and order; and a strict attention to the directions of the Matron, and the rules of the House. These efforts have not in every instance been crowned with that success which the Committee could desire; but the exceptions have been so few, that, instead of diminishing, they have stimulated to renewed and increased exertions.

The sympathies of the Ladies' Committee, have been peculiarly and strongly elicited on behalf of those girls who cannot be bound out, in consequence of having been sent to the Refuge when nearly arrived at the limited age, and are therefore discharged and again exposed to temptation, without friends or the honest means of immediate support. The Committee cannot conceive a case in the "whole range of human destitution," that presents a stronger claim on our compassion, than a penitent female thus circumstanced.

The committee are aware that when such cases have occurred in the Refuge, the private benevolence of individuals connected with the Institution, has applied at least a partial remedy; but they respectfully suggest whether some permanent arrangement cannot be made to provide this interesting class of female delinquents with the means of support, till they can place themselves in situations beyond the reach of their former associates. Without some such provision, there is reason to fear that many on whom the discipline of the House, and the admonitions received within its walls, had exerted a beneficial influence, may become so disheartened by the hopelessness of their condition, as to yield to the pressure of circumstances, and again resort to those haunts of vice from which they had been rescued.

The average number of girls in the House of Refuge during the past year, does not exceed one half of the number for which there are accommodations. Could the Committee believe that this resulted from a deficiency of suitable objects, it would indeed be cause of thankful acknowledgment; but their daily walks through the city, furnish conclusive evidence that this is not the fact, for they are met at almost every corner by numbers of vagrant female children, whose ragged appearance and disorderly conduct shew that they are destitute of Parents or Protectors, or what is even worse, under the influence of such as urge them to the commission of crime. Deeply impressed with the importance of snatching as many as possible of these unfortunate children from that course of life, which our Records abundantly shew they are persevering in, the Ladies' Committee earnestly solicit the attention of the Managers to the subject. They will not permit themselves to doubt the existence of a disposition on the part of our City Authorities to co-operate and lend them assistance in a cause like this. The Committee need scarcely advert to the fact, that applications for girls to be placed in respectable families, remote from large towns or cities, are much more numerous than the means of supply. That the conditions of the class of girls referred to, would be improved by the change, is too self-evident to admit of dispute: and the Committee indulge the hope that the period is not remote when the existing accommodations, at least, shall be fully occupied by these houseless children of want.

The Committee feel bound, before closing this report, thankfully to acknowledge the goodness of the Great Disposer of Events, in continuing to the inmates of the Refuge, the blessing of health.

SARAH C. HAWXHURST, *Secretary, pro tem.*

12th mo. (December) 4th, 1829.

WORK DONE BY THE BOYS.

CANE CHAIR BOTTOM MANUFACTORY.

Cane chair bottoms, 750 dozen plain seats.
" " 145 Curled Maple flush back seats,
" " 41 doz. raised back, solid front, curled maple,
" " 59 plain maple solid front seats,
" " 20 settee seats,
2025 pounds of cane, (after dressed) from the Rattan.

BRUSH MANUFACTORY.

3515 dozen Shoe Brushes.
90 dozen Flesh Brushes.
700 dozen Hair Brushes.
300 dozen Horse Brushes.
780 dozen Cloth Brushes.
100 dozen Plate Brushes.
186 dozen Tooth Brushes.
120 dozen Hat Brushes.
1030 dozen Scrubbing Brushes.
400 dozen Horse Brushes.

4500 pound Bristles, assorted and combed.
1400 pound Bristles picked.
1300 pound Bristles washed and bleached.
200 pound Whalebone cleaned.
1500 dozen Shoe Brushes finished.
300 dozen Hair Brushes finished.
200 dozen Cloth Brushes finished.
300 dozen Horse Brushes finished.

SHOE SHOP.

Cacks, or Children's Shoes, - - -	2,034
For the use of the House, - - -	350

Besides double that number mended.

CARPENTERS' SHOP.

Soap boxes, for Shipping - - -	12,500
Windsor do. - - - - - -	1,550
Large brown do. - - - - -	4,000
Candle do. - - - - - -	2,500
	20,550

TAILORS' SHOP.

By the girls, 250 Suits, jacket and trowsers for winter use.
By the boys, 100 } 350 pairs canvass trowsers for summer
By the girls, 250 }
By the boys, 150 Cloth Hats or Caps for boys.

DRUGS PREPARED FOR APOTHECARIES.

400 pounds roots cut up.
180 pounds Gum broken up.

CABINET SHOP.

500 Cradle Bottoms, for willow cradles.
500 Wagon do. do. do.
800 pair Cherry Rockers.
500 pair pine Rockers.
1 dozen Wash Stands.
3 dozen Pine Tables.
10 dozen Safes, (wire)
20 dozen Wash Boards.
200 pair small Rockers, for toy cradles,
20 dozen Spitting Boxes.
2 dozen Knife Boards.
6 dozen Paste Boards.
3 dozen Wash Benches.
40 dozen Bottoms for willow chairs.
40 dozen Tables for do.
12 dozen Knife Boxes.
200 Segar Boxes.
4 dozen Foot Benches.
6 dozen Boot Jacks.
12 dozen Step Ladders.
6 dozen Clothes Horses.

OTHER WORK DONE BY THE BOYS AND GIRLS.

Tilling the grounds; working in the gardens. All the cooking for the Male House, has been done by the boys, except the baking; that is done by the girls. The boys whitewash and cleanse their own apartments; mend the greater part of their own clothes, save their shirts and stockings. The girls make and mend all the shirts; knit a part, and mend all the stockings. The girls do all the washing for the whole establishment, which is said to be eight hundred pieces per week. The girls make and mend all their own clothes, and in some instances, they have become quite decent mantuamakers in making their plain garments.

STATEMENTS.

		Subjects.
There were in the house when the last report was made,		161
Of those previously disposed of, there have been returned		26
Former escape, returned,		1
Received during the past year		154
		342
Of whom there have been indentured	148	
Escapes	8	
Returned to friends	12	
Returned to the Alms-House	3	
Of age	5	
Now in the House	166	
		342

Of the 26 returned, 7 came to the House for protection, having been unfortunately situated. One was a little girl 7 years of age, and proved too small for the purposes for which she was wanted. Two in consequence of indisposition.

The number of subjects received into the House of Refuge since our last report as above - - - - - 154

Committed by the following authorities, viz:

Commissioners	76	
Police	33	
New-York Sessions	16	
Brooklyn Sessions	6	
Albany Sessions	11	
Monroe Sessions	4	
Washington County Sessions	2	
Green County Sessions	1	
Rensselaer County Sessions	1	
Tompkins co. Oyer and Terminer	1	
Orange County Sessions	1	
Westchester Sessions	1	
Dutchess County Sessions	1	
		154

Of the above number, eighty-five are foreigners, or the children of foreigners, and the remaining sixty-nine are of American parentage.

COUNTRIES OF FOREIGNERS, OR CHILDREN OF FOREIGNERS.

Ireland 47, Scotland 2, England 24, France 1, Spain 1, Germany 4, Wales 1, Italy 1.

STATES OF AMERICA—PARENTS OR CHILDREN OF DITTO.

Massachusetts 2, Connecticut 2, New-York 54, New-Jersey 9, Pennsylvania 1, Maryland 1.

The ages of the Children received into the Refuge since it was opened on 1st January, 1825, to 1st January, 1830.

BOYS.

Years of age. - -	7	8	9	10	11	12	13	14	15	16	17	18	19	20
1825														
to 1826,	1	1	2	4	5	6	6	13	14	7	5	1	1	
to 1827,		1	4	7	4	6	9	20	25	10	11	5	9	3
to 1828,			4	8	13	14	13	16	11	12	8	4	1	
to 1829,		3	5	11	12	18	13	32	12	11	5			
to 1830,			3	10	7	17	6	25	23	10	5	1	2	1

GIRLS.

Years of age. - -	7	8	9	10	11	12	13	14	15	16	17	18	19	20
1825														
to 1826,	1	1				2	4		3	4				
to 1827,				3	2	4	3	4	5	6	7			
to 1828,	1		1		4	5	7	6	5	9	3			
to 1829,	3		3	1	3	7	10	3	5	5	3			
to 1830,		2	4	2	4	4	5	5	10	4	1			

Classification of the Children received into the House of Refuge since it was opened on 1st January, 1825, to 1st January, 1830, in literary improvement.

	BOYS.									GIRLS.								
Class, - -	1	2	3	4	5	6	7	8	9	1	2	3	4	5	6	7	8	9
from 1825																		
to 1826,	6	5	24	2	16	10	1	1	1	3		6		5	1			
to 1827,	10	9	13	15	19	10	13	21	4	6	5	8	5	2	4	3	1	
to 1828,	9	11	9	7	12	8	25	19	4	3	5	3	4	6	3	17		
to 1829,	10	10	12	7	7	8	38	26	4	5	5	7	4	2	5	3	8	4
to 1830,	6	10	20	10	9	13	20	16	6	6	3	5	5	7	1	6	7	1

SCHOOL REPORT.

The School was re-organized 1st January, 1829.

The following Tables are designed to show the improvement of the children, for the past year, and embrace as well those that were in the House at the period of re-organization, as those received during the past year.

Of those who entered the following reading classes, there have been promoted from the

	2d,	3d,	4th,	5th,	6th,	7th,	8th,	9th,
1st to the	3	4	3	1	1	0	0	0
2d	-	8	8	4	1	1	0	0
3d	-	-	14	8	10	2	0	0
4th	-	-	-	16	9	8	0	0
5th	-	-	-	-	16	8	0	0
6th	-	-	-	-	-	16	5	0
7th	-	-	-	-	-	-	40	4
8th	-	-	-	-	-	-	-	28

Of those who entered the Arithmetic classes, there have been promoted from the

		2d,	3d,	4th,	5th,	6th,	7th,	8th,	9th
Combination,	1st to the	20	12	12	2	0	0	0	0
Addition,	2d	-	27	24	4	0	0	0	0
Subtraction,	3d	-	-	16	6	0	0	0	0
Multiplicat'n,	4th	-	-	-	20	4	0	0	0
Division,	5th	-	-	-	-	12	0	0	0
Comp. Rules,	6th	-	-	-	-	-	9	2	0
Reduction,	7th	-	-	-	-	-	-	5	3
Rl. of Three,	8th	-	-	-	-	-	-	-	5

In the ninth class there are twenty-nine children* who read History and study Geography.

Fifty-two write on paper; 114 write on slates.

With this exhibit of the improvement of the children, the teacher would remark, that the regular and stated employment of the children, eight hours per day, does not appear in any wise to militate against as successful a prosecution of their studies during the time allotted them, as is observed in our Public Schools.

The Sabbath School is also under the sole care of the teacher, and it is gratifying to say, the attention given to the reading and searching the Holy Scriptures, affords reason to hope, that many of our children will hereafter (as many already have) date their acquaintance with that "salvation" which is no where taught save in the "lively oracles," to Sabbath School instruction received in the House of Refuge.

It appears due in this place to advert, with thankfulness, to the very liberal donations which have been made from time to time, by the Young Men's Bible Society of New-York, Auxiliary to the American Bible Society; nor should the monthly visits of the friends of Sabbath Schools, who are careful to present us with their monthly rewards, for the encouragement of such children as are diligent in searching the Scriptures, be forgotten.

The number of children received into the Refuge, since it was opened, 1st January, 1825, to 1st January, 1830, that have been in places of confinement, viz: In Bridewell, Prisons, Penitentiaries, &c. &c., and the length of time they were confined, before being sent to the Refuge.

Bridewell.—47 have been in once, 23 twice, 11 three times, 3 four times, 5 five times, and 1 ten times.

Penitentiary.—13 have been in six months, 3 twelve months, 4 eighteen months, 1 thirty months, 2 thirty-six months.

State Prison.—1.

Character of the Parents of Children received into the Refuge.

Parents been in Bridewell, 25; Penitentiary, 6; State's Prison, 2; Intemperate, 401; Houses of Ill Fame, 9; Parents allow children to steal, 8; Parents receiving the avails of stealing, 8.

* This exhibits the state of the schools, male and female.

Statement of the *ages* of the Children *now* in the House of Refuge, up to 31st December, 1829.

Boys.—1 eight years, 2 nine, 6 ten, 14 eleven, 16 twelve, 19 thirteen, 25 fourteen, 15 fifteen, 21 sixteen, 6 seventeen, 3 eighteen.

Girls.—1 eight years, 2 nine, 4 eleven, 1 twelve, 6 thirteen, 7 fourteen, 8 fifteen, 5 sixteen, 4 seventeen.

Since the opening of the House there have been received, 690. Of whom there have been indentured,

Boys,	326		
Girls,	92		
		418	
Of the above there have returned,		17	
			401
Returned to friends, Boys,	34		
Girls,	17		
			51
Returned to Commissioners, Boys,	3		
Girls,	14		
			17
Of Age, Boys,	6		
Girls,	18		
			24
Deceased, Boys,			1
Sea Service, Boys,			14
Escaped permanently, Boys,	15		
Girls,	1		
			16
Now in the House, Boys,	128		
Girls,	38		
			166
			690

TO WHAT TRADE OR BUSINESS—BOYS INDENTURED.

YEAR.	Farmer.	Shoe Maker.	Blacksmith.	Chair Maker.	Brush Maker.	Tailor.	Hatter.	Potter.	Silversmith.	Carver.	Tinman.	Pump and Block Maker.	Brass Founder.	Tanner and Currier.	Wheelwright.	Carpenter.	Cabinet Maker.	Printer.	Comb Maker.	Miller.	Baker.	Paper Maker.	Boat Builder.	Glass Blower.	Mason.	Sugar Maker.	Cloth Manufactory.	Returned to Parents.	To Commissioners.	Of Age.	Sea Service.	Whaling.	Stocking Weaver.	Deceased.	Summary.
from 1825 to 1826.	3																											1			2				6
from 1826 to 1827.	13	1						1	1									1										8	1		2				28
from 1827 to 1828.	30		2	2		1	1			1	1			1	3		1	1				2						12	1	4		32		1	96
from 1828 to 1829.	45	12	2	1		2	4				2			2			1	1		3	1	1					2	7	1	1	1	21			110
from 1829 to 1830.	68	6	5	1	2	3	2				2	1	1	2	2	2	1	1	2			2	1	1	1	2	1	6		1	9	18	1		144

Total 384

TO WHAT TRADE OR BUSINESS—GIRLS INDENTURED.

YEARS.	Domestic.	Milliner.	Tailoress.	Returned to Parents and Friends.	To Commissioners.	Of Age.	Total.
from 1825 to 1826.	4				1	1	6
from 1826 to 1827.	8				1	3	12
from 1827 to 1828.	20	1		3	8	6	38
from 1828 to 1829.	34	1	1	8	1	3	48
from 1829 to 1830.	23			6	3	5	37
							141

IN WHAT STATES INDENTURED.

YEARS.	*Boys.* New-York.	Connecticut.	New-Jersey.	Pennsylvania.	Ohio.	Massachusetts.	Illinois.	Maryland.	Florida.	*Girls.* New-York.	Connecticut.	New-Jersey.	Pennsylvania.	Ohio.	Massachusetts.
from 1825 to 1826.	3									3	1				
from 1826 to 1827.	13	2			2					8					
from 1827 to 1828.	36	1	8			1				16	2	2		1	
from 1828 to 1829.	44	11	8	2	14					26	3	2	1	3	1
from 1829 to 1830.	71	21	7		4	2	1	1	2	13	4	2	1		3

SUMMARY.

	Indentured.	Escaped.	Returned to friends	Returned to A. H.	Of age.
1829.					
January,	3	–	–	–	–
February,	7	–	–	1	1
March,	10	–	1	–	–
April,	19	2	1	–	1
May,	14	–	–	–	1
June,	19	2	–	–	1
July,	17	–	2	–	1
August,	13	–	1	–	–
September,	9	1	1	–	–
October,	9	–	2	–	–
November,	17	1	3	2	–
December,	11	2	1	–	–
	148	8	12	3	5

A table showing the weekly report of the number of children in the House, with the average number, for the year 1829.

DATE.	1829.	boys	girls	total	DATE.	1829.	boys	girls	total
January,	6	131	34	165	July,	7	139	33	172
"	13	133	35	168	"	14	144	35	179
"	20	135	36	171	"	21	138	37	173
"	27	136	36	172	"	28	135	36	171
February,	3	138	35	173	August,	4	136	36	172
"	10	139	36	175	"	11	138	39	177
"	17	139	36	175	"	18	137	41	178
"	24	141	36	177	"	25	139	41	180
March,	3	141	35	176	September,	1	137	41	178
"	10	143	34	177	"	8	136	42	178
"	17	145	35	180	"	15	134	41	175
"	24	148	38	186	"	22	135	40	175
"	31	144	37	181	"	29	135	39	174
April,	7	137	36	173	October,	6	139	38	177
"	14	142	38	180	"	13	140	36	176
"	21	138	39	177	"	20	139	36	175
"	28	141	39	180	"	27	140	37	177
May,	5	136	36	172	November,	3	138	37	175
"	12	131	37	168	"	10	140	40	180
"	19	130	37	167	"	17	134	40	174
"	26	137	37	174	"	24	127	38	165
June,	2	138	37	175	December,	1	134	37	171
"	9	140	34	174	"	8	135	36	171
"	16	133	32	165	"	15	130	36	166
"	23	139	33	172	"	22	128	38	166
"	30	134	32	166	"	29	129	36	165

The Society for the Reformation of Juvenile Delinquents, in Account Current with Cornelius Du Bois, Treasurer.

Dr.

Date		$	cts.
1829 Jan. 1 to 1830 Jan. 1	To Cash, Repairs and additions to the buildings upon the premises,	$513	10
	" Clothing, for the Children	1157	26
	" Food and Provisions, for the Children	3872	71
	" Furniture, Beds Bedding, &c.	601	84
	" School and Hospital Expenses, Books, Paper, Stationary, Medicine, &c.	955	94
	" Coal, Wood, Oil, Stoves, Pipes, and fixtures,	926	16
	" Horse, Cows, &c. for the use of the Institution,	335	70
	" Salaries of the Superintendent, Assistants, Schoolmaster, Matron, &c.	3749	85
	" Premium of Insurance against Fire on the buildings,	92	88
	" Interest on Money loaned to support the Institution,	30	33
	" Printing Annual Report, Account Books, Stationary, &c.	98	76
	To Balance carried down,	5797	12
		$18131	65

Cr.

Date		$	cts.
1829	By Balance in the Treasury	766	86
Jan. 1 to 1830 Jan. 1	By Cash, grant from the Legislature of the State of New-York, for 1829,	2000	00
	By Cash received for the Labor of the Children in the different Work Shops	2115	83
	By Nett amount received from collection of Donations and Subscriptions from the Citizens of New-York	1417	29
	By Cash from Marine Hospital Fund, towards the annual support of the House of Refuge, (a part of the Surplus Funds arising from a tax upon Foreign Passengers,	6000	00
	By Cash, tax upon three Theatres,* ($500 each,)	1500	00
	By Cash, tax upon 2842 Tavern Licences, and Licences to sell ardent spirits,* ($1¼ each.)	4263	00
	By Cash, for horse, &c. sold,	68	67
		$18131	65
1830 Jan. 1	By Balance brought down, († See note 2, next page.)	$5797	12

* See note 1, on the following page.

* NOTE 1—*Upon Tax on Tavern Licences, and Theatres.*

It will be noticed in the preceding statistics, how large a proportion of the Parents of children sent to the Refuge, are *intemperate:* more than one *half* of the whole number: viz. of 690 children received, 401 of their parents drink ardent spirits to excess. The examination and histories of the children, furnish the melancholy fact, that upwards of 150 children of both sexes, commenced stealing, and other vices, for the purpose of being furnished with the means to frequent Theatres, and to obtain Rum.--There are now *two children* in the Refuge, (of the ages of 12 and 14 years,) who were previous to being sent there, in the daily practice of drinking from 8 to 12 glasses of rum or whiskey, and one of them has drunk *a quart of ardent spirits* in a day, when they were successful in pilfering property, which could be exchanged for it, or which they could sell for the value of 20 to 30 cents.

† NOTE 2—*In relation to the balance of Funds on hand.*

The Building at the Refuge, appropriated for the Boys, has 128 Dormitories, or sleeping rooms. It will be noticed in the "Weekly Report of the number of boys in the House," that a larger number has constantly been in the Institution during the past year, than could be accomodated with *separate* sleeping cells, (an object very important in the system of Reformation,) and that from 6 to 20 of the smaller Boys, have been compelled to sleep upon the floors of the School-hall, (for the want of additional accommodations,) which is very unsafe, inconvenient and unhealthy. At several periods, during the past year, the managers were obliged (reluctantly) to notify the police and commissioners of the Alms House, to withhold sending Boys to the Refuge, not having accommodations for them. The interest of the Institution requires an additional building, for sleeping apartments, an eating room, and bake house. And the managers have authorised their Acting Committee to contract for the erection of a building, to connect the two present houses, which will furnish accomodations for 100 more Boys. The Building will probably be ready to be occupied by the 1st of May next, and will cost, furnished, (from estimates received) about 8000 Dollars: which will absorb all the funds now on hand, and the balance will have to be paid from the receipts of the year 1830.

Officers of the Society.

CADWALLADER D. COLDEN, *President.*

STEPHEN ALLEN,
CORNELIUS DUBOIS,
JOHN GRISCOM,
HENRY I. WYCKOFF,
JAMES LOVETT,
PETER SHARPE, } *Vice Presidents.*

CORNELIUS DUBOIS, *Treasurer.*
FREDERICK SHELDON, *Secretary.*

JOHN STEARNS, M. D.
ANSEL W. IVES, M. D. } *Physicians and Surgeons.*

House of Refuge.

NATHANIEL C. HART, *Superintendent.*
RICHARD WYMOND, *Assistant Superintendent.*
REBECCA ORAM, *Matron.*
SARAH ANN ORAM, *Assistant Matron.*
DAVID TERRY, Jun. *Teacher.*

Indenturing Committee.

ROBERT C. CORNELL,
NATHANIEL RICHARDS,
JAMES LOVETT.

Acting Committee.

WILLIAM W. FOX,
MYNDERT VAN SCHAICK,
RUFUS L. LORD,
JOHN HUNTER,
ROBERT D. WEEKS,
FREDERICK A. TRACY,
JACOB HARVEY.

Managers.

STEPHEN ALLEN,
HEMAN AVERILL,
ARTHUR BURTIS,
C. D. COLDEN,
ROBERT C. CORNELL,
CORNELIUS DUBOIS,
WILLIAM W. FOX,
JOHN GRISCOM,
JOHN HUNTER,
JOHN E. HYDE,
JACOB HARVEY,
ANSEL W. IVES,
JAMES LOVETT,
RUFUS L. LORD,
WILLIAM F. MOTT,
HUGH MAXWELL,
DENNIS M'CARTHY,
RALPH OLMSTED,
NATH'L RICHARDS,
FRED'K SHELDON,
PETER SHARPE,
JOHN STEARNS,
M. VAN SCHAICK,
HENRY I. WYCKOFF,
JOHN W. WYMAN,
SAMUEL WOOD,
RUSSEL H. NEVINS,
J. I. ROOSEVELT, Jun.
FREDERICK A. TRACY,
ROBERT D. WEEKS,
WILLIAM L. STONE.

Ladies' Committee.

REBECCA M'COMB,
SOPHIA WYCKOFF,
ANN WARNER,
DEBORAH L. EMBREE,
ALMY CORNELL,
MARGARET BEERS,
ANN L. MOTT,
ISABELLA BULOID,
PHEBE MOTT,
CHARLOTTE L. FOX,
SARAH C. HAWXHURST,
MARIA L. HYDE,
MARTHA WILLIS,
ESTHER SEYMOUR.

SIXTH ANNUAL REPORT, &c.

1831.

The Managers of the House of Refuge, proceed to lay before the "Society for the Reformation of Juvenile Delinquents," the Sixth Annual Statement of the Institution committed to their charge. It would be an easy task for the Managers, at the present time, to extend their Report by a renewed, or an enlarged exposition of the nature and importance, of the system of Juvenile Reform, which has now been steadily prosecuted by them, throughout a period of six years. But, so fully have these points been illustrated, by the early Reports and publications of the Society, and so distinctly were they recapitulated in the last Annual Report, that it is deemed to be altogether inexpedient, at the present time, to occupy the attention of the Society, or the public, with a repetition of these arguments. The minds of all those of our citizens, who have taken the trouble to read our Reports, and to examine, deliberately, the question of a Juvenile Penitentiary, distinct from that of adults, and governed in conformity to the clear distinctions which separate the two classes of public offenders, will, we confidently believe, unite with one voice, in the importance of such a distinction. If there are any of our fellow citizens, whose judgment and character, claim for them an influence in the community, who have declined their assent, to the value of such an institution as ours, we venture to believe, that they are among those who have never visited our establishment, and examined the history of its inmates.

It is no small satisfaction to the Managers, to be able to say, that the experience they have gained, in the knowledge of juvenile crime, and the causes which lead to it, have greatly tended to increase their convictions, of the humanity and necessity of such a charity.

They are not aware, that any of their anticipations have proved too sanguine—that any of those expectations, which, prior to the foundation of the Refuge, rested chiefly upon theoretic views, have been disappointed or defeated. There was nothing in the scheme, which suggested such a mode of relief, for some of the most alarming evils, which have proved to be of an impracticable nature.

The incomparably greater influence of moral and religious treatment, over the minds and habits of the young, than in the case of adult criminals, has been amply confirmed. The prospect of being able to rescue hundreds of children and youth, of the finest natural endowments, from almost inevitable ruin, has been fully realised. The possibility of inculcating a love of literary improvement, and habits of industry and honesty, upon the idle and profligate, has been well established. The readiness with which even young boys can be taught mechanic arts, has been demonstrated in our work shops. The advantage of appropriating from two to four hours per day, to literary instruction, has been manifest by the progress in spelling, reading, and writing, of many of the boys, who otherwise would have remained destitute of this knowledge, throughout their lives. The efficacy of religious instruction in meliorating the character, and changing the dispositions, of some of the most abandoned youth, has most clearly appeared, by their good conduct after leaving the Refuge, and by their grateful acknowledgements, that it had been to them, as an ark of safety, and a rescue from destruction. The short history of our establishment, has proved, that it is possible to convert juvenile thieves and vagrants, gamblers, and pick-pockets, the most profane and abandoned, into honest farmers, good sailors, ingenious and faithful mechanics. It has also proved, that a House of Refuge, while it effects these salutary changes in the character of its subjects, is nevertheless, a house of improvement. It has thus gained for itself, a name in the community, well known throughout the various ranks of juvenile depravity. Its name imposes a wholesome terror upon disobedient and vicious youth; and it appears evident, to the managers, from the small number of commitments which they now receive from the city police, and the Court of Sessions, compared with those of the Commissioners of the Alms House, that the influence of the Refuge, is highly auspicious to the peace of the city, and the security of our dwellings. It is an institution also, which with other concommitant circumstances, enables its managers to trace to their earliest effects, the causes of those crimes, which in their punishment, occasion to the municipal and State governments, so heavy an expense of time, and labor, and taxation; and it must be, by a judicious attention to facts, thus developed, that the criminal laws of a country, can be made to approximate the most nearly to a perfect system of prevention and cure. The Managers therefore, beg leave to invite the attention of the Society, as opportunities occur, to the record of cases on the books of the Refuge, a number which have been printed in the Annual Reports.

They would earnestly invite all respectable citizens, who entertain doubts of the value of this institution, to visit the Refuge,—to witness, on working days, the activity and ingenuity of the young mechanics—the order and economy of the table—the good condition of the School, and, on the Sabbath, the decency and devotion of the Chapel; and then seriously to inquire, whether it is possible, by any other mode, to lay the needful restraint upon the vicious propensities of young criminals,—of children, corrupted or abandoned by their parents,—to reform their habits, and to train them to usefulness and respectability.

So obvious is the necessity, and so palpable the benefits of a reformatory for Juvenile delinquents, in every populous city. It is well known, that the principles upon which our House of Refuge is conducted, have been approved in all parts of the Union, and that similar establishments are now in operation in Boston and Philadelphia, and that humane individuals in Baltimore, have taken some steps for the erection of one in that city.

Since the last Annual Report, the Managers have completed an additional building of stone, 120 feet by 38, and three stories high, which, besides other important accommodations, affords 138 additional dormitories; and being constructed with a view to greater security than those previously in use, they are much better adapted to the nightly confinements of older and larger boys, and will thereby supply a want, which has long been felt.

The Managers cannot well avoid again calling the attention of those who may favor this Report with a perusal, to the two most fertile sources of juvenile profligacy and crime—the Theatres and Grog Shops. Very few are the instances on their books, which do not go to demonstrate, that the earliest departure from honesty and filial duty, is immediately connected with, if it does not result from, the allurements of those two capital sources of "*public amusements*." They are emphatically, the Scylla and Charybdis of the current of life, to the youth of this metropolis. Could we abstract from the various incentives to evil which abound in the city, the vicious excitement produced by these places of resort; we know of nothing, which could be found as a substitute, that would be productive of half the amount of crime and misery which so evidently result from them.

In the preceding remarks, we have endeavored to give a brief general view of the prosperous condition, and the moral effects of the Institution. But there are some points, respecting which, it will be necessary to descend more into particulars.

The cause of elementary instruction, has been prosecuted as usual, in both departments of the Refuge, and with flattering success. The Sunday schools have likewise been continued, and, it is believed, with happy results. The course of religious and biblical instruction, which it is the primary object of Sunday schools to impart, may be counted first among the means of effecting a reformation of vicious youth. Among numbers of the inmates, there have been decided evidences, not only of outward reformation, but of sincere piety. And it is hoped that numerous others, who do not afford a confident hope of such a change, previously to their departure from the Refuge, will carry thence many precious lessons from the scriptures, which will be freshly remembered, and productive of much good, in after years. In aid of the religious instruction given, the Managers have to acknowledge the receipt of donations of Bibles, from the Young Men's Bible Society. It would be a work of supererogation, at this day, to urge the necessity of continuing these schools, and rendering them as interesting and effective as possible. But were it otherwise, and should we attempt to illustrate their utility and importance, and to show the close affinity existing between vice and crime, it would only be necessary for the Managers to state, that of the commitments during the last year, of boys alone, fifty-five could not read a syllable. Fifteen of this number knew not a letter of the alphabet. The ages of these latter, were from eight to sixteen—averaging eleven and a half years. The remaining forty were from ten to sixteen years of age, averaging twelve and a half.

In speaking of the House of Refuge in his late Message to the Legislature, His Excellency the Governor remarks:—"The funds provided by the Government, are ample for all the purposes of the institution." This declaration of the Chief Magistrate, whose views and feelings are decidedly in favor of the institution, when taken in connexion with the present embarrassing condition of our Treasury, seems to require some explanation from the Managers. The erection of the large new building already referred to, required heavy disbursements. This addition to our accommodations, was already necessary to the enlarged and increasing usefulness of the institution; but the law of the last session of the Legislature, authorising the Governor to transfer minors from the state prisons to the House of Refuge, rendered the new edifice indispensable to the comfort, convenience, and safety of the establishment. For the means of paying for its construction, the Managers have confidently relied upon the funds by law appropriated to their use, but which, without the knowledge of His Excellency the Governor, as it is presumed, have for many months been retained in the hands of the Mayor, under the direction, (as regards far the greater sum,) of the Common Council. The funds here referred to, are those derived from the additional excise imposed by the act of 1829, upon the grocers and tavern keepers of this city, for the especial benefit and support of the House of Refuge; and likewise the money derived from the licences of theatres, circuses, &c. Every member of the Society is probably aware of the fact, that the constitutionality of this additional excise upon the venders of ardent spirits, has been contested by those required to pay it; and although the tax was collected, yet the money has been withheld by order of the Common Council, and is to be withheld, until the question in litigation shall have been finally disposed of. In order to save expenses, however, and bring the question to a more speedy decision, a case was made up in the first instance, and submitted, by consent of parties, to the Supreme Court; by which tribunal the constitutionality of the law has been sustained, and judgment awarded in behalf of the House of Refuge. That such would be the decision of this enlightened tribunal, the Managers never entertained a doubt; and on hearing of the decision, they supposed the money would be paid over without further difficulty or delay. But they have been disappointed in this reasonable expectation; and because of an intimation, (though as yet unofficial, as your Managers believe,) that the cause is to be carried up to the Court of Errors by an appeal, His Honor the Mayor still withholds the money from our treasury, to the amount of between four and five thousand dollars, of which the Managers are in the utmost need.

The amount due the institution, accruing from licences granted to theatres and circuses, is twelve hundred and fifty dollars. No constitutional difficulty has been raised by those who have taken these licences. Nor do any pending or threatened legal proceedings afford an excuse for retaining the money from the House of Refuge. But his Honor the Mayor, and, as it is understood, without the direction of the Common Council, has thus far declined paying it over, upon the ground that, under the best opinion he has been able to form, if the additional excise upon grocers and tavern licences is unconstitutional, so also must be the tax upon places of public amusement. His Honor therefore expresses a determination to retain these moneys also in his hands, until the question involved in another, and, as your Managers believe, a very different and distinct case, shall have been definitively adjudicated.

In stating the foregoing facts, the Managers feel that they have been in the discharge of their duty, not only to the Society in whose service they are engaged, but to the Chief Magistrate of the state, and to the government by which it has been so liberally endowed. But in doing so, they would by no means be understood as questioning the motives of the Mayor. Still, they cannot but regret the embarrassments to which they have been subjected by these unexpected proceedings. Their treasury is not only empty, but they have been compelled to draw upon the private funds of their treasurer, to the amount of upwards of three thousand five hundred dollars.

No apprehension, however, is entertained by the Managers, as to the ultimate result of the legal controversy mentioned above; but every week of delay must necessarily add to their pucuniary difficulties. The constitutionality of the law has been sustained, not only by the opinions of men of great legal eminence, but by the ablest judges on the bench. But while the Managers feel it to be unnecessary to enter upon any argument as to the equity of the law, they are constrained to repeat their belief, that it is the consumption of ardent spirits, and the influence of the theatres, which contribute, more than all other causes, to the numbers sent to the Refuge. Intemperate parents, being unfit for the care and management of their children, suffer them to grow up in idle and vicious habits—the criminal infirmity of the parents, too often begets a like infirmity in the children, while the pestilent atmosphere of the theatre, conspires to hasten the work of destruction.

Although the Managers feel that they have but little to fear from such an application, yet they have learned with regret, that a renewed effort is to be made during the present session of the Legislature, to deprive the treasury of the House of Refuge, of the monies hitherto, during the last few years, derived from the Health Commissioners' department—being a comparatively small portion of the receipts from passengers arriving in this port. The pretext under which it is hoped to deprive the Refuge of this portion of its revenue, is the old and unfounded complaint, that it is encroaching upon the contributions of mariners, and perverting their hospital money to a purpose foreign to that for which such contributions were originally, and are yet professedly levied. This is by no means a fair or correct statement of the case, as the members of this society, the public, and the Legislature, must all by this time very well know. It would be unnecessary, were it otherwise proper, to go into the argument here. The facts are simply these: The hospital funds, so called, are derived as well from *passengers* as *mariners*. Nay, the receipts from passengers will always approximate near, if they do not swell beyond, the amount derived from the mariners Such has been the fact for several years past; and during the year now just closed upon us, it is estimated that the receipts from passengers alone, will amount to nearly thirty thousand dollars—say twenty-eight thousand. The act of the Legislature of 1829, appropriates the sum of eight thousand dollars from the moneys so collected, and no more. So that the hospital fund will have received about twenty thousand dollars during the past year, from passengers alone, over and above the amount paid to the House of Refuge, and in addition to the contributions of the mariners; for, notwithstanding the clamors upon this subject, it is nevertheless a fact, that not one dollar of the money arising from such contributions, has ever been asked for, or received, by the Refuge. Nor is there any more reason, so far as your Managers can perceive, why the mariners should exclusively enjoy the benefits accruing from the contributions of the *passengers* arriving at this port, than there is that the latter should in some way participate in the benefits of the tax upon the former. But there *is* a very substantial reason why the House of Refuge should receive a portion of these funds. By referring to the series of the Annual Reports of this Society, it will be seen that a very large proportion of the inmates of the Refuge, are the children of foreigners—

of the same passengers who have contributed towards this fund. Of one hundred and forty-four inmates committed during the past year, sixty only were children of American parents, while eighty-four were children of foreigners. Of these forty-one were of Irish, and twenty-three of English extraction—the countries, which, more than all others, have contributed to the fund of which we are speaking. This simple statement of facts is deemed amply sufficient to prove the peculiar propriety of the enactment of the State Legislature, which appropriate a part of the revenues thus accruing, to the House of Refuge.

There is one other subject to which, though a matter of some delicacy, the Managers feel constrained to invite the attention, not only of the members of the Society, but of the community at large, and of the state government. Whenever it has so happened that fresh depredations have been committed upon the property of individuals, or the peace of the public, by persons who may have formerly been inmates of the Refuge, the cases have been eagerly seized upon by certain persons, who, from interested or some other motives not apparent, are opposed to the institution, magnified beyond measure, and employed as means of exciting unfriendly feelings towards the Institution, and distrust as to its utility. Such, in particular, has been the fact on two occasions during the past year, viz: on the return of a couple of sailor-boys last summer, who had been inmates of the Refuge, and in the recent case before the Court of Sessions, of John Lace. In regard to the former, the Managers are persuaded, that the larceny charged upon one of them, was imputed to him by mistake. He had most worthily performed a long sea-voyage, and returned here with his earnings in his pocket, to visit his relatives, and in particular to thank the Superintendent of the Refuge, for his kindnesses towards him. He was moreover, at this very time, under a profitable engagement for a second whaling expedition, upon which he is now absent. The case of Lace was a hard one from the beginning. When first thrown upon the hands of the managers, and conveyed to the Refuge, he was old and skilful in crime. Indeed his case was one of the few which seemed altogether hopeless in the outset: and it is now several years since he left the Refuge. He was bound out to a trade, but soon ran away from his master, and has at length found a situation in the State Prison, where he ought to have been in a state of discipline long since. But is it just or generous to raise a clamour against an institution of this peculiar description, on account of three or four, or even of a dozen unfortunate cases? There have been eight hundred and thirty Juvenile Delinquents received into the Refuge, since its commencement, six years ago. Six hundred and fifty of these have been disposed of in different ways;—and is it to be supposed that in so great a number, a thorough moral reformation could, by human means, have been wrought in every one? Such a general and radical transformation, it is apprehended, however desirable, could not have been produced, save by the immediate and visible interposition of Divine Power. It is to be recollected, however, that when the Refuge was founded, it was an experiment. There was no other institution of the kind in America; and errors both in judgment and practice were to be expected, until time and experience should have enabled the Managers to discover the most wholesome principles upon which to build their moral edifice, and to devise the best practical system for the effective administration of its affairs. When moreover, its doors were first opened, and for a year or two thereafter, many of the larger classes of the delinquents sent to the Refuge, were already adepts in crime, and not a few of them had previously been in the penitentiary, once, twice, and in some cases, even thrice. Was it reasonable, then we repeat, to suppose, that in each and every of these cases, a radical, perfect, and permanent reformation was possible;—or, in default of having effected such reformation, in such cases, is it just to question or deny the utility of the institution? If so, the age of human perfectibility might have been considered very near, since nothing more would have been necessary to banish sin and shame, crime and sorrow, than to transform all the dwellings in the world into houses of Refuge for Juvenile Delinquents. But notwithstanding the disadvantages which all new and untried establishments for improving the moral and intellectual condition of man, must encounter, and in despite of other untoward circumstances, so far from the existence of any just cause of censure or disappointment, the wonder is, that so much has been accomplished; that so many hopeful reformations have taken place; that so much real, substantial, and, to all human appearance, enduring good, has been effected. If the Managers of this institution can already point to hundreds of cases, in which idle and dissolute, and even criminal, children, of both sexes, have been reclaimed—snatched, as it were from the steep leading to inevitable destruction,—and moulded into well-behaved, sober, moral, industrious and modest young artizens, farmers, seamen, seamstresses, &c,—some of them already grown up, married, and respectably settled in life,—then surely may the Institution appeal with confidence, to the favor and support of the public. That such have been the fruits of the salutary moral and religious discipline of the House of Refuge, and in very numerous instances, too, its archives are supplied with abundant testimony to prove. A portion of this testimony, which is constantly accumulating, has been laid before the Society, from year to year, in its annual reports; and some additional items of evidence to the same effect, are hereunto annexed. That some of the inmates have proved irreclaimable, and that others, after an apparent reformation—speaking contrition for the past, and promising well for the future,—have again relapsed into immoral and vicious practices, the Managers feel no disposition to conceal or deny. But such cases, they are warranted in saying, are comparatively rare—comprising but a small proportion of the whole number who have fallen under the care of the institution. On the contrary, if the assurances of their officers are to be believed, some of the finest young seaman in the navy, have been taken from the Refuge. Others have been entered in the whaling business, to the entire satisfaction of their employers, and with profit to themselves. There has been general good conduct among these, and some of them are at the present time engaged as officers in that hardy and lucrative service.. Others, again, are seamen, engaged in different branches of commercial enterprise; and one of the reformed inmates of this Institution, has recently sailed from one of our ports, the second mate of an Indiaman. Many are now engaged, under very favorable circumstances, as apprentices in the art of husbandry. The term of service of some has expired, and they have grown up respectable young men. One of these has married, and settled down a good citizen. Some of the number have become respectable mechanics. One of these, a very hard, but ultimately a very interesting case, became decidedly devout while in the Refuge. His whole temper and disposition were changed to mildness and docility. He was bound out to a trade—has acquired it—and having married a respectable girl, is now established, and engaged in the successful prosecution of a lucrative business. Several cases have occurred, where young girls, guilty of different offences, have been thoroughly reclaimed from the paths of iniquity. Of these, some have been bound to service at distant places in the country, where their deportment was in all respects so excellent, that they have married respectably, and are now discharging the duties of affectionate and virtuous wives and mothers. And the reports from great numbers of others, of both sexes, whose periods of service have not expired, are of the most gratifying, and even animating description. With these facts before us, is there not much cause for rejoicing that Providence has in such numerous instances, smiled upon the labors of this institution! And is there not large encouragement for the continuance of our exertions, in a cause which has already been attended with such gratifying results, and which is so rich in promise for the future!

In conclusion, the Managers have only to express the very great obligations they are under to the ladies who have the supervision of the Female Department of the Refuge, for their continued and efficient services in that interesting branch of this important public charity. It is peculiarly pleasant to contemplate the spirit of philanthropy, resting upon virtuous and accomplished women, enabling them, as her ministers, to forego the luxuries and refinements of elegant homes, to watch over the management of an institution like the House of Refuge—filled, as it must be, with beings often rendered loathsome by their vices and their crimes, and seeking to bring back the erring wanderer to the paths of virtue, and to elevate even the most degraded to a state of comparative moral purity. It is woman who invests charity with her most beautiful drapery, while her deeds of beneficence increase her own loveliness. Could there be an excess of true charity, woman would be prodigal; "but in charity there is no excess; neither can man or angel come in danger by it."

To the physicians of the institution, likewise, Doctors STEARNS and CARTER, the thanks of the Managers are eminently due, for their gratuitous services rendered during the past year, in the hospital of the Refuge.

Confidently relying upon the continuance of the public and legislative favor, and determined to spare no exertions themselves to render this institution, if not all that can be desired, at least much more than could, a very few years since, have been anticipated by the most sanguine, the Managers close their sixth year's labors, with the consolation arising from what they have believed a faithful discharge of their public duty, and are prepared to enter upon the seventh with renewed confidence, and with still brighter prospects of success in proportion to their means.

APPENDIX.

LETTER FROM THE SUPERINTENDENT.

In reply to a note addressed by the Committee appointed to prepare this Report, to the Superintendent of the Refuge, requesting the necessary facts and documents to be incorporated therein, the following letter was received with the other papers. It was not written for publication; but as it embraces many statements proper for the public eye, the Committee have thought it advisable to include it in this Appendix.

"You ask, gentlemen, the causes of the commitment of our inmates. I would first refer you to the number of intemperate parents ascertained—doubting not, but if the truth was known, there are many more of this class than the parents of the sixty-three I have mentioned. The consequence is, the children are neglected, and suffered to run about the streets, to form acquaintance and connexion with older and idly trained boys and girls. They next begin to pilfer—sleep out nights, around the market places, &c.; and as their depravity naturally leads them from one step of vice to another, they begin to find the power of money, not only to gratify their appetites, but by degrees are led to different places of amusement, which in their nature are very seducing. Indulgence does but create stronger dispositions to obtain the means for attending Circuses, Theatres, &c., and we rarely receive a child of any years, which is not quite familiar with either the one or the other, or both. We have one of the strongest instances of the infatuation produced by theatrical amusements, in a boy now in the House, that we recollect to have witnessed. He is a youth of highly respectable parentage, and his father had the means and disposition to give him a liberal education. Much pains and expense were expended to qualify him for college, and he actually entered one of those seminaries, where he spent part of two sessions. But while quite young, he was taken to the theatre, by a person unknown to his parents, and continued to attend there for a length of time, before it was discovered by them. When it became known to them, they set their faces strongly against it;—but such was his propensity thitherward, that, in the first instance, if means could not be obtained, he would sell his school books—then his mother's silver spoons, and books from his father's library; and when these were not obtainable, would change away his best clothes for inferior ones, to obtain the difference, for the purpose of gratifying himself in these amusements. It had such an influence upon him, as to become a perfect infatuation. He would not attend to his literary pursuits, and would stop at nothing to obtain money, that he might indulge his passion. To prevent greater disgrace, his friends interfered, and had him sent here. We have not discovered that this youth is beset by any other propensity. And had it not been for this, there is no probability that his parents' hearts would have been wounded in so tender a point, and one of our colleges would doubtless now have had one more respectable and promising young man enrolled upon its catalogue. And while we look over our large family, we see many under our care, who, had they been blessed with sober and industrious parents, would doubtless have made such children as we all would have been proud of, had they been sons of our own. We consider the inculcation and practice of industrious habits, a powerful means of restoring to a good state of feeling, this young class—connected with those moral and religious precepts taught in the Bible. Notwithstanding we do not always see the fruits of religious instruction; still, feeling the influence of a kind father's precepts and example upon my own mind, we pursue our labors cheerfully, believing the impressions will be lasting and powerful in more mature age.

"Of the larger and more hopeless class, we have sent them on long voyages to sea, where they will arrive to manhood in this honest and industrious calling—hoping that on their return, those bubbles and toys, that in their youth glistened in their eyes like the diamond, will have lost their charms. Some, it is true, have disgraced themselves, and brought sorrow to the hearts of the managers of this institution, who devote much of their time by day and by night, for the interest of these unfortunate Juvenile Delinquents, without fee or reward, other than the satisfaction they must experience, at having done all in their power to reclaim and to save them, by placing them in a way to obtain a respectable and honest livelihood. Yet, on the other hand, they are cheered to see now and then a hearty and hardy Tar return from his voyage—and passing even his own relatives to come up with his certificate of good conduct from his captain, or the merchant, first to greet his kind benefactors at the Refuge. I now recollect two boys who once afforded but little hope. They are now mates of ships out of this port, one of whom is entrusted with large amounts of valuable property, and is considered to be a young man of the strictest integrity.

"As to the children occasionally returned upon our hands, while we are compelled to say some are unworthy of the stations they were placed in—yet with all the vigilance and industry of our Indenturing Committee, who spare no pains to obtain information, not only of the respectability, but fitness of the families of persons applying to them for apprentices from the Refuge, yet sometimes children are unhappily located—or more is expected from them than it is reasonable to require of children of their age. A striking instance at this moment occurs to my mind. A gentleman of respectability obtained a little girl. His family became so dissatisfied with her, that the gentleman put her out to board for a short time, until he could make application to the Indenturing Committee, and have an opportunity of returning her to the Refuge, which he did with an appearance of strong dislike, &c. All were fully satisfied that his complaints were without just grounds, and after retaining her a few months, another favorable opportunity offered to send her to the West. After she had been out several months the second time, the gentleman's brother came (a few days since) nearly three miles, to tell us how highly his brother and family were pleased with the little girl, and that she was the admiration of the neighborhood.

"From one neighborhood in Massachusetts, we have lately had an account from five boys, who are all doing well, and were very much beloved. In one place in Connecticut, six of our boys are all doing well; and, gentlemen, I could fill a little volume with interesting facts like the foregoing, as we always keep an account of parentage, former life, conduct in the House, reports from their masters after being indentured, and even after they are free, married and settled in business, with great care and precision, and have now rising eight hundred of these histories of cases that have fallen to our care. I will close by furnishing you with a few extracts from the books of the past year, showing the effects of this beneficent public charity.

"Respectfully yours,

N. C. HART."

SELECTION OF CASES AND LETTERS

From Apprentices, and from Persons to whom Apprentices have been bound.

BOYS.

September 18, 1829

C. D., from a court of Oyer and Terminer, held in Albany, in and for the county of Albany, aged 18 years the 11th inst., born on the island of Guernsey, of English parents; his mother died in Guernsey, twelve or thirteen years ago; his father moved to P. several years since. Not long after, moved back to V. Some short time previous to his father's death, he had put C. D. as an apprentice to Mr. ——, where he continued four years; had learned the trade so that he could make cream cups, silver spoons, &c.—became acquainted with a boy about 15 years of age. M. C. proposed leaving that place for the north; C. D. said he had no money; C. replied that he had sixty dollars. They started the 7th of June last. The first stop they made was with P. M. in Broadway, four days; they then went to Albany, put up with Mr. J. They stayed there about a week, and then cleared out without paying their board; went to Troy, put up with Mr. P. three days, paid their board and started for Waterford: put up with Mr. H. F. a short time, and cleared without paying their bill. They then started for Albany, took lodgings with Mr. C., told him they had no money, but they were to write to Washington for some; stopped one week, walked out to Rensselaer Ville, and put up with C. T. Not having any cash, they were asked for money; C. D. pawned his watch, which, according to calculation, would defray their expenses for several days, (subject to be redeemed for $8); but in about two days they arose before day, contrived to get into the bar room, took the landlord's pocket book containing $12 50 cents in cash, and several promissory notes. C., as it rained, helped himself to a cloak, and on they started, (this was the 4th of July.) They were pursued and taken near Cocyman's Landing, with the money on them, having thrown away the pocket book and papers. C. was bailed out for $500; went home, and forfeited the bond. C. D. remained and was found guilty, and sentenced here. He says during the four years that he was with his master, he in a few instances picked up scraps, made gold rings and sold them; his master knew of it twice, but only reproved him. Entered the 8th class.

On the re-examination which took place, I judge about three months after the foregoing, he says that he was a bad boy, would play truant from school, &c.; feels deeply impressed that his bad conduct was the leading cause of his father's death, and shows much contrition for his past misconduct.

When this boy first came here, he was very troublesome, and showed a strong disposition to avail himself of the first opportunity to make his escape, and gave us much anxiety; but in a few months, we can truly say, the Lion became (from every appearance) a Lamb; he became humble and pliable, of a quiet and meek spirit; a lover of his Bible and of his closet; would gather the smaller boys around him during play hours, in the school hall, read some good book, and converse so sweetly about good things, that he had much influence with them; as he was large and somewhat advanced in years, we felt it our duty to give him a fair probation. He was in due time, indentured to a Blacksmith in U. I saw a gentleman from that neighborhood, who informed me that he was an admirable boy, his life was an example for the neighborhood.

The following is the copy of a letter from E. F., a little Irish boy, whose father is dead, and whose mother is very intemperate: in consequence of which she was expelled her humble abode, not being able to pay her rent; they were found in the street, without house or home, by the Commissioners. This boy having been guilty of some little improprieties, was sent here as a vagrant, in July, 1828; and in about nine months was indentured to Mr. B. M., farmer of M.

M. December 7, 1830.

"My Dear Mother.—Your letter dated the 26th of January last, was received by my friend, Mr. M., it has given me great pleasure. I have been well through summer and fall: I have attended Sunday School regularly; I am well pleased with my place; yet, dear mother, I wish you good health, and sister, and uncle, and friends; likewise I wish you to let me know how you are; I like my master and his family very well so far; I expect to go to day school this winter; I am going to have a suit of new clothes this christmas; I have learned to ride on horseback pretty well; I have plenty of good food and raiment; I have seen D. F., he is well, and lives two miles from us; if I live, and be a good boy, I expect to go to New-York, and see you and my sisters, and perhaps some of my friends too; we have had a very fine fall in this country; we are privileged with plenty of nuts and apples.

Mr. M., has a large fine ox, and when he takes him to New-York, he will be dressed with ribbons.

Dear mother, I give my best respects to all my friends and acquaintances. Dear mother don't give yourself any uneasiness on my account. I am hearty, well, and contented, and hope to see you again before long.

I remain your affectionate son.

E. F.

The following is at the bottom of E. F's letter, written by his master, Mr. M.

E. appears to be well pleased with his place, and we like him very well; we think he is full as smart, and trusty, as common for boys of his age. This letter is his own hand writing and composition.

Yours, &c.

N. C. Hart. B. M.

The following letter was received from G. S., who was indentured to a Mr. S., in D. Co., New-York, farmer, nearly four years ago, and may be interesting. His father is dead, and his mother is a poor, low, miserable drunkard.

Mr. N. C. Hart,—Dear Friend, I take this opportunity to write to you these few lines. I am well, and hope this will find you so too, and all my mates, and I hope they will all behave well, and get good places, and when they get them, I hope they will stick to them. I have stuck by Mr. S., and have "done as well as I knew how" so far. I have got the promise of a farm when my time is out. My dear mother, I hope, is well, and my brothers and sisters too. My time will soon be out, and I will come and see you all.

Mr. Hart, please write to me, and tell me where my mother and brothers and sisters are, and how they are doing. I should like to hear from all. Yours, &c. J. M.

[This poor boy's prospect of having a farm on shares when his time is out, connected with the tender interest manifested in behalf of his mother, brothers and sisters, comes home to our feelings. N. C. H.]

1826, Dec. 2, H. C., from the Commissioners, aged 15 years, born in New-York. He, commenced a wild career very young, was, by his father, turned over to the Commissioners of the Alms House as a vagrant. Alderman Burtis bound him out in the country. He soon ran away from his place, and returned to his father, who sent him to school; but he played truant about the streets. He was then put with a cabinet maker, as an apprentice, in a short time was sent with a piece of furniture, received the money, and ran away, and in fact he could not be kept by his father nor masters from running at large. He said his first theft was committed five years ago, by stealing a shilling from his father. He stole a silver watch from one of his father's boarders. In offering it for sale, he was mistrusted, and taken. The watch was obtained by the owner, and he severely punished by his father. Soon after, he procured a key that opened a trunk belonging to the same man from whom he had stolen the watch, where he found a sum of money in bank bills;—he took them, but was detected before he left the house. His father then locked him up for two or three months, and kept him on bread and water; but notwithstanding, he frequently afterwards pilfered small amounts from his father, and sometimes when sent on errands with money, would run away with it, and be gone from home several days at a time. The last time, he was absent a month, carrying wood, begging, &c., when his friends had him taken up, and sent here as a vagrant.

H. was not a bad dispositioned boy, nor was he very troublesome to manage; yet, after keeping him here two years and a half, we could not feel that confidence in his integrity, which warranted us in binding him out in the country. Consequently, in June, 1829, as an opportunity offered, he was sent on a whaling voyage.

The following is a copy of a letter sent by him to the Superintendent:

Sante Jago, July 23, 1830.

Mr. N. C. Hart,—Dear Friend, I take my pen in hand to inform you that I am well, and hope you enjoy the same blessing.

I am now on my second voyage;—when I return, I will come and see you. There being a brig near us bound to New-York, I thought it a favourable time to let you know where I was, and how I come on. I am hearty as a buck; I never will forget what you have done for me. I remember what you told me—"H, you are going to sea,* but remember there is seldom a rose without a thorn."

*At which he was very much pleased.

If I live, when I return I shall come and see you with pleasure. I saw J. M., who has gone round Cape Horn the second voyage. I am on board the same ship, the old Congress forever. We got last year, 1300 barrels of oil. We have three pots and four boats. We are determined to get a voyage. We are going to the Cape of Good Hope; of late we call it the Cape of Storms, where there is many a bitter blow. If we do not get a load, we are going to double the Cape, and cruise for the Spanish coast. We are in hopes to return by next March, with a full cargo of oil. When I return to Nantucket, I will let you know. I leave my blessing with you.

H. C., a Refuge boy in the ship C.

Feb. 18, 1830.

H. J. was received from the Police, aged 10 years, the 4th of July† last; born in New-York, of Irish parents. They are both dead, and he has been two years in the Orphan Asylum.

His sister, the wife of J. S., took him, thinking that she could do for him. But it appears that her husband drank. He received a coat to mend, which he pawned, and for which he was sued; he threw all the blame and disgrace upon his wife, wrongfully. Feeling herself so disgraced, she told her husband to clear out, and went herself to service. Consequently, the care of H. devolved on his brother T., a stone cutter; but he not being married, put him as an apprentice, first to G. W., a butcher, to whom he was so disobedient and saucy, that he would not keep him. Next his brother put him to live with a Mr. ——, a shoe maker, where he remained two weeks, and ran away. On application of his brother to the Police, they sent him here as a vagrant. He hardly knew his letters, and a more scurvy looking little object of pity, we have seldom received. But it was soon found, that all that he required to make him a first rate boy, was proper discipline, with regularity and some encouragement. He soon rose to the class of honor, and a more faithful, respectful, industrious child, we could not desire. In about nine months, he was indentured to ——, of ——, who has sent us the following letter:

Dec. 13, 1830.

Dear Sir,—I now sit down to drop you a few lines respecting the boy who was indented to me by you on the 23d of October last, and thereby fulfil my promise. As respects the boy, I certainly am much pleased with him; and as far as my observations have extended, must say, that his willingness to make himself useful, exceeds the ordinary run of boys. As yet, I have not selected a school for him, but think of doing so in a few days, as the winter is the most convenient time for me to spare him. He tells the family he would rather stay than return, notwithstanding he has to work hard. Should you, or any other person, who is, (or ought to be,) interested in the boy's welfare, be passing through this section of the country, I should like you to call.

Your Obedient Servant, ——

Mr. N. C. Hart, Superintendent of the House of Refuge.

August 21, 1829.

O. P., from a court of Special Sessions held in this city, aged 12

† When we cannot ascertain what month or day they were born, we always put it the 4th of July.—N. C. H.

years the 4th of July last, born in ——— County, of American parents. His father resides in ——— street; does occasionally drink too much. His mother died about four years ago. His father married again in about two years. He appears to have been at loose ends for some time. The boy has been in the practice of playing truant from school, running about the markets, &c. He commenced stealing by taking fruit from different markets, at different times, such as apples, peaches, melons, &c. Next he went into a cellar kitchen, with S. J., where a table was standing and took two small silver spoons, which they sold for three shillings: then a sleigh from another boy, which he sold for two shillings: then in company with his brother H. and others, two vests and a silk handkerchief: then again with S. J. in another cellar kitchen, two large silver spoons. He was taken up in offering them for sale. Could not read.

One of the largest of his associates has since been sent to State Prison, for Burglary, known as a leader and teacher of little boys in crime.

O. had been here but twelve days, before he secreted himself under the floor of one of the work-shops, with an intention to escape, for which he was punished; but it appears it had not its desired effect, for the sixth day following, bent on making his escape, being very active, he ran up a tin leader on the side of the house, got on the roof, down another tin leader, on the other side of the same building, and ran like a little deer, but was discovered by one of the Superintendent's domestics, was chased into a swamp, and re-taken in a few minutes. He was then locked up in solitude for several days on bread and water, which had its desired effect. He soon after, by his quiet, meek and respectful manners, connected with punctuality in the faithful performance of all his labor and duty, not only gained a high degree of esteem and confidence from his care-takers, but was esteemed by his fellows, whose society was courted by the first class of boys, was in due time promoted to the highest class of honor, by the unanimous vote of all his mates, which vote is always taken when offered by the Superintendent for so high a rank among his fellows, nor did he ever disgrace his badge while he remained in the House; but his former associates having been of a base kind, and his crimes having been considerable, for a little boy, it was thought proper to give him a pretty good probation in the Refuge.

After remaining in the House from the 21st of August, 1829, to the 8th of October, 1830, he was indentured to a respectable mechanic in D. C. who in a short time, being much pleased with his boy, has written to know if he could procure a girl from the Institution. After describing the age and qualifications of the girl he wants, he concludes by saying, "one of your choice girls, as you called the boy that I took from your Institution. And sir, I do really consider him a choice boy."—But his request was not granted, as the Managers think it imprudent, generally, to place two of our children in one family.

A few days since we received the following letter, in the boy's own hand writing, which is fair and every word spelt correctly.—

Mr. Hart.—As you requested me to write you, to inform you how I was pleased with my place and trade; I am certain I think you have obtained a good place and trade for me. Mr. B., puts me to work with a journeyman, who instructs me well. I attend to writing and arithmetic, evenings. You will not expect more the first time. I look to you for good advice.

My thanks to you and good wishes, and to my former co[illegible]ions.

Yours Truly,

O. P.

As we report one death during the year, in the House, it may be gratifying to some to have an account of the case.

His name was John Gillen—between 11 and 12 years of age. He was naturally a good dispositioned child, but his former habits were such as might be expected from a child living in one of the most abandoned parts of the city—without father or mother, or any other care-taker than an aunt, who wished him away from her, unless he could bring her some money. He was sent here by the Commissioners, on the 8th of August, 1829. About five months previous to his death, he was taken with the scarlet fever, which terminated in the consumption. During his illness, he was frequently admonished of his approaching dissolution, and of the necessity of a preparation to meet the change; and occasionally prayers were offered up with him, and he was pressed to look to his Redeemer for mercy; which, for some time, he was daily in the practice of. He appeared to die in a very happy frame of mind. A few minutes before his death, he was asked if he thought he should go to heaven. He answered, "I wish I was there now," and requested the children standing round his bed, to sing the following lines:

O how happy are they,
Who their Saviour obey,
And have laid up their treasure above;
Tongue can never express,
The sweet comforts and peace
Of a soul in its earliest love, &c.

He made an effort to join in singing; but his strength would not allow. After they had sung three verses, he strove to say something; but was too far gone, and immediately breathed his last, without a struggle or a groan.

GIRLS.

April 20, 1830.

G. H., from the Commissioners, aged 13 years the 13th of Oct. last, born in New-York of English parents. Her mother as well as her father, drank hard, and he quitted her and went to W. S. C. where he died a short time since.

This child says she was at loose ends, and had nothing but bad examples before her, running about the streets, forming acquaintance with loose girls, &c. Entered 8th Class.

From the time the child first came here, her deportment appeared to show that the bent of her mind was to reform, and to try to re-establish her character, by "doing as well as she knew how." She soon, not only gained the confidence of her care-takers, but their esteem and affections.

She was, the 19th of August, indentured to a pious family in O. C. who are delighted with the girl, and call her "a charming child."

May, 1828.

B. C., from the Commissioners, aged 7 years the 4th of July last: born in this country, of Irish father and English mother, who died about one year ago. Since which time, she and her sister, about eleven years of age, have been their father's principal housekeepers: he, by trade, is a soap boiler and starch manufacturer, and drinks very hard; when intoxicated is very cruel. The children thus having no one to look after them but a drunken father, would run about from place to place, forming acquaintances with wicked, swearing, thievish girls, who put them up to steal their father's goods and sell them—tear up his shirts and sell them for old rags. This course they kept until they found their way to the House of Refuge. This one did not know her letters. She being young, with proper management soon bid fair to make a desirable child; and an opportunity offered to place her in a good pious family, where we had no doubt she would be trained up in the way she should go. The Indenturing Committee ordered her Indentured in a few months. After remaining in her place about two years, the following letter was received.

December, 1830.

Dear Sir, Thinking you would be pleased to hear from B. C., whom we received from your institution about two years ago, I would inform you that she has enjoyed good health since that time, and has learned to *read*, knit and sew. Her conduct in general, has been good. She is perfectly contented with us, and does not express a wish to return to New-York.

Respectfully Yours, T. W.

F. G. H. from the Commissioners of the Alms House, aged 13 years the 10th of September last, born in New-York of American parents. Her father was a ship carpenter by trade; died about three years ago. Not long after, her mother commenced keeping a bad house in R. street, but removed to L. street, where after this course for nearly three years, she died, leaving three orphan daughters. This and the next youngest, about 11 years of age were taken charge of by girls of ill fame, where the Commissioners found them about a week after her mother's death. The youngest, about seven years of age, was taken possession of by her mother's washer-woman. When she first came here, she was very wild, exhibiting that kind of deportment, which was natural for her to acquire from the examples of lewd girls.

After a few months, she become very industrious and obedient, and gave much hope, that she would yet make a fine woman. The Ladies' Committee recommended, that she be indentured, when a suitable place in the country should offer. She was so indentured, to a gentleman residing in the state of Massachusetts, who has written the following letter, relative to the child.—

October 19, 1830.

Mr. Hart—Dear Sir,—It is with pleasure that I am able to state to you and the Board of Managers of the House of Refuge, that the girl that you bound to me last spring, has uniformly conducted herself with propriety, and to my satisfaction. From her conduct thus far, I trust, and think that she will prove to be superior to most girls. She appears to be pleased with her situation, and does not wish to return to New-York.

I am Dear Sir, Your Ob't Servant.

October 21, 1829.

A. B. a girl from the Police, aged 14 years, the 2d of April last. Born in S. N. J. Her father left her mother with ten children to look after, all of whom are now living.

A. B. left her mother contrary to her wishes, about twelve months ago, thinking that she could do better by herself. First lived three months with Mrs. H. at three dollars per month: next with Mrs. O. who kept a small shop nearly opposite, four months, at three dollars per month; then with her aunt, Mrs. R. about five months, at three dollars per month and other presents. * * *

Her going out so often without having any errand to do, raised the suspicions of her aunt and sister; this led her sister to watch her one evening, when she saw her join a stranger in her walk—headed her, and directed her to go home. Her aunt then interceded with the Police and had her sent here. Entered the eighth class.

Soon after she came here, she united with another girl in forming a plan to escape, but was detected and punished; after which, her deportment was very satisfactory; she became contented and satisfied, and would converse freely upon her condition and state, and manifested by degrees, much thoughtfulness.

It pleased Divine Providence, to visit the females in such a manner as to produce much religious excitement among the children, at which time A. B. became a subject of hopeful conversion, nor do we believe she ever swerved from the path of piety afterwards. Last summer she became quite indisposed, and her sickness baffled the skill of our Physicians. She loved her Bible, and was strict in her private devotions, and occasionally, while confined to her bed of affliction, would break out in humble but modest acclamations of praise to her Blessed Saviour—blessing God that she had ever seen the House of Refuge.

In September last, her friends made application to the Indenturing Committee, to return her to them; feeling, as they should do, a solicitude for their dying relative. It was granted. Some of the Ladies' Committee, the Matron, and myself, frequently called to see her—always found her in the same sweet and even frame of mind. A few days since she breathed her last, in the triumph of faith; blessing and praising her Maker, that ever she saw the House of Refuge, and came under the care of Mrs. Oram, the present matron. Her last request, was, that her friends should send for the Matron and Superintendent.

REPORT OF THE LADIES' COMMITTEE.

To the Managers of the House of Refuge, the Ladies' Committee respectfully Report—

That, since their last Annual Report, the Monthly Meetings of the Committee have been regularly held, and the House has been visited at least once in each week by sub-committees, appointed for that purpose. From the Minutes of these Committees a summary of which will be laid before the Managers, it appears, that, with the exception of a few months during which the matron was seriously indisposed, general good order has prevailed, and the usual routine of duties been well performed.

By the detailed Report appended to this, it will be seen, that in addition to the every-day occupations of cooking, washing, and mending their own and the boys' clothes, attending school, and family devotions, &c., the girls have made upwards of twenty-five hundred garments for themselves and the boys.

At the date of our last Annual Report, there were thirty-eight girls in the House; of whom twenty-three have been Indentured; two returned to the Commissioners of the Alms House—three to their parents—six released, being of legal age, and four remain in the House.

During the past year 31 girls, have been committed to the House, and 5 returned who had been indentured, *in previous years*: leaving 40 in the House at this time.

The exertions of the Matron to reform the habits and characters of the girls, have, we believe, been attended with salutary effects; an evidence of which is furnished by the fact, that in no previous year has there been so entire an exemption from gross misconduct in the female department of the Refuge.

The practice of committing to memory portions of the Holy Scriptures, and reciting them to the weekly Committees, is continued, and frequently furnishes opportunities for admonition and reproof, which we trust has not been without its share of influence in promoting the objects of the Institution. Indeed the neglect of this practice, has generally been accompained by a corresponding deviation from the rules of good order and propriety.

It cannot be doubted that there are in this city a large number of female children, destitute of the means of moral instruction, and exposed to the contaminating influence of corrupt example; and that their condition would be greatly improved and the community relieved, by placing them in the House of Refuge; we are so increasingly and deeply impressed with the importance of the subject, that we again call your attention earnestly to it. We do still indulge the hope that our Public Authorities may be induced to apply to this acknowledged evil, at least, a partial remedy—and earnestly desire that your exertions for the attainment of this object may not be relaxed.

In taking a retrospective view of their labors during the past year, the Ladies' Committee cannot but advert with feelings of regret to cases in which their efforts have been fruitless. These have not, however, been numerous, while, in many instances, the cheering reflection remains, that their labors have, with the Divine blessing, been crowned with success.

They are therefore encouraged to persevere in the good work, remembering the injunction, "In the morning sow thy seed, and in the evening withhold not thy hand, for thou knowest not which shall prosper."

SARAH C. HAWXHURST, *Secretary.*

12th mo. (December) 27th, 1830.

STATEMENTS.

		Subjects.
There were in the house when the last report was made, Boys,	128	
Girls,	38	
		166
Of those previously disposed of, there have been returned Boys,	20	
Girls,	5	
		25
Received during the past year, Boys,	113	
Girls,	31	
		144
		335
Of whom there have been indentured, Boys,	105	
Girls,	23	
		128
Returned to friends, Boys,	8	
Girls,	3	
		11
Returned to the Alms-House, Boys,	5	
Girls,	2	
		7
Of age, Girls,		6
To the General Sessions, Boys,		1
Deceased, (sick with consumption when received,) Boy,		1
Now in the House, Boys,	141	
Girls,	40	
		181
		335

The number of subjects received into the House of Refuge during the past year,

Boys,	113	
Girls,	31	
		144

Committed by the following authorities, viz:

Boys,—Commissioners of the Alms House	31		
Police of New-York county,	53		
Special Sessions of do.	1		
General Sessions of do.	10		
Erie County Sessions	3		
Albany county Sessions	3		
Kings County Sessions	7		
Herkimer County Sessions	1		
Auburn State Prison,	2		
Sing Sing State Prison,	1		
		113	
Girls,—Commissioners of Alms House,	17		
Police of New-York,	11		
Court of Special Sessions	1		
Albany County,	2		
		31	
			144

Of the above number, are children of

American Parentage,	60
Irish,	41
English,	23
German,	7
Scotch,	3
Italian,	1
French,	1
Unknown,	8
	144

The parents of sixty-three of the above children are *Intemperate.*

Indentured during the past year,

Boys—To Farmers,	30	
Sea Service of various kinds,	31	
Blacksmiths,	6	
Cloth Manufacturers,	10	
Hair Dresser,	1	
Cabinet Maker,	1	
Piano Forte Maker,	1	
Bellows Maker,	1	
Paper Maker,	1	
Shoe Makers,	4	
Sugar Manufacturers,	12	
Whip Manufacturer,	1	
Tailors,	2	
Saddler,	1	
Comb Manufacturer,	1	
Mason,	1	
Hatter,	1	
		105

Girls,—Domestic Service, Tailoresses, &c., 23

WORK DONE BY THE BOYS.

CANE CHAIR BOTTOM MANUFACTORY.

Cane chair bottoms, 351 dozen plain Maple Seats.
" " 294 dozen plain solid fronts.
" " 143 dozen Curled and Birds Eye fronts.
" " 18 dozen curled sewing chair fronts.
" " 24 dozen curled solid front, raised back, and box seat.
" " 17 dozen large seats and backs caned for arm chairs.

847 dozen.

39 settee seats.

BRUSH MANUFACTORY.

1000 dozen Shoe Brushes.
200 dozen Scrubbing Brushes.
600 dozen Hair Brushes.
500 dozen Cloth Brushes.
100 dozen Horse Brushes.
50 dozen Hat Brushes.

50 dozen Flesh Brushes.
10 dozen Nail Brushes.
10 dozen Table Brushes.
2000 pound Bristles, assorted and combed.
1400 pound Bristles picked.
1400 pound Bristles washed and bleached.
1000 dozen Shoe Brushes finished.
200 dozen Scrubbing Brushes finished.
600 dozen Hair Brushes finished.
500 dozen Cloth Brushes finished.
100 dozen Horse Brushes finished.
50 dozen Hat Brushes finished.
50 dozen Flesh Brushes finished.
10 dozen Table Brushes finished.

SHOE SHOP.

The boys make and mend all the shoes used by the subjects in both houses.

New shoes made for the use of the house, past year, 400 pair.

Mended, a large quantity.

CARPENTERS' SHOP.

Soap and Candle Boxes, 20,175.

OTHER WORK DONE BY THE BOYS.

Tilling the grounds; working in the gardens. All the cooking for the Male House, has been done by them: they whitewash and cleanse their own apartments, and mend all their woollen clothes; pick wool; cut roots and sarsaparilla; clean and sort gums and drugs for Apothecaries, &c. &c.

WORK DONE BY THE GIRLS.

Shirts made, - -	300	Pillow Ticks, - -	16
Pantaloons, - -	702	Bolsters, - - - -	1
Roundabouts Jackets,	527	Stockings run, (pair) -	439
Chemises, - -	106	Stockings footed, " -	16
Frocks, - - -	151	Spreads made and quilted,	18
Aprons, - - -	82	Brown Rollers, - -	125
Waistcoats, - -	45	Diaper Towels, - -	12
Petticoats, - -	44	Brown Towels, - -	12
Night caps, - -	116	Pantaloons mended, -	2178
Vandikes, - -	104	Shirts mended, - -	2628
Pillow Cases, - -	104	Bed Ticks mended, -	114
Sheets, - - -	209	Blankets mended, -	360
Pillows, - - -	8	Sheets made for Hospital,	24

Pieces Washed, 46,800.

SCHOOL REPORT.

From the 1st of January to December 31, 1830, one hundred and forty-four children have entered school.

71 of the above number could not read.

20 of the 71 did not know a letter. They were from 8 to 16 years of age: average, 11 years 6 months.

51 were in the second, third, and fourth classes; they were from 10 to 16 years of age: average, 12 years 6 months.

45 entered the first reading classes, viz: sixth and seventh.

28 in the more advanced, or eighth and ninth.
33 of the 144, are all that knew any thing of Arithmetic.
22 of the 33 were in addition.
During the past year the promotions have been as follows:—

20	have been promoted	from	the	1st to 2d class,
19	"	"	"	2d to 3d class,
28	"	"	"	3d to 4th class,
31	"	"	"	4th to 5th class,
36	"	"	"	5th to 6th class,
47	"	"	"	6th to 7th class,
31	"	"	"	7th to 8th class,
21	"	"	"	8th to 9th class.

Of those who entered the Arithmetic classes, there have been an equal number of promotions.

In the ninth class there are twenty-one children* who read History and study Geography.

Forty-two write on paper; 110 write on slates.

With this exhibit of the improvement of the children, the teacher would remark, that the regular and stated employment of the children, eight hours per day, does not appear in any wise to militate against as successful a prosecution of their studies during the time allotted them, as is observed in our Public Schools.

The Sabbath School is also under the sole care of the teacher, and it is gratifying to say, the attention given to the reading and searching the Holy Scriptures, affords reason to hope, that many of our children will hereafter (as many already have) date their acquaintance with that "salvation" which is no where taught save in the "lively oracles," to Sabbath School instruction received in the House of Refuge.

It appears due in this place to advert, with thankfulness, to the very liberal donations which have been made from time to time, by the Young Men's Bible Society of New-York, Auxiliary to the American Bible Society; nor should the monthly visits of the friends of Sabbath Schools, who are careful to present us with their monthly rewards, for the encouragement of such children as are diligent in searching the Scriptures, be forgotten.

* This exhibits the state of the schools, male and female.

The ages of the Children received into the Refuge since it was opened on 1st January, 1825, to 1st January, 1831.

BOYS.

Years of age. - -	7	8	9	10	11	12	13	14	15	16	17	18	19	20
1825 to 1826,	1	1	2	4	5	6	6	13	14	7	5	1	1	
to 1827,		1	4	7	4	6	9	20	25	10	11	5	9	3
to 1828,			4	8	13	14	13	16	11	12	8	4	1	
to 1829,		3	5	11	12	18	13	32	12	11	5			
to 1830,			3	10	7	17	6	25	23	10	5	1	2	1

to 1831, 113—average age 12 years 2 months.

GIRLS.

Years of age. - -	7	8	9	10	11	12	13	14	15	16	17	18	19	20
1825 to 1826,	1	1				2	4		3	4				
to 1827,				3	2	4	3	4	5	6	7			
to 1828,	1		1		4	5	7	6	5	9	3			
to 1829,	3		3	1	3	7	10	3	5	5	3			
to 1830,		2	4	2	4	4	5	5	10	4	1			

to 1831, 31—average age 12 years.

The number of children received into the Refuge, since it was opened, 1st January, 1825, to 1st January, 1831, that have been in places of confinement, viz: In Bridewell, Prisons, Penitentiaries, &c. &c., and the length of time they were confined, before being sent to the Refuge.

Bridewell.—57 have been in once, 26 twice, 14 three times, 3 four times, 5 five times, and 1 ten times.

Penitentiary.—13 have been in six months, 3 twelve months, 4 eighteen months, 1 thirty months, 2 thirty-six months.

State Prison.—4.

Character of the Parents of Children received into the Refuge.

Parents been in Bridewell, 35; Penitentiary, 16; State's Prison, 2; Intemperate, 464; Houses of Ill Fame, 9; Parents allow children to steal, 10; Parents receiving the avails of stealing, 8.

Since the opening of the House of Refuge, there have been committed and received into it eight hundred and thirty-four children.

Boys, 628
Girls, 206
——834

The Society for the Reformation of Juvenile Delinquents, in Account Current with Cornelius Du Bois, Treasurer.

Dr.

Date		$	cts.
1830 Jan. 1 to 1831 Jan. 1	To Cash, paid on account of the erection of a new building for boys,	$6882	23
	" Clothing, for the Children	1218	28
	" Food and Provisions, for the Children	3382	24
	" Furniture, Beds Bedding, &c.	572	05
	" Coal, Wood, Oil, Stoves, &c.	512	33
	" School and Hospital Expenses, Books, Paper, Stationary, Medicine, &c.	427	38
	" Salaries of the Superintendent, Assistants, Schoolmaster, Matron, &c.	3195	94
	" Premium of Insurance against Fire on the buildings,	76	63
	" Interest on Money borrowed,	32	83
	" Printing Annual Report, Account Books, Stationary, &c.	95	50
	" Horse, Cows, &c. for the use of the Institution,	277	28
	" Chair Shop, Maple plank and boards, rattan and tools, to furnish mechanical employment for the boys,	2354	81
		$19027	50
1831 Jan. 1	To Balance brought down due the Treasurer,	2242	67
	To Cash paid draft of the Acting Committee, balance due on new building, and supplies for the children,	1675	13
		$3917	80

Cr.

Date		$	cts.
1830	By Balance in the Treasury	5787	12
Jan. 1 to 1831 Jan. 1	By Cash received for the Labor of the Children in the different Work Shops	1283	36
	By Cash from Marine Hospital Fund, balance due on annual appropriation for 1829, $2000		
	By Cash from Marine Hospital Fund, on account of the annual appropriation for 1830, (a part of the Surplus Funds arising from a tax upon Foreign Passengers) $6000	8000	00
	By Cash, tax upon 270 Tavern Licences, and Licences to sell ardent spirits. (Balance due on Licences granted for 1829.)	405	00
	The Tax upon Tavern Licences, granted for 1830, amounting to about $4500, collected by the Commissioners of Excise, and due the Society, is withheld by the Mayor, per order of the Corporation of the City.*		
	The Tax upon two Theatres and one Circus for 1830, amounting to $1250, collected by the Mayor, and due the Society, is withheld by him.*		
	By Cash for sales of Chair Bottom Seats, manufactured by the boys,	1299	35
	By balance due the Treasurer,	2242	67
		$19027	50

* Note.—Suits have been commenced by the Society against the Mayor, for the payment of the above monies collected.

Officers of the Society.

CADWALLADER D. COLDEN, *President.*

STEPHEN ALLEN,
CORNELIUS DUBOIS,
JOHN GRISCOM,
HENRY I. WYCKOFF,
JAMES LOVETT,
PETER SHARPE, } *Vice Presidents.*

CORNELIUS DUBOIS, *Treasurer.*

FREDERICK SHELDON, *Secretary.*

JOHN STEARNS, M. D.
GALEN CARTER, M. D. } *Physicians and Surgeons.*

House of Refuge.

NATHANIEL C. HART, *Superintendent.*
JOSEPH B. ROE, *Assistant Superintendent.*
REBECCA ORAM, *Matron.*
SARAH ANN ORAM, *Assistant Matron.*
CHARLES CECIL, *Teacher.*

Indenturing Committee.

WILLIAM F. MOTT,
HEMAN AVERILL,
MYNDERT VAN SCHAICK.

Acting Committee.

WILLIAM W. FOX,
MYNDERT VAN SCHAICK,
HEMAN AVERILL,
JOHN HUNTER,
ROBERT D. WEEKS,
FREDERICK A. TRACY,
RUSSEL H. NEVINS.

Managers.

Stephen Allen,
Heman Averill,
Arthur Burtis,
C. D. Colden,
Robert C. Cornell,
Cornelius Dubois,
Jacob Drake,
William W. Fox,
John Griscom,
John Hunter,
Jacob Harvey,
William Kent,
James Lovett,
Rufus L. Lord,
William F. Mott,
Hugh Maxwell,
Dennis M'Carthy,
Russel H. Nevins,
Ralph Olmsted,
Nath'l Richards,
Fred'k Sheldon,
Peter Sharpe,
John Stearns,
P. R. Starr,
William L. Stone,
Charles Town,
Frederick A. Tracy,
M. Van Schaick,
Henry I. Wyckoff,
John W. Wyman,
Robert D. Weeks.

Ladies' Committee.

Rebecca M'Comb,
Sophia Wyckoff,
Ann Warner,
Deborah L. Embree,
Almy Cornell,
Margaret Beers,
Ann L. Mott,
Isabella Buloid,
Phebe Mott,
Charlotte L. Fox,
Sarah C. Hawxhurst,
Maria L. Hyde,
Martha Willis,
Esther Seymour.

SEVENTH ANNUAL REPORT, &c.

1832.

IN obedience to the act incorporating the Society for the Reformation of Juvenile Delinquents in the city and state of New-York, the Managers respectfully Report:—That

				Subjects.
There have been received into the House of Refuge during the past year,	Boys,	101		
	Girls,	24		
		125		
Of those who had been previously indentured, there have been returned,	Boys,		11	
	Girls,		2	
				13
There have been also returned, two boys who had escaped,				2
There were in the House, at the date of the last Annual Report,	Boys,		141	
	Girls,		40	
			181	
Thus making, of all the children under the care of the Society during the past year, the total of				321
Of these there have been Indentured,	Boys,		102	
	Girls,		20	
			122	
Returned to friends,	Boys,		12	
	Girls,		2	
			14	
Of Age,	One Girl,			1
Escaped during the year,	Boys,			2
And there are now remaining in the House,	Boys,		139	
	Girls,		43	
			182	
				321

Those received into the House, were committed by the following authorities, viz:—

Boys:—By the	Commissioners of the Alms-House,	6
"	Police of the City and County of N. Y.	63
"	Special Sessions of do.	6
"	General Sessions of do.	7
"	Albany County Sessions,	7
"	Kings County Sessions,	4

" Orange County Sessions,	3	
" Rensselear County do.	1	
" Monroe County do.	2	
" Ulster County do.	1	
" Oneida County do.	1	
		101
Girls:—By the Commissioners of the Alms-House,	5	
" Police of New-York County	18	
" Special Sessions of do.	1	
		24
		125

Of the above number, there are,

Of American Parentage,	61	
Of Irish do.	32	
Of English do.	15	
Of German do.	2	
Of Scotch do.	3	
Of French do.	8	
Of Welch do.	3	
Of unknown do.	1	
		125

Those committed were of the following ages, viz:

One of	5	years,
One of	7	"
Five of	8	"
Five of	9	"
Six of	10	"
Seven of	11	"
Thirteen of	12	"
Eighteen of	13	"
Twenty-one of	14	"
Twenty-nine of	15	"
Twelve of	16	"
Five of	17	"
One of	18	"
One of	19	"

Total, one hundred and twenty-five.

There have been Indentured during the year;—

Boys,—To Farmers,	35	
South Sea Whale Fishery, and other Sea Service,	24	
Shoe Makers	8	
Blacksmiths,	9	
Tailors,	2	
House Carpenters,	4	
Ship Carpenters,	3	
Mason,	1	
Chair Makers,	4	
Tanners and Curriers,	4	
Baker,	1	
Carriage Makers,	2	
Carried over,		97

Brought over,	97	
Hatter, - - - - -	1	
Printer, - - - - -	1	
Cloth Manufacturers, - -	2	
Cabinet Maker, - - - -	1	
	—102	
Girls,—House-wifery, - - - - -	20	
		—122

It will be observed in the foregoing Tables that in a few instances, children have been returned to their friends. This course has never been pursued, except under peculiar circumstances, which appeared to the Managers not only to justify the proceeding, but to render it more advisable than the ordinary mode of indenturing apprentices. It was done, for example, in one instance, in which a child's parents of respectable characters had removed from the city to the country, and settled on a farm with a view to permanent agricultural pursuits, and offered perhaps the most advantageous apprenticeship, which it was in the power of the Managers to procure. In another instance, it was satisfactorily proved that the charge on which a boy had been sent to the Refuge was utterly unfounded, and the Magistrates before whom he had been arraigned, united in a certificate of his innocence. One little boy of very tender years, afflicted by a disease which ultimately terminated in his death, was surrendered, temporarily, to the care of an anxious mother. This departure from the usual disposition of the children, has been allowed only when on the best consideration, it seems preferable to any other course which could be pursued in relation to the child.

In *indenturing* the Children, committed to the Managers' care, the most patient consideration is bestowed upon the selection of suitable occupations and places of abode, and every means within the power of the Managers is diligently employed in the investigation of the character and circumstances of the person to whom an apprentice is indentured. The wishes of the child are carefully attended to, and an apprenticeship rarely takes place without the perfect accordance of his feelings. The execution of this important branch of the Directors' duties, involves in it perhaps the greatest degree of labor attending the management of the Institution. Three of the Managers, forming what is termed the *Indenturing Committee*, are specially charged with this employment. This Committee meets always once, and frequently twice or three times a week at the House of Refuge, often spending the greater part of a day in a meeting. Before this Committee are laid the applications for apprentices; and all such certificates and evidence as it is possible to obtain of the character and circumstances of the applicants, are required and minutely examined: and as far as a personal investigation into every circumstance connected with the proposed Indenture is within their power, it is industriously prosecuted by the Members of the Committee in the recess of their Meeting.

It is felt by the Managers, to be due to the gentlemen to whom this important department of the management of the Institution has been confided, to bestow a further remark upon the additional labors with which they charge themselves. The supervision of this Committee over the children of the Refuge, ceases not with the departure of the latter from our walls. As far as is practicable, a tutelary observation is still maintained over the situation of the youth who have been indentured, and particularly over the treatment which they receive from their employers. And in some instances, where an interference on behalf of the apprentice was demanded, as where it was discovered that he had been cruelly treated, or that his morals had been neglected, or that the character of his master was different from what it had been represented, and likely to affect injuriously the welfare of the indentured boy, a change was effected by the exertions of the Committee, and the child transferred to a more humane and advantageous situation.

The discipline and government of the children within the House of Refuge, are enforced and improved by the collateral labors of the Indenturing Committee. In guiding their judgments in the selection of Apprentices, the Members of the Committee render themselves minutely acquainted with the individual character and circumstances of the different children, and are enabled to assist the Officers of the Institution by their counsel, in the details of their treatment of the inmates of the House. The children are separately called before them, and examined in private; their good or bad standing is inquired into, and its causes ascertained; those who are subject to censure are exhorted, advised and reproved, while the meritorious are commended and encouraged to persevere in the performance of their duties: and a regular classification of all the persons in the House is made, with a view to the relative standing of each individual, and the distribution of rewards or the application of punishments. The effect of these services is perceived by the Managers, on the whole operation of the Institution, and draws from them this acknowledgment to the gentlemen whose gratuitous labors, at the cost of so much time and active exertion, have been faithfully and unremittedly performed.

The tables above given, exhibit the different occupations selected by the Managers for the Apprentices whom they have indentured.

One of the occupations, which may strike the observer on the first consideration, as the most hazardous and doubtful in its effects on youth—we allude to that of a seaman—has been proved by experience to be among the most benign and favorable. The young men, (for those indentured as seamen were the oldest boys in the establishment,) shipped as sailors were mostly sent on the South-Sea whaling voyages, of which the results appear to have been favorable to their morals, as well as to their pecuniary interests. The Superintendent, in a letter to the Managers, of which we give an extract, has pointed out this class of our boys as deserving of particular notice. "I shall," he remarks, "feel much gratified in speaking "of the happy results of sending our boys on the long "South-Sea whaling voyages. A large number have "returned this season, and almost uniformly come to "see us; dressed without exception like gentlemen; "some with watches in their pockets, the fruits of "their own industry. The greater part of them re-"turn to the same employ again. Many are shipped "as boat-steerers, and one, I am informed, has been "made second mate of one of the whaling ships."

During the past year, the inmates of the House of Refuge have been engaged in the following mechanical employments: In the manufacture of Brushes for clothes, shoes, hats, &c.; in Cabinet work, making bedsteads, pine and cherry tables, wash stands, &c.; in the manufacture of bead ear-ring, safety-chains, and necklaces; and, principally, in the manufacture of seats for chairs and settees. The amount of work performed by the boys in these branches, will appear in the statements of the Superintendent annexed to this Report. Shoes for the use of all the children are made within the walls, as are also clothes for the use of the whole establishment. The cooking of the Male and Female Houses, is done exclusively by the inmates of the respective Houses; and the washing for all the children is done by the girls. By a recent arrangement, fifteen of the girls are now employed by a tailor in making clothes, on wages of a shilling each per day. And in the above mentioned trades, (except the making of shoes and clothes,) the boys are, in like manner, hired by contractors at wages of 12 1-2 each per day. This method has been adopted by the Managers, after a trial of different dispositions of the children, as on the whole the most advantageous. It is free from the losses and risks attendant on the carrying on of trades for the account of the Society, and enables the Officers of the Institution to bestow more time, and greater attention on the moral government of the children, who remain, by the terms of the contracts, exclusively under the discipline and control of the Society.

It is with great satisfaction that the Managers advert to the health of the Refuge. During the past year not a single death has occurred among the children within the House, nor scarcely a case of serious disease; and at the present moment, there is not in our Hospital a child whose sickness excites the least apprehension. In a season like the present, of unusual sickliness in the city of New-York, the healthy state of the House of Refuge cannot but be considered as a convincing proof of the propriety of the regimen and treatment observed in it. The Managers have, however, some time during the late year, felt much solicitude at the existence in the Refuge of a disease of the eyes, which at one period assumed an alarming aspect. At the commencement of 1830, about thirty boys were afflicted with this Opthalmia.* The attention of the Managers, and of the Physicians of the Society, was particularly turned to it, and a system of sanitary regulations, under the advice of the latter, adopted, which has been followed by a reduction of the number of those affected by the disease to four, all of whom appear to be on the recovery. In no instance has the eye-sight of an individual been lost, and the Managers now confidently anticipate the speedy extirpation of this disorder among the children.

The judicious management and skill of Dr. Power, the Resident Physician of the House of Refuge, in relation to this disease, have been felt and appreciated by the Managers; and they avail themselves also, of this opportunity, to renew to Doctors Stearns and Carter, their grateful acknowledgments for their gratuitous services, rendered in the past, as during the preceding year, with indefatigable and persevering attention.

The nature of the *government* and *discipline* exercised over the children, will perhaps be better illustrated by a summary account of the routine of a single day in the House of Refuge, than by any other description which it is in the power of the Managers to give.

At sun-rise of every day in the year, a bell rings to rouse the children. In fifteen minutes the cells are opened, and each of the children, having made up his own bed, and arranged his little apartment, steps forth at a signal into the Hall. They are then marched in order to the wash-room, where the utmost attention to personal cleanliness is required and enforced. From the wash-room, they are called to parade in the open air (the weather permitting) when they are ranged in ranks, and undergo a close and critical in-

* As far as it could be traced, it was introduced into the House by three boys, who had been subject to this distemper in the City Alms-house.

spection as to cleanliness and dress. The Parade finished, they are summoned to Morning Prayers. These various operations consume about a half-hour; and at half-past five o'clock, in the summer, the Morning School commences. In school, they remain till seven o'clock, when they are dismissed for a few minutes, and until the bell rings for breakfast, which consists, according to the dietary regulations of the Managers, of bread, molasses, and rye coffee, occasionally varied by the substitution of indian meal for bread, and milk for coffee. A half-hour is allowed for breakfast, at the expiration of which, the signal for labor is given, and the children are conducted to their respective work-shops, to remain there until noon. By an allotment of tasks, however, these hours of labor are shortened to the industrious. The working day for this purpose is considered as commencing at one o'clock in the afternoon, when a certain task, proportional to his years and capacity, is assigned to each child, and if this task is performed before twelve o'clock at noon of the succeeding day, the child is rewarded by the allowance for his recreation of whatever time he thus gains before twelve and after eleven o'clock, until which hour all are kept in the workshops. The benefit of this arrangement is sensibly perceived upon the spirits and industry of the boys, and there are few among them, who do not thus gain, what all but the wilfully idle are able to gain, some extra time for their own amusements.

At twelve o'clock, a bell rings to call all from work, and one hour is allowed for washing (which is again scrupulously attended to) and dinner. The dinner, by the Managers' regulations, consists [for five days in the week,] of nutritious soups, meat, potatoes and bread. On Fridays, fish is substituted for soup and meat; and on Sunday, a dinner of Beef and a vegetable of superior quality to those of the other days is allowed. At one o'clock, a signal is given for recommencing work, which continues till five in the afternoon, when the bell rings for the termination of the labor of the day. A half-hour is allowed for washing (which is once more enforced) and supper, consisting of mush and milk, molasses and rye coffee. At half-past five, the children are conducted to their Evening School, in which they are kept till 8 o'clock. Evening prayers are now attended to by the Superintendent, and the children, ranged in order, are then marched to the Sleeping Halls, where each takes possession of his separate apartment, and the cells are locked, and silence is enforced for the night.

The above is the history of six days of every week in this year, except that duriug the short winter-days, morning school is suspended, and the work-shops are closed at four o'clock in the afternoon. On Sundays labor, of course, ceases, and instead of the Morning School, the time allotted on other days for this purpose, is taken up in the classification of the children according to their conduct during the preceding week, and the distribution of Badges of Merit. Religious Service is performed twice during the day in the Chapel, in the presence of a Committee of the Managers, by the clergymen of the city in rotation. In the interval between the church services, a Sunday school is held for the children; and after the Evening Service, they are allowed to walk about the grounds under the observation of the officers until eight o'clock.

The children have been instructed during the past year by the Assistant Superintendent of the respective Houses, in reading, writing and arithmetic. Their progress has been on the whole satisfactory; but the Managers have it in contemplation to extend and improve the system of instruction. The duties of the Assistant Superintendent are necessarily varied and pressing, and it is deemed advisable to appoint a well qualified person to discharge the single duty of instructing and watching over and promoting the moral and religious improvement of the children.

The discipline exercised over the inmates of the House of Refuge, is of a mild and simple character. The children are divided, with reference to their merit, into four classes, the most worthy being placed in class No. 1. Each wears on his arm a badge of the class to which he belongs. To a station in the third class, is annexed a certain slight deprivation of play; and to the fourth class, which consists of the worst boys, who have been guilty of flagrant offences against the rules of the House, is attached, during the first week, the penalty of the third class, with an additional one, consisting of the deprivation of Sunday supper. A second week's continuance in the fourth class, which is the consequence of further bad conduct during the first week, brings with it the additional punishment of confinement after evening service on Sunday. On the other hand, four weeks maintenance of a station in class No. 1, which is the result of continued good conduct during this period, entitles a boy to a blue ribbon, and certain slight but highly appreciated privileges: four weeks of further good conduct, entitles the wearer of the blue ribbon to the higher honors of the red and blue:—and if after this, he shall, without any special limitation of time, prove himself worthy of the confidence of the officers, he receives the highest reward of merit in the tri-color badge.

This simple system of rewards and punishments, suffices, in the main, to preserve in contented and cheerful obedience the two hundred little beings confided to our care. Cases however do arise, which require severer punishments. Bold and daring attempts to escape, and rude and obstinate disobedience do occasionally occur, when corporal punishment—never however of a severe character—and solitary confinement—rarely of a protracted duration—are found indispensably necessary. The misconduct which renders necessary punishments of the last description, is almost invariably committed by those of the youth who are approaching the years of manhood. The experience of our Institution fully confirms the common opinion, that the hope of a delinquent's reformation is inversely as his years; and that the benefit which an offender of mature age derives from the discipline of the Refuge, is greatly counterbalanced by the evil which he spreads around him. It must indeed be an obvious truth, that a youth of either sex, who has passed the years of childhood—who adds a thorough acquaintance with vice to the untutored passions of early life, and who has felt all the attractions, and but slightly the bitter consequences of guilt, is not included among those Juvenile Delinquents, whom, it was the design of this Institution, to receive, and cherish, and reform. The means of coercion and government possessed by the House of Refuge, were intended moreover for children, in the ordinary meaning of the term, and not for those who in bodily strength, temper, fixed habits, determination of character, and every thing except the legal definition of infancy, are separated from this class. It will be remembered, by those who have attended to the history of the House of Refuge, that some years since, a desperate plan of escape was formed and nearly executed, which cost the blood, and almost the lives of several of the officers. This was the work of a boy of nineteen years of age. In the past year, several daring plans of escape by violent means, have been detected among the older boys. It is of importance that these facts should be understood and appreciated by the community, as, by a late statute, amendatory of the act incorporating this Society, every court in the state is empowered to send to the House of Refuge, such convicted children as shall be deemed by them to be proper objects. And under this authority, the Managers are very frequently compelled to receive boys, sentenced hither by courts influenced by deceptive statements of the ages of the offenders, or by the suggestion, as they respectfully conceive, of ill-judging compassion, who would have been excluded by a due consideration of the nature and objects of this Society.

A statement of the receipts and expenditures of the Society during the past year, by Cornelius Dubois, Esq. the Treasurer of the Society, is annexed to this Report.

Subjoined to this Report, will be also found a few histories of children who have heretofore been under our charge, and who were indentured under our supervision. The selection is made from a mass of cases, perhaps equally interesting, and could have been extended far beyond its present limits. In these short and simple annals, no attempt has been made by the Managers to alter or suppress the language of the communications of the children whose cases are given, under the belief that their own artless, if imperfect narratives, are the best form in which their stories can be presented to the public eye. But in histories of these children, preceding their entrance into the House of Refuge, the Managers have been compelled to throw a veil over many details, which would have heightened the contrast of the present situation of these little beings, snatched from the midst of vice of the deepest, and in some instances, most unnatural depravity.

The Managers invite attention to the annual report of the Ladies' Committee, of whose services to the Institution—particularly the Female Department, it is difficult to speak in terms of adequate commendation, and sufficiently grateful acknowledgment.

In closing this report, the Managers have only to observe that they are aware of no circumstances in which this Institution has failed to fulfil the wishes and hopes of its Founders and Patrons: and, on the contrary, they feel encouraged by every view of this Society and its effects, to persevere in their direction of this noble attempt on the part of the community, to stay the contagion of corrupting guilt, and to direct to paths of virtue and peace, the footsteps of erring and deserted childhood.

The Society for the Reformation of Juvenile Delinquents, in Account Current with Cornelius Du Bois, Treasurer.

Dr.

Date		$	cts
1831	To Balance due the Treasurer,	$ 2242	67
Jan. 1	To Cash, Clothing, for the Children	1492	50
to	" Food and Provisions, for the Children	4807	56
Jan. 1	" Furniture, Beds Bedding, &c.	961	29
1832.	" Coal, Wood, Oil, Stoves, &c.	1100	76
	" School and Hospital Expenses, Books, Paper, Stationary, Medicine, &c.	189	12
	" Salaries of the Superintendent, Assistants, Schoolmaster, Matron, &c.	3346	45
	" Premium of Insurance against Fire,	76	63
	" Interest on Money borrowed,	34	97
	" Printing Annual Report, Account Books, Stationary, &c.	110	72
	" Horse, Cows, &c. for the use of the Institution,	447	84
	" Chair Shop, Maple plank and boards, rattan and tools, to furnish mechanical employment for the boys,	2489	83
	" Building, Repairs, Additions, &c.	2582	54
	" Paid Finance Committee per order of the Board,	6787	73
		$26620	61
1831 Jan. 5	To Balance brought down due the Treasurer,	$1046	10

Cr.

Date		$	cts
1831 Jan. 1	By Cash received for the Labor of the Children in the different Work Shops	2953	36
to 1832 Jan. 1	By Cash from Marine Hospital Fund, (a part of the Surplus Funds arising from a tax upon Foreign Passengers)	8000	00
	By Cash, tax upon Tavern Licences, due and collected in 1830—(paid this year.*)	4564	50
	By Cash, Tax upon two Theatres and one Circus, due and collected in 1830—(paid this year,)	1250	00
	By Cash, Tax upon four Theatres for 1831,	2000	00
	By Cash from Corporation of City of New-York, from Excise Fund,	4000	00
	By Cash for sales of Chair Bottom Seats, manufactured by the boys—and stock of Raw Materials, Tools, &c.	2524	82
	By Cash, donations, subscriptions, &c.	281	83
	By balance due the Treasurer,	1046	10

* The law imposing the above Tax has been repealed.

APPENDIX.

REPORT OF THE LADIES' COMMITTEE.

To the Managers of the House of Refuge, the Ladies' Committee Report—

THAT since their last Annual Report, the Monthly Meetings of the Committee have been regularly held, and a Sub-Committee of their number have visited the House of Refuge at least once in each week during the past year.

Minutes have been kept by the Committee and Sub-Committees, a summary of which will be laid before the Managers; and to this summary they refer them for particulars of their proceedings.

By a reference to our Minutes of the past year, we find general satisfaction is expressed with the order and management of the House. We believe the several Committees have endeavored as far as they could, to assist and advise with the Matron on the arrangements necessary for the improvement and comfort of the females committed to their superintendence, and to convince them that the path of virtue is the only one to happiness, while they acknowledge the necessity of Divine agency to make their counsel effectual.

The usual duties of washing, making and mending the boys' and their own clothes and bedding, have been accomplished by the girls with general satisfaction; which, together with school-exercises, family devotion, and moral and religious instruction, have fully occupied them; and we may notice an improvement in industry and order, although we have to lament that we cannot, in every case acknowledge success. We believe, however, that the past has not been a year of particular discouragement, but that we have the usual incitements to perseverance, leaving consequences with Him who alone can bless our efforts for the amelioration of these children of sorrow.

The Committee express their pleasure with the effort now making, to give our larger inmates a more perfect knowledge of the tayloring business than they have hitherto had. We have long wished for a more profitable application of time for many of them, than the routine of the family furnishes. There will always be several of them, who, from various causes, will continue under our care until they are of age, and we feel very desirous, that when they leave us, they may be sufficiently instructed to gain a respectable living, if so disposed, with but little exposure.

The subject of classification has long engaged much of our attention, and we earnestly solicit your co-operation with our wishes on this subject. We know that it involves many difficulties, but not more than you have already encountered and successfully combated. We think our usefulness would be much increased by a judicious separation between girls of sixteen and children of ten years of age, who are at present promiscuously instructed; the former of whom must naturally be older in delinquency than the latter.

We have before said to you, how pained we frequently are, in our walks through this city, with the sight of disgusting pauperism, which must almost with certainty eventuate in crime, if not prevented by adequate care; and we do feel how much better and easier prevention is than reformation. And when we reflect that almost one half of our comfortable House is untenanted, we greatly desire for these children of destruction, so safe and effectual a Refuge from contamination and suffering.

We have painfully to acknowledge, since the date of our last Annual Report, the separation, by death, of our esteemed friend, Sophia Wyckoff. She is the first so separated from our Committee since its formation. She was indeed one of those who fed the hungry, clothed the naked, and visited the sick and imprisoned; and we humbly hope she has her inheritance with those who are blessed of God our Father. Her last moments were consoled with the belief that she should be permitted, through the merits of her Redeemer, to join the Heavenly company in praising and adoring the King of Kings and Lord of Lords.

Before closing this Report, we note with gratitude, the general health of our inmates during the past year, and hope, as we persevere in attention to the objects of the Institution, we shall be encouraged by beholding future improvement amongst them.

SARAH C. HAWXHURST, *Secretary.*

12th mo. (December) 26th, 1831.

SELECTION OF CASES AND LETTERS

From Apprentices, and from Persons to whom Apprentices have been bound.

The following cases were furnished by the Superintendent. It is his practice to write down the history of each child, taken from his own narration, on his advent to the House. After the lapse of some time, the child is re-examined, and the accuracy of his first account is thus tested. In the following cases, it will be perceived, that the history of the child, preceding its entrance into the House of Refuge, consists of the narrative thus taken down by the Superintendent.

The statements, &c., following the cases of the boys, were also furnished by the Superintendent.

BOYS.

September 17, 1830.

A. B., from the Police, aged 14 years the 22d of December last; born in New-York, of Irish parents. His father is an old porter; he occasionally drinks too much; then, the boy says his father will swear off for a year at a time, but when the time is past will pay for all in excess of drinking.

He has two sisters and one brother. A. and one of his sisters lived about two years in Paterson, where he was a good boy; but his father took him home to go to school, when he soon commenced playing truant and going round the markets (Washington and Fulton) stealing fruit.

He commenced, in junction with two others, stealing eggs from barrels standing by grocery stores, in which they were very successful, and one would pass and take a handful, and another would receive them at a convenient place, and sell them to a woman who keeps a victualing stand, by the name of ——, who gave them one shilling for eighteen eggs. This woman would give them three shillings per piece for smoked beef, and from four to eight shillings for hams by the lump; these articles, this boy and his companions were very successful in stealing. He stole hats occasionally, sometimes they stole cocoa-nuts from stands and vessels, lead frequently, and sometimes old rope; but his associates told him that was too low, that he could make more at more honorable stealing. He once stole an umbrella in Maiden-lane, once he stole from the pocket of a drunken man three shillings, and at another time one shilling and eleven-pence from a money drawer in Hudson-street.

He was very successful in selling stolen handkerchiefs about the markets: they frequently stole clothes when they would be out to dry. A. was in the act of stealing a pair of pantaloons from a yard near the white fort, North River, when he was detected, taken and sent here. He would be frequently away from home, first one night, then a week and three weeks at a time, sleeping in shavings in new buildings, lumber yards, &c.

He and his companions had curious names for different articles that they stole, so as not to be understood by honest men: for instance, smoked beef or hams were smokers, hats cadies, shoes and boots crabs, handkerchiefs wipers, vests garvises, trowsers kickers, watches thimbles, shirts and other articles taken from yards were gooseberries; when they proposed to plan to get articles of this kind, they would say we will go a gooseberrying; crockery and glass from crates would be tapping crates, a trunk they called Peter.

They often deposited their goods in lumber yards and slept in them. He often went to the Theatre.

By the above, we see that this unfortunate, interesting boy, had learned many lessons in one year, and was in the broad road to destruction. On re-examination, the boy thinks it likely that he stole many other things; that he cannot remember all. Enters 6th class—could not read in the New Testament.

September 27th, 1831.—He was indentured to Mr. V. D., Printer, of ——.

It was a matter of much pleasure to the Managers, to witness the great improvement in this boy, snatched from the haunts of vice, rapidly running into such crimes as must, had there not been a House of Refuge, have soon added to the number in our Penitentiary or State's Prison. The moral influence used in our Institution, had a visible effect upon his mind, and by degrees he became a good boy. He selected such company as prided themselves in doing as well as they knew how: and before he left the House, arrived to the highest grade of the Class of Honor.

It will be observed, that when he came here, he could not read intelligibly the New Testament; but to show his advancement, we will here insert a letter from his master, relative to the boy.

N——, Nov. 14, 1831.

N. C. Hart,

Dear Sir,—You no doubt wonder at my silence with respect to the boy A. B. I did expect to have visited you ere this, or I should certainly have answered yours of the 26th October, previous to this time: with respect to him, I have the satisfaction to inform you, and the rest of his friends, that his conduct, so far, has proved entirely satisfactory. He is obedient, active, willing, and very apt, and appears to do every thing that he is requested to, with cheerfulness. Considering the time he has been with us, he has made very great progress, certainly more than we did expect of him; although he has not been with us two months yet, he can set very near a column of our paper per day, which, I am proud to say, I consider rather extraordinary. He appears to be perfectly satisfied with his situation, and says he has no desire to associate with his former street companions. I have no doubt, sir, he will prove an honor to your house and to himself.

I am, Dear Sir,

Yours, Respectfully,

J. V. D——.

July 15, 1830.

C. D., from the Police, aged 15 years the 9th of May, last; born in Ireland, his father is a stone cutter by trade, and carries on the business in ——, keeps journeymen and apprentices, at which business he put this boy, but he would not work with his father. Said that he first began to run away from home about five years ago; would be absent from one week to a month at a time, sleeping in stables, &c.—would steal old rope, copper, iron, lead, &c.: in fact, almost any thing that he could lay his hands upon: frequently was very successful in stealing old copper from the Dry Dock; not uncommon to make six shillings per day. Says the opportunities for stealing old copper at the Dry Dock, make many boys thieves. He stole money several times from his father, from two shillings to two dollars at a time; sometimes would go over to Long Island and pick peas, &c. He contracted an ardent thirst for rum, which was to him a serious harm.

He states, as one reason why his home was disagreeable to him, that his father drank hard, and would often go home intoxicated, quarrel with his mother, and raise mobs about the house.

He used to find market for his stolen goods at ——, in —— street. After an absence of three weeks, his father discovered where he was, had him taken up and sent here.

C. D. entered the 7th Class—that is, could read moderately in the New Testament.

After he had been here a few months, the Superintendent made the following written remarks to his history, which is his custom to do to every case occasionally, as their cases may be.

"C. D. has a good deal of natural cleverness about him, we are sometimes almost ready to confide in him, but fear his habits have been so long badly fixed, as to require a longer probation."

However, a mason by trade, who was represented to be a religious man, wanted an apprentice, and it was thought as he had some knowledge of stone cutting, it would be to his advantage to put him to this business, he was selected for that purpose—when called to converse with the gentleman and to ascertain whether he would be pleased to go with him and learn the Mason's trade, (as the Managers are careful never to compel a child to go with any person, nor to any trade contrary to their wishes,) his first remark was that he would be willing to go providing liquor could be kept from him; that being easily disposed of, he was indentured accordingly, and in rather less than a year after he came to the house. It appears that his Master last summer built a large stone House for M. in Connecticut, brother to one of our Managers, who wrote to him recently, "we have so far progressed towards finishing the "house, and not a drop of ardent spirits has been used by any of "the workmen, but we have been greatly favored with the out "pouring of the Spirit of the Lord," enumerating how many of his workmen and neighbors had become the subjects of grace, he says "C. D. is one of the members, and his light shines daily, his de- "portment corresponds with his profession, he is a fine boy, has "joined a Christian Church, and is much beloved."

August 18, 1829.

E. F., from the Police, aged he says 16 years, but we judge 14 the 4th of July last, born in Ireland, his father sells potatoes, clams, &c. his parents both drink, but his mother is very intemperate, his father (the boy says) used to beat him very unmercifully, for being a bad boy, he often ran away from home, once he was absent 15 months in different parts of New Jersey, Pennsylvania, Paterson, Lehigh &c. used to steal different articles from his father and others, would often sleep out nights, would drink very hard, often get very drunk, a few days since in company with ——— went into a house while selling clams, saw a man lying drunk, they concluded to sound him, and stole a Pocket Book containing six dollars, but were so profuse in spending it in the neighborhood that it led to their detection. He was in the practice of driving a Horse and Cart or Wagon to sell the above articles, consequently could get as much rum as he wanted, often drank 10 and 12 glasses per day. Entered 8th class.

We find that after he had been here about 5 months, the Superintendent remarked under his history that E. improved, and had become a boy that afforded some promise, and professed to have lost his desire for ardent spirits, but to the regret of all concerned, he was persuaded some time after to unite with two larger boys in making arrangements to escape, in which he was detected; this, connected with his former very intemperate habits, caused the Managers to think it best to give him a long probation before they parted with him. For several months before they parted with him, he evinced a uniform, industrious, moral course, showing much contrition for his errors; consequently after remaining in the House about 20 months M. of ——— made application for a boy as an apprentice to the shoe-making business. The indenturing Committee made thorough investigation as to the character of the man, his family, &c. They were not only satisfied that M. was a very suitable man to have an apprentice, but that all his apprentices had joined the Temperate Society, in the place where he lived, as well as their Master, and were suitably zealous in this good cause, consequently they thought this a very suitable place for the boy who was formerly in the practice of drinking 10 and 12 glasses per day.

Some months after M. called and informed the gentleman who furnished him with the boy, that E. was a very fine youth, moral, modest, sober and industrious, and that he had frequently sent him to collect money, and had never discovered any thing improper in his apprentice, that he attended Sabbath School, &c. and was so much pleased with him, that he would be glad to have another from the Institution.

Oct. 21, 1830.

G. H. from the Commissioners, aged 10 years the 4th of July last, born in Philadelphia of Irish parents, his mother died about 5 years ago, and his father a shoe-maker, died about 4 or 5 months since, he then was left in charge of his step-mother. It appears that when his friends made application to the Commissioners to have him sent here, they represented him to be a disobedient bad boy, running about the streets, playing truant from school, sleeping out at night, going with bad boys, who would occasionally steal &c. they sent him here.

On examining the boy himself, he says that he ran away because his step mother beat him, he would sleep almost any where, when night overtook him, in sand and coal boxes, &c. then up in the morning, away to the Dry-Dock, steal copper, or any thing that he could get, and when he could not supply the calls of nature by stealing, then he would beg. Entered the 7th class.

The following remark was made by the Superintendent some months after he had been in the house, under the head of *remarks* on the page of his history.

G., is a bright, intelligent, interesting, little fellow, and we set much store by him.

On the 6th of Oct. 1831. He was indentured to Mr. J. D. of ——— town ——— County, State of New York.

Since which the following letter has been received from the boy in his own hand writing:

Nov. 24, 1831.

Dear Sir,—I with pleasure inform you that I am in good health, and like my master and mistress well. They are very kind to me. We have every day something that is good. He has given me two suits of clothes. I have a good bed to sleep in: but he is very angry if I tell him a crooked story. He has once boxed my ears for telling him that I had watered his horse, when I had not watered him. I drive the horse for him when he goes abroad with his one horse wagon; then my fingers got cold, but now I have got a new pair of mittens to keep my hands warm. I have learned the printed instructions you gave me by heart, and I intend to follow them, for my master has promised me that if I be a good boy, he will be a good master, if I be a bad boy he will be a hard master. But I choose the good part. I intend, as much as in me lies, to follow your good advice, for which I kindly thank you. I am going to school on Monday next. Our school house is near by.

I remain your obedient boy, G. H.

To Nathaniel C. Hart.

Jan. 8, 1831—J. J. K., from the Police, aged 13 years, the 29th of August last, born in New-York, of American parents. His father was a carpenter by trade, died 6 or 7 years ago; after which his mother took in sewing and washing, but she died about three years ago. Since which time he has been principally under the care of his uncles residing in ——. He once lived with —— who keeps stages, &c. at ——, returned to his uncle in —— and went to school, rendering assistance as the cases required. Last February, being a tolerable scholar, he, by the influence of Mr. ——, got a situation with Mr. ——, where he remained some months, and he thinks gave satisfaction. Would often have several thousand dollars given him to deposit in the bank, or pay away. His aunt, with whom he boarded, was very strict with him, allowing him but 20 minutes to be at her house after he shut up his office at 3 o'clock. Towards the close of July, the boy took a notion to go to —— after he closed his office—did not return until 6 o'clock in the evening—his aunt scolded him very hard, and gave him to understand that he might clear out, and go about his business, and let his uncles take care of him, if he was running there, neglecting to come home at the appointed time. He felt rather dissatisfied with the reception he met with, and left his aunt the next morning. It appears that his wages were drawn by his aunt to pay board, &c.; there being $17 due, he forged an order for $10 of it, and ran away. Went to ——, worked a little while in one place, and then to another; was doing very poorly: shunned his relatives, and was doubtless in the broad way to destruction, when they interfered, and had him taken before the authorities, and sent here.—Entered the 9th class.

He was indentured, the 27th of September last, to Mr.—— of ——Co. Conn. Shoe-maker. The following letter was recently received from him.

——. *Conn., Dec.* 12, 1831.

Mr. Nathaniel C. Hart,—I take my pen in hand to inform you that I am well, and hope these few lines will find you the same. I have got a good place, and am doing well. I am going to school at present to a good man. I am used well, and have every advantage that can be wished for. I had the pleasure of seeing my sister before I left New-York. I also had a meeting with my old school-master at Wilton, who has often given me good advice; and if I had taken it, I should never have been in the House of Refuge. But I feel it a blessing that I have seen the House of Refuge. Had it not been for the good instructions I have received there, I might long ago been ruined. My eyes got well in about three days, so that I could work as well as ever, by washing them morning and evening in eye water procured by Mr. ——

I like the country, and enjoy liberty with thanks, and with pleasure, and thank you and Mr. Roe for the good instructions which I have received from you both: though I confess with shame and with sorrow, that I did not deserve it as well as I ought to have done. I am now at work a little, closing shoes at night and go to school in the day time. Give my respects to Mr. Monmouth B. Hart, Mr. Roe, and Mr. Joseph Belden, when you see him again. Tell G. D. that I hope he will conduct himself so that I may have the pleasure of seeing him at liberty.

Please send me an answer as soon as you get this letter.

I am your humble and obedient servant,

I. J. K.

Extract of a letter from the Rev. David Terry, jun. to one of his friends in this city.

"Please tell Mr. Hart, that E. F. and G. H. are living on the circuit that I travel. I saw E. F. with his master; he was dressed like a gentleman. G. H. "is all alive in religion, and I understand is very gifted—that is, he exhibits superior talents for a boy of his years," &c.

This boy was brought up in one of the most dissolute parts of our city, (the Five Points.) His mother kept a brothel: the child of course was suffered to run about the streets without restraint. Being very active, with rather a winning address, and withal cunning, he became the successful leader of a little band of thieves. From this deplorable condition he was rescued, and placed in the House of Refuge. On the 12th of March, 1829, it pleased the Lord, by the influence of his Holy Spirit, in the fall of the same year, to cause a considerable religious excitement among the children; and although but between 13 and 14 years of age, he was one of the number that gave the strongest evidences of a happy change by grace.

Notwithstanding we loved the boy, we deemed it most prudent, in consequence of his past life, to give him a good probation; and after remaining in the House better than a year, an opportunity offered to bind him to a pious man, which was embraced. During the 20 months that he has been absent from us, we have occasionally heard verbally that G. H. was doing well, but had heard nothing particularly as to his religious state of feeling, before we saw the above letter.

April 23, 1829.—M. N. from the Commissioners of the Alms-House, aged 12 years the 4th of July last. Born of American parents, at ———, Long Island. His father, ———, moved to this city about five years ago, and drives a cart. Resides in ——— street, No. ———.

This boy has been sent to different schools, but would stay at none. Was a notorious truant; running about, he said, every where; would sleep out at night, in stables, &c. to avoid his father and others. Would watch the opportunity, when his father would be gone to work, to go home and get something to eat, as his *mother* never punished him, and then would clear out again; has picked old copper on shares for three days together, would sometimes take his pockets full of copper nails, has often stolen old iron and rope from about the docks; he once stole two dollars from his sister, that she had earned at sewing, spent it for toys, going to the Theatre and Circus, where he often went. Entered 5th Class.

For a year or more, this boy evinced a most unyielding stubborn temper, was naturally smart, but would get in his ugly turns occasionally, and we became almost discouraged with him, but during the second year of his stay with us, I can compare his change to nothing so striking, as that witnessed when the sun breaks through a motley flying cloud; he became kind, industrious, pleasant and contented, and while we write, we can bring before us the cheerful smile often discovered by him.

April 26, 1831. After remaining in the House three days over two years, he was indentured to ——, of ——, farmer, leaving us with a Bible under his arm, and capable of writing a letter to his friends, who in a few months became very anxious to hear from M. We wrote to his master, desiring that his apprentice might write to his family, &c.

The following was copied from his own hand writing, and child-like composition.

—— *Town, Sept.* 24, 1831.

Dear sister Armenia,—I send my respects to you, I am well, and hope that you are enjoying the same health, I should be glad to see you all, I have neglected writing, I have been pretty busy in working in the fields this summer, picking fruit, and busying myself with some oats, &c. M., the man I live with, has six girls, and no boys, but myself, and a little boy of his brother's; I feel quite contented, I live about two miles from T. B. and frequently see him; give my respects to father, mother, and the rest of my friends, give my love to Mr. Hart, and Mr. Roe. M. N.

The following was written by his master, at the bottom of the same letter.

This may certify, that M. is a good boy, and merits the love and good will of his employer, and all that are acquainted with him; he has been very steady at his work, I have not had occasion to speak a short word to him since he has lived with me, he appears to be well suited, and we are all much pleased with him.

Yours with respect,

J. S.

GIRLS.

March 18, 1829.

N. O., from the Commissioners, aged 12 years the 3d of May last, born in Ireland, her father and family moved to America seven years ago. He took to drink in Eastport about five years since—brought his family to disgrace and poverty: went to dig on the canal about twenty months or two years ago, when a bank of earth caved on him, and he lost his life.

This child, I should judge a fair subject for reformation; she is very candid and frank, says she was a good girl until she became acquainted with W. X., about sixteen months ago. She then was led to run about the streets and market places, until a late hour at night, use profane language, &c. Would leave her places of service, and be impudent to her poor mother, who has to labor for her support. Enters 8th class.

REMARKS.

January 11, 1830.—N. is a stout, able-bodied girl, with a strong temper, inclined to be impudent, but on the whole is governable.

Perhaps we never had a child in the House possessing such a Herculean mind as this girl. After she became somewhat settled in the course of her duties, there being opportunities for every child to read and study the scriptures, she gave her attention to it, and recited regularly to the Ladies' Committee every week, from

150 to 190 verses of the New-Testament. Here we would remark that some would be ready to judge, that it might be in certain parts where she had previously studied; but this was not the case, she would go on with one gospel or epistle after another in regular rotation.

After remaining nearly 17 months, she was indentured to Mr. ——, of ——, a farmer.

The following is a copy of a letter from N. to the Matron.

U. Co., Oct. 20, 1831.

Mrs. Rebecca Oram,

Dear Madam,—I take this favorable opportunity to inform you that I am well, and hope you enjoy the same blessing. I am much pleased with my situation. Mr. and Mrs. —— are very kind to me, and I am very well satisfied. When I first came, I felt very lonesome, but however, I soon got over that. It is a very handsome country, and to use my own language, it is a charming place.

I saw the gentleman on board the boat, to whom W. was indentured; he says that they have no fault to find with her, only she has no pride about herself, and has not ambition enough to make her own linen; otherwise she does very well. He says she has no inclination whatever to come back.

I should like to hear from you and Miss Oram, also Miss Nichols.

I go across the creek every Sunday to school, and like it very well. I have learned how to milk since I have been here,—Suckey is the name of the cow that I sometimes milk, and Flora is her calf's name. I have now seven geese to make as fat as butter. We have a sow with eight pretty little pigs.

Please give my love to Eliza Thompson, and tell her I wish she would write, and let me know how she is. Please give my love to Miss Nichols and all the girls.

I remain your Refuge Girl,

N. O.

Please favor me with an answer.

April 26, 1826.

W. X., from the Police, aged 14 years the 5th of February last, born in Philadelphia, of Irish parents; about 9 years ago the family moved to New-York. Her mother died about three years ago, since which her father married a woman who proved to be in the daily practice of drinking to intoxication, since which the family appeared to go to destruction with rapid strides: her father became intemperate, and substituted habits of industry, for drinking and stealing, and when under such influence led his poor children to the same practices, the step-mother not being backward to do her part in these vile practices. The father and eldest son were taken up for stealing, and put in Bridewell to await their trial. The father found guilty of grand larceny, and the son sent to the House of Refuge, (N. Y.) During this time the mother was in the continual practice of drinking, and took her poor child to market and required her to steal two heads of cabbage, they were directly taken up and sent to Bridewell. The subject of my story was sent to the House of Refuge, which proved a home to her, and a happy escape from wretchedness and bad example; she would no doubt from constant example, if she had been permitted to remain with her parents, have become fixed in habits of intemperance and dishonesty; she however showed that she only wanted good precept and example to make her a good and pious girl.

In consequence of a feeble state of health, she was not indentured when she was considered in a suitable state of mind to part with, in 1828. While in the House she professed to meet with a happy change of mind, and indeed her deportment while she remained with us, spake loudly of the religion she professed; she was very trusty, and acted more like a matron as to womanly deportment, and the discharge of the trust committed to her, than like a Refuge Girl; an opportunity offered to put her in a situation suitable to her state of health at the south. Such has been her correct deportment since she left, that increased confidence is placed in her as to unvarying integrity, and she now receives a salary for certain duties in a Public Institution of much respectability.

Extract from the Weekly Report of the Superintendent, to the Acting Committee, showing the number of children in the House in each week.

1831.		No. of Children in the House.	1831.		No. of Children in the House.
January,	4	180	July,	5	184
"	11	179	"	12	185
"	18	179	"	18	189
"	25	181	"	26	189
February,	1	188	August,	2	187
"	8	185	"	9	189
"	15	189	"	16	193
"	22	191	"	23	196
March,	1	193	"	30	200
"	8	194	September,	6	200
"	15	195	"	13	205
"	22	191	"	20	205
"	29	189	"	27	208
April,	5	189	October,	4	208
"	12	184	"	11	202
"	19	182	"	18	203
"	26	178	"	25	198
May,	3	174	November,	1	197
"	10	176	"	8	190
"	17	177	"	15	191
"	24	178	"	22	191
"	31	177	"	29	195
June,	7	178	December,	6	193
"	14	179	"	13	194
"	21	183	"	20	197
"	28	184	"	27	198
			January,	2	182

WORK DONE BY THE BOYS.

BRUSH MANUFACTORY.

600 dozen Shoe Brushes.
120 dozen Scrubbing Brushes.
400 dozen Hair Brushes.
300 dozen Cloth Brushes.
70 dozen Horse Brushes.
30 dozen Hat Brushes.
30 dozen Flesh Brushes.
6 dozen Nail Brushes.
5 dozen Table Brushes.
1200 pound Bristles, assorted and combed.
900 pound Bristles picked.
800 pound Bristles washed and bleached.
600 dozen Shoe Brushes finished.
120 dozen Scrubbing Brushes finished.
400 dozen Hair Brushes finished.
300 dozen Cloth Brushes finished.
70 dozen Horse Brushes finished.
30 dozen Hat Brushes finished.
30 dozen Flesh Brushes finished.
6 dozen Nail Brushes finished.
5 dozen Table Brushes finished.

CABINET SHOP.

675 Bedsteads made,
75 Pine Tables made,
25 Cherry Tables made,
50 Wash Stands made.

JEWELLER'S SHOP.

1680 dozen pairs of Black Bead Ear Rings or drops,
20 dozen Safety Chains.

CANE CHAIR BOTTOM MANUFACTORY.

Cane Chair Bottoms or Seats made as follows:
67 dozen plain or thin Maple Seats,
536 dozen plain solid front do.
165 dozen curled maple, do. do.
18 dozen sewing chair do.
3½ dozen curled maple raised back do.
48½ dozen curled maple box seats,
1 dozen seats and backs caned for large arm chairs,
22 dozen small seats for children,
5 dozen old chairs re-bottomed,
53 dozen stools for steam boats,
1 dozen counter stools,
14 oval stools for Piano Forte seats,
32 dozen frames for thin seats, made for shipping,
9 dozen birds eye solid front seats,
68 settee bottoms,

Making 916 doz. seats made complete, besides the settees, old chairs, &c.

18000 pounds rattan knotted and scoured,
1800 pounds of cane dressed fit for seats,

The frames of the seats are cut from rough plank and boards—made and polished complete by the children. Also, the rattan as imported, cleansed, split and dressed by do.

SHOE SHOP.

About 400 pairs new shoes, for both houses. A large number of do. mended.

Boys do all their own cooking.

SCHOOL REPORT.

[*From the Superintendent.*]

In consequence of sickness, &c. it has been necessary to make a change in our Teachers during the past year, which has prevented my receiving a correct account of the promotions from the school department for the whole year; therefore, that you may judge of the present rapid improvement of our well organized school, I shall only give you an exhibit of the advances of the children for the last three months in their various departments.

In Spelling and Reading there have been promoted

From	1st to 2d class,	Boys' department,		2
"	2d to 3d class,	"	"	9
"	3d to 4th class,	"	"	20
"	4th to 5th class,	"	"	31
"	5th to 6th class,	"	"	38
"	6th to 7th class,	"	"	30
"	7th to 8th class,	"	"	32
"	8th to 9th class,	"	"	22

It will be understood that those who enter the 1st class do not know their letters, &c.; the 9th class are understood to be those who read with much ease, and a good degree of elegance.

PROMOTIONS IN ARITHMETIC.

From	Addition to Subtraction, - -	53
"	Subtraction to Multiplication, -	43
"	Multiplication to short and long division,	39
"	Division to the Compound Rules, -	25
"	The Compound Rules to Reduction,	3
"	Reduction to the Rule of Three, -	2
"	The Rule of Three to Interest, -	2

There are now 139 boys in the School. All write on Slates, 45 on Paper.

In looking over the Girls' School, I find seven now in the House that have been received during the last year, who could not read when they came here, but who can now read the Scriptures, and write a fair hand.

There are 43 Girls in the House; 18 of that number write on paper. The girls have been taught by the Assistant Matron for about nine months past.

ARTICLES MADE BY GIRLS IN 1831.

[Furnished by the Matron.]

Chemises, - -	75	Spreads made and quilted,	18
Shirts - - -	439	Stockings run, (pair) -	311
Pantaloons, - -	511	Stockings knit, " -	10
Roundabouts Jackets,	307	Stockings footed, " -	16
Petticoats, - -	29	Carpeting made, (yards)	243¼
Frocks, - - -	116	Silk Shades for Eye Infirmary,	60
Bed Ticks, - -	68	Waistcoats for girls,- -	30
Brown Rollers, - -	56	White Vandikes, - -	7
Brown Aprons, -	54	Bed Gowns for Hospital,	2
Sheets for cells, - -	117	Night caps, - - -	50

ARTICLES MENDED.

Shirts, - - -	2350	Blankets - - -	98
Pantaloons, - -	1359	Bed Ticks, - - -	58
Chemises, - -	57	Pieces Washed, -	52,000
Stockings, (pair) -	1222		

Officers of the Society.

STEPHEN ALLEN, *President*

CORNELIUS DUBOIS, JOHN GRISCOM, HENRY I. WYCKOFF, JAMES LOVETT, PETER SHARPE, HUGH MAXWELL, *Vice Presidents.*

CORNELIUS DUBOIS, *Treasurer.*

FREDERICK SHELDON, *Secretary.*

JOHN STEARNS, M. D., GALEN CARTER, M. D. *Physicians and Surgeons.*

Indenturing Committee.

ROBERT C. CORNELL,
WILLIAM F. MOTT,
HEMAN AVERILL.

Acting Committee.

JAMES LOVETT,
WILLIAM KENT,
FREDERICK A. TRACY,
JACOB DRAKE,
JOHN HUNTER,
WILLIAM W. FOX,
P. R. STARR.

Managers.

STEPHEN ALLEN,	JAMES LOVETT,	JOHN STEARNS,
HEMAN AVERILL,	RUFUS L. LORD,	P. R. STARR,
ROBERT C. CORNELL,	WILLIAM F. MOTT,	WILLIAM L. STONE,
CORNELIUS DUBOIS,	HUGH MAXWELL,	FREDERICK A. TRACY,
JACOB DRAKE,	DENNIS M'CARTHY,	M. VAN SCHAICK,
WILLIAM W. FOX,	RUSSEL H. NEVINS,	HENRY I. WYCKOFF,
JOHN GRISCOM,	RALPH OLMSTED,	JOHN W. WYMAN,
JOHN HUNTER,	NATH'L RICHARDS,	ROBERT D. WEEKS,
JACOB HARVEY,	FRED'K SHELDON,	SILAS BROWN,
WILLIAM KENT,	PETER SHARPE,	B. L. WOOLLEY.

Ladies' Committee.

ISABELLA BULOID,	ANN L. MOTT,
MARGARET BEERS,	REBECCA M'COMB,
ALMY CORNELL,	ESTHER SEYMOUR,
DEBORAH L. EMBREE,	MARTHA WILLIS,
CHARLOTTE L. FOX,	ANN WARNER,
MARIA L. HYDE,	ELIZA TOMLINSON,
SARAH C. HAWXHURST,	SARAH LAVENDER.
PHEBE MOTT,	

House of Refuge.

NATHANIEL C. HART, *Superintendent.*
W. SAMPSON, *Assistant Superintendent.*
REBECCA ORAM, *Matron.*
CLARISSA NICHOLS, *Assistant Matron.*
MONMOUTH B. HART, *Teacher.*

RULES AND REGULATIONS FOR THE GOVERNMENT OF THE HOUSE OF REFUGE,

Requisites which the House of Refuge possesses for the Reformation of Juvenile Delinquents.

1. THE MEANS OF SECURITY.
2. INSPECTION.
3. CLASSIFICATION.
4. CONSTANT EMPLOYMENT.
5. RELIGIOUS AND MORAL INSTRUCTION.
6. ALLOWANCE OF FOOD AND CLOTHING.
7. SPACE FOR EXERCISE CONDUCIVE TO HEALTH.
8. SEPARATION OF THE SEXES.
9. ATTENDANCE UPON THE SICK.

THE introduction of labor into the House of Refuge will be regarded principally with reference to the moral benefits, and not merely to the profits, to be derived from it.

Preference will be given to those trades, the knowledge of which may enable the delinquents to earn their subsistence, on their discharge from the House.

LABOR.

The Children shall be employed every day in the year, except Sundays, at such labor, business, or employment, as may from time to time be designated by the Acting Committee; and, in order that the children may be properly instructed in the Arts or Trades at which they may be employed, the Superintendent shall, with the approbation of the Acting Committee, engage as Assistant Keepers, persons who are properly qualified to give such instruction.

A LIST OF EMPLOYMENTS AT PRESENT CARRIED ON IN THE HOUSE OF REFUGE.

BOYS.

Tailoring.
Shoe Making.
Brush Making.
Basket Work on Bottles, &c.
Brass Nail Making and Plaiting.
Box Making.
Chair Making.
Turning.

GIRLS.

Cutting out and Making Wearing Apparel for Boys and Girls.
Washing, Ironing, and Mending for Boys and Girls.
Plain Cooking, and House Work generally.

These may be increased or changed for other employments, as circumstances may require and the Committee direct.

FOOD.

The Children shall be fed with a sufficient quantity of coarse, but wholesome Food, and in conformity with a Dietary to be established by the Acting Committee.

The greatest economy and plainness shall be used in furnishing food for the children. The Superintendent shall inspect every article, and take care that nothing unsound be admitted into the House, and that the contracts made for its supply are fairly executed.

CLOTHING.

The Children shall be clothed in coarse, but comfortable apparel, of the cheapest and most durable kind. The cloth to be of a uniform color, and the clothes of the same cut or fashion. All the clothes, garments, shoes, &c. must, if practicable, be made on the premises, and by the children.

FEMALES AND MATRON.

The Females shall eat their meals and lodge in separate apartments from the males, with whom they shall have no intercourse or communication.

The Females shall be placed under the immediate care and superintendence of a Matron or Female Keeper, who shall reside in the House, and shall at no time absent herself from the premises, without the permission of the Acting or Visiting Committee.

None but the Matron shall search or examine the Female Delinquents. She shall superintend their work, and take charge of their clothes and bedding. She shall accompany the Superintendent or Physician, whenever it may be necessary for either of them to visit the apartments of the Females. She shall endeavor to unfold to those under her charge, the advantages of a moral and religious life, and to impress them with a conviction of the evils and miseries that attend the wicked and profligate. She shall, at the season set apart for the purpose, teach them the rudiments of education, and instruct them in the business of Housewifery, &c. She shall be authorized to punish them for offences against the rules of the House, or for indecorum in their behavior towards herself or one another, and she shall regularly report to the Superintendent such matters relative to their deportment and conduct, and the punishment she has inflicted, with the nature of the offence committed, as will be proper for him to lay before the Acting Committee.

No female subject shall pass out of the female yard or house, into the public yard or any of the adjoining tenements, upon any pretext whatever. And no boy, except the messenger, specially approved of by the Visiting Committee, shall go into the female house or yard, except to attend Divine Service on Sunday, or unless he is accompanied by an officer of the Institution.

PUNISHMENTS.

If any child shall refuse or wilfully neglect to perform the work required of him or her, or to obey the orders of the Superintendent or Assistant Keeper or Keepers, or shall use profane or indecent language, or shall assault or quarrel with a fellow delinquent, or shall make a noise or talk after having retired to the sleeping room, he or she shall be punished at a suitable time; and if, after this, such child persist in disobedience, he or she shall be confined in solitude for such time as the Superintendent may direct.

If any child shall strike or resist the Keeper, or attempt to escape from the House, or shall wilfully injure any article belonging to the Society, he or she shall be punished.

The Superintendent shall possess a discretionary power in awarding the punishment to offenders; but this must be exercised with great caution and judgment, and never under the influence of passion. He shall in all cases enter on the daily Journal, and report to the Acting Committee, a brief detail of the offence, and the punishment inflicted for the same.

If it should ever be necessary to inflict corporal punishment upon *females*, it shall only be done by or in the presence of the Matron.

KINDS OF PUNISHMENTS THAT MAY BE USED IN THE HOUSE OF REFUGE.

1. Privation of play and exercise.
2. Sent to bed supperless at sunset.

3. Bread and water, for breakfast, dinner, and supper.
4. Gruel *without salt*, for breakfast, dinner and supper.
5. Camomile, boneset, or bitter herb tea, for breakfast, dinner, and supper.
6. Confinement in solitary cells.
7. Corporal punishment, if absolutely necessary.
8. Fetters and handcuffs, only in *extreme cases.*

WARDSMEN OR MONITORS.

The Superintendent may, whenever in his opinion it shall be useful, appoint for each ten or more children, one of the delinquents as Wardsman or Monitor, who shall be selected from the most orderly, well behaved, and best qualified for the purpose.

The general duty of the Wardsmen shall be, to observe the behavior and conduct of their respective classes; to see that they daily wash their persons: that their sleeping and work rooms are regularly swept every morning, and washed or scrubbed once in each week; that the rooms and bedding be ventilated and aired, and the night utensils removed and cleansed; and that decency and good order prevail throughout the class.

The Wardsman shall be authorised to select from his class, in rotation, one of the number to perform the duty of sweeping, scrubbing, &c. and it shall be an offence against the rules, for any of the class to disobey the reasonable commands of the Wardsman. He shall report to the Superintendent any improper act committed by a member of his class immediately after its occurrence, in order that it may be corrected forthwith.

ARRANGEMENT OF TIME.

A bell shall be rung every morning one quarter of an hour before the unlocking of the lodging rooms, and also at the hour of unlocking, when every child shall be prepared to leave his room, in order to wash &c. previous to going to work.

The time of beginning and leaving off work, of eating breakfast, dinner, and supper, of attending school, and of retiring to sleep; shall be in conformity with a table prepared by the Acting Committee, and each time shall be designated by the ringing of the bell, as the Superintendent may direct.

CLASSIFICATION.

The Boys and Girls shall be classed according to their moral conduct, and as soon as practicable there shall be four grades of classes formed, viz: Nos. 1, 2, 3, 4.

Class No. 1, shall include the best behaved and most orderly Boys and Girls: those who do not swear, lie, or use profane, obscene, or indecent language or conversation, who attend to their work and studies, are not quarrelsome, and have not attempted to escape.

Class No. 2. Those who are next best, but who are not quite free from all the foregoing vices and practices.

Class No. 3. Those who are more immoral in conduct than Class No. 2.

Class No. 4. Those who are vicious, bad, and wicked.

Badges bearing the number of each class, shall be worn on the arm, at all times in the day.

In case of improper and bad conduct, the children in Classes, Nos. 1, 2, or 3, shall be transferred or degraded by the Superintendent to the lower or lowest Class. And for improvement, or good conduct, in Classes 4, 3, or 2, they may be transferred or promoted to a higher class.

The children in Class No. 1, who behave well, and are orderly and correct in their conduct, may be rewarded by the Superintendent, in the presence of all the children, and of the Acting Committee.

Those children who have behaved well for three months in succession, shall be allowed to wear a badge of distinction and approbation.

SUPERINTENDENT AND KEEPER.

The Superintendent and Keeper shall have the general superintendence of the House of Refuge, and shall carry into effect all the rules and regulations adopted by the Acting Committee for its management and government.

He shall keep a register of every child committed to his custody, the name, age, and description of person; when received, by whom committed, on what charge, in what part of the House confined, when discharged, and such other remarks as may be proper and useful, including a brief historical sketch.

He shall keep a regular aud separate account of the expense incurred for the keeping of the children placed under his charge, with every item properly designated; also, an inventory of the whole personal property within the House belonging to the Society, and the manner in which the same may have been disposed of, to be submitted to the Acting Committee, every half year, or oftener if required.

He shall keep a record of the events worthy of note, that may occur daily during the recess of the Committee, and submit the same for inspection at every meeting.

He shall daily inspect every part of the House and premises in person, and shall not absent himself from the establishment for a night without permission from the Acting or Visiting Committee.

He shall exercise the authority delegated to him with firmness, moderation and discretion: but in order that the certainty of punishment may deter from a repetition of offence, he shall permit no offence against the rules to pass without some punishment.

He shall, under the instruction of the Acting Committee, procure the necessary supplies for the House, and purchase such materials as may be necessary and indispensable for the employment of the children; and he shall dispose of such manufactured articles, as the Committee, may direct, and credit the Society for all receipts from such sales.

By the direction and sanction of the Committee, he may contract with mechanics or others for the services of the children under his charge, or any number of them, to be employed within the walls of the establishment, at such business as may be mutually approved by the parties.

He shall allow none of the children to be absent from the premises, without special permission in writing first obtained from the Committee for that purpose

He shall have the uncontrolled direction of the Matron and Assistant Keeper or Keepers, in all matters relative to carrying into effect the rules, regulations, and discipline of the House; and he shall be responsible for their acts and conduct while on the premises, and in the employ of the Society.

The Superintendent shall render quarterly to the Acting Committee, a detailed account of receipts and expenditures on account of the House of Refuge.

TEACHER AND ASSISTANT KEEPERS.

The Matron and Assistant Keeper or Keepers shall conduct themselves in strict conformity with the rules of the Establishment; they are to receive their orders from the Superintendent, and to obey his directions. They shall not absent themselves from the House, without the leave of their principal.

ACTING COMMITTEE.

The Board of Managers, shall choose, from their own number, an Acting Committee consisting of seven members; one of whom shall go out of office monthly, and a new member be chosen to supply his place.

The Acting Committee shall meet four times a month, for the transaction of business, once at the House and three times in town.

The Acting Committee shall appoint a sub-committee of two, to visit the House of Refuge weekly, one of whom shall retire each month, and a new one be appointed. The visiting committee shall record in a book, to be submitted to the Acting Committee, such observations on the cleanliness of the House, and the conduct of the officers and children, as may seem to them proper. From these records, summary minutes shall be made by the Acting Committee, and laid before the stated meetings of the Managers.

The Acting Committee shall be empowered to appoint a temporary Assistant or Assistants, for the purpose of instructing the children in the House of Refuge in any work, manufacture, or useful employment, which they may deem expedient to introduce into the House.

The Acting Committee shall be authorised to enter into such contracts, as they may think proper, with any person, for the employment of the children in any work, manufacture or trade.

The Acting Committee shall appoint in rotation, one of its number, to attend at religious service in the chapel of the House of Refuge, on Sundays. The person appointed, shall furnish a substitute from the Board of Managers in case of unavoidable absence.

Whenever any work above the value of five dollars is authorised to be done at the House of Refuge, when any of the boys or girls are put to labour at a stipulated price, or when a Superintendent, matron or other officer or servant of the House is hired, or a collector employed, contracts in writing shall be made by the Visiting Committee, with the party or parties respectively, which contracts shall be copied by the Superintendent into the contract book, kept at the House for that purpose, and delivered by him to the Acting Committee at their next meeting.

LADIES' COMMITTEE.

The Managers will annually appoint a Committee of thirteen Ladies, to visit the Female Delinquents. It shall be the duty of the Matron to attend upon the Ladies' Committee, to afford them every facility in their investigations, and give them all the information she possesses respecting the conduct of the female house, the clothing and property belonging to it, the character and conduct of the girls, their proficiency in learning and good manners, and generally to advise and confer with the Ladies, relative to the affairs and management of this Department.

The Committee of Ladies will visit the House of Refuge monthly, and they will appoint in rotation a sub-committee of two of their number to visit it once in each week, to inspect the Female Department, to excite in the girls a sense of virtue and piety, to inculcate habits of industry, cleanliness, and strict attention to the directions of the Matron and the rules of the House, and to reward those who shall distinguish themselves for industry and good conduct.

Minutes will be kept by the general and visiting committee, in a book, provided for that purpose, in which they will note the order, cleanliness, and improvement of the girls, and make such suggestions and remarks as they may deem proper and useful. These minutes will be read at the meetings of the Acting Committee, and a summary of them also at the stated meetings of the Managers.

Should vacancies occur in this Committee by death or resignation, the Committee may appoint such Ladies as they shall have previously ascertained will, if elected, attend to the important duties devolving on them.

The Committee of Ladies, will recommend to the Superintendent, the most suitable materials of clothing for the male delinquents, and he will confer with them on the subject, when new clothing is required for the use of the male Refuge.

They shall be empowered to purchase or procure, or may recommend to the Acting Committee, the most suitable clothing for the female Delinquents.

The Committee of Ladies will report to the Superintendent, for the use of the Indenturing Committee, such girls as may be fit to be bound out. In any other emergency, the Ladies will report to the Acting Committee.

INDENTURING COMMITTEE.

The Board of Managers shall annually choose from their own body an Indenturing Committee, to consist of three persons, who shall be (ex-officio) members of the Acting Committee.

The Indenturing Committee shall meet weekly at the House of Refuge, they shall keep regular minutes of the business transacted by them, and shall monthly report to the Board of Managers a detailed statement of the number of children indentured, to whom indentured, place of residence, and references, and such other information, connected with their duty, as they may consider expedient and proper.

The Indenturing Committee shall examine into the character and qualifications of the children, and at proper times endeavor to procure for them suitable places, as apprentices, to mechanics, manufacturers, and farmers, and as domestics, and in some cases as mariners.

The Committee shall obtain the best information practicable of the fitness of applicants to have children indentured to them, and when satisfied on this important head, they shall give permission in writing to the Superintendent to have the indentures executed, and deliver the child.

No child shall be indentured in the city, or delivered up to its parents or guardians, without the consent of the Acting Committee.

When any boy is to be indentured as a mariner or for the sea service, the consent of his parent or guardian, if he has any, shall first be obtained, if practicable, by the Indenturing Committee.

The Superintendent shall present all written applications for apprentices and servants to the Indenturing Committee, by whom they shall be approved before they are granted; and no child shall be put to service out of the House, unless under regular indentures from the Society.

A Bible and printed paper of advice relative to his or her future conduct, shall be given to each delinquent when so apprenticed.

The term of the apprenticeship of the Girls shall not extend beyond the age of 18 years; they shall not be apprenticed to unmarried men, nor placed in boarding-houses, or academies for boys.

It shall be the duty of the Superintendent, under the direction of the Indenturing Committee, to correspond, as often as they may think necessary, with those to whom children have been indentured, to ascertain the general character and conduct of the child.

DIVINE SERVICE.

Divine Service shall commence in the Chapel, on the Sabbath at half past ten in the morning, and from the 1st of March to the 1st of November, at three o'clock in the afternoon, and from the 1st of November to the 1st of March, at half past two o'clock in the afternoon; and may be continued for one hour and a half each.

There shall be no meetings held at any other time or place, experience having shewn that many of the children are unfit to attend, after their daily schooling and labor are finished.

Respectable visitors and the neighboring families, may be admitted to attend religious service in the Chapel, at the discretion of the Superintendent and upon his responsibility, but they are not to be suffered to remain on the premises, or to talk to the children, or have any intercourse with them. It is made the duty of the Superintendent to publish this rule to the audience, as often as may be necessary.

No person shall be allowed to address the children at the meetings for worship, without the permission of the Superintendent or the Committee in Attendance.

GENERAL REGULATIONS.

No spirituous liquors shall, upon any pretence whatever, (excepting by order of the Physicians,) be brought into any part of the premises of the House of Refuge.

No species of gambling, nor of plays or games having a tendency thereto, shall be permitted at the House of Refuge.

The wall, and ceilings of the wards, cells, rooms, and passages, used by the delinquents throughout the House of Refuge, shall be white-washed and thoroughly cleaned at least twice in each year; which work shall be done by the delinquents, except on particular emergencies.

Every morning the day-rooms, work-rooms, passages and cells shall be swept; the pans emptied, the dirt and ashes, and all filth and rubbish collected in the yard, removed to the place appropriated for the same. The day-rooms, working-rooms and sleeping cells, shall be washed once a week, or oftener if requisite. The doors of all the sleeping cells, and also the windows, when the weather will permit, shall be kept open during the day.

The bedding of the House shall be hung up to air, whenever the Superintendent shall require it. The straw in the Mattresses shall be changed, and the corn-husk Mattresses scalded and washed as often as the Physicians may think proper. The blankets and coverlets shall be washed, at least once in three months, and in all cases clean bedding shall be provided for every new delinquent.

No delinquent of any description shall, on any account whatever, be confined in any apartment under ground, or where there is not sufficient light and ventilation.

Every delinquent, seized with any disorder, shall be forthwith removed to the Infirmary; and in case of any putrid or infectious disorder, to the Fever Ward therein. The cell, from which he or she was taken, shall immediately after such removal, be cleansed, fumigated, and white-washed.

Bibles and Testaments, and such elementary books as may be thought necessary, shall be provided for the use of the children, to be distributed among them, at the discretion of the Acting Committee.

The admission of visitors during the week, shall be restricted to Wednesdays and Fridays, excepting strangers, not residing in the city, and persons accompanied by or having a written permission from a manager.

Parents and guardians shall be permitted into the Refuge, to see their children, once in three months, upon the days appointed, under the inspection of the Superintendent and Teacher, and their visits shall be confined to the hours between 12 and 4 o'clock.

The Superintendent shall make weekly reports of the sums he receives from the contractors for the labor of the boys, together with the balances due, and the names of those contractors who do not pay every Saturday.

The Superintendent shall pay over to the Treasurer, at least once a month, all the monies he receives belonging to the House.

It shall be the duty of the Visiting Committee to call upon the contractors, whenever it may be necessary, and to see that they pay with punctuality.

Not less than from three to four hours shall be devoted to the literary instruction of the subjects of the Refuge. The Superintendent shall report the hours of employ, every month, so that new arrangements may be made by the Acting Committee to suit the changing seasons.

No boy or girl shall be permitted to receive money or presents of any kind, while a subject of the Refuge.

The Superintendent shall keep a notice of this regulation, on the boys' house and the gate, for the government of parents and visitors.

As no person can be received into the premises who is not engaged under contract, or committed according to law, it is made the duty of the Superintendent to report the name of any person or persons, male or female, who shall have staid in the Refuge during the week, or any day or night of the week preceding his report. And the Acting Committee shall take cognizance of the case without delay.

The gate-keeper shall not admit any person, without permission of the Superintendent, or by his express orders, unless he bears a permit from, or is introduced by, a manager. Any violation of this rule shall be reported to the Acting Committee, and will subject the gate-keeper to immediate dismission.

The person who may be appointed collector to the House, shall once a month furnish the Treasurer with a list of the subscribers and donors, from whom collections may have been made; and at the same time shall pay the moneys collected, into the hands of the Treasurer.

It shall be the duty of the Treasurer, to examine the collector's books and accounts, at the period above named, and if any omission or defalcation is discovered, he shall immediately report the same to the Acting Committee.

The Treasurer shall, once a year, publish a list of subscribers and donors, in any two or more of the public papers.

At their meeting next after the annual election, the Board of Managers will appoint a Finance Committee, to consist of two members to serve for one year. Any vacancies in this committee will be filled up at the discretion of the Board.

The securities and vouchers taken by the Finance Committee, shall, as soon as received, be delivered by them to the Acting Committee, who shall cause them to be copied into their book of minutes, and then to be transferred to the Treasurer for safe keeping and collection when due.

A DISCOURSE

ON OPENING THE NEW BUILDING IN THE HOUSE OF REFUGE, NEW-YORK; ESTABLISHED FOR THE REFORMATION OF JUVENILE DELINQUENTS. DELIVERED DECEMBER 25TH, 1825, IN PRESENCE OF THE MANAGERS OF THE INSTITUTION, THE HONORABLE THE MAYOR AND COMMON COUNCIL OF THE CITY, SOME OF THE MEMBERS OF THE LEGISLATURE, AND MANY OF ITS PATRONS AND FRIENDS.

BY JOHN STANFORD, A. M.

Once rude and ignorant we were,
With natures prone to stray!
Blest now by Pity's kindest care,
We hear of Wisdom's way.

The soul untaught is dark as night,
Where every evil dwells;
All hail Instruction's sacred light,
Which all this night dispels!——SS.

New-York, Jan. 10, 1826.

At a meeting of the Board of Managers of the Society for the Reformation of Juvenile Delinquents, the following Resolutions were passed:—

Resolved—That the thanks of this Board be presented to the Rev. JOHN STANFORD, for his very able and appropriate Discourse, on the opening of the House of Refuge, on the 25th of December last.

Resolved—That the Rev. Mr. Stanford be requested occasionally, and when his other public engagements will allow, to visit the House of Refuge.

Resolved—That the Rev. Mr. Stanford be requested to furnish a copy of his late Discourse, delivered at the opening of the New Building, for the use of the Delinquents at the House of Refuge.

Copied from the Minutes,
ROBERT F. MOTT, *Secretary.*

To the Honorable Cadwallader D. Colden, **President,** *and the Gentlemen composing* **the Board of Directors** *of the* **HOUSE OF REFUGE,** *for the Reformation of Juvenile Delinquents,* **This Discourse** *is Most Respectfully DEDICATED, by*

JOHN STANFORD.

ADVERTISEMENT.

THE HOUSE OF REFUGE owes its origin to the Society for the Prevention of Pauperism in the City of New-York:—a voluntary association, formed by a number of citizens for the purpose of tracing the evils of poverty to their actual sources, and of suggesting and urging such remedies as might be deemed practicable, for a certain portion of those evils.

The results of the investigations and deliberations of this Society, were given to the public in several successive annual and special reports, which excited among the benevolent citizens of the metropolis, no inconsiderable share of solicitude that the city might avail itself of those suggestions; inasmuch as it was plainly perceived, that without some energetic efforts to arrest the progress of vice and its attendant poverty, the burthen of the city for the maintenance of its poor would increase to an alarming degree. Among those evils, the subject of juvenile delinquency presented itself to the Society in a formidable shape. The report on that subject, detailing the nature and amount of the evil, and proposing an establishment, separate from the City and State Prisons, for the confinement and reformation of juvenile criminals and vagrant youth, elicited so much cordiality of feeling, that the sum of $15,000 was promptly subscribed by the citizens, and a special Society formed, for carrying the plan into operation. These objects have been so fully approved by the Governor and Legislature, that the Society has been incorporated, and a legislative provision made for its support, which, with the liberality of the citizens, will, it is presumed, prove sufficient to secure its continuance and prosperity. The Institution was opened on the first of January, 1825, with nine subjects, sentenced by the police to the control of the Society. The number at the present time, (July, 1826,) is, 94 boys and 24 girls. When the buildings which are now in progress shall have been completed, the Institution will accommodate 140 boys, and 70 girls.

Four hours of each working day are devoted to literary instruction; and the remainder, with the exception of meals, and a moderate portion of time for relaxation, to the work shops.

The Managers are abundantly encouraged, from the success already obtained, to hope for extensive usefulness in the reformatory influence of the Institution, over the minds and characters of its subjects: most of whom, without such a timely agency, would in all probability be led, by the force of corrupt associations, into habits of deep and irretrievable criminality.

DISCOURSE.

EXODUS II. 9.

Take this child away and nurse it for me, and I will give thee thy wages.

It has frequently been asserted, that when a child is destined for some eminent station and usefulness in life, its birth is usually accompanied with some strong marks of distinction. This certainly was the case with Moses, who was designated by the Almighty to be the deliverer of the Israelites from their bondage in Egypt; and afterwards to become their Lawgiver, Prophet, and General through the wilderness to inherit the land of Canaan. About the 320th year of the Hebrew captivity, it is said, *There arose up a new king over Egypt, which knew not Joseph.* Which I presume, is not to be understood, that he was ignorant such a person had lived in Egypt, was raised from obscurity to dignity, and preserved multitudes alive amidst the ravages of famine: but, that he had no esteem for him, because he was an Hebrew; and therefore cultivated an implacable enmity to Joseph's brethren, who had so exceedingly increased that it alarmed his fears for the safety of his kingdom. This excited his cruelty to lay unjustifiable burdens upon this people; but *the more he afflicted them, the more they multiplied and grew.* Disappointed in this measure, he commanded, that when the Hebrew women should bring forth their male children, the midwives should destroy them in their birth. In this also the king was disappointed; for, to the humanity and honour of those females it is said, *the midwives feared God, and did not as the king of Egypt commanded them, but saved the men children alive*; and then made an excuse for their conduct. This so exasperated the king, that, *he charged all his people, saying, Every son that is born ye shall cast into the river, and every daughter ye shall save alive.*—Cruel wretch, in the character of a king! his edicts are here recorded as perpetual brands of his infamy.

At this time lived Amram and Jochebed, two pious

Israelites of the tribe of Levi. God had already blessed them with a son whose name was Aaron, and a daughter called Miriam. Now, a third child is added to the number; it was a son of a beautiful countenance, and excited the most ardent affections of his parents. But, the edict! the cruel mandate of Pharaoh, which sentenced the lovely child to death in the waters of the Nile, overwhelmed them with sorrow. The fond parents determined to conceal the infant as long as possible, and retained it within their arms for three months, but could do so no longer. God, who foresees all events, to accomplish his own purposes, no doubt dictated to the mother the expedient of making an *Ark*, or close basket of bulrushes; and it is said, *she daubed it with slime and with pitch*, to keep out the water. Into this ark, she laid her tender infant, closed the lid, and in faith on the God of Israel, laid it in the flags by the river's brink, whether for life, or death.* Say, ye tender mothers! what were your feelings, when on the loss of an infant by death, it was laid in the coffin, and before the lid was closed, you gave with your lips, the last token of affection! Ye best can tell the feeling of the mother of Moses, when in tears she closed the lid of the ark, and left him in the waters of danger.

On this very day, the providence of God directed the feet of Pharaoh's daughter, in company with her maidens, to go down to the river and wash. Whether this was for the purpose of pleasure, for health, or as an act of idolatrous worship, is not so material for us to determine. As she walked by the river, she saw a something among the flags; curiosity prompted an order to her maidens to fetch it; the lid was opened; she saw the child; and behold! *the babe wept.* Had we been present, we should have perceived her surprize; the tears of Moses in distress awakened her sympathy; her generous bosom glowed; she had compassion on him, and instantly exclaimed, *This is one of the Hebrews' children!* A nurse was immediately provided, and the princess honoured her own feelings by thus addressing her: *Take this child away, and nurse it for me, and I will give thee thy wages.* This was accepted, *And the woman took the child and nursed it.*

* Hebrews xi. 23.

Those who have read the sequel of this history, need not be told, that from this most striking occurrence, Pharaoh's daughter adopted this rescued child as her own son; she caused him to be instructed in all the learning of Egypt; and, that he afterwards became one of the most distinguished and honoured characters that adorn the pages of the Old Testament.

As we are this morning assembled in this new building, to offer our prayer to the Almighty for his gracious benediction upon this benevolent Institution: perhaps I may not better perform the duty assigned me, than by drawing a few lines of comparison between the forlorn exposure, and the relief of little Moses, and those young unfortunates whom this Society rescues from misery, granting them protection in this House of Refuge.

I. Let us recollect the danger to which the infant Moses was exposed.—He was laid among the flags which grew on the brink of the Nile, and in danger of being carried away by the stream, and seen no more. And who does not know, that iniquity has too long run down our streets like water; and that the floods of the ungodly, like the rising of the waters of the Nile, have frequently overflowed the safety and peace of our city? The rising generation, for successive years, have been exposed to this polluting current, and many of them have been carried away and destroyed. Often have we seen the children of the lower orders of society, for the want of education and restraint, plunging into this iniquitous stream; and such are the force of example and the fascinations of vice, that we are not without some instances of other young persons, of respectable connections being unhappily carried away from the paths of virtue, lodged in houses of criminal confinement, lost to all expectation by their parents of retrieving their characters, and becoming useful members of society. But now, the pitying eye, like that of Pharaoh's daughter, is directed to such young offenders; and, the hand of kindness is extended, at once to rescue them from destruction, and safely conduct them to this House of Refuge.

Let us not forget that little Moses was also in danger of being devoured by the crocodile. This amphibious animal is a native inhabitant of the Nile, living both on land and water; it frequently grows to an enormous size, is of great strength, and extremely voracious. It has the largest mouth of all monsters, opens both his jaws at once, which, being furnished with a great number of sharp teeth, can snap a man asunder in a moment, and gorge the body. To this dreadful monster the infant Moses was exposed; and we cannot but shudder at the apprehension of his exposure. Perhaps you may inquire, Have we any such dangerous animals in our city, or in its rivers? We have only seen them exhibited in show, and so confined, as to admit of no danger to the visiters. Where then can be the correctness of this comparison between little Moses, and the miserable young beings who wander in our streets? I venture to affirm, that among us, we have crocodiles in human shape; persons whose conduct is as dangerous to the interest of civil society, as are the ravages of the monsters in the Nile. They may well be denominated amphibious, for they are capable of committing their ravages upon the land, or on the water. Indeed, it is well known that by various methods, such unhappy characters form their criminal practices into a system. They first learn the rudiments of their art in secret; perhaps in some obscure cellar, and there form combinations. Occasionly, a party sally forth to try their skill in less crimes; till eventually, some of them are detected, and sentenced to the penitentiary. There, for the want of room to make the necessary classification, they horde too much in mass, and soon find those who are more proficient in criminal practices than themselves; from whom they receive greater aid to carry on the course of bad instruction. So true is it, that *evil communications*, not only *corrupt good manners*, but certainly make bad manners much worse. Here too, they formerly met with the juvenile offender; perhaps sentenced for his first offence. As with the false tears of the crocodile, they pretended to commiserate his misfortunes, ingratiate themselves into his tender feelings, and by such insinuations, he gradually listens to the story of their own vicious conduct;

and, finally imbibes those depraved principles, which soon make him to resemble their own likeness. Thus advanced in their vicious education, no wonder they should resolve to form a new gang on their liberation; so that, on the expiration, it may be said of some of them, they are competent to take their first degree of Bachelor in the Art of crime.

Now, a new scene appears. Instead of cultivating repentance for past offences, such is the strength of sinful habits, they improve their criminal system, and form stronger combinations to execute their purposes. Their rapacity, like that of the crocodile, increases; and, with extended jaws they lay in wait to catch the young offender that he may aid in their dark designs. This becomes indispensably necessary, in order to perform those operations of which a grown person is incompetent. The little boy must watch the opening door; climb the fence; or, urge his way through the cellar bars. Having gained admission, the urchin conceals himself, perhaps beneath the bed; within the vacant closet; or, in the garret's corner, until all is hushed in silent sleep; when, behold! he descends the stairs, unlocks the door, and admits the gang to accomplish their plunder. This is no false representation; facts like these have too frequently occurred; and I personally know a youth, of about fifteen years of age, now in one of our prisons, who, by such early instruction and practices, has been pronounced competent to take the lead of a gang. What generous soul but shudders on beholding scenes like these, and ardently wishes to rescue such young delinquents from the jaws of total destruction! Such public depredations, however, seldom go long without detection; and, the perpetrators are deservedly conveyed to the State Prison. Here, likewise, for the want of adequate means to classify the criminals, their intercourse with each other, especially in the shades of night, is favorable for that conversation, which, can only produce a stronger growth of vicious principles, and which outbraves the watch of their keepers, and the moral lessons which they constantly receive. And here too, the old offenders seldom fail to ensnare the young, and instil stronger principles of mischief into their minds, and thus stimulate them to the perpetration of more flagrant offences. From such a mass of criminals, so long in the cultivation of vice, no wonder that some of them should become so proficient, as at the expiration of their sentence, they may be said to take their second degree, of MASTER in the ART of criminality.

Let us look again at the infant Moses, and we shall perceive him exposed to danger from the Officers of Pharaoh's court. Had they passed along by the river side, and perceived something in the shape of a basket, they would have been excited to ascertain its contents. Opening the lid, they would have found the Hebrew child; and although they might have been affected by perceiving its tears, the inexorable edict of their king would have compelled them to take away its life by drowning him in the river. This is similar to the case of our delinquent children; for, the civil law of our country knows no distinction in the detection of crime, whether committed by old or young. When therefore our officers of justice perceive the unwary youth, wading in the stream of iniquity, notwithstanding they may have compassion for his tender years, they are bound to arrest. And, although the natural life of the offender be not in danger, like that of Moses, still, the condemnation, and criminal confinement of a young person, generally produces the moral death of his character, and destroys the hope of society in his favor. How generous then is that hand, which can rescue a fallen youth from such extreme danger!

What adds a final grade to the distressing exposure of poor little Moses, is, that he was unconscious of his danger. Is not this the case with our unwary youth? Ignorant of the criminality of their conduct; their offences against God; and their accountability to the laws of society, they go astray, regardless of its fatal consequences. Like as Moses knew not his danger of being carried away by the stream, or devoured by the monster of the Nile: so our unfortunate children are insensible of the current of vice, or of those older, abandoned characters, whether male or female, who lay in wait to destroy them! Nor is it uncommon for such old offenders, having succeeded in decoying the young under a promise of gain, on their detection, to turn evidence against them, and thus seal their condemnation.

Let this general statement of our dissipated youth, and the dangers to which they are exposed, produce the necessary impression upon our mind, and we shall instantly perceive the importance of the laudable efforts of this Society in rescuing them from the paths of the destroyer, and giving them a place in this House of Refuge. As the means which the Almighty employed to extricate the infant Moses from his danger are so remarkably interesting; and, as the circumstances attending it are so admirably calculated to afford us a few lessons of instruction on the design of the present assembly, we will make them the subject of the second part of this discourse.

II. By the intervening providence of God, the feet of Pharaoh's daughter were directed to the waters of the Nile. How minutely does the Almighty perform his operations! Had the Princess, with her maidens, come down on the morning before, Moses had not been there; had she been confined to her chamber, and visited the river on the following day, the child might have been drowned, or devoured by the monster. This therefore was the very *set time* for God to favor Moses; and all circumstances combine to produce the event.—Permit me to say, that many years ago, I cultivated a commiseration for the vagrant children in our streets; and especially for those miserable little creatures who were confined in our prisons. In the year 1813, I presented to the Honorable the Common Council, the outlines of a plan for the establishment of an Asylum for their relief; but, it was like the morning, too soon! The set time for such an operation had not arrived; now, the providence of God appears in their favor, and the public mind is generously excited to rescue them from the pulluted waters of destruction, and employ every possible means for their restoration to usefulness and happiness.

The address of the Princess of Egypt to the nurse, is as expressive as it is kind and benevolent; and affords us a charming impression of the strong interest which she took in the future welfare of the infant. *Take this child away*, said she, from its present danger, though it be an Hebrew. Carry it to your home, *and nurse it for me*, as though it were my own. I require not this care at your own expense; for I am able, and promise to *give thee thy wages*. Excellent Princess! what more could she have said! How justly may all these items be applied to the good intention of the Society now assembled. Let us examine them?—*Take this child away;* remove the miserable little objects from the paths of idleness, beggary, vanity, and inducement to crime, by the crafty and the wicked who lay in wait to allure and destroy them. But whither shall these juvenile delinquents be conveyed? Where is the hospitable door that will open to receive them? Here it is! The House of Refuge is now open: its door unfolds to receive and protect them, as the arms of the nurse were extended to embrace the rescued Moses.—What attention are they here to receive? They are to be nursed. What this means, is easy to be understood. They come to you in rags, and you must clothe them; they are hungry, and you will feed them; destitute of virtuous friends, you clasp them to your bosom; mentally diseased by idleness and sin, you afford them the religious means for restoration. Nursing is indeed anxious labor; and those who have the government of this Institution, will frequently find a sufficiency of care to fill both their hands and their hearts.—Still, who is to supply? From whence are the necessaries to be obtained to feed, and to clothe so large a family? Remember, Pharaoh's daughter said unto the nurse, I will give thee thy wages; and if the nurse could trust the Princess of Egypt, surely we may confide in the providence of the Almighty, for the silver and the gold are his to bestow. Besides, the public mind has already been so benevolently interested in its favor, that, methinks I hear their voice to you this morning, "We will give thee thy wages." For, indeed, you nurse these poor miserable creatures for the public peace and safety; and therefore they will not fail to give you the most ample supply.

The reflections I have already made, lead me to institute an inquiry:—What may be the public expectation of benefits arising from this new establishment? The first I will name, is, the extraction of THE CORE OF PAUPERISM. It is well known, that we seldom see men and women, with baskets on their arms, going from house to house, soliciting charity; for the trade of mendicity has been carried on, principally by the children of the indolent and worthless. While this practice was pursued, Societies for the cure, or prevention of Pauperism, may hold their meetings, and publish their annual reports, without any other benefit than what would accrue to the paper mill, and the printing press. Remove such children from the streets, and nurse them well; then, though the strings of the core of pauperism may draw hard in its extraction, it is the best, if not the only method of cure.—The public will likewise expect these children will be instructed in the rudiments of plain education; the importance of cultivating habits of industry; and some of the more useful mechanic arts; by which, hereafter, they may obtain an honest livelihood, whether on the land, or on the seas.—To which must be added, their reformation, and improvement in morals; without which, very little good will be obtained. No man will expect that you can change their vicious little hearts; for this is alone the prerogative of God, by the operation of the Holy Spirit of his grace. But, as this is frequently produced by the use of means, you can teach these ignorant children to read their once neglected Bible; show them the nature and danger of sin and transgression in the sight of God and man; you can point them to a compassionate Saviour, who not only died for our sins, but in the days of his flesh, took children in his arms and blessed them. And, it will be easy for you to contrast their former state of ignorance and degradation, with the privileges of instruction and good examples which they now receive, in the cheering hope of their interest and happiness in the world. These are some of those duties which you owe to them, and to the public; and if faithfully performed, I hope God will succeed your endeavors, and the expectation of our citizens will be happily realized.

ADDRESSES.

The Ladies who have so generously engaged their services to visit and to watch over the female department of this House of Refuge, will accept my congratulation upon this occasion. You have no need for me to intimate the duties you have to perform. You possess a parental feeling; and nothing but motives of tenderness and kindness could have prompted your exertions to aid in this noble design of restoring the fallen children of your own sex, to the paths of virtue and happiness. Permit me to remind you of Pharaoh's daughter, as your noble example. True, she was an Egyptian; an Idolatress; no matter for the color of her complexion; she came to the brink of the river; she saw the helpless infant; she had compassion, and she saved him! Had that distinguished woman lived in a Christian land; and had her heart been enriched with the Gospel of Christ, I would exhibit her in the attitude of relieving the distressed, and then say to you, BEHOLD THE LOVELIEST PICTURE OF CHRISTIAN CHARITY!—Go, worthy Ladies, and do likewise.

The Honorable the Mayor, and the Members of the Common Council of the City; and the Gentlemen of the New-York Delegation to the State Legislature, who have honored this Society with their presence, cannot but feel a lively interest in beholding this rising Institution. You must be convinced, Gentlemen, that this is not an object of simple charity. It is strongly combined with the safety, honor, and happiness of the whole community. If such little offenders were permitted to range at large, their criminal habits would grow with their years; their number by example would increase; and, by these means, town and country would be overrun, and our public prisons be crowded, not failing to produce an enormous expense to the state! To prevent these calamitous consequences, the House of Refuge is erected, and makes a strong appeal for public support. But, my humane friends, the prevention of the growth of crime is not all that is intended by this Society; it is their moral design, by every method possible, to reclaim these juvenile delinquents, that they may become useful and honorable members of society. This enhances the value of the Institution so highly, that I have no language sufficiently to express its importance! While therefore we cherish the hope that our own CORPORATION will look with a benign aspect on the House of Refuge: our CITY DELEGATION also will make such a favorable representation of it, that our STATE LEGISLATURE will form a sort of echo, "We also will aid, and pay thee thy wages."

THE MANAGERS OF THIS ESTABLISHMENT. I cannot but congratulate you, Gentlemen, on the completion of this new building. The smiles of heaven have thus far succeeded your efforts, in favor of the young unfortunates committed to your care. The duties requisite in every new institution, must generally be known as the result of observation and experience; of course you will have much to learn, as well as much to perform. Begin your services in the fear of your God; duly reflect on the magnitude of the object for which you are engaged; while you combine tenderness and faithfulness in all your operations; it is my sincere wish, that the whole may be crowned with the most abundant success.

THE CHILDREN.

CHILDREN! I must not omit claiming your attention, and soliciting you to indulge the most serious reflections on the privileges you now enjoy. The erection of this building, together with your support, must give you strong conviction, how much a benevolent public are interested in your present and future welfare. Had you been left alone to yourselves, in poverty, idleness and sin, instead of ensuring you peace and pleasure, iniquity would have proved your final ruin. You are to look at the walls which surround this building, not so much as those of a prison, as an hospitable dwelling, in which you enjoy comfort, and safety from those who once led you astray. And, I may venture to say, that in all probability, this is the best home many of you ever enjoyed! You have no need for me to tell you, that the consideration of all these favors should stimulate you to submission, industry, and gratitude. You are not placed here so much for punishment, as to produce your moral improvement. By these indulgent means, we hope, that instead of your spending your days in idleness, disgrace, and misery, you may become useful to yourselves, honorable in society, and share in the true happiness of your fellow creatures. Although you are now young in years, you must have some consciousness that the errors of life, and the evils of your heart, expose you to the displeasure of the Almighty; that you need the tender mercy of the Saviour to pardon your iniquities; to renew your depraved minds by the virtue of His grace, and thus save you from the desert of your transgressions. We hope, therefore, that while you are within these walls, the Lord may command his merciful kindness upon you, and enable you to devote yourselves to his adored Name, and his most delightful service! Moses could never forget the humanity and kindness of Pharaoh's daughter, in delivering him from the danger to which he was exposed; and I would indulge the charming impression, that, there is no youth in this House of Refuge, but what will bear in devout remembrance the deliverance and the favors which you have here received, and evince the sincerity of your gratitude by the amiableness of your temper, and the virtue of your future conduct.

CONCLUSION.

The time on which we have now assembled, is usually called "Christmas Day." Whether this recognizes the very day on which *Jesus* was born in Bethlehem, is not now my business to examine. If any man prefers keeping this, or any other day to the Lord, I am not disposed to interrupt him in the enjoyment of his privilege. The text on which I have this morning addressed you, combined with the narrative of Moses laid among the flags on the brink of the river, remind me of the Angel's address to the Shepherds in the field while watching their flock by night. *Fear not: for, behold, I bring you good tidings of great joy, which shall be to all people. For unto you is born this day in the city of David a Saviour, which is Christ the Lord. And this shall be a sign unto you; ye shall find the babe wrapped in* *swaddling clothes, lying in a manger.* Immediately the Shepherds left their flocks; *and they came with haste, and found Mary, and Joseph, and the babe lying in the manger.** This is that true Moses, the Prophet, which the Lord our God promised to *raise up, like unto him in all things, whom his people should hear.*† How singularly striking were the circumstances which attended their infancy! Yes, the babe of Bethlehem, found in a manger, was Christ the Lord; and, *his name was called Jesus, for he was to save his people from their sins.* If Moses that was found in the ark of bulrushes, was born to deliver the Israelites from their bondage in Egypt, and conduct them through the wilderness on their way to Canaan: we are certain, that our blessed Saviour was born to deliver from the more dreadful bondage of sin and misery, and safely conduct his redeemed to the rest of immortality and glory. Yes, Jesus was born to live, to suffer, and to die upon the cross for our sins; and after he was laid in the grave, he burst the bands of death, ascended up to heaven, and sat down on the right hand of the Majesty on high, from thence to shower down the multiplicity of his mercies upon mankind. And who, on this occasion, but what will most devoutly pray—LORD, RESERVE A BLESSING FOR THIS HOUSE OF REFUGE! Amen.

The service was concluded by the children, *alone*, singing an hymn. The recollection that those sixty-three unfortunates, had just been rescued from vice, and the paths of the destroyer; and now employed in singing the praises of the Lord; together with the melody of their voices, produced a most impressive effect upon the whole assembly!

*Luke ii. †Deut. xviii. 15. Acts vii. 37.

Acts of the Legislature of the State of N. York,

RELATING TO THE HOUSE OF REFUGE.

AN ACT *to Incorporate the Society for the Reformation of Juvenile Delinquents in the City of New-York.*

Passed March 29, 1824.

WHEREAS, by the petition of several inhabitants of the city of New-York, it is represented, that they are desirous of establishing a Society, and House of Refuge, for the Reformation of Juvenile Delinquents in the said city, and have prayed to be incorporated;

Therefore, Be it enacted by the people of the State of New-York, represented in Senate and Assembly: that all such persons as now are or hereafter shall become Subscribers to the said association pursuant to the bye-laws thereof, shall be and hereby are constituted a body corporate and politic, by the name of "the Managers of the Society for the Reformation of Juvenile Delinquents in the city of New-York; and by that name they shall have perpetual succession, and being in law capable of suing and being sued, defending and being defended in all courts and places, and in all manner of actions and causes whatsoever, and may have a common seal and change the same at their pleasure, and shall be capable in law by that name and style, of purchasing, holding, and conveying any estate real or personal for the use of the said corporation. Provided, that such real estate shall never exceed the yearly value of ten thousand dollars, nor be applied to any other purposes than those for which this incorporation is formed.

And be it further enacted, That the estate and concerns of the said corporation, shall be conducted by a board of thirty Managers to be elected by a plurality of ballots of the members resident in the City of New-York, being Subscribers as aforesaid, and present at such election yearly on the third Monday in November, at such place in the said City and at such time of the day as the Board of Managers may from time to time appoint, and of which public notice shall be given, and if any vacancy shall occur by the resignation, removal, or otherwise, of any one of the said Board, the same shall be filled for the remainder of the year by such person or persons being subscribers as aforesaid, as the Board for the time being or a major part of them shall appoint; and until the election on the third Monday in November in the year one thousand eight hundred and twenty-five, the following persons shall compose the said Board of Managers, to wit:—Cadwallader D. Colden, John Griscom, John Duer, Jonathan M. Wainwright, Isaac Collins, Thomas Eddy, Ansel W. Ives, John T. Irving, John E. Hyde, Cornelius Du Bois, James W. Gerard, Joseph Curtis, John Stearns, Ralph Olmsted, Robert F. Mott, Stephen Allen, Henry I. Wyckoff, Samuel Cowdrey, John Targee, Arthur Burtis, Joseph Grinnell, Hugh Maxwell, Henry Mead, Peter A. Jay, Gilbert Coutant, Cornelius R. Duffie, and James Lovett; and it is hereby further enacted, that no Manager of the said Society shall receive any compensation for his services.

And be it further enacted, That if the annual election shall not take place on the stated days for that purpose, the said Corporation shall not thereby be dissolved, but the Members of the said Board shall continue in office until a new election, which shall be had at such time and place and after such notice as the said Board shall prescribe, and in case of an equality of votes for any one or more persons as a Member or Members of the said Board of Managers, the said Board shall determine which of such persons shall be considered as elected, and such person or persons shall take his or their seats, and act accordingly.

And be it further enacted, That the said Managers shall have power in their discretion to receive and take into the House of Refuge, to be established by them, all such children who shall be taken up or committed as vagrants, or convicted of criminal offences in the said City, as may in the judgment of the Court of General Sessions of the peace, or of the Court of Oyer and Terminer in and for the said City, or of the Jury before whom any such offender shall be tried, or the Police Magistrates, or of the Commissioners of the Alms-House and Bridewell of the said City, be proper objects, and the said Managers shall have power to place the said children committed to their care, during the minority of such children, at such employments, and to cause them to be instructed in such branches of useful knowledge, as shall be suitable to their years and capacities; and they shall have power in their discretion to bind out the said children with their consent as apprentices or servants during their minority, to such persons, and at such places, to learn such proper trades and employments as in their judgment will be most for the reformation and amendment, and the future benefit and advantage of such children: *Provided*, that the charge and power of the said Managers upon and over the said children, shall not extend in the case of females beyond the age of eighteen years.

And be it further enacted, That all and singular the clauses and provisions in the act entitled an act concerning apprentices and servants, relating to the covenants to be inserted in the Indentures of apprentices and servants, made by the overseers of the poor, and the provisions of the Sixth, Ninth, Tenth, Eleventh, Twelfth, and Thirteenth Sections of the last mentioned act, shall apply to the apprentices and servants, and the persons to whom they may be bound, under, and by virtue of this act.

And be it further enacted, That the said Managers under this act, may, from time to time, make bye-laws, ordinances, and regulations relative to the management and disposition of the Estate and Concerns of the said Corporation, and the management, government, instruction, discipline, employment, and disposition of the said children, while in the said House of Refuge, or under their care not contrary to law, as they may deem proper, and may appoint such officers, agents, and servants as they may deem necessary to transact the business of the said Corporation, and may designate their duties; and further, that the said Managers shall make an annual report to the Legislature, and to the Corporation of the City of New-York, of the number of children received by them into the said House of Refuge, the disposition which shall be made of the said children by instructing or employing them in the said House of Refuge, or by binding them out as apprentices or servants; the receipts and expenditures of the said Managers, and generally all such facts and particulars as may tend to exhibit effects, whether advantageous or otherwise of the said Association.

And be it further enacted, That this act shall be and is hereby declared a public act, and that the same shall be construed in all courts and places benignly and favorably for every humane and laudable purpose therein contained.

And be it further enacted, That the Legislature may at any time hereafter, alter, modify, or repeal this act.

State of New-York, Secretary's Office.

I certify the preceding to be a true copy of an original act of the Legislature of this State on file in this Office.

ARCHABALD CAMPBELL,
Dep. Secretary.

Albany, April 1, 1824.

AN ACT *in aid of the Managers of the Society for the Reformation of Juvenile Delinquents in the City of New-York.*

Passed April 9, 1825.

BE it enacted by the People of the State of New-York, represented in Senate and Assembly, That the Treasurer shall, on the warrant of the Comptroller, pay to the Treasurer or the Managers of the Society for the Reformation of Juvenile Delinquents in the city of New-York, out of any money in the treasury not otherwise appropriated, the sum of two thousand dollars annually, for the term of five years: that the first payment of two thousand dollars shall be made on the first day of May next, and the like sum on every first day of May thereafter.

AN ACT *to amend the act, entitled " An act to incorporate the Society for the Reformation of Juvenile Delinquents in the city of New-York," passed March* 29, 1824, *and for other purposes.*

Passed January 28th, 1826.

BE it enacted by the People of the State of New-York, represented in Senate and Assembly, That the Managers of the Society mentioned in the act hereby amended, shall receive and take in the House of Refuge, established by them in the City of New-York, all such children as shall be convicted of criminal offences, in any city or county of this state, and as may in the judgment of the court before whom any such offender shall be tried, be deemed proper objects; and the powers and duties of the said Managers in relation to the children which they shall receive in virtue of this act, shall be the same in all things, as are prescribed and provided by the act entitled, "An act to incorporate the Society for the reformation of Juvenile Delinquents in the city of New-York," passed March the 29th, 1824, in respect to children which the said Managers have received, or may receive in virtue of that act.

And be it further enacted, That the commissioners mentioned in the thirty-eighth section of the act entitled "An act to provide against infectious and pestilential diseases," passed March the 21st, 1823, shall account annually to the comptroller of the state, for all monies received by them, for the use of the Marine Hospital, and if the same shall, in any one year, be more than sufficient to defray the expense of executing the trust committed to them, exclusive of such expenses as are to be borne and paid as part of the contingent charges of the city of New-York, and including the annual compensations granted to the said commissioners by the said act, then, and in such case, the said health commissioners shall pay such surplus over to the treasurer of the Managers of the Society for the Reformation of Juvenile Delinquents in the city of New-York, for the use of the said Society; and the said commissioners shall also pay to the said treasurer, for the use of, and to be expended by the said Society, in the erection of a House of Refuge, for female Juvenile Delinquents, so much of the balance, or surplus, now in their hands, or which may be invested, pursuant to the said thirty-eighth section, to meet any deficit of the receipts of the said commissioners for the purposes of the said marine hospital, or for the building of such other stone or brick hospitals in the place of the present wooden ones, as the person administering the government of this state may from time to time think necessary, and that the said thirty-eighth section, so far as the same is inconsistent with the provisions of this act, and no further, be, and the same is hereby repealed.

And be it further enacted, That the sheriffs of the several counties of this state, shall be allowed for the transportation of any Juvenile Delinquents according to the provisions of this act, the same compensation as is now given by law for the transportation of convicts to the state prisons, to be audited and paid by the supervisors of the respective counties, as part of the contingent expenses of the said counties: *Provided*, That after notice shall be given by the Managers of the said Society, that there is not room for the reception of any further delinquents, it shall not be lawful to transport any other delinquents, until notice shall be given that they can be received.

And be it further enacted, That the legislature may at any time, repeal, amend, or modify this act.

Chapter 1st, *Title* 7, *Sections* 17 *and* 18 *of the Revised Statutes, Page* 701, *Vol.* 2.

Whenever any person under the age of sixteen years, shall be convicted of any felony, the court, instead of sentencing such person to imprisonment in a state prison, may order that he be removed to and confined in the House of Refuge, established by the Society for the Reformation of Juvenile Delinquents in the city of New-York; unless notice shall have been received from such Society, that there is not room in such House for the reception of further delinquents.

Such convicts shall be removed by the sheriff of the county, pursuant to such order, and he shall be allowed the same compensation therefor as is provided by law for the transportation of convicts to the state prison, to be audited and paid as part of the contingent expenses of the county.

AN ACT *to create a Fund in aid of the Society for the Reformation of Juvenile Delinquents, in the city of New-York, and for other purposes.*

Passed April 29, 1829.

The People of the state of New-York, represented in Senate and Assembly, do enact as follows:

§ 1. The commissioners of health mentioned in the eleventh and twelfth sections of Title fourth of Chapter fourteenth of the first part of the Revised Statutes, shall pay out of the monies received by them for the use of the marine hospital, eight thousand dollars annually, in quarterly payments of two thousand dollars each, commencing on the first day of May next, to the treasurer of the society for the reformation of juvenile delinquents in the city of New-York for the use of said society, which sum of eight thousand dollars, shall be part of the surplus, and not in addition thereto, directed to be paid said treasurer by the above mentioned eleventh section, and the said commissioners of health shall pay over annually to the comptroller of the state, on or before the first of April, the balance that may remain of the said surplus fund, after paying the eight thousand dollars as aforesaid; and the balance of the said surplus, so paid to the comptroller, shall be invested by him in some secure manner at interest, and the said fund shall be kept distinct and separate, and shall be denominated the "Mariner's Fund."

§ 2 So much of the said twelfth section of Title fourth of Chapter fourteenth of the First Part of the Revised Statutes as applies to the balance of hospital monies in the hands of the commissioners of health, is declared to apply only to such balances as were in their hands at the time said chapter took effect as a law; and any part of said section inconsistent with this declared construction, is hereby repealed.

§ 3. The commissioners for collecting the duty of excise in the city of New-York, designated by the act entitled "An act to lay a duty on strong liquors, and for regulating inns and taverns, so far as relates to the city of New-York, and for other purposes," passed April 10th, 1824, shall demand and receive one dollar and fifty cents, in addition to the sum now required by law, upon every licence granted by them after the passing of this act, to any tavern keeper, grocer or keeper of an ordinary or victualling house or public garden, in pursuance of the act above mentioned, and the acts amendatory of the same, which additional sums the said commissioners shall pay over to the treasurer of the society for the reformation of juvenile delinquents in the city of New-York, for the use of said society.

§ 4. No theatre or circus, or building for exhibiting theatrical or equestrian performances in the city of New-York, shall be opened for such exhibitions after the first day of May next, unless the manager or proprietor thereof shall annually obtain from the Mayor of the said city, a license therefor; which license the said Mayor is authorised to grant, to continue until the first day of May ensuing the grant thereof; and every manager or proprietor offending in the premises, or consenting or allowing the same to be done, whether there be one or more managers or proprietors of such theatre or circus, shall be guilty of a misdemeanor, and shall be subject to a fine of one hundred dollars for each day it shall be so opened, or imprisonment not exceeding three months.

§ 5. Upon granting every license authorised by the preceding section, the mayor shall receive from the person to whom the same shall be granted, the sum of five hundred dollars for each theatre, and the sum of two hundred and fifty dollars for each circus: which sums when so received, shall be paid over to the treasurer of the society for the reformation of juvenile delinquents in the city of New-York, for the use of said society.

§ 6. The said commissioners of health shall render to the comptroller annually, a minute and detailed account of all monies denominated "Hospital monies," which shall be received, and also of all such monies disbursed by them or either of them, for the marine hospital; for the expenses of their trust, so far as the same are payable out of this fund for their own salaries, and the commission allowed by law to the health commissioner for collection, and also of the surplus, if any, of such monies paid over to the treasurer of the society for the reformation of juvenile delinquents in the city of New-York.

§ 7. The comptroller is hereby authorised to allow to the health commissioner for the collection of "Hospital Money" from coasting vessels, a commission at his discretion, of not less than two and a half, nor exceeding ten per cent., which allowance he is authorised to make, as well upon the collections made from such vessels during the past year, as upon those hereafter to be made.

AN ACT *concerning convicts under the age of seventeen years, and other purposes.*

Passed April 16, 1830.

The People of the State of New-York, represented in Senate and Assembly, do enact as follows:

§ 1. The person administering the government of this state, is hereby empowered to direct the agent of either of the state prisons of this state, whenever the inspectors thereof shall recommend the same, to convey any convicts who shall be under the age of seventeen years, to the house of refuge in the city of New-York; and they shall there be confined according to the rules and regulations of said house of refuge: The expenses of such removal shall be the same as allowed to sheriffs for like services, and a charge upon such prison, as part of its ordinary expenses to be certified by the inspectors.

AN ACT *to amend "An act to create a fund in aid of the Society for the Reformation of Juvenile Delinquents in the city of New-York, and for other purposes," passed April* 29, 1829.

Passed April 21, 1831.

The People of the State of New-York, represented in Senate and Assembly, do enact as follows:

§ 1. There shall be paid annually by the treasurer of the city of New-York, on the first Monday of July, to the treasurer of the Society for the Reformation of Juvenile Delinquents, in the city of

New-York, the sum of four thousand dollars, for the use of said society, out of the moneys appropriated for the support and maintenance of the poor of the said city, by the act, entitled " An act to amend an act, entitled "An act to lay a duty on strong liquors, and for regulating inns and taverns, so far as it relates to the city of New-York, and for other purposes," passed April 10th, 1824.

§ 2. The third section of the act, entitled "An act to create a fund in aid of the Society for the Reformation of Juvenile Delinquents in the city of New-York, and for other purposes, passed April 29, 1829, and which directs the commissioners for collecting the duty of excise in the city of New-York, to demand and receive one dollar and fifty cents in addition to the sum then required by law for a license to any tavern keeper, grocer, or keeper of an ordinary or victualling house, or public garden, shall be, and the same is hereby repealed.

PART OF AN ACT passed April 22, 1831.

The People of the State of New-York, represented in Senate and Assembly, do enact as follows:

§ 13. The eight thousand dollars appropriated by the act entitled "An act to create a fund in aid of the Society for the Reformation of Juvenile Delinquents in the city of New-York, and for other purposes," passed April 29, 1829, shall continue to be paid to said society in the manner and at the time therein specified, out of the moneys collected from passengers by the provisions of Title four, Chapter fourteenth, Part first of the Revised Statutes: but if the amount collected from passengers should be insufficient (after paying all the expense of the quarantine establishment at Staten Island,) to meet the eight thousand dollars now appropriated from the "Hospital Funds" for the support of the Society for the Reformation of Juvenile Delinquents in the city of New-York, then the balance to make up said eight thousand dollars shall be appropriated annually from the state treasury.

A List of Life Subscribers and Donors

TO THE

HOUSE OF REFUGE

NOT PREVIOUSLY PUBLISHED.

B. Auchincloss, & Co.	$10
Charles Anthon,	20
Heman Averill,	50
Benjamin Bailey,	20
Simeon Benjamin,	6
Wm. Blakeley,	6
Silas Brown,	5
John M. Bruce,	6
J. Boyd, jun.	5
H. Beekman,	5
Wm. Banks,	5
D. I. Boyd,	5
R. S. Brown,	6
J. Benedict,	10
James Brown,	50
James Brewster,	50
John Bolton,	10
C. Beers,	15
Wm. & T. C. Chardovoyne,	6
Joseph Corlies,	6
John Crumby,	20
Thos. G. Cary,	5
Benjamin Corlies,	5
D. M'Cormick,	10
Nathaniel Coggeswell,	5
F. Depeyster,	50
J. S. Dolan,	6
James W. Dominick,	10
John A. Davenport,	6
E. Dayton,	6
Ogden Edwards,	10
James Fellows,	10
Ferris Finch,	6
D. A. Frost,	6
Chas. Pregure & Frassire,	5
E. T. Franklin,	5
G. Froute,	5
Henry Grinnell,	6
Fred k. Gebhard,	10
John Greenfield,	5
F. G. 69 Wall-st.	50
Geo. Griswold,	50
J. W. Gerard,	10
Geo. Gardiner, (on account of life subscription,)	30
George Griffin,	50
J. Houseman,	10
John Hunter,	9
Hugh Holmes,	6
Willet Hicks,	15
H. Hinsdale,	6
J. S. Hyer,	5
O. Holmes,	5
J. K. Hamilton,	5
Jeromus Johnson,	50
W. S. Johnson,	6
H. P. Jones,	6
Jackson & McJimsey,	5
John D. Keese,	6
J. & W. Kelly,	6
J. D. King,	6
R. Lockwood,	6
C. W. Lawrence,	10
E. W. Laight,	6
Henry Laverty,	10
Allen C. Lee,	10
James W. Lent,	10
Thomas F. Livingston,	9
P. Lorillard,	20
Valentine Mott,	20
Morland Mecholl,	6
B. P. Melick,	6
Robert I. Murray,	10
Thos. W. Moore,	9
Wm. W. Mott,	5
Petersen and Mensch,	5
Samuel Marsh,	6
H. Maxwell,	12
David Marsh, jun.	20
N. Norris,	6

C. Oakley, - -	5	A. Seton, - - -	6
Wm. Prior, - -	10	G. P. Shipman, - -	6
F. Place, - -	6	C. Swan, - - -	10
J. Post, - - -	10	T. R. Smith, - -	20
G. C. Peterson, - -	10	Seabury Tredwell, -	5
E. Prince, - -	6	George Tredwell, -	5
P. 169 Front-st., -	50	Wm. Thomson, -	6
R. L. P., 101 Front-st.,	10	Wm. W. Todd, -	6
Henry Rogers, - -	10	A. Tredwell, - -	5
Bailey & Remsen, -	5	E. Townsend, - -	5
P. H. Rhinelander, -	5	S. A. Talcot, - -	5
R. Ray, - . -	6	Martin E. Thompson, -	50
A. C. Rossire, - -	6	Joshua S. Underhill, -	6
N. Richards, - -	10	H. Vanwagenen, -	6
Rev. — Robinson, -	10	W. Vandewater, -	6
Peter Sharpe, - -	50	Wm. Waring, - -	6
B. Sterrill & Co. -	5	Wm. Wright, - -	10
Benjamin Strong, -	10	Elizabeth Walsh, -	7
Mrs. G. Smith, - -	10	Henry S. Wyckoff, -	10
Wm. Stevens, - -	6	Salem Wines, - -	6
Fred'k Sheldon, - -	10	John Wheelwright, -	5
H. H. Scheiffelin -	5	C. P. White, - -	5
W. Stewart, - -	5	Stephen Whitney, -	50
F. S. & P. Schlesinger,	50	Mead Wheeler, - -	6
Thos. L. Servoss, -	5	E. White, - -	5
Ruel Smith, - -	10	R. D. Weeks, - -	20
S. P. Staples, - -	6	John Ward, jun. -	10

THE END.

Titles in This Series

1 *Children's Hospitals in the Progressive Era: Two Investigations of Substandard Conditions*. David J. and Sheila M. Rothman, eds. New York, 1986

2 *The Consumer's League of New York: Behind the Scenes of Women's Work, Three Reports*. David J. and Sheila M. Rothman, eds. New York, 1986

3 *The Dangers of Education: Sexism and the Origins of Women's Colleges, An Anthology of Nineteenth Century Sources*. David J. and Sheila M. Rothman, eds. New York, 1986

4 *Divorce: The First Debates, A Collection of Articles*. David J. and Sheila M. Rothman, eds. New York, 1986

5 *Low Wages and Great Sins: Two Antebellum American Views on Prostitution and the Working Girl*. David J. and Sheila M. Rothman, eds. New York, 1986

6 *Maternal Mortality in New York City and Philadelphia, 1931–1933, Two Studies*. David J. and Sheila M. Rothman, eds. New York, 1986

7 *National Congress of Mothers, the First Conventions, 1897–1899*. David J. and Sheila M. Rothman, eds. New York, 1986

8 *The Origins of Adoption, Two Reports*. David J. and Sheila M. Rothman, eds. New York, 1986

9 *The Origins of Day Care: Selections from the Conferences on Day Nurseries, 1893–1925*. David J. and Sheila M. Rothman, eds. New York, 1986

10 *Risks for the Single Woman in the City, An Anthology of Studies by Late Nineteenth-Century Reformers*. David J. and Sheila M. Rothman, eds. New York, 1986

11 *Saving Babies: Children's Bureau Studies of Infant Mortality, 1913–1917*. David J. and Sheila M. Rothman, eds. New York, 1986

12 *The Sheppard-Towner Act, the Record of the Hearings*. David J. and Sheila M. Rothman, eds. New York, 1986

13 *Women in Prison, 1834–1928, An Anthology of Pamphlets from the Progressive Movement*. David J. and Sheila M. Rothman, eds. New York, 1986

14 Azel Ames, Jr., *Sex in Industry: A Plea for the Working Girl*, Boston, 1875

15 Robert South Barrett, *The Care of the Unmarried Mother*, Alexandria, 1929

16 Elizabeth Blackwell, M.D., *The Laws of Life, with Special Reference to the Physical Education of Girls*, New York, 1852

17 Alida C. Bower and Ruth S. Bloodgood, *Institutional Treatment of Delinquent Boys*, Washington, D.C., 1935–36

18 New York Assembly, *The Girls of the Department Store*, New York, 1895

19 Committee on the Infant and Preschool Child, *Nursery Education*, New York, 1931

20 Robert Latou Dickinson and Lura Beam, *The Single Woman: A Medical Study in Sex Education*, Baltimore, 1934

21 G. V. Hamilton, M.D., *A Research in Marriage*, New York, 1929

22 Elizabeth Harrison, *A Study of Child Nature from the Kindergarten Standpoint*, Chicago, 1909

23 Orie Latham Hatcher, *Rural Girls in the City for Work*, Richmond, 1930

24 William Healy, Augusta F. Bronner, et al., *Reconstructing Behavior in Youth*, New York, 1929

25 Henry H. Hibbs, Jr., *Infant Mortality: Its Relation to Social and Industrial Conditions*, New York, 1916

26 *The Juvenile Court Record*, Chicago, 1900, 1901

27 Mary A. Livermore, *What Shall We Do With Our Daughters?* Boston, 1883

28 *Massachusetts Society for the Prevention of Cruelty to Children: First Ten Annual Reports*, Boston, 1882

29 Maude E. Miner, *Slavery of Prostitution: A Plea for Emancipation*, New York, 1916

30 Maud Nathan, *The Story of an Epoch-Making Movement*, New York, 1926

31 National Florence Crittenton Mission, *Fourteen Years' Work Among "Erring Girls,"* Washington, D.C., 1897

32 New York Milk Committee, *Reducing Infant Mortality in the Ten Largest Cities in the United States*, New York, 1912

33 James Orton, ed., *The Liberal Education of Women: The Demand and the Method*, New York, 1873

34 Margaret Reeves, *Training Schools for Delinquent Girls*, New York, 1929

35 Ben L. Reitman, M.D., *The Second Oldest Profession*, New York, 1931

36 John Dale Russell and Associates, *Vocational Education*, Washington, D.C., 1938

37 William H. Slingerland, *Child Welfare Work in California*, New York, 1916

38 William H. Slingerland, *Child Welfare Work in Pennsylvania*, New York, 1917

39 *Documents Relative to the House of Refuge, Instituted by the Society for the Reformation of Juvenile Delinquents in the City of New York, in 1824*, New York, 1832

40 George S. Stevenson, M.D., and Geddes Smith, *Child Guidance Clinics*, New York, 1934

41 Henry Winfred Thurston, *Delinquency and Spare Time*, New York, 1918

42 U.S. National Commission on Law Observance and Enforcement, *Report on Penal Institutions, Probation and Parole*, Washington, D.C., 1931

43 Miriam Van Waters, *Parents on Probation*, 1927

44 Ira S. Wile, M.D., *The Sex Life of the Unmarried Adult*, New York, 1934

45 Helen Leland Witmer, *Psychiatric Clinics for Children*, New York, 1940

46 Young Women's Christian Association, *First Ten Annual Reports, 1871–1880*, New York, 1871–1880